D1570189

San Carlo Borromeo

San Carlo Borromeo (1538–84), by Ambrogio Figini.*(Courtesy of the Pinacoteca Ambrosiana, Milan.)*

San Carlo Borromeo

Catholic Reform
and Ecclesiastical Politics in the Second Half
of the Sixteenth Century

EDITED BY
John M. Headley
AND
John B. Tomaro

Folger Books

Washington: The Folger Shakespeare Library
London and Toronto: Associated University Presses

© 1988 by Associated University Presses, Inc.

Associated University Presses
440 Forsgate Drive
Cranbury, NJ 08512

Associated University Presses
25 Sicilian Avenue
London WC1A 2QH, England

Associated University Presses
P.O. Box 488, Port Credit
Mississauga, Ontario
Canada L5G 4M2

The paper used in this publication meets the requirements
of the American National Standard for Permanence of Paper
for Printed Library Materials Z39.48-1984.

Library of Congress Cataloging-in-Publication Data

San Carlo Borromeo : Catholic reform and
    ecclesiastical politics in the second half of
    the sixteenth century.

    "Folger books."
    Papers originally presented at a conference held
in Washington, D.C., in Nov. 1984, to celebrate the
fourth centennial of San Carlo Borromeo's death.
    Includes bibliographies and index.
    1. Charles Borromeo, Saint, 1538–1584—Congresses.
2. Counter-Reformation—Congresses.   I. Headley,
John M.   II. Tomaro, John B.
    BX4700.B74S36   1988   282'.092'4   86-83052
    ISBN 0-918016-92-4 (alk. paper)

In Memoriam
Eric W. Cochrane (1928–1985)

PRINTED IN THE UNITED STATES OF AMERICA

Contents

CONTENTS

Introduction

JOHN M. HEADLEY

PERHAPS NOTHING SEEMS SO INCONGRUOUS AS AN AMERICAN EFFORT TO celebrate the fourth centennial of San Carlo Borromeo's death in 1584; one might better expect an anniversary celebration in Palermo for George Washington's birth. The editors, however, continue to be impressed by the historiographical and conceptual need to expose the period under consideration to reinterpretation; and at the same time because of the uniformly high quality of the papers presented, an unusual situation for a conference, they hope that the potential effectiveness of these proceedings may serve to promote such a reevaluation. And although there were moments of lively exchange at the time of the conference, it is only after the papers have received their full annotation and been submitted that their interrelationship and impact can begin to be perceived.

Much of what follows in this volume had to do with image making and how the perceptions others have of a person, an event, or a period can sometimes crystallize, for reasons not altogether unworldly, into fashionable, apparently unbreakable orthodoxies. For human perceptions, particularly when politically motivated, can frequently obscure more than illuminate. In the present instance the conference organizers did not set forth as professional iconoclasts, but, drawn to a new generation of scholarship on the subject, they were impressed by how San Carlo Borromeo, the heart and soul of Catholic Tridentine reform in his own time, had been allowed to become a stuffed saint, safely embalmed and removed, the object of passing, if profound respect. For although Borromeo's piety has long been the object of veneration, even awe, the specifics of his reform program long remained relatively unknown and unexplored. Indeed not until after World War II and the emergence of ecumenicity did some scholars stop treating Borromeo in hagiographical terms—whenever the cardinal-archbishop has been the focus of research—or in passing and rather superficially—whenever his role in Catholic reform was touched upon in the context of a larger study on the Catholic or Counter-Reformation. Not until the Second Vatican Council (closed 1965) did scholars begin to assess critically and comprehensively the work and impact, within and outside the Roman Catholic Church, of the cardinal-archbishop of Milan.

The fact that a hagiographical mist has come to obscure the man, his work, and particularly the ecclesiological implications of his reform may well not be entirely accidental or unrelated to the triumph of papal centralism and to a prevailing Roman interpretation of the Council of Trent. Thus the primary and overriding purpose of the conference was to examine the distinctive features and goals of Borromeo's work in its historical context. To accomplish this would require more than simply dusting off the old tired image. It would require breaking into that image, as it were, and in the words of one participant rehistoricizing it. In doing so the conference had no interest in questioning or debunking San Carlo's credentials for sanctity or sanctity in general. The design was to get beyond the halo of the saint as well as the splendid vestments of the cardinal to the man as he understood himself—to Carlo Borromeo, archbishop of Milan, and to his total historical ambience.

In short, given the opportunity to capitalize upon a new generation of scholars more nuanced in their interpretations and less bound to Roman centralism, the conference sought to mobilize these resources in order to paint a landscape of the Catholic Reformation that contains deeper and richer hues than the traditional monochromatic still life of the Counter-Reformation which tends to feature two magnitudes—the Jesuits and the papacy. In Borromeo, despite all his loyalty to the papacy, one discovers a commanding figure who was hardly a proponent of Roman centralism. On the contrary, he sought to extend his Milanese experience of provincial reform to Rome, the Curia, and the remaining Catholic world at large. To a considerable extent he succeeded, even to the degree of having his provincial legislation accepted in other contexts wherein they promoted, ironically, a new immobility in the life of the church. Nevertheless, the direction of his policies, which sought to enhance episcopal authority, the jurisdiction of metropolitans, and the regularity of provincial councils, conflicted with Roman centralization. For this reason it becomes more understandable why the historical dimensions of Borromeo have remained under a blanket of intense praise and universal, but uninformed, respect.

There were other reasons for such a conference. In a world of shrinking budgets and shrinking historical horizons, the American academic perception and presentation of European history after the Italian Renaissance generally narrows to England, France, and Germany: the so-called Forgotten Years extend alas well beyond Florence and tend to include all Mediterranean lands, even Spain. A determined effort to correct this neglect would be useful to the profession. Furthermore, what better way to accomplish this end than to introduce an English-speaking world to some of the exciting achievements and scholarly excellence of what we might briefly refer to as a Bolognese school—historians coming from the University of Bologna, the Istituto per le Scienze Religiose, and the Istituto Storico Italo-Germanico in Trento (for Paolo Prodi), supplemented by representatives from the University of Rome and the Ambrosian Library at Milan, all distinguished by their contributions to the field and subject under consideration. Also including American scholars, most of whom were equally distinguished by length of time and quality of scholarship in the same endeavor, the conference sought to present a fresh view of the post-Tridentine period: such issues as ecclesiastical reform, lay and clerical discipline, ascetic piety and administrative refurbishment of the type manifested in the work and person of Borromeo; and finally the image of the man as conveyed in history.

In order to set the tone and direction for the conference the organizers placed Eric Cochrane in the lonely role of providing an introduction for the entire period. With characteristic forcefulness, supported by a command of Italian historiography, Cochrane challenged the received notion of the "Counter-Reformation" in Italian history as referring to the period that broadly runs from the peace of Cateau-Cambrésis in 1559 to the condemnation of Galileo in 1633. Cochrane early raises the problem of perceptions and how an age might be experienced in one way by its participants yet seen in another light by a later age. The Iron Age, a term sometimes applied to this period, has no place in Cochrane's picture of the Italian peninsula. The age is marked by creativity and magnificence, by pious popes replacing warrior prelates, and by an exemplary order in the pursuit of learning that persists certainly to the end of the sixteenth century. This favorable appreciation of our period continues into the Enlightenment, and it is not until the second third of the nineteenth century that a reversal of attitude develops, crystallizing in the mid–twentieth century. Here, upon the evidence is inflicted the term Counter-Reformation, by which is to be understood an age of brittle hypocrisy, hard repression, authoritarian conformism, and foreign (bad) domination. One might recognize here the obvious revenge of nationalism and republicanism upon an earlier world of courts, aristocratic patronage and Catholic reform. But what impresses Cochrane is the perceptual damage done by imposing a procrustean periodization, in this instance the Counter-Reformation, acquired by a later experience in the form of a fashionable orthodoxy upon the material. What results is a sonorous hash. Cases that do not fit become inexplicable exceptions to the general rule of what the Counter-Reformation is claimed to constitute and signify. An atomistic research dealing with individual cases compels new research to embrace uncritically the dominant paradigm. In concluding, Cochrane leads us to the threshold of a potential historiographical openness that he compares to that impending upon the Aristotelian philosophical and scientific cosmos on the eve of the *Sidereus Nuncius;* further patching up of the old paradigm simply will not do. Instead he offers a new name, the Tridentine Reformation, as serving to capitalize upon and resolve the incongruities, distortions, and suffocation produced by the orthodoxy of "the Counter-

Reformation" and thus to break out and effect the exploration of new
dimensions in the age of Borromeo.

After such an introduction to the purposes of the conference, its first
session sought to present San Carlo in his largest, perhaps best-known
European ambience—in connection with the Council of Trent whose interpretation and implementation would dominate his own life and those of his
contemporaries. While the first paper dealt more narrowly and intensively
within a segment of the short period when he served as cardinal-secretary,
the second paper ranged more widely over his years after the Roman sojourn
in order to define the style, character, and import of his reforming activity in
the archbishopric of Milan as an interpretation of Trent. Robert Trisco may
be better known to the field of American church history, but he has recently
put European historians of the early modern period in his debt by his study
of the Emperor Ferdinand's relations to Trent and the papacy[1] with which
this present lecture forms a diptych. He begins his contribution with the
picture of the young, dutiful, obedient cardinal-nephew at the levers of
power at Rome just as the Council of Trent moves into its final, critical,
almost fatal phase. Although recent work on the practice of nepotism has
corrected some of our instinctive prejudices and allowed us to see it as the
age's answer to the perennial need for trustworthy and reliable service,[2]
there still remains something breathtaking about an inexperienced twenty-
four year old at the top of the papal secretariat, as chief implementer of papal
policy. Carlo is represented here simply as the docile instrument of his uncle,
Pius IV. He shares his uncle's view of the council as being a potential enemy
of the papacy. As the fateful debate at Trent over the question of episcopal
residence becomes more protracted and heated, something approaching
panic evinces itself in the correspondence of Borromeo. There are certain
indications of rawness and lack of experience such as a manifest lack of
influence over the pope and, much to his bewilderment, some of his letters'
giving offense at Trent. Yet young Carlo seems to settle into the role of main
wire-puller: as the pontiff's chief minister he has recourse to some expedients
that reflect little credit on the papacy. He instructs the papal nuncio at
Madrid to complain to Philip II in order to prevent an alliance of Spanish
and French bishops at the council and to restrict its freedom. On the arrival
of the Cardinal of Lorraine at Trent, he instructs the new president, Cardinal
Morone, to pull the wool over Lorraine's eyes, while traducing him behind
his back, "giving his head a good washing in the general congregations by
pointing out his imperfections"—all this to be done in the most seemly
fashion, of course. Inducements, or what a more moralistic age would
understand as bribes, are pressed on those needing to be influenced: from
pistachio nuts and tunny roes to promises of a cardinalate. As the crisis
deepens a barrage of instructions is sent up from Borromeo to the experienced Morone at Trent not to spare the expense; the key figures are to be

pelted with gold *scudi*. Particular attention is bestowed on the French envoy, Du Ferrier, to get him to behave. Apparently the latter did not oblige, despite the circumspection of Morone: striding militantly across the bridge of Gallicanism, enunciated at the council, Du Ferrier shortly afterward became a Calvinist on the yonder shore. After so much arm twisting, one could hardly blame him.

In the emerging picture of Carlo Borromeo, the arrant curialist, the impact of Father Trisco's presentation is all the greater. There is no dazzling methodology here nor is such methodology needed. He lets the documents pretty much speak for themselves and proceeds at a responsible, even pace. Yet a surprise and reversal are impending. In its criticism of abuses related to the sacrament of orders the council would impel Borromeo's being ordained to the priesthood in July 1563, thereby promoting his own spiritual reform instead of his promoting a general reform through the council. Then a concatenation of events beginning with the death of Carlo's brother in the previous November, the visit of De Martyribus to Rome in the autumn, and the successful closing of the Council of Trent contribute to an astounding transformation in the deportment of the cardinal-nephew, a fact noted by contemporaries. A different perspective on Borromeo's conversion, about which we know too little is provided by a later participant, but the apparently conflicting pictures of Carlo during these months are by no means irreconcilable.

With the subsequent paper the ecclesiological implications of Borromeo's reform, with respect both to Trent and to Rome, come sharply into focus. Its author, Dr. John Tomaro, wrote his dissertation, bearing the same title as the present paper, on the subject of the congregations of the Council and of the bishops, culminating with a study of Borromeo.

Tomaro begins with the critical year 1563: the crisis of the council intersects with Borromeo's own mounting spiritual crisis that had been apparently initiated by the death of his brother in the previous November. Under the influence of the Jesuit Ribera, Carlo emerges from his spiritual transformation with a commitment to becoming the model reformed prelate. While proceeding to enact the conciliar decrees in Rome and through his vicar, Ormaneto, in Milan, Borromeo realizes that Trent can only be implemented by his episcopal residence at Milan. Here he works to restore the almost forgotten authority of the archbishop, for he sees the reformed dioceses as the building blocks of the renewed church. In giving passing attention to Borromeo's conflicts with the civil and Spanish authorities, Tomaro maintains his focus on the great archbishop's interpretation of Trent in relationship to Rome. For Borromeo, reform is to be effected by episcopal initiative; Rome, while respected, is not to intrude. His posture is devout, obedient, but never abject; Rome's is marked by esteem that falls well short of license. With the pontificate of Gregory XIII this relationship of mutual regard begins to wither: for almost three years (1576–79) the papacy never responds to Borromeo's submission of the decrees of the fourth provincial council of Milan, thus necessitating Borromeo's personal appearance in Rome. At his death he knew that his relationship to Rome had radically changed. In the posthumous image that Rome contrived for Borromeo, he was depicted always as cardinal, never as archbishop. He was seen as a model bishop because he was a loyal servant and agent of Rome. The whole intermediate and considerably independent authority of the bishop between Rome and the faithful was conveniently allowed to fade. And with it faded a specifically episcopal interpretation and implementation of the Council of Trent.

There is a measure of fateful inevitability in this submerged conflict between Borromeo and Rome that Tomaro defines here. The episcopally based, potentially particularist interests and initiatives of Borromeo presented a reform whose success depended upon a thousand like-minded, dedicated, driven bishops. In short, although for a moment in church history such resources for reform seemed available, that extraordinary situation could not survive the generation of the Tridentine fathers and Borromeo's Milanese school of lieutenants. The Roman interpretation of Trent would prevail because Rome alone through her extensive bureaucratic structures could provide a measure of systematic and continuous realization. Moreover the question in this drama is not spirit versus structure but of spirit in which structure—a potentially universal or a specifically local one? Ultimately the archiepiscopal structure would prove too local and dependent upon an unsustainable vitality. For in any decisive conflict between the mortal self and whatever system, the system can always invoke a greater duration and even eternity itself: the bureaucratic answer must always prevail.

Moving the focus from the wider world of Rome and the Council of Trent to Milan and to that intense experience of such momentous consequence to later Catholicism, the second session turned its attention to the great Lombard capital and ecclesiastical province, the most highly developed area of sixteenth-century Europe, and to the events unfolding there. Agostino Borromeo, whose own field of specialization is the Philippine bishops and the relations between Madrid and Rome during this period, addressed the matter of the heightened strain in relations between the ecclesiastical and civil authorities of Milan. Determined to enforce rigorously the Tridentine decrees, Carlo Borromeo considered it necessary to procure all possible means of coercion over the clergy, and in some cases over the laity as well. The archbishop reclaimed the right to indict laymen of specified crimes in the episcopal court of justice and also the liberty to deploy his own police force. This presumption on Borromeo's part that justice could be exercised over the secular sphere within the judicial system of the church was bound to be checked by the Spanish authorities, whether in Milan or Madrid, who feared that an excessive strengthening of ecclesiastical power over their subjects would endanger the stability of Spanish domination in Lombardy. In turn, a strenuous opposition against the activity of the archbishop was raised by the civil authorities, based on the argument that the alleged customs of the Milanese church were not sufficiently proven or, in any case, that they had fallen into disuse. From such adversarial positions, various confrontations naturally occurred, some of which were particularly violent. The situation was to some degree tempered only after 1580, when Borromeo dispatched his own representative to the royal court at Madrid. The study of these confrontations demonstrates that, despite their frequency, they did not impede collaboration between the two spheres of authority, such as was to occur in their common struggle against heresy.

To the task of assessing lay-clerical relations and the religious-social import of Borromeo's activity, Adriano Prosperi brings a record of distinguished scholarship in the religious history of the period; he is probably best known for his biographical study of G. M. Giberti, whose early reform work at Verona exerted considerable influence on the entire Tridentine age. For Prosperi Carlo Borromeo is not the initiator but rather the heir and chief interpreter of a tradition stemming from midcentury that seeks a vigorous restoration of the dignity and function of the clergy and that understands reform to be measured in pastoral and diocesan activity. In a church that is becoming narrower and more uniform, providing a structure of control for the mass of the faithful, Borromeo emerges as the leading exponent and interpreter of a daily asceticism that is no longer the prerogative of the monk but extends through the secular clergy to the people at large; likewise he stands as advocate of the sharp demarcation of the clergy from the laity. Borromeo's preoccupation as evinced in his sermons is not with the heretic or the Turk or apocalyptic themes but with the daily struggle against the evil within that characterizes the Christian life and imparts to this work a modern quality. Likewise his model of bishop is not that of the combatant-martyr but more that of the magistrate determined to have his authority respected against all backsliding. For this reason the bishop must be hard and exacting. Prosperi criticizes the very use of the term reform as representing Borromeo's work, for there is never any grand plan—how could there be in fact?[3]—but rather precise proposals relating to rules, customs, and forms of religious life. Yet if the ultimate reference is to the individual Christian, it assumes the dimensions of a collective struggle on the part of the clergy against a lay world before whose revival of paganism the clergy feels itself embattled. In the cleric-lay relationship, Borromeo would provide the definitive interpretation of the Tridentine decrees. If the clergy was to be superior and apart, it must by its heroic model continuously win its prestige; only a later period would divorce the clergy's dignity and superiority from its heroic function of stimulus and model to the laity. This heavy charge falls to the secular, which is now clearly preferred to the regular clergy. As is evident from a number of clashes in these Milanese years, Borromeo strives successfully to bring the religious orders within his effective jurisdiction. In this study of the meaning of Borromeo's pastoral activity for religious-social relationships, Prosperi concludes with the family in the parish and the long-neglected subject of lay confraternities. Finally he returns to his doubts as to the correctness of using the term "reform" to understand Borromeo's work: again there was no grand plan to institute but rather a hard, daily asceticism that now applied to clerics and the laity alike. Milan would indeed begin to compete with Geneva.[4]

The Church Militant acquires here flesh and bone: the comportment of the secular clergy is designed from the eye-level of the laity; to this clergy is imparted the heroic role of conquest of the world, a conquest that involves the subordination and disciplining of the laity and the control of the regular clergy by the episcopal authority. If not reform, we experience nevertheless the exhilarating effect of an ideal as it makes its way into the vast inertia of the world. Something of the wonder of the Milanese initiative is captured in the stunning statement of one of Borromeo's correspondents, writing on the reception of the decrees of Milan's first provincial council in Rome, December 1566: "La riforma romana è figliuola della milanese."

The third session took us further into the matrix of the Milanese context and the nature of Borromeo's pastorate. All the speakers had recourse to the fact of the freshly redefined special status of the clergy apart from the laity that figured significantly in Professor Prosperi's paper. John O'Malley, who is presently engaged in a full-scale history of Christian preaching, turns to Borromeo's exercise of the "preeminent function of bishops"—preaching. His interest here is in the history of treatises on how to preach, the relation between Borromeo's theory and practice regarding these treatises, and the factors that conspired to give him a unique position for his day in the presentation of the Christian message. Although Erasmus' *Ecclesiastes* is the first major departure from the scholastic *Artes praedicandi*, the age is slow to arrive at a viable alternative. Only during the 1570s in the confluence of studies treating the subject is the rupture with the old schema realized and the humanistic element, which would constitute the hallmark of the Counter-Reformation, incorporated. Borromeo himself lacked formal theological training; his education had been in law and literature and his Noctes Vaticanae had evinced particular interest in Stoicism and the *Enchiridion* of Epictetus. Borromeo's *Instructiones* of 1576 contributes to the formal revamping of practices and goals accomplished in these years. His preaching lacks a theology of the Word; it tends to the moralistic and suggests a special, perhaps narrow ecclesiastical culture that sets the preacher apart from the general culture. Borromeo's preaching emphasizes so much the respect due to the clergy and the evil of any criticism of the church that the insistence on ecclesiastical order prevents any impulse to prophetic criticism. While Borromeo's preaching avoids Pelagianism, O'Malley believes the prevailing moralistic tone to breathe an optimistic view of man's spiritual capabilities. The evident anti-Ciceronianism and severe ideal derive partly from the contemporaneous Spanish theorists on preaching and also from the simpler style of the Fathers. Sensing the lack of any manual to implement the Tridentine command to the bishops to preach, Borromeo encouraged his friend Agostino Valier, bishop of Verona, to publish in 1574 a work on ecclesiastical rhetoric that would meet the religious and aesthetic tastes of the age. Together with the comparable works of Diego de Estella and especially Luis de Granada, they constituted the age's successful replacement for the *Artes praedicandi*. By his stimulus, his own practice, and by bringing good preachers to Milan, Carlo Borromeo because of his particular eminence was able to define, establish, and consolidate a distinctive preaching for the Counter-Reformation in a way that no other Catholic could. O'Malley makes clear that although not as well known and recognized heretofore, the ministry of the Word in the sixteenth century was just as characteristic of Catholicism as of Protestantism.

To address the subject of elementary education under Borromeo the conference was fortunate to engage the participation of Paul F. Grendler, who is presently bringing to completion a study on primary and secondary education in the Italian Renaissance. His subject for the conference is the Schools of Christian Doctrine established by a lay confraternity in 1539. Their instruction was directed toward the children of the Milanese laboring classes and sought therefore to present the basic elements of Catholicism in an uncomplicated way to lay persons with modest goals. The books of the schools were well designed to instruct the laity in the rudiments of the faith so that one might live well and attain to heaven. Before Borromeo's entry on the scene the movement, originating in Milan, was so successful as to have spread across northern Italy. Yet according to Bascapè and the biographical-hagiographical tradition the schools were relatively insignificant until Borromeo took charge. In actual fact the archbishop at first seems to have deliberately kept his distance from the movement for reasons that will have seemed obvious to most readers of this material by now: namely, Borromeo's basic opposition to lay initiative and lay involvement in religion. Grendler prudently, however, does not rush to this conclusion and emphasize it, for while admitting Borromeo's aristocratic background and his real lack of sympathy or understanding for popular life, the author is equally struck by the unusual restraint the archbishop manifested, given his predilections. For if he brought the movement under clerical direction, he did not change the format or content of the instruction, and he permitted lay persons to teach the catechism. If we are amused or even dismayed at the

appearance of social differences when individual nobles embark on charitable missions to the lowly, one may well ask with the author how could it be
otherwise, given the quasi-feudal society of late sixteenth-century Italy.
Before concluding, the author presents an anecdote that is possibly worthy
of greater attention in order that we may be better prepared to assess
Borromeo's most recent reinterpretation: regarding Borromeo and the catechism schools, tradition tells that when he went to teach the boys Christian
doctrine, he carried with him, perhaps reminiscent of the schools' founder, a
sack of red apples to reward the children. If it is just possible that the
cardinal-archbishop of Milan and apostolic legate of all Italy could unbend
thus far, it would seem that we should be better prepared to have him
unexpectedly unbend into the twentieth century, when we come to examine
the case of Pope John XXIII.

Perhaps because of sociological implications, already evident in the earlier
contribution of Prosperi, Grendler's paper produced the liveliest discussion
and exchange. Some of the more fruitful questions asked were: Did the laity
want clericalization? What was their reaction to it? And most suggestive:
Does the laity impel the clergy to be the model? In this last we are reminded
of that late medieval layman, priest manqué, Thomas More, who had imputed this specific role to the regular clergy at the beginning of the century.[5]

Cecilia Voelker, who has been working on an English translation of
Borromeo's *Instructiones fabricae,* addressed the question of his influence
upon sacred art and architecture. The evidence of architecture and art history
provides the ordinary historian with a tangible force and directness that are
usually lacking to written evidence. This concreteness is particularly true of
architecture, intrinsically the most social of all the arts. Voelker's lecture
reinforced some of the points and notions already adumbrated: the increased
dignity and remove of the clergy; the careful separation of the sexes here by
means of a wooden partition running down the aisle and different arrangements for seating; the eye that must legislate every detail. While Borromeo's
intention was to restore dignity and functionality, there is manifest
throughout this extraordinary work a comprehensive mind bearing on every
aspect of the structure, its furnishings, and the liturgical service, attesting at
the same time to a meticulous attention in its minute specifications down to
the exact amount of space to be allotted each of the faithful, the placement of
a hook for the beretta or the ring for raising the cover of a sepulcher, and the
precise materials to be used in each instance. Painters and sculptors were to
be called in and informed as to the rule pertaining to sacred images; to these
rules they must adhere. No matter how alien may appear to a modern mind
the stupefying detail and immoderate zeal imparted by all these specifications, leaving it impatient, bewildered, exhausted, we need to be reminded
that the priorities of one age are not those of another.

In the early stages of planning this conference, the organizers were grateful to receive from Professor Agostino Borromeo the suggestion that one session should be devoted to the archbishop's influence outside the Milanese context. The subsequent session was designed to meet that need: to suggest not simply the apparent influences of Borromeo abroad but to indicate what specific features of his pastorate at Milan were transmissible, what readily appropriated, what rejected in three diverse, alien contexts—Spain, France, and the empire. Finally, to hazard the seemingly improbable—to what extent might an authentic Borromean type of church be realized outside of Italy in early modern Europe?

Having very recently published a general study of the Counter-Reformation with particular attention to Spain, Anthony Wright probably knows the Spanish archives with reference to Catholic reform in this period better than any other English-speaking historian. Grounded in the archival evidence, Wright is actually less concerned with tracing specific influences than in perceiving parallels and similarities with occasional appeals to the Borromean image of severity and rigor. Particularly conscious of the great Milanese archibishop are Juan de Ribera, archbishop of Valencia, and his successor Fray Isidro Aliaga, Archbishop Pedro de Castro of Granada, and Cardinal Quiroga. Wright finds the liturgical service of many Spanish churches regulated with an exquisite detail worthy of Borromeo. In their admiration for the Caroline Acts the Spaniards reveal a concern for clerical education notably similar to that of Borromeo. Likewise the Borromean separation of the sexes in parish churches is reproduced in the post-Tridentine decrees of Spanish bishops. Sermons of definite Milanese inspiration are published, and at Granada De Castro, in citing specific Borromean provincial legislation, tries to establish Borromean standards for the female conventual life. The attempt to exclude the laity from the chancel is rejected, reminding us of the monarchy's grip upon the Spanish church. In Granada as well as Valencia the conscious example of Borromeo was valued for the assertion of independent episcopal authority in accordance with Trent, not as a jurisdictional goal in itself but rather as the means for realizing and maintaining true standards of ecclesiastical reform and religious life. In the Spanish kingdoms episcopal jurisdiction was circumscribed by royal defense of the secular tribunals' jurisdiction in appeals. Before the Habsburg monarchy his Spanish exponents lacked Borromeo's extraordinary combination of authorities. Nevertheless the Spanish case impressively reveals in this period a strict, detailed episcopal regulation of diocesan life.

In trying to find the right person to treat our problem for France, we encountered a number of difficulties and disappointments. Only when far advanced in our search did we learn that Marc Venard was in fact the right historian for the task, given his wide-ranging command of the diocesan life of France in this period and his study of the church in Avignon. We spent the better part of the year pursuing him with letters through the upper echelons of the French educational system. When he was finally reached at Rouen, time was short and our invitation could only appear to be cordially blunt: we want you for only one purpose—to give a paper on Borromeo's influence on the church in France. The response to our invitation read that the only grounds on which he would come to such a conference would be to give a paper precisely on the topic specified. Judging from the personality involved and from the results, one could hardly desire a better meeting of minds.

In his methodical, thorough exposition Venard first addresses the question of how Borromeo comes to be known in France.[6] Here the vehicles of transmission are first members from the larger circle of the Milanese school, then books, particularly lives of Saint Charles and the *Acta* and the *Instructiones pastorum*. The Constitutions of the Assembly of the Clergy at Melun in 1579 incorporate almost verbatim sections from the *Acta* and thereby establish a practice used by other French ecclesiastical assemblies of the period. Furthermore the initiative of Melun at this time is, with respect to the reception of Trent, equivalent to what historians usually attribute to the French church only later in 1615. Secondly, in noting the specific points in the diocesan and religious life of France, where Borromeo's influence is discernible, Venard finds the most striking impact to have been confession and the confessional; generally from 1650 to 1850 all France is confessed according to Borromean principles. Determinative for the entire presence of Borromeo in France is that, never a popular saint, he triumphs in the clerical context, being readily assimilable among the greatest saints of all time for immediate imitation. In the course of his analysis of Borromean penetration into the pastoral machinery of the diocese, Venard finds evidence of the earlier achievements of Giberti in more than one instance. In watching the author pile up his precious evidence, the reader has the experience of the scales seeming to fall suddenly from his eyes: "*Idealement, l'Église de France du XVIIe siècle est toute borroméene.*" And to a great extent practically, we are now persuaded to add. On the final level of interrogation, the reasons for this influence, Venard's answers are most fascinating: (1) the vital congruence between the distinctively episcopal character of Borromeo's reform and absolute monarchy, each mutually reinforcing and affirming the other; (2) the assertion of the superiority of the secular clergy over the regular; and (3) the appeal of rigorism, of distance, discipline and good order. He ends by noting the apparent congruence of Borromean spirituality—austere, distant, severe, a touch of arrogance with the spirit of Port Royal; indeed what we have taken too easily in this period to be Jansenist can sometimes better be understood as a part of the general Borromean envelopment.

Only on one point might we take exception to this extraordinary and most admirable paper and even then only to place its achievement in a different perspective. In concluding, Venard sees the great paradox to be that from the Milanese model the Gallican Church would make a rampart against

Ultramontanism. But beyond the mountains in Italy at least as late as 1584 there exist not one but two ecclesiologies or, more modestly, vehicles for the interpretation and implementation of the recent council: a Roman centralist and an archiepiscopal. Although not opposed, nor even in competition, nevertheless there are occasional tensions of which Borromeo's friend, the archbishop of Bologna, eloquently can remind us. If therefore Ultramontanism is a somewhat more complex phenomenon for a moment at the end of the sixteenth century, then what comes to find a home in the Gallican north is that distinctively archiepiscopal, Borromean version. Otherwise stated, Borromeo's ecclesiology, his vision of an episcopally responsible church, or better an interpretation of such a church, became a historical fact only outside of Italy in a Gallican context. At the same time the Milanese and the Gallican ecclesiologies present us with a remarkable congruence rather than paradox, as Professor Venard's paper has so beautifully demonstrated.

The third contributor to this session, John Headley, was unique to the conference in possessing no credentials in this particular subject, having done all his work in the early sixteenth century. Nevertheless the case of Borromeo's close associate and friend, G. F. Bonomi, appears to be quite instructive to the ecclesiological issues here presented by the historical problem of Trent's interpretation and implementation. The very anomaly of a fervent Borromean bishop serving as papal nuncio, the period's most concrete expression of Roman centralism, produces incongruities and paradoxes that may illuminate the ecclesiastical tensions and possibilities of the age. The present study attempts to assess within the forbidding terrain of the empire the ecclesiological implications of Borromean reform and its bearer with respect to Rome and Trent. What does it mean to have a Borromean bishop, turned papal nuncio, seeking to effect Tridentine reform in an alien, intractable context? Lacking an episcopally supportive and relatively unobstructed landscape, such as Milan afforded, in which to operate, Bonomi had to have repeated recourse to papal authority, if the Council of Trent was to be advanced. What develops, first in a fascinating encounter with the Swiss canons of Uri, Schweiz, and Unterwalden in September 1579 and shortly afterwards in central Germany, is the fact that the episcopal implications of the council would have to be forsaken if piecemeal Catholic reforms were to be effected. In the process the modest bishop of Vercelli becomes a veritable proconsul of papal jurisdiction and of Catholic revival, decisively contributing to the maintenance of Catholicism in northwestern Germany and on the lower Rhine. But we are left with a paradox: that Trent would have to be violated in order to be realized. The paradox itself may provide a clue to the historical impossibility of any extensive episcopal realization of Trent outside of northern Italy, other than what a Gallican context can apparently offer.

With the final session, "The Image of Borromeo in History," we return to the question of perceptions in various time periods. Giuseppe Alberigo, who

is well known for his knowledge of religious and ecclesiastical history both
in this period and more generally for the entire modern period and is
particularly recognized for his study of the Italian bishops at Trent, addressed the subject of two models of bishop in Borromeo's development. He
begins by defining three periods for his study, the first being the all too easily
ignored Roman years, 1560–66, of the young Carlo, the second the period of
maturation associated with Borromeo's entire ministry in Milan, 1566–84,
and then that of the posthumous workings of the image. Although there is
much still lacking and much that we will never know about Carlo's Roman
years, Alberigo's analysis reveals in the young prelate both the emergence of
a distinctively voluntarist temperament and a rising sensitivity to the degeneracy of the church. Presumably his observations pertain to the period after
1563, when Carlo is usually believed to have had some sort of conversion
experience. Late 1563 with the transformed Carlo is where Robert Trisco
ended his study; his very different picture of the young Borromeo can be
reconciled with Alberigo's not only in that each is emphasizing a different
half of this six-year period but that also there would have to have been some
stage of spiritual and psychic overlap occasioning tension. Both scholars
agree in admitting at this stage the apparently decisive intervention of De
Martyribus, archbishop of Braga. Another point raised early by Alberigo
that needs to be noted and assessed is that he shares Prosperi's misgivings
about the use of the term "reform" applied to Borromeo's work. Alberigo is
making what appears to us to be a very important observation that yet could
be easily overlooked when he says that "the past did not provide a plan,"
even though he reinforces the thought in a note by observing that "a
fashionable literature has frequently presented Borromeo as a restorer, while
his attention is exclusively dedicated to the present." If the whole period of
the Renaissance and Reformation, minus the immense bulk of Martin
Luther, can be understood in terms of a series of resorts to the past for
supposed norms that in the present will exercise a reforming influence, then
Borromeo's presentism may signal to us the end of this great period of
intellectual and institutional ferment. In precisely the same decade Jean
Bodin draws the same conclusion that the past does not provide any normative answer for the needs of the present and that the resolution lies instead
in the legislation of the prince.[7] Yet while the Angevin arrives at his realization from a mounting sense of crisis, the Milanese would find himself
traditionally restrained from any such recourse to the past by his perception
of working within a divinely established, hierarchically structured church
where the operation of any dialectic of reform can only be extremely limited
and normally focused upon the individual.

Yet, if we may obtrude, it is the individual both in history and in
historiography that has now entered the limelight. As Prosperi had observed
earlier, we discover in the case of Carlo Borromeo those personal interven-

tions that modify reality. Such modifications might have been ignored or obscured by a historiography that exploited quantification and social structures, thereby inadvertently contributing to the traditional embalmment of our present subject, the archbishop of Milan. Now in Alberigo's representation of the young Carlo's deliberate assumption of the role of bishop with its commitment to the pastoral ministry and the quest for holiness, together constituting the substance of his conversion, have we not here in this Epictetean aristocrat's transformation a most momentous case of Renaissance self-fashioning?

There is something both arresting and clarifying in Alberigo's bold statement that the decision to go to Milan is the sole authentic conversion of Borromeo. There his voluntarist temperament is furthered in conflict with the civil and political authorities. Alberigo divides this second period into two phases demarcated by the event of the plague; he hypothesizes that in the latter phase, 1577–84, Borromeo achieves a new level of maturity and liberty: toward the end of his journey he reveals a deepened commitment as well as a more complex and dynamic vision of episcopacy and the life of the church. The emerging model bespeaks prayer, asceticism, penitence not as individual exercises but as energies placed at the service of the pastoral community. In the process of his winning this new model, however, we obtain an interesting glimpse of Borromeo and his work as perceived by one of his less enthusiastic lieutenants, the bishop of Brescia: wearied by his mounds of decrees, he finds the archbishop impractical, exhaustingly zealous, full of holy willpower and an imprudent rigor.

In discussing the third period following Borromeo's death, Alberigo treats this reconsolidation of the ideal of the bishop in the age of the Counter-Reformation; he seems to understand it in an expanded and extended sense of including Catholicism in the entire modern period virtually down to Vatican II. The new age is distinguished by a crystallization of that confessional division of European Christianity and at the same time the passing of that creative stage which marked the minds of the fifteenth and sixteenth centuries. In the last two decades of the sixteenth begins a phase of normalization and order. One is here reminded of Cochrane's reference to Borromeo's age as that of consolidation, although Alberigo intends by it more a sense of inquiry giving way to certainty in spiritual and theological statement. Here he effectively expresses what later generations wrought upon the Council of Trent in their need systematically and totally to wall off the Reformation and modern culture: "All the spaces left open by the council were closed and almost always in its very name." Likewise the memory of Carlo Borromeo is so blurred and dismembered that the virtues and piety are separated from that pastoral commitment later to be recovered by Roncalli.

Although in a somewhat reduced form, the paper of Niels Rasmussen,

O.P. is presented here with the deliberate intention of preserving the immediacy and freshness of a lecture delivered with slides. Because the complete study had previously been committed and the scholar is asked to consult the *Analecta Romana Instituti Danici* 15 (1986) for the full text and annotation, we consider ourselves fortunate to be able to include in this volume a reduced version of the lecture with reproductions of a few of the slides. No effort has been made to depart from the original by translating quotations.

Integrating iconographic evidence with liturgical data, Rasmussen's paper provides a detailed description and analysis of Carlo Borromeo's canonization on 1 November 1610. Picking up on Alberigo's point regarding the church's need to reinterpret by way of amputation and selection, Rasmussen shows that the process had already begun: Rome decreed that Borromeo was always to be depicted as a cardinal. The author examines canonization as a distinct ecclesiastical ceremony and this particular one, which in its baroque lavishness and grandeur surpassed all previous canonizations; the exponential increase in expenditures provides concrete evidence for this fact. The apparent loss of proportion and inordinate, abrupt growth in this sort of celebration in general are explained as features of liturgical development. By means of a sensitive as well as lively presentation, the author affords us an insight into a stupendous baroque ceremony.

By the time Alberto Melloni rose to speak on A. G. Roncalli (Pope John XXIII) and Borromeo, the conference had probably managed to secure in all minds at least one certainty thus far: the image of Borromeo as severe, rigorous, harsh in personality and in performance. Dr. Melloni, a former student of Professor Alberigo, has been preparing a computer concordance of Roncalli's writings and has written on their sources. More directly related to the purposes of the conference is Melloni's work on the massive five-volume Roncallian edition of Borromeo's Bergamese visitation of 1575, a document that would have a significant impact on the future pope both for the development of his own historical culture and for his Borromean model of pastoral care.

Melloni begins by announcing that Borromeo's harshness is a myth. He proceeds to chart Roncalli's development out of the clerical culture of the late nineteenth century toward the acquisition of a dynamic perception of history that will lead to the unraveling of the "myth." Important in his evolution is his becoming secretary of Bishop Radini Tedeschi of Bergamo, through whom he will encounter Borromeo both in pastorate and in thought. For the Lombard episcopal scene at this time was beginning to open up to provincial councils, synods, and to an increasing emphasis on visitation. In 1906 Roncalli found in the Ambrosian Library the manuscript of Borromeo's Bergamese visitation, and he embarked upon its publication. The future master of *aggiornamento* recovered a living Carlo who lacked for him the traditional ruthlessness. Here the author cites the case of Borromeo instructing Bonomi not to press too hard and be too harsh in requiring some clerics to shave their beards. Although Melloni claims no direct link between Carlo and the famous *aggiornamento,* it is in the light of Borromeo and as the product of Roncalli's historical approach that we can understand the emergence of John XXIII as a Tridentine pope. Here presumably Tridentine signifies an interpretation of Trent that emphasizes its pastoral and even episcopal implications.

In the ensuing discussion Paul Grendler rose to challenge the notion of the unraveling of a myth: the image of Borromeo is that of a very stern task-master; his synodal decrees are replete with prohibitions and penalties for every kind of clerical and lay transgression. How can the severe Borromeo of the decrees be reconciled with the mildness and charity of Roncalli's apparent image? Melloni responded that Borromeo exhibited mildness toward erring priests on a number of occasions. The severity of his synodal decrees was essentially a "pastoral strategy" to persuade priests and people toward reform. Professor Alberigo supported this view with examples and urged that Borromeo was not so severe as his decrees and reputation might suggest. Indeed an undercurrent of criticism, directed at the traditional image of Borromeo's severity, runs like a silver thread through Alberigo's own paper.

Whether John XXIII was right or not in his interpretation of Borromeo is beside the point. In the act of perception there is inevitably involved a transfer of needs and desires for the purpose of appropriation. The late sixteenth century needed harsh rules and a severe temper that is abundantly found in that commanding and spiritually moving eminence which was Carlo Borromeo. But these same qualities, so necessary for social existence four centuries ago, would prove in all their boldness intolerable today, especially in a declericalized, largely secular society. Although elements of gentleness, mildness, and charity are certainly discoverable in Borromeo, one cannot help suspecting that Roncalli as a product and interpreter of his own age put much of himself into his perception and appropriation of Borromeo. What seems incontrovertible is that this modernization of Borromeo served as a stimulus and inspiration to produce something far more anomalous and certainly far more momentous than a Borromean nuncio in the sixteenth century: namely, a twentieth-century Tridentine pope.

No matter how impressive and apparently definitive some of the findings of our conference may prove for the understanding of Borromeo, Catholic reform, and ecclesiastical politics, the whole purpose of our efforts was to open up the subject rather than close it down. Although Adriano Prosperi could darkly observe that this conference, like other centennial celebrations, will probably fail to lift the veil of obscurity that covers our subject, Giuseppe Alberigo could point to subjects that are crying for examination, such as the Council of Trent in Borromeo's thought and work or his relationship to the Jesuits at the seminary. At any rate the only fitting way

that a conference such as this could end would be to hear from a doctor of
the Ambrosian Library on the opportunities for research. Carlo Marcora's
continuous record of Borromean publications from the recognized center for
such studies makes him the father of modern research on Carlo Borromeo.
His report emphasized the correspondence present at the Ambrosiana:
35,971 letters addressed to San Carlo and twenty-four volumes of drafts of
letters expedited, the drafts revealing Borromeo's meticulous interventions
and presiding care. The Ambrosiana has compiled a card index of correspondents that awaits funds for publication. Such a catalog would prove to be a
most useful instrument for the recovery of the true physiognomy of Borromeo as well as of the church in this period.

In concluding, the planners of this conference would like to confess that
they experienced one major disappointment in their efforts to include the
best persons in the field: Paolo Prodi was approached at the very outset and
had agreed to come; only later did he find it necessary to withdraw. And yet
because his work has opened up so many windows to scholars in the field,
Prodi affirmed another sort of presence within the gathering. Therefore it is
not altogether inappropriate to shape our final reflections upon the conference in accordance with his most recent work, *Il sovrano pontefice*.

As the sixteenth century drew to an end, it was becoming evident to the
Tridentine fathers that the development of Catholic reform and of the
church's life in general had taken a course different from that of episcopal
control. Rome's need to overhaul and blur the image of Borromeo reflected
the unexpressed challenge presented by archiepiscopal reform and ecclesiastical initiative at Milan that had flowered briefly and must now be quietly
buried. Profoundly associated with the heightened universal pretensions of
the papacy, cresting at the beginning of the next century, went a process of
territorial state building that had increasingly preoccupied popes since the
mid-fifteenth century. The fact that the papal office during these years
possessed a dual role of prince/pastor, *papa/re*, could not conceal the fact
that the inner logic and dynamic of the ecclesiastical territorial state asserted
its own priorities and redefined the universal mission of the church according to its needs. Thus it would appear that the Roman church became one
more territorial state in a European world that was defining itself in terms of
territorial sovereign states. In this dangerous game the papacy survived with
increasing precariousness and with an increasingly compromised univer-
salism. If Prodi's analysis is correct that the political was preeminent in papal
policy from 1450 to 1650 and that nothing had really changed at Rome from
Renaissance to Counter-Reformation, then the Catholic reform of this
period together with the Council of Trent and the pastoral revival effected by
the Milanese school are episodes in the otherwise general European strait-
jacketing of life by the Leviathan state. Yet, if on the other hand the Counter-
Reformation and Borromeo's pastorate apparently constitute a subordinate

theme in the period, by fastening upon the properly catholic pastorate of the church and upon a longer tradition than statism can offer, the work of Carlo Borromeo becomes from this larger perspective not just the more important but the most vital and necessary for the survival of Catholic Christianity.

Initially the organizers of the conference had thought in much more modest terms of a small gathering to present a few papers on a Saturday morning nearest to 4 November 1984. But once having knocked on the door of O. B. Hardison, then director of the Folger Shakespeare Library, we soon partook of a far more grandiose vision. In the process of developing the program and realizing its goals, the planners have acquired many debts which they can only repay in expressing here their profound gratitude: principally and *sine qua non* the Division of Research Programs of the National Endowment for the Humanities whose head, Dr. Harold C. Cannon, had the courage and imagination to support such a project, and whose funds have also made possible the preparation of the conference's proceedings for the press; Georgetown University, the John Jacob Roskob Foundation, and the Maryland Province of the Society of Jesus, each for its timely financial aid in launching the conference; Lena Cowen Orlin and her staff of the Folger Institute for their wise counsel and vital assistance; the untiring, prudent, and good-natured support of Dr. Robert Schwartz, Office of Sponsored Programs, Catholic University of America, who administered the funds both for the conference and for the preparation of the proceedings for the press. We also wish to thank the Research Council of the University of North Carolina at Chapel Hill for providing supplementary financial support for the preparation of the proceedings for publication. In this task the labors of Boris Teske, graduate student in history, were appreciated. Finally, at crucial moments throughout this entire enterprise we received the counsel, aid, and support of Paul Grendler, John O'Malley, and Nelson Minnich, which in all instances proved decisively beneficial.

A word about the translation. The papers by Marc Venard, Adriano Prosperi, Giuseppe Alberigo, Carlo Marcora, all the quotations appearing in Alberto Melloni's paper, and the annotation to Agostino Borromeo's paper have been translated by John Headley. The text of Professor Borromeo's paper was translated by its author with the help of Dr. Kai Hørby of the University of Copenhagen. The editors found it necessary to reduce in a few instances the wealth of annotation to Dr. Marcora's paper in the belief that for the interested researcher what we present here would provide at this stage a sufficient conspectus of the Ambrosiana's holdings.

Notes

1. For the complete reference see n. 5 in the article by the same author, p. 64.

2. Wolfgang Reinhard, "Nepotismus. Der Funktionswandel einer papst-geschichtlichen Konstanten," *Zeitschrift für Kirchengeschichte* 86 (1975): 145–85.

3. According to Gerhart B. Ladner on the patristic period, reform could only pertain to the individual's *renovatio* of his original image-likeness to God, and not to "church reform" as such, although it might involve the monastic sphere. Only with Gregory VII did this change so as to apply to the *Ecclesia*, but the individual character of reform in the Catholic tradition remains uppermost. See his *The Idea of Reform* (New York, 1967), pp. 3–4, 277, 423–24.

4. On this last point see the interesting observations on discipline by John Bossy, *Christianity in the West, 1400–1700* (Oxford, 1985), pp. 126–40, esp. 132–33.

5. Etenim mihi meique similibus, qui misero fluctuamur orbe, vos profuerit velut inferne suspicere, vestraque instituta non aliter atque Angelicae vitae exemplar admirari, quo quasi stupore quodam virtutis alienae nostra nobis vita vilescat impensius. "Letter to a Monk," in *The Correspondence of Sir Thomas More*, ed. E. F. Rogers, (Princeton, 1947), p. 203, ll. 1433–37.

6. Perhaps the only aspect of the problem of Borromeo and France that most historians know about is the personal relationship between the Milanese archibishop and Henry III—a point which Venard did not care to treat. See Francis A. Yates, *The French Academies of the Sixteenth Century* (London, 1947), pp. 152–54, 172, 214, 217. But cf. also the revisionist judgment on their relationship by Robert J. Sealy, S.J., *The Palace Academy of Henry III* (Geneva, 1981), pp. 175–76. Although it has little bearing on Venard's argument, it is of interest that the Library of Congress possesses one of the three known copies in the United States of a work entitled *Traitté contre les Danses et les Comedies* (Paris: George Soly, 1664) which is attributed to Borromeo. According to the prefatory letter, the book dealer received the manuscript from the bishop of Montpellier who during his sojourn in Rome had faithfully had the work transcribed from a manuscript notebook, kept carefully in the library of Cardinal Francesco Barberini, with the understanding that it would be printed. While it purports to have San Carlo as its author and naturally would only gain greater currency by the attribution, the immense deployment of learned opinion on dance from Ecclesiastes to Plato, and from Basil and Cyprian to Alexander of Hales, makes it appear unlikely that the busy archbishop of Milan was its author. The first prefatory letter of the printer, Soly, to the princesse de Conti associates the work with a much larger contemporary debate raging over the immorality of the theater. André Deroo, *Saint Charles Borromée* (Paris, 1963), pp. 492–93, with considerable uncertainty suggests that a Theatine, P. François Caffaro, was the author.

7. In his preface to the first edition of the *République*, Bodin conveys the image of the ship of the French state foundering and the need for all to close ranks around the prince, his magistrates, and his laws. Plato and Aristotle appear too summary and leave us unsatiated, according to Bodin; furthermore there have been two thousand years of experience since they wrote and *la science Politicque* still remains shrouded in the same darkness, for political discourse has ignored a sound knowledge of the laws and of public law in general. I use here the Paris 1583 edition, sigs. aij–aiijv, whose preface follows the original Paris, 1576, edition.

Counter Reformation or Tridentine Reformation? Italy in the Age of Carlo Borromeo

ERIC W. COCHRANE

THE AGE OF WHICH CARLO BORROMEO WAS ONE OF THE PRINCIPAL PRO-
tagonists—that is, the age that opened with the Peace of Cateau-Cambrésis,
the fall of the Carafa, and the reconvocation of the Council of Trent and
which ended with the Interdict controversy, the Monferrato War, and the
astronomical discoveries of Galileo Galilei—was hailed by most of those
who lived through it as one of the greatest, if not the greatest, in the whole
history of Italy. This age enjoyed, contemporary observers maintained, the
most sustained external and internal peace that the peninsula had known
since the Gothic invasion of A.D. 410. Its cities had never been more
prosperous, more populous, and more magnificent. Well-organized com-
monwealths administered by well-trained law school graduates had at last
put an end to the internecine rivalries and endemic civil war that had
characterized all previous attempts at political organization since the myth-
ical Edens of the first communes; and momentary outbursts of civil discord,
like those in Genoa in 1575–76 and in Naples in 1585, were quickly suppressed or resolved. Pious and reform-minded popes, like Pius V and
Clement VIII, had replaced warrior and nepotistic popes, like Julius II and
Alexander VI, while continuing to live up to the still normative example of
Pius II and Leo X as patrons of the arts and letters. Paternalistic princes had
replaced predatory princes. Artists faithful to the doctrines of the art theorists had rejected the theoretically unjustified experiments of the "Man-
nerists" and had returned to the well-trodden ways of the masters of the
High Renaissance. Poets fully versed in the rules of Aristotelian aesthetics
were producing a creative literature quite the equal—so everyone thought—

I am most indebted to the members of the informal Renaissance colloquium at the
University of Chicago, and particularly to John Willis, for their many stylistic and
substantive criticisms of the penultimate draft of this paper.

of Vergil and Petrarch. And artists and writers in almost all the canonical genres of culture were confident of having at last realized the greatest ambition of all the humanists since Petrarch: surpassing the ancients.

This favorable view of the age of Borromeo was largely forgotten during the ahistorical age of the baroque that followed. But it was revived a century later by the founders of the Italian Enlightenment. For Giambattista Vico, the sixteenth century was the age "of the Patrizi, the Scaligers, and the Castelvetro," comparable in stature to the age of "Plato and his pupil, Aristotle." For the neo-Tridentine Pope Benedict XIV, it was the age of the scholar-prelate Marcello Cervini, to whom he looked for inspiration in his own campaign for ecclesiastical and religious reform and of whom he commissioned a biography. For Ludovico Antonio Muratori, it was "the best century of our language" as well as of the great historians whose work he sought to continue. It stood in the same relationship to the century of Petrarch and Boccaccio, Muratori proposed, as did the century of Cicero to the centuries of Homer, Hesiod, and Terence—that is, at the culmination of a long, progressive development.[1]

This view was still acceptable as late as 1825, notwithstanding the upheaval of the political and economic reforms of the later Italian Enlightenment. According to the historian of Ligurian culture, Giovan Battista Spontorno, the sixteenth century remained the most exemplary of all centuries for "the ardor shown by Italians" of the age "in the pursuit of learning."[2] By the middle of the nineteenth century, however, this view had come to be seriously questioned. Francesco De Sanctis, the influential historian of Italian literature, consigned to a limbo of "Foreign Domination" the entire period between what he deplored as the immorality of Pietro Aretino and what he hailed as the "New Literature" of Metastasio; and he wrote off even its best-known poet, Torquato Tasso, as a manifestation of "the frivolous and unsubstantial (scarso) base of Italian life" at the time, "the repose of a tired society."[3] By the mid–twentieth century, whatever was left of a once positive evaluation was wiped out by the concurrent attacks of Benedetto Croce, Antonio Gramsci, Bernard Berenson, Ferdinand Schevill, and Federico Chabod. The heirs of Machiavelli, Raphael, Savonarola, and Niccolò Capponi were decried for their subservience to foreign rulers and tastes, for their infidelity to Albertian principles of disegno, for their blindness toward the progressive nature of the Protestant Reformation, for an antieconomic "return to the land" from their previous occupations in commerce and industry, and, above all, for their lack of a "national" spirit. The age in which they lived was represented no longer as the culmination, but as the antithesis, of the two great ages that preceded it: the age of the republican communes and the age of Renaissance humanism.

This morally and aesthetically negative view of the age of Carlo Borromeo is still the one that guides most historical research in the late twentieth century. According to this view, Italian statesmen of the sixteenth century gave up an active (i.e., aggressive) role in European politics and submitted ingloriously to the hegemony of a Flemish emperor and then, worse yet, of a Spanish king. Men of letters became the sycophantic courtiers of princes. Formerly independent scholars abandoned solid scholarship for the empty oratory of frivolous academies. Protodemocratic republics were remolded into absolutistic monarchies.

Of all the charges levied against this unfortunate age, the most severe have been those associated with the term "Counter-Reformation." This term was originally coined to describe certain local phenomena in the religious history of Germany. It was formally introduced into the history of religion and the church in Italy by Hubert Jedin, who sought to distinguish the religious movements that preceded the Council of Trent from those that followed it. It was then elevated to the rank of a major periodic concept; and in this form it was broadened in scope to cover all the more important political and cultural, as well as religious and ecclesiastical, aspects of Italian life during the same eight decades after the reestablishment of the Roman Inquisition— the first major manifestation, according to Jedin, of the religious and ecclesiastical Counter-Reformation.

To be sure, it is still not entirely clear just which of these aspects can properly be characterized by the term "Counter-Reformation" and which, on the other hand, should be considered anachronisms. Most historians agree that the term should not be applied to those persons whose religious beliefs differed from those proclaimed as orthodox by the Council of Trent—those persons, in other words, whom Delio Cantimori called "heretics" or "Nicodemites." Some historians also exclude all those who, on the basis of a "key" that supposedly unlocks the hidden meaning of their otherwise innocuous writings, must have been at least crypto-Protestants.[4] Others would exclude even those whose earlier interests in ecclesiastical or spiritual reform did not lead them to support a conciliar solution to the abuses they deplored; and they usually exclude as well those who, after the council, continued to be inspired by pre-Conciliar ideals. All historians agree in including Gian Pietro Carafa, Pope Paul IV, even though he refused to call the council back into session; some of them exclude such protagonists of the council as Reginald Pole and Giovanni Morone for the very reason that Paul, the prototype of all Counter-Reformation popes, persecuted them.

What has made this term particularly attractive to historians, however, is not so much its capacity for assembling within a single category a large number of otherwise unrelated events, ideas, actions, and personalities. Its attractiveness consists rather in its capacity for supplying many different phenomena with a single, and easily comprehensible, cause. Whatever it may have been, the Counter-Reformation has been held responsible, first of all, for having perverted, even destroyed, Renaissance humanism. "Trent," says one recent historian, put "the seal of authority upon the cultural and theological synthesis of Christian faith and Aristotelian reason, of theology and philosophy"—that is, upon the exact opposite of the patristic-biblical-Ciceronian synthesis sanctioned by the humanists. What little of "humanist culture the Jesuits made their own" was transformed into a very unhumanist "instrument in the hands of a restored dogmatic and disciplinary tradition"; and it survived "only as nostalgia, as a memory not yet dimmed by the clouds of oblivion."[5] "The uncontested supremacy assumed by reformed Catholicism" thus succeeded "in neutralizing the last remnants of sixteenth-century culture and in imposing itself as a totalizing model upon every religious or social innovation." "The collapse of Renaissance humanist values" then assured the emergence "of an ideal theocratic system within which lords and potentates could occupy the place of God on earth": so says one eminent art historian; and his judgments bear the imprimatur of no less prestigious an organization than the Venice Biennale.[6]

The Counter-Reformation has also been held responsible for the destruction of Jedin's "Catholic Reform"; and the gravity of that charge has been exacerbated by the considerable sympathy with which several of the more eminent "Catholic Reformers" have been presented in recent monographic and biographical studies. "The history of the Catholic Reform is truly the history of a great defeat," says the current historiographical dean of one of Italy's largest political parties; and "to try to see in the Council of Trent . . . a continuation of that reform" is to ignore the ideological formula that the reformers invented in response to the problems of their times—namely, "Justification in Christ" (rather than, presumably, justification *in fide* or *in operibus,* which most other historians believe to have been the chief doctrinal concern of most of the reformers).[7] "The end of religious liberty in the peninsula" coincided with "the end of Italian political liberty" and "the fall of the Florentine Republic"—supposedly the last free state in Italy—"after the famous siege of 1530." As in politics, so also in religion Italy became "the object," no longer "the subject" of "initiative"—that is, "the object of disputes and the field of application of disputes and proposals of foreign origin" (the term *foreign* in this context still bears its nationalist connotation of "bad").[8]

Thus whoever among the "Reformers" managed to survive the first wave of the "everywhere victorious repression" soon succumbed to "exactly what Contarini had wanted to avoid: a drastic, profound rupture [with] the spiritual climate that had [once] prevailed in the religiously more dedicated circles of Italy."[9] Even the indomitable Roman Oratorio, which had stood up to the harsh hand of Paul IV himself in the late 1550s, put up not the slightest resistance in the 1570s, when an otherwise obscure Milanese neophite decided to transform it from "a community open to all the experiences of its members" into "a congregation rigidly regulated toward precise and exclusive ends."[10] The only consolation amid these repressive acts is the one offered by those few recent historians who find the "reformers" as distasteful as the "counter-reformers." Those historians believe that only true Reformation, the only one capable of "changing the doctrinal and pedagogical structure of . . . Christendom and offering a new image of the church," was the one promoted by Luther. Therefore, none of those "reformers" who failed to follow Luther can be considered as anything but "conservative, if not reactionary." Since they could resolve their numerous contradictions only by disguising them under the code word *beneficio*, they were unable to constitute themselves as anything but a tiny group of timid individuals—a group that scattered to the winds the moment an Ambrogio Catarino Politi growled in their direction.[11] If they remained outwardly faithful to the church, it was only because of their fascination with "the mirage of an ecclesiastical career" and their expectation of the "tangible satisfaction, in the form of prestige or riches," that such a career inevitably bestowed. For no intelligent person could ever pretend that "the prize of blessedness in the next world" was anything but a rationalization for the "conspicuous harvest of monetary profit [to be expected] in this one."[12]

The Counter-Reformation has been held responsible for much else besides. "The closed, hierarchical, and authoritarian conformism [that it] established" prevented sixteenth-century Italians from taking an interest in the recent overseas discoveries, notwithstanding, apparently, the example of such formidable geographers among them as Pietro Martire d'Anghiera, Giovan Pietro Maffei, and Giovan Battista Ramusio.[13] Its "encyclopedic spirit absorbed and systematized all branches of knowledge" into "an oratorical and propagandistic base" for "the absoluteness of [its] dogmas."[14] Its pedagogical demands forced Grand Duke Ferdinando de' Medici to establish a chair in Bible studies at the University of Pisa in 1589; he thereupon abandoned the "lay policies" of his supposedly pre- or anti-Counter-Reformation brother Francesco in favor of "bigotry"—the bigotry that continued to afflict the court of Florence even, apparently, after Galileo was appointed tutor to Ferdinando's children.[15] The Counter-Reformation "suppressed what was left of the culture that the old political order had supported" after "local tyranny and Spanish domination" had destroyed "republicanism" in all the states of Italy except Venice.[16] It forced literary culture "to close itself in a narrow isolation," notwithstanding the welcome accorded to such illustrious visitors as Jacques Callot and Rubens. It made men of letters renounce their once productive "osmosis with the intellectual and religious life [of the rest of] Europe."[17] Worst yet, it wiped out what some anthropological historians have discerned as an autonomous "popular" culture in accordance with the elitist, anti-"people" formula dictated in the name of Trent's war against superstition:

nihil quod . . . a doctoribus Ecclesiae probatis dissentiat, proferant, historias ex apochryphis scriptoribus populo ne ennarrent, neq. miracula, quae
probata scriptoris fide non commendentur, ineptas et ridiculas fabulas ne
recenseant nec supervacanea et infructuosa.[18]

Worst of all, the Counter-Reformation forced the Italian economy, previously the most "capitalist" in Europe, back into "feudalism." It deprived
Italians of "any incentive to work . . . and to invest." It cut them off from
"the grand directions of the march of international commerce." It thus
prevented them from accomplishing what was their principal obligation to
historical progress: first a bourgeois and then a proletarian revolution.[19]
Indeed, so powerful and so all-pervasive does the Counter-Reformation
seem to have been that it was able to replace "gaiety" with "somber horror"
in mid-sixteenth-century funeral ceremonies, to force one of Ludovico
Carracci's Roman imitators to be "much more constrained" in his work, to
induce Giovan Paolo Lumazzo to rail against the portrayal of saints "in
clothing that was never worn by them" ("here Counter-Reformistic preoc-
cupations are ever more evident," says the editor), and, finally, to mislead
Francesco Verino into supposing that "good morals" were an important
requirement for nominations to university chairs.[20]

This view of the age of Carlo Borromeo has been accorded canonical
status by almost all historians who concern themselves with Italian affairs.
On their authority, it has also been accepted as axiomatic by most of those
who have had occasion to refer to Italy in other contexts. According to
Hellis Yiortopoulo Sisilianou, the current authority on the history of Corfù,

> the Counter Reformation climate was . . . exacerbated by the increase of
> political influence in Italy of the intolerant Spanish monarchy. . . . With
> its center in Rome, and particularly in the Vatican, it brought about a
> profound rejection of humanist ideals.[21]

According to an *équipe* of American historians headed by Crane Brinton in
the 1981 revision of their widely used textbook of European history, the
Council of Trent was most notable for having "forbidden individuals to
interpret the Scripture contrary to the teaching of the Church"—to the
sorrow, it seems, of "liberal Catholics, who have always felt that the Council
was a mere instrument [in the hands of] of the popes and the Jesuits."[22]

*   *   *

Widely accepted though it may be, however, this canonical view of the age
of Carlo Borromeo has not proven to be entirely satisfactory. First, it has
failed to give an adequate account of the origins of the "Counter-Reformation." For example, it has not been able to explain why those who are called
"Evangelicals," in deference to their supposedly anti- or ante-Counter-

Reformation character, should have been just as intransigent as the "intransigents" when confronted with the "arrogance and pride joined with great ignorance" (to use the words of Gaetano Contarini) of the intransigent dissenters in Modena. In fact, those who most frequently use the word do not state clearly what the "intransigents" were intransigent about, since before Trent there was very little consensus concerning the orthodoxy of most of the doctrinal hypotheses then being brought forth. Nor does this view explain the willingness of most of the "Evangelicals" to accept the council's doctrinal decisions once they were formulated, to remain the good personal friends of those responsible for the formulations, and to sacrifice what some modern theological historians treasure as an essential "space of freedom" in theological matters.[23] Before such apparent anomalies, some recent historians have been forced to take refuge in Romeo De Maio's condemnation of all the "Evangelicals" as *gretti*—as narrow-minded individuals who, "had they prevailed against the sanguine and intolerant Paul IV, would have given the church a turn still more devastating to fundamental human liberties."[24]

Similarly, the application of this view to different aspects of the same issue has occasionally yielded contradictory theses. A good example is the issue of the relation between religion and politics, state and church. If Venice closed itself off from the Counter-Reformation that had engulfed the rest of Italy, how is it that, according to one recent historian, "orthodoxy triumphed in the whole territory of the *Serenissima* . . . thanks to the repressive work of the tribunal of the Venetian Inquisition" and thanks to the support given the Inquisition by "the Venetian administration"?[25] If "the ideology expressed by the Counter Reformation was a function of"—and thus a cover-up for— "the new forms of political power,"[26] how is it that a "minister of the Holy Roman Church" and a "consultant of Borromeo" like Lelio Gavardo could have written a dissertation on politics of which the "notoriously utilitaristic"—i.e., Machiavellian—character has puzzled even so seasoned a historian of economics as Aldo DeMaddelena?[27] How is it that the "*Casacce* and the confraternities" of Liguria could have "flourished explosively" and embarked upon a myriad of "Christian-social services" just at a moment when they should have been "suffocated" by "ecclesiastical centralization"?[28] One dilettante of the currently fashionable subdiscipline of the history of printing has been so upset by the abundant evidence recently assembled concerning the quantity and variety of literature then in circulation, that she has chastized the ecclesiastical censors for being "overburdened, inefficient, or easily bribed."[29] A well-known historian of political ideas has chastized the chief assembler of such evidence, Paul Grendler, for failing to identify the free circulation of all ideas with the free circulation specifically of Protestant theological doctrines.[30]

Even more contradictory have been the results reached in the history of

natural philosophy. Did the Counter-Reformation favor the further elabora-
tion of Aristotelianism? It "must have," answers one historian:

> The re-evaluation and exaltation . . . of the Aristotelian-scholastic systems
> aimed at the restoration of the principle of authority was brought about by
> means of the scholastic method, of which the Jesuits became the most
> authoritative depositories."[31]

The "dogmatic, erudite, Counter-Reformationistic" Aristotelianism of the
"citadel of the learned," answers another historian, along with "the Accademia degli Infiammati, . . . Sperone Speroni . . . , the critics, ico-
nographers, popularizers, and poligraphers [who were] always ready to
serve the authorities with any kind of eulogy," constantly opposed the
"popular, rustic, dialect, interest in the real and the concrete," an interest
that led nascent natural science from Copernicus through Cardano to
Galileo."[32] Indeed, "the empty remnants of Aristotelianism, the Counter
Reformation and baroque scaffolding by which Italian thought had been
suffocated" did not finally "dissolve"—to continue the admirably baroque
metaphor—until the age of Pietro Giannone.[33] Quite the contrary, answers
no less an authority on Renaissance Aristotelianism than Charles Schmitt.
"In Italy, the Counter Reformation successfully cut off the drive toward the
discovery of self-consciousness. It successfully encouraged the . . . produc-
tion of a vast series of manuals . . . based on a retrograde and prosaic version
of Aristotle's philosophy." As a result, "the Aristotelian tradition in the
universities became exhausted, confined as it was not only by the regulations
of the Inquisition, but also by the new aspirations for a culture ever more
clerical and subservient to the church."[34]

Did the Counter-Reformation also block the emergence of modern science? Most certainly, answer almost all the current specialists: the church,
with the help of the Index and the Inquisition, stamped out the last flicker of
free discussion, and it put acritical acceptance of authority in the place of an
objective search for the truth. But when faced with the considerable number
of technical manuals that issued from the Italian presses in just those years,
these same historians are forced to imagine that the manuals "must have been
submerged" by a similar growth in the number of religious manuals. When
faced both with the amazing productivity of such an original and innovative
scientist as Ulisse Aldrovandi and with Aldrovandi's equally fervent Tridentine religious piety, they are forced to make of him an inexplicable exception
to a general rule. They are also forced to suppose, on the basis of what has
been written about the "Nicodemites," that Aldrovandi's "return to the
tracks of orthodoxy could not have been the fruit of a wholly spontaneous
and deeply felt choice."[35]

In the field of literature, the search for the effects of the Counter-Reformation has forced historians to chop up persons, institutions, and classes into separate pieces. Tasso, for instance, becomes a *barone dimezzato:* "Only the deteriorated parts of his personality belong to the Counter Reformation and the Counter Reformationist spirit."[36] Giovan Battista Strozzi wrote some madrigals that were "grave" and "bizzare" and others that were "pastimes, . . . somewhere between Counter Reformation and baroque"; only the latter managed to pass through "the silent operation of censorship" adopted by his heirs "in the suffocating climate of Tridentine conformism brought to Florence in 1586."[37] Men of letters, whom the church had appointed solely for their literary accomplishments early in the century, were subsequently separated into two distinct groups: "lay intellectuals and ecclesiastical intellectuals." If any of the latter happened to show up also among the former, that must be attributed to "the mechanisms of integration between the church and civil society," or, more precisely, to the success of "the Counter Reformation . . . in making lay culture a subsidiary of ecclesiastical culture."[38] Even the Tridentine decrees have been split into two categories: those which enabled "Tridentine oppression" to exercise its "ideological violence," and those, like the exclusion of Ovid and Catullus from the Index, which made it "a masterpiece of hypocrisy."[39]

In another area of Italian culture, that of art and art theory, most of the supporting evidence for the deleterious effects of the "Counter-Reformation" comes from no more than three or four documents: the two dialogues of an otherwise obscure Umbrian named Giovanni Andrea Giglio, some deathbed remarks by the famous architect Bartolomeo Ammannati about the inappropriateness of nudes in ecclesiastical paintings, and the elaborations of Carlo Borromeo and Gabriele Paleotti upon the admittedly very generic guidelines set down hastily in the last days of the council. But what are these among the so many treatises, paintings, and statues that constituted the most important aesthetic revolution in the history of Italy between the time of Pontormo and Alessi and the time of Winckelmann and Mengs? Giglio's dialogues appeared in only one small, haphazardly printed edition in tiny Camerino. They had the nerve to proclaim, after all that Vasari had written some fourteen years earlier, that "this excellent art has neither book nor rule which give painters the means and procedure for doing all kinds of figures." And no one seems to have paid any attention to them until they were picked up and turned into a paradigm of all "Counter-Reformation" art theory by Federico Zeri in 1957.[40] Similarly, Ammannati's relationship with the Society of Jesus, whose college in Florence he built and endowed, is best documented not by any set of structural or stylistic commands, but by a respectful letter from the general, Claudio Acquaviva, in 1590.

> Your design of the facade of the College on the side toward S. Lorenzo has pleased us very much; and we have nothing else to do but to entrust

ourselves to your great prudence, since you yourself know very well what is suitable for our company.[41]

Finally, an unguided reading of selected chapters of Paleotti's *Discorso intorno alle imagini sacre e profane* of 1582 may well seem to justify labeling as "Counter-Reformistic" certain recommendations regarding those works of art which were destined for "the glory of God, the discipline of ourselves, and the edification of our neighbor." But a reading of other chapters will reveal that the rules for sacred art were not meant to apply to works of art destined rather for the glory of the artist or his patron. Those ends, admitted Paleotti, were equally legitimate; but they were to be realized with the help not of the Tridentine decrees, but of the same, wholly nonreligious, principles that had been sanctioned by all the non-Counter-Reformation art theorists since Leon Battista Alberti. Moreover, providing that they are read in the light of what Paolo Prodi discovered about their genesis some twenty-three years ago, a reading even of the chapters on sacred art will reveal the hand not of an authoritarian bishop, but of the literary and artistic avant garde of his diocese, to whom the bishop turned for advice on matters within their special field of competence. Since the diocese happened to be Bologna, and since Bologna was just then emerging as the most creative art capital of Italy, it is not surprising that those chapters contain *in nuce* most of the principles that were to revolutionize all Italian art during the following two decades.[42]

To imagine, therefore, that "in the rigoristic and austere climate" of Tridentine "neo-feudalism, neo-medievalism, and primitivism" artists "descended to shoddy qualitative levels" is to overlook the "tremendous joie-de-vivre," the "new blossoming of vitality and of energy" that Rudolf Wittkower discovered in the gallery commissioned by that staunch protagonist of the Tridentine Reformation, Odoardo Farnese.[43] To suppose that "minor artists bore with passivity the directives of the church" and that "artists suspected of promoting a radicalization of religious demands coming from the bottom of society" were "pushed aside *(emarginare)*" is to set up a bifurcation of the late Renaissance artistic community that no one at the time, and no sociological historian since, has yet discerned.[44] Not even Father Pietro Pirri of the Society of Jesus, after all, was able to find a trace of "Jesuit architecture" in the works of the Jesuit architect Giovanni Tristano.[45]

From one area of culture, finally, the Counter-Reformation has been totally excluded: music. For Palestrina's decision "to dedicate all my efforts to adorning the most holy Sacrifice of the Mass with new modes" was clearly the result not of his submission to ecclesiastical authority—much less of Paul IV's fixation about married musicians in the Sistine Chapel—but of his recognition that his own aspirations for the further development of polyphony coincided with Trent's recommendations concerning church music:

that it be comprehensible, not just entertaining.[46] Glareanus's proclamation of the demise of medieval liturgical modes demonstrates not that music was about to lose its autonomy, but that "the evolution of music had come together with the liturgical requirements exposed in the Council's Canon VIII."[47] The musicians themselves agreed, in accordance not with the dictates of the clergy but with the rhetorical principles of their own theorists, that "the temple of God [ought not to become] a place for reciting lascivious and ridiculous things." Their ecclesiastical patrons obliged them by admitting that "on the stage, it is perfectly permissible to recite every kind of clown-like, ridiculous, and lascivious music."[48] "The church music declarations of Trent" thus turn out to be, in the words of no less an authority on music history than Karl Gustav Fellerer, "the outcome of theological and musical development rooted in humanism; and they became the guiding principle for further musical and liturgical innovations."[49]

It is not surprising, then, that only one non–music historian has dared to assert, not having read the music historians, that music retrogressed everywhere in late sixteenth-century Italy except in Venice because there it was "preserved . . . from Tridentine puritanism." After all, the same historian, not having read his non–music historian colleagues either, also thinks that "there is no question that by the 1590's Florence"—the Florence of Jacopo Peri, Ludovico Cigoli, and Pietro Tacca—"had become an artistic backwater."[50] Nor is it surprising that only one of the many recent historians of music in Italy has seen fit to use the term "Counter Reformation" in a title: Lewis Lockwood. But Lockwood's account of Vincenzo Ruffo's collaboration with Carlo Borromeo does not demonstrate the subservience of the Milanese musicians to one prelate's pretended omniscience. It demonstrates rather "the connection [between] the post-Tridentine argument for intelligibility [and] the ideas espoused by musicians"—even purely "secular" musicians like Vincenzo Galilei—"with problems of expression."[51]

∗ ∗ ∗

The recognition of these and other difficulties involved in applying the concept "Counter-Reformation" to the history of the sixteenth century has brought protests from a few brave scholars in the field. Mario Rosa has attributed them to "the pulverization of research into the atomism of single individualities and single situations," a pulverization that obliges monograph writers to accept uncritically general paradigms handed to them from the outside.[52] Thomas Buser has insisted that "a definite relationship between the Counter Reformation and the arts had never been determined" and that the textbooks which assume such a relationship merely "repeat the same undocumented generalizations."[53] Arnaldo D'Addario—in a detailed study of Florentine religious life of the period—has objected to the "repetition of historiographical commonplaces on the theme of Counter Reformation";

and he has blamed the consequent deformations upon "the ideological preconception that this historical period was a moment of involution . . . or of the mortification of moral commitment."[54] Paolo Prodi—in a study of the relation between religion and politics in the Papal State—has denounced what he calls "a veritable iron cage, which suffocates even the most recent studies, forcing them into schemes that are now old and fruitless."[55]

Given the paucity, the rarity, and the apparent ineffectiveness of these voices of protest, however, a more incisive remedy may be necessary. It may be, indeed, that the entire framework within which the study of Italy in the age of Carlo Borromeo has been carried on for the last century or so is now in a condition similar to that of the Aristotelian philosophical and scientific cosmos on the eve of Galileo's discovery of the satellites of Jupiter. If so, then patching up the ever more numerous holes in what has lost its potentiality to stimulate new scholarship will do little but mislead even more scholars in the future.

Names, to be sure, do not determine things. But getting rid of a name that has now become hopelessly overburdened with prejudicial connotations would at least be a good beginning. Replacing a charged term with a still relatively neutral term like "Tridentine Reformation" would have at least one practical advantage: that of freeing the protagonists of current Italian political polemics from the fear of provoking—with such tactical blunders as the flight of the terrorist Toni Negri—another "huge Counter Reformation in an authoritative direction."[56] But a new name of this sort might be equally advantageous in the realm of scholarship. It would make possible bringing together under a single denomination all those various religious movements, persons, and institutions that led up to, paralleled, were sanctioned by, or issued from the Council of Trent. It would encourage a reassessment of the humanist content of such typically "Counter-Reformation" phenomena as the pedagogical program of Silvio Antoniano, whose recommendations to Carlo Borromeo for making saints of the children of Milan were based as much upon Plutarch and Sadoleto as upon the Roman catechism.[57]

To be sure, this change of names would necessitate a considerable redrawing of the overexpanded boundaries previously assigned to the "Counter-Reformation." For it would have to take account of one of the chief assumptions of Renaissance humanism: the mutual autonomy of the various areas of human endeavor. Tridentine piety and theology, along with Tridentine art and music, may thus turn out to have constituted one, two, but by no means all of the many different components of late Renaissance culture—just as the Christian religion has turned out, in the most recent scholarly studies of such key figures as Lorenzo Valla and Cristoforo Landino, to have constituted one of the principal components of the supposedly "lay" culture of the early Renaissance. At the same time, that part of late Renaissance culture which properly falls within the definition of a "Tridentine Reformation" may be shown not to have destroyed humanist culture, but rather to have promoted the generation of such latecomers to the humanist disciplines as archaeology and ecclesiastical historiography, those favorite enterprises of Filippo Neri's—and Cesare Baronio's—Roman Oratorio.[58] When the evidence collected years ago by Federico Chabod is at last put together with such subsequently published documents as the diary of Giambattista Casale and the petition of the *parlamento* of Celle in western Liguria, the Tridentine Reformation may prove to have been the work not only for certain arbitrarily selected "Counter-Reformation" prelates, but also of the ordinary citizens of Milan and Celle, who willingly cooperated with anyone willing to transform the earthly city of Milan or village of Celle into Trent's version of the heavenly city of God.[59]

Thus Roberto Bellarmino's *summa*, Francesco Panigarola's sermons, Gregory XIII's calendar, and Clement VIII's Latin Bible may well be recognized as monuments of the Tridentine Reformation. But they seem to have had little or nothing to do with Battista Guarini's *Pastor fido*, Annibale Carracci's *Butcher Shop*, Giacomo Zabarella's *Opera Logica*, Lionardo Salviati's *Lo 'Nfarinato secondo*, Alessandro Farnese's fiscal reforms, the Strada Nuova of Genoa, or many of the other literary, political, and artistic monuments of the age. Out of respect for its variety, its productivity, and its polymorphous character, the age can no longer be called the Age of the Counter-Reformation or even the Age of the Tridentine Reformation. It may have to be rebaptized, in accordance with what now seems to have been its most pervasive character, as the Age of Consolidation.

Notes

1. Vico, *Prima scienza nuova*, Sec. 253; Pietro Polidoro, *De Vita, Gestis, et Moribus Marcelli II Commentarius* (Rome, 1744); Muratori to Anton Maria Salvini, 1 August 1704, in *Opere*, ed. Giorgio Falco and Fiorenzo Forti (Naples-Milan: Ricciardi, 1964), 2:1817.
2. *Storia letteraria della Liguria* (Genoa, 1825), 3:1–2.
3. *Storia della letteratura italiana,* ed. Benedetto Croce and A. Parente (Bari: Laterza, 1939), 2:161.
4. Eric Cochrane in *Catholic Historical Review* 68 (1982): 501–4. For exactly the opposite opinion of the monograph in question, see the eulogy ("il bel volume . . . ha offerto l'indubbia testimonianza della profondità e della minuziosità della ricerca compiuto [by the author], e questo suo . . . singolare lavoro non può non essere accolto con vivo interesse dagli storici della cultura e delle idee") by one of the author's junior colleagues, Giovanni Cipriani, in *Il pensiero politico* 17 (1981): 118.
5. Vittorio Facchietti in *Il Rinascimento: Aspetti e problemi attuali* (Florence: Olschki, 1982), p. 371; Gino Benzoni in *Storici e politici veneti del Cinquecento e del Seicento,* ed. Benzoni and Tiziano Zanato ("La letteratura italiana: Storia e testi," 35, pt. 2) (Milan-Naples: Ricciardi, 1982), p. 494.
6. Zorzi in *I teatri pubblici di Venezia* (Venice: Biennale, 1971), p. 25; on the dangers of isolating the study of the "reformation" in Italy from other aspects of the

culture of the age, see Silvana Seidel Menchi, "Lo stato degli studi sulla riforma in Italia," *Wolfenbütteler Renaissance Mitteilungen* 5 (1981): 35–42.

7. Nicola Badaloni, *Cultura e vita civile tra Riforma e Controriforma* ("Letteratura Italiana Laterza," 24) (Bari: Laterza, 1974), p. 110.

8. Maurilio Adriani, *Storia religiosa d'Italia* (Rome: Biblioteca di Storia Patria, 1968), p. 351.

9. Giovanni Miccoli, "La storia religiosa," in the Einaudi *Storia d'Italia*, vol. 2, pt. 1, p. 1001.

10. Maria Teresa Bonadonna Russo, "Le 'Memorie' del p. Pompeo Pateri," *Archivio della Società Romana di Storia Patria* 97 (1974).

11. Romeo De Maio, *Riforme e miti nella Chiesa del Cinquecento* (Naples: Guida, 1973), here quoted on p. 14; Paolo Simoncelli, *Evangelismo italiano del Cinquecento* (Rome: Istituto Storico Italiano, 1979), esp. pp. 113–15.

12. Benzoni in *Storici e politici* (above, n. 5), p. 495.

13. Massimo Firpo, *Pietro Bizzarri* (Turin: Giappichelli, 1971), p. 153.

14. Manfredo Tafuri in *Studi sul Borromini* (Rome: Accademia Nazionale di San Luca, 1967), 2:40.

15. Giovanni Cascio Pratili, *L'università e il principe* (Florence: Olschki, 1975), p. 167.

16. William Bouwsma, "Venice, Spain, and the Papacy," in *The Late Italian Renaissance*, ed. Eric Cochrane (New York: Harper & Row, 1970), p. 358.

17. Antonio Rotondò in "La censura ecclesiastica e la cultura," in the Einaudi *Storia d'Italia*, 5, quoted on p. 1404.

18. Archbishop Scipione Gesuado on preaching, quoted by Pasquale Lopez in *Riforma cattolica e vita religiosa e culturale a Napoli dalla fine del '500 ai primi del '700* (Naples: Istituto Editoriale del Mezzogiorno, 1964), p. 25.

19. Sergio Zoli in *La Controriforma* (Florence: La Nuova Italia, 1979), pp. 23–24, where he accepts the theses of Josef Macek in *Il Rinascimento italiano*, trans. Hana Kubistova-Casadei (Rome: Edizioni Riuniti, 1972).

20. Eve Borsook, "The Funeral of Cosimo I de' Medici," *Mitteilungen des Kunsthistorischen Instituts in Florenz* 12 (1965): 40–41; S. J. Freedberg, *Circa 1600* (Cambridge: Harvard University Press, 1983), p. 84; *Scritti d'arte del Cinquecento*, ed. Paola Barocchi (Milan-Naples: Ricciardi, 1971–73), p. 2244; Alessandra Del Fonte in *Nuova rivista storica* 64 (1980): 401–3.

21. Ἀντώνιος ὁ Ἐπαρχός: Ἕνας Κερκυραῖος ουμανιστής τοῦ ΙΣΤ΄αἰῶνα (Athens, 1978), pp. 146–48.

22. Crane Brinton, John B. Christopher, and Robert Lee Wolff, *Civilization in the West* (Englewood Cliffs, N.J.: Prentice-Hall, 1981), p. 248.

23. Quoted (and explained) by Massimo Firpo in "Gli 'Spirituali', l'Accademia di Modena e il formulario di fede del 1542," which the author kindly permitted me to read in the typescript presented at a meeting at Lucca in October 1983.

24. *Michelangelo e la Controriforma* (Bari: Laterza, 1978), p. 8.

25. Armando Pitassio, Facoltà di Scienze Politiche, Università di Perugia, *Annali* (1970), p. 7.

26. Gian Paolo Brizzi, "Educare il principe," in *Università, Principe, Gesuiti* (Rome: Bulzoni, 1980), p. 141.

27. DeMaddelena, "Fragilità delle istituzioni," *Rivista storica italiana* 45 (1983): 314–31.

28. Edoardo Grendi, "Le confraternite liguri in età moderna," in *La Liguria delle casacce* (Genoa, 1982), p. 49.

29. Elizabeth Eisenstein in *The Printing Press as an Agent of Change* (Cambridge: Cambridge University Press, 1979), 1:145.

30. Gaetano Cozzi in *Journal of Modern History* 50 (1979): 90–98, reviewing Grendler, *The Roman Inquisition and the Venetian Press* (Princeton: Princeton University Press, 1977).

31. Maria Rosa Di Simone, *La 'Sapienza' romana nel Settecento* (Rome: Ateneo, 1980), p. 81.

32. Michelangelo Murano, *Le pitture della chiesa di S. Tommaso Apostolo* (Albignasego, 1980), pp. 20, 23–24.

33. Raffaello Ajello in *Pietro Giannone e il suo tempo*, ed. Ajello (Naples: Jovene, 1980), 1:98.

34. *Cesare Cremonini* (Centro Tedesco di Studi Veneziani: Quaderno 16) (Venice, 1980), pp. 7–8.

35. Giuseppe Olmi, *Ulisse Aldrovandi: Scienza e natura nel secondo Cinquecento* (Università di Trento, Quaderni di Storia e Filosofia della Scienza, Quaderno 4), pp. 46–48 and 61; Manlio Brusatin in the Einaudi *Storia d'Italia*, 3:60.

36. Giambattista Salinari in the introduction to *Novelle del Cinquecento*, 2d ed. (Turin: UTET, 1976), p. 23.

37. Marco Adriani in the introduction to his edition of Giambattista Strozzi il Vecchio, *Madrigali inediti* (Urbino: Argalle, 1975).

38. Alberto Asor Rosa, *La cultura della Controriforma* ("Letteratura Italiana Laterza," 26) (Bari, 1974), p. 31; Vincenzo De Caprio, "Aristocrazia e clero dalla crisi dell'umanesimo alla Controriforma," in the Einaudi *Letteratura italiana* (1983), 2:351.

39. Nicola Longo, "Prolegomeni per una storia della letteratura italiana censurata," *Rassegna della letteratura italiana* 78 (1974): 402–19.

40. Zeri, *Pittura e Controriforma: L'arte senza tempo di Scipione da Gaeta* (Turin: Einaudi, 1957). *Scritti d'arte del Cinquecento*, ed. Paola Barocchi ("Classici Ricciardi," 82) (Milan-Naples: Ricciardi, 1971), p. 835.

41. Published by Filippo Baldinucci in *Notizie dei professori del disegno* (Florence, 1846: reprint, S.P.E.S., 1974), 2:394.

42. Prodi's *Ricerche sulla teorica delle arti figurative nella Riforma cattolica* (Rome: Edizioni di Storia e Letteratura, 1962) is not mentioned in the harangue against the "il nuovo canone dell'autocensura dell'artista minuziosamente tenuta d'occhio . . . da Paleotti . . . , i cardinali legati e da tutto un apparato clericale conformista e soffocante" in Piero Camporesi's preface to his edition of *La maschera di Bertoldo* (Turin: Einaudi, 1976). I quote from the text published by Barocchi in *Scritti d'arte* (above, n. 40), pp. 916, 190, 902.

43. Luigi Salerno in the Einaudi *Storia dell'arte italiana*, 2d ed. 2:449–50; Wittkower, *Art and Architecture in Italy, 1600–1750* (Pelican History of Art, 1958), p. 64.

44. Annalisa Bristot in *Saggi e memorie di storia dell'arte* 12 (1980): 35.

45. *Giovanni Tristano e i primordi della architettura gesuitica* (Rome: Institutum Historicum S. J., 1955).

46. Palestrina quoted by Karl Gustav Fellerer in *Der Stilwandel in der abendlandischen Musik um 1600* (Oplander: Westdeutscher Verlag, 1972), p. 13.

47. Fellerer in Lino Bianchi and Fellerer, *Giovanni Pierluigi da Palestrina* (Turin: RAI, 1971), p. 260.

48. Vicentino quoted by Henry William Kaufmann in *The Life and Works of Nicola Vicentino* (American Institute of Musicology, 1966), p. 39.

49. "Wandlungen der mehrstimmigen Kirchenmusik im 16. Jahrhundert," *Kirchenmusikalisches Jahrbuch* 61–62 (1977–78): 2.

50. These are the opinions of H. G. Koenigsberger in "Republics and Courts in Italian and European Culture in the Sixteenth and Seventeenth Centuries," *Past and Present* 83 (1979), here quoted on p. 47.

51. *The Counter-Reformation and the Masses of Vincenzo Ruffo* (Venice: Universal Edition, 1970), p. 130.

52. In "Geografia e storia religiosa," *Nuova rivista storica* 53 (1969): 1–43.

53. In *Art Bulletin* 58 (1976): 424.

54. *Aspetti della Controriforma a Firenze* (Rome: Archivio di Stato, 1972), p. ix.

55. *Il sovrano pontefice* (Bologna: Il Mulino, 1982), p. 8.

56. Marco Pannella quoted in *La repubblica*, 19 October 1983, p. 8.

57. *Tre libri dell'educazione christiana scritti ad instanza di mons. illustriss. cardinale di S. Prassede Archivescovo di Milano* (Verona, 1584).

58. Eric Cochrane, *Historians and Historiography in the Italian Renaissance* (Chicago: University of Chicago Press, 1981), pp. 458–63.

59. Casale, *Diario*, ed. Carlo Manacorda, in *Memorie storiche della diocesi di Milano* 12 (1965): ample selections in English translation will soon appear in the University of Chicago *Selected Readings in the History of Western Civilization*. (University of Chicago Press, 1985), vol. 5. The decree of the Parlamento of Celle is published by Gian Luigi Bruzzoni in *Analecta Augustiniana* 45 (1982): 299.

Carlo Borromeo and the Council of Trent: The Question of Reform

ROBERT TRISCO

HISTORIANS HAVE LONG RECOGNIZED THAT CARLO BORROMEO, THE CAR-
dinal-nephew who directed the papal secretariat during the third period of
the Council of Trent, was exceedingly faithful and tireless in carrying out
Pius IV's wishes, but they agree that because of his youth and lack of
experience he had little influence on his uncle's policy and made no important decisions without his permission. The Venetian ambassador, Girolamo
Soranzo, expressed that conclusion in his final report to the Senate of the
Serene Republic in June 1563, saying that Pius did not consult the other
cardinals, because most or all of them were bound to some prince, and made
use only of Borromeo and Tolomeo Galli (the secretary of the papal chancery and private secretary of the pope as well as bishop of Siponto), who was
several years older than Borromeo; Soranzo stated that these two, being
young and having little or no experience and deferring to the pope's least
hint, could be called simple executors rather than counselors. The ambassador acknowledged, however, that the pope did handle all affairs through
his nephew.[1] In the same vein, Josef Šusta, who edited Borromeo's correspondence with the legates at the council, concluded that in contrast to the
cardinal-nephews in earlier pontificates, such as Carlo Carafa and Alessandro Farnese, who had impressed the stamp of their own personality on
papal policy, Borromeo was pictured only as the dutiful assistant of his
uncle, who with indefatigable diligence was occupied with the administration of the Papal States and the management of the chancery but was unable
to make any independent decision in affairs of state; on the contrary, even in
the smallest matters he had first to ascertain the will of the pope. He did not
take advantage of the great favor in which Pius held him to increase his
power.[2] Similarly, Pio Paschini observed that because of his youth Borromeo
(born on 2 October 1538), who had just finished his studies, was not in a
position to exercise a strong influence on Pius IV, an expert jurist and skilled
curialist who had wielded public authority for so many years.[3] Finally,
Hubert Jedin, the distinguished historian of the Council of Trent, wrote that

Carlo considered himself only a collaborator and an instrument of his uncle and added that during the two great crises of the council—in April 1562, and in the winter of 1562–63—he cannot be shown to have favored the reform party at Trent and its leaders, the cardinal-legates Ercole Gonzaga and Girolamo Seripando, nor to have opposed the party of the *zelanti* or extreme papalists; rather it was the council and the reform movement that animated it which pointed out to Borromeo the way that he was to follow later and which contributed to the spiritual development that he initiated in 1562.[4]

As the one who composed on behalf of the pope most of the dispatches from Rome regarding the council, Borromeo was intimately involved in the great assembly from the beginning of his uncle's pontificate until the final papal confirmation of its decrees. Through his correspondence with the legates at Trent and with the nuncios at the several Catholic courts, as well as through his relations with the ambassadors in Rome (who, of course, reported his words to their sovereigns), he could not avoid revealing to some extent his own attitude toward the controversial question of ecclesiastical reform that preoccupied the council during these years. It is true that his dispatches to the legates and nuncios are filled with such expressions as "His Holiness says," "His Beatitude desires," or "Our Lord is pleased," but in some passages he does not invoke the pope's authority to support his directive or advice. In those cases it is more difficult to determine whether he simply did not wish to cite the pontiff lest he implicate him in dubious dealings or was stating his own position.

Basically Borromeo shared his uncle's fear of the council as a potential enemy of the papacy. Although they could rely on the Italian bishops who were loyal to the Holy See out of conviction or self-interest, and more of that kind could always be sent to Trent as needed, they knew that many of the non-Italians and even a few of the Italians still harbored conciliarist theories or obeyed governments that disputed the papacy's claims to rule the church in their countries. Even many prelates who did not contest the papal primacy were convinced by recent history that the needed reforms would never be enacted unless the council undertook the task without restraint. The pope and his court wished to limit the discussions lest the council infringe on the rights and prerogatives of the Holy See, and they denied that the council had any competence over the Roman Curia, which the pope would reform independently through his own decrees.[5]

To put this policy into practice, Borromeo as the chief minister of the Supreme Pontiff had recourse to certain expedients that reflected little credit on the papacy. Pius did not fully trust even all the legates whom he had appointed to direct the council; his only confidant among them was his fellow Milanese, Cardinal Lodovico Simonetta, a "clever canonist"[6] and a zealous defender of the papal supremacy. Only he, although a junior legate, and the president of the council (Ercole Gonzaga, the Cardinal of Mantua) were provided with a code for secret correspondence with Rome. Borromeo wrote Simonetta many letters apart from the other legates; in one of them, in April 1562, he begged him to pardon him if he was too forward in speaking and then to give him his opinion regarding a certain matter; he added, "and if for the future you will take particular care always to write the opinion of each one of the illustrious legates and the inclination and mood, especially when certain doubts will occur, since it will be something worthy of your illustrious Lordship's diligence and fidelity, I know that it will be most pleasing to Our Lord [the pope]."[7] This habit of dealing separately with a lower-ranking member of the college or board of legates inevitably provoked disharmony among them and diminished their mutual trust, unintentionally throwing sand into the gears of the council.

Eventually in the spring of 1562 a crisis arose at Trent over the question of whether the bishops' obligation to reside in their dioceses was *de jure divino* or merely of ecclesiastical law (from which the pope could dispense); Pius IV did not want the council to define that residence was obligatory by divine law because the Holy See would then be criticized, especially by Protestants, for having granted dispensations from a divine law. Reports from numerous prelates at Trent who wished to prove their devotion to the Holy See painted the dissension in the council in such vivid colors that the whole Curia was alarmed. Several reports of Simonetta, who, of course, had been firmly opposed to any declaration of a basis in divine law for the duty of residence, created a profound impression on the pope. As the conciliar discussion became more and more protracted and embittered, Pius lost confidence in the ability of the cardinal-president, Gonzaga of Mantua, to control the situation and decided to appoint two more legates, one of whom would outrank Gonzaga and thus assume the presidency of the council.[8] Borromeo transmitted to Simonetta the pope's directive to resist *"etiam in faciem"* any of the legates in whom there was no improvement or if anything was attempted "against us."[9]

The Cardinal of Mantua, who had come close to being elected pope in the last conclave and still had ambitions to succeed Pius IV, had to be treated very circumspectly. Borromeo, therefore, tried to soften the blow by writing the cardinal a lengthy letter. He said that the pope was so upset by this strident controversy that he was thinking of sending the Cardinal of San Clemente, Giovanni Battista Cicada, an expert canonist familiar with the Curia, who would help Mantua to maintain the dignity of the Holy See against any assailants, especially the French who were expected to arrive shortly. Borromeo wrote that he and Cardinal Francesco Gonzaga, Mantua's nephew who was trying to protect his interests in the Curia, had done everything that seemed appropriate to prevent the pope's decision, but they were outdone by "many both in the council and at Rome, who have converged from every side to indicate to His Holiness by mouth and with letters that, unless provision be made, the total destruction of this see and of this court will come to pass." Borromeo recognized "that many through wickedness, many through simplicity, many who have been seduced by the violence of the intrigues, are all united" in blaming the legates. All that Francesco Gonzaga and Borromeo could obtain with much effort was that the pope's letter informing the legates of his dissatisfaction and of his intention was not dispatched immediately and that Pius was willing to declare in a general congregation that he had been asked by Mantua to make this provision. The fact that Borromeo and Mantua's nephew, who were his very devoted servants, as he called them, could not achieve more for him showed, he asserted, how much trouble this affair was causing. He assured Mantua, "Indeed, I see in the pope so much love for your illustrious Lordship that greater cannot be desired. . . ; but on the other hand, the importance of the business at hand, in which it would be a great matter that His Holiness would never fail to do anything that would be for the benefit of this see and the preservation of its dignity, makes him go very cautiously. . . ." Borromeo was sure that if "the public interest" made the pope stand firm in his intention, he would on another occasion always show his desire to promote Mantua's greatness and honor. He promised on Francesco Gonzaga's and his own behalf to safeguard Mantua's dignity in every way possible and added that this devotion was merited by Mantua's virtues as well as by Borromeo's obligations to him and those of his house.[10] Here he was probably alluding to the fact that his sister Camilla was the wife of Cesare Gonzaga, count of Guastalla, brother of Cardinal Francesco and nephew of the Cardinal of Mantua.

The Cardinal of Mantua did not accept Borromeo's advice and threatened to leave Trent if Cicada should come to assume the presidency. The pope yielded and abandoned the plan of sending more legates, and Mantua remained in office. Borromeo's initial failure to save the cardinal, who had been made the victim of the curialists' wrath because he had tolerated freedom of discussion in the council, illustrates the papal nephew's lack of influence over Pius IV. At the same time it must be recognized that Borromeo bore part of the responsibility for this excitement by encouraging the prelates in Trent who were ardent champions of the Holy See. In fact, at the same time (11 May 1562) as he wrote to the Cardinal of Mantua, he also privately informed Simonetta that it would be pleasing to His Holiness if the legate would confirm in their good intention all those prelates who had shown themselves devoted to and zealous for the authority of the pope and of the Holy See in regard to the question of the divine law of residence. For that purpose he sent Simonetta letters for those who expressed a desire to be recognized as such. Three publicly ostensible letters were prepared in which Borromeo commissioned Simonetta to express to three bishops papal recognition of their good services.[11] Such letters of Borromeo, not addressed directly to the individual bishops, caused considerable umbrage in Trent. Soon he was informed that his letters were being shown to others and interpreted in a wrong way. He then wrote confidentially to Simonetta that although everything he had put in such letters was phrased in general terms and by way of reply and compliment, still, in order to remove any occasion for murmuring, in the future when Simonetta would give such letters he should warn the recipients if he thought it necessary.[12] The legates in common had complained to Borromeo that laudatory letters sent to individual council fathers had produced gossip and comments at Trent, and other cardinals had told him the same thing. Hence, the pope had decided that from then on, Borromeo should be very sparing in writing to those prelates and that when it would be necessary either to thank them or to answer their letters, Simonetta should do so orally. To the legates as a body Borromeo replied that he was not aware of having ever written anything that could reasonably irritate anyone, never having answered in other than the most general words, and he professed himself ready to render a more detailed account if the legates would indicate some particular letter of his. He suggested that the offending letters had been written by other cardinals of the court, among whom there may have been diversity of opinion just as there was among the fathers of the council.[13]

Still the prelates of the council who were currying favor in Rome continued to write to their friends or patrons in the Curia about the events occurring in Trent. The legates advised Borromeo that he would find no better or surer or prompter remedy than to give such writers no answer and to send their letters to the legates, because the writers were emboldened by receiving letters from the papal nephew and would never cease to trouble him while they would never reveal to the legates what they wrote to Rome in order not to deprive themselves of the favor that nourished their ambitions and vanity.[14] It is not known to what extent Borromeo followed this sage advice.

Besides supporting the conciliar fathers who advocated the papal positions in the debates, Borromeo tried underhandedly to silence the opposition as much as possible. For example, after Simonetta had reported to him that the bishop of Brugnato, Antonio Cognor (Antonius du Cucurno), O.P., had favored the wrong side in the discussion of the sacrament of orders, Borromeo directed Simonetta: "If the Bishop of Brugnato is still, as you have written several times, little inclined to the public service [i.e., to the defense of the rights of the papacy] and is eccentric (stravagante), perhaps it will be good adroitly to give him permission to go to take the cure for his ailment, as has been done for [Giambattista] Osio [the bishop of Rieti], in order not to nourish, as they say, the serpent in one's bosom." Borromeo left it to Simonetta's good judgment to tell Cogorno that the pope would be pleased to grant him the favor of uniting a certain chapel to his diocese even though some persons had accused him of simony and other misdeeds in the past, which he could dilute with his good behavior in the council; but if he were unwilling to mend his ways, the legates could give him permission to depart if he should request it again.[15] In spite of his illness, Cogorno remained at Trent. Even the following spring Borromeo charged the legates to keep the adherents or dependents of the Curia in Trent with every skill and contrivance but to give the others leave without hesitation as soon as they might request it under a legitimate pretext.[16]

Even bishops known for their loyalty to the Holy See felt themselves endangered if they were denounced to Rome as having deviated from the curial line. Thus Muzio Calini, archbishop of Zara (now Zadar) in Dalmatia, was reported to his patron in Rome, Cardinal Luigi Cornaro, as having sided with the anticurialists in the debate on episcopal residence and as having led others to that position, as well as having held that bishops are constituted *jure divino*. He justified himself in one of his regular letters to Cornaro, saying that he was conscious of having always acted with an upright and sincere intention and in such a way that he hoped to be able to give a good account of himself and of his actions before a benign judge, such as he trusted he ought to find in Cornaro and Borromeo.[17]

The Spanish bishops caused particular consternation at Rome, especially before the French delegation arrived at Trent in November 1562, by their efforts to reaffirm the authority of the diocesan bishops that was unduly limited by the centralizing claims of Rome and by the encroachments of their civil governments. Some Italian bishops, especially those who were not subjects of the pope as a temporal sovereign, let themselves, as Borromeo wrote to his trusted observer at Trent, Carlo Visconti, the bishop of Ventimiglia, be carried on the shoulders of the Spaniards. After the twenty-first session was celebrated on 16 July 1562 without a reform decree on episcopal residence, and the council went on to discuss the Sacrifice of the Mass, the Spaniards desisted for the time being from demanding a decree on residence, mainly because their king, Philip II, had ordered them not to pursue the matter.[18] Borromeo hoped that the like-minded Italians would follow their example, but since he was not sure that the Cardinal of Mantua, who had much influence on those bishops, would dissuade them from continuing the effort, he directed Visconti to talk to certain Italian bishops whom he knew to be intimate with Mantua and to explain to them that since the Spaniards would not strive to have the question of residence discussed any further, the Italians could know that Rome had no doubt about or distrust of Mantua's mind on this matter; however, they could better understand that if this intrigue were not completely laid to rest now, it would be thought in Rome that Mantua and his followers had not wished to carry out their duty with the fervor with which they appeared and ought to. Borromeo summarized the task he was enjoining on Visconti as giving this little spur to the Cardinal of Mantua and his friends without arousing the mistrust of any of them.[19]

Actually, the Spaniards had not abandoned their goals but were waiting until the sacrament of orders should come up for discussion, as it did in the autumn. Thereupon Borromeo, informed about their conduct, directed the nuncio in Spain, Alessandro Crivello, to complain to the king. He asserted that the archbishop of Granada, Pedro Guerrero, from the beginning of this period at Trent had made public and open profession of detracting from the authority and dignity of the Holy See and through private meetings had drawn many others of that nation in the same direction, and that he had now entered into discussions with the imperial and French ambassadors, who were advocating changes of ecclesiastical discipline which Borromeo knew Philip disapproved of. The nuncio was to point out to the king the great disorder, harm, and ruin that could result not only for the church but also for the states and personal affairs of the king unless it were remedied in all ways possible, at least by separating the Spanish prelates at Trent from the imperial and French ambassadors "and making them unite with those who are in that place for the pure service of God and of the Catholic religion" and who were devoted to King Philip as were the legates and many Italian prelates. Borromeo insisted that for the public and private interest of the pope and the king together, it was "more than necessary" that the latter make provision, and that it be of such a nature and so prompt and vigorous as to forestall the troubles into which they would all otherwise fall. The nuncio was not to prescribe the exact remedy, but he was to aim at the breaking of the contacts between the Spanish and the French as suspect to all good men and full of a thousand consequences pernicious for the public safety, and he was also to aim at the union of the Spaniards with the legates.[20] Since this diplomatic effort produced no result, Borromeo repeated it in December and again in January and February 1563.[21]

From the papal point of view the situation became more dangerous after the French bishops arrived at Trent and formed close bonds with the Spaniards, who were alienated by the intransigence and extravagance of the *zelanti*.[22] Borromeo directed the nuncio to inform King Philip and his ministers that with three or four exceptions all the Spanish bishops at Trent had "made profession of our enemies against the commission [they had received from the king] and against every duty and perhaps also against their own consciences, taking much more pleasure in exercising a certain rabid venom that they have conceived against the Court of Rome only out of jealousy or [self-] interest, than in doing what they ought."[23] Besides unjustly attributing base motives to those who held a different but still tenable ecclesiology, Borromeo was obviously trying to have the king of Spain dictate the course for his bishops to follow and thus to restrict the freedom of the council.

It was the Cardinal of Lorraine, Charles de Guise, however, who caused the Curia the greatest preoccupation during the first six months and more of his sojourn in Trent. He was suspected of scheming to foster Gallicanism in opposition to the papal primacy and to change the procedure of papal elections, as well as of working against the new president of the council, Cardinal Giovanni Morone, who had been appointed after the death of the Cardinal of Mantua and had gone immediately to Innsbruck to win the support of Emperor Ferdinand I. After Morone arrived in Trent and took up the reins of the council, therefore, Borromeo instructed him on behalf of the pope in regard to the way in which he should deal with the Cardinal of Lorraine. He should speak "good words" to him and show that he hoped for every good from him, "giving him in appearance all those satisfactions" that he could, but in secret Morone should have no regard for him and should hand him all those insults that his insolence and inconstancy deserved. For this purpose Borromeo suggested that Morone encourage some of the bishops who were learned and eloquent friars and loyal to the Curia to resist him to his face and give his head a good washing in the general congregations by pointing out his imperfections, which were too numerous to mention. Borromeo advised Morone, however, not to communicate this intention to anyone except Simonetta and to concert with him the most seemly measures.[24]

A week later Borromeo put into practice the first part of his own directive to Morone, writing to the Cardinal of Lorraine fulsomely and almost servilely and assuring him of his entire devotion and of his lively desire to be helpful to the Frenchman in everything. "Your most illustrious Lordship," he professed, "does me a distinct favor every time . . . you avail yourself of my efforts in matters of your satisfaction and service." He promised, in obedience to him, to promote with all his might the appointment of a certain French bishop, and he begged the Cardinal of Lorraine to be convinced that it was not necessary for others to remind him of what he was bound to do to merit the cardinal's good grace.[25]

Meanwhile Morone had reported to Borromeo that Lorraine spoke "infinite good words and promises" to strive to bring the council to a close to the pope's satisfaction, to the dignity of the Holy See, and to the benefit of Christendom.[26] These assurances pleased the pope, who then trusted that Morone would draw the desired results from all his visits to, conversations with, and courtesies to the Cardinal of Lorraine.[27] In the meantime, in response to Borromeo's original, militant position, Morone reminded him that the Cardinal of Lorraine really had a large part in the council, because he conferred not only with the French but also with the Spanish and others before speaking and then was the first to speak; thus he easily won many supporters. Wiser than Borromeo and the pope, Morone preferred to try every means before breaking with the Cardinal of Lorraine or exasperating him more.[28] By then Pius and his nephew were willing to adopt this conciliatory policy, and in the end the leader of the French delegation was induced to collaborate with the papal legates for the successful completion of the council.

In addition to bringing pressure to bear on the fathers at Trent, Borromeo resorted to bribes for royal envoys and imperial counselors known for their anticurial views. This practice, of course, was common at that time; most of the curial cardinals received pensions from princes to look after their interests. Borromeo first aimed at winning the favor of the imperial counselors who had compiled the great reform memorial or *libellus* that Ferdinand I had had his ambassadors present to the legates in June 1562.[29] In the following month the cardinal-nephew wrote to the nuncio at the imperial court (then in Prague), Zaccaria Delfino, bishop of Lesina, that the pope, knowing how important it was for the affairs of the council to have the emperor's advisers well disposed *(amorevoli)* toward him and the Holy See, ordered Delfino to make every effort to win them over, and if for this purpose he should think it might be opportune to give them or some of them some presents, the pope would not fail to send him the means. "And with this assurance," he continued, "you may tell them that whatever they wish to be given is already on the way, and furthermore, they can be promised His Holiness's ample favor."[30] Executing this directive, Delfino offered gifts to the counselors, but the only things they would accept were certain Italian delicacies—pistachio nuts, salamis, botargos (a relish of salted mullet or tunny roes), Malmseys, and similar items of small value. Through his nephew Pius ordered the nuncio to proceed and promised to reimburse him for the expense and for others that he might incur "for the public service." Borromeo added that he would order some things from Naples, although, because of the distance and because the objects were not on hand and orders were not filled with the desirable promptness, he doubted that they would be delivered on time.[31] Perhaps it was at Delfino's suggestion that Borromeo wrote to the Cardinal of Mantua in November when the count de Luna, Claudio Fernández de Quiñones, the Spanish ambassador at the imperial court who had been appointed to the council in the same capacity, was expected at Trent: "His Holiness says that you should not fail to do everything you can to win over the Count de Luna, even if it should be necessary to promise him something great, even as much as the cardinalate for some relative of his."[32] Mantua could not act on this advice because he died before Luna arrived in Trent.

In the following month, December 1562, Borromeo wrote to the Cardinal of Mantua that the bishop of Viterbo, Sebastiano Gualterio (formerly nuncio in France), who had been sent to Trent to cultivate relations with the Cardinal of Lorraine and to report on his activities to Borromeo, had suggested that some money be given to one of the French envoys to the council, Arnaud du Ferrier, president of the Parlement of Paris, who was suspected of Protestant leanings. The papal nephew asked Mantua to discuss the matter with Gualterio, and if it seemed possible to win du Ferrier over in this way, to give him *"una buona mancia"* that should not be less than five hundred scudi. He advised the cardinal-president to spend heedlessly *(alle-gramente)* as much as he might see fit, because Borromeo would not let him lack money.[33] It was true that du Ferrier was in financial straits because he had suffered severe losses when his property had been damaged by the Huguenots in the religious war in France. It should be noted, moreover, that five hundred scudi was a considerable amount in comparison with the normal subsidy that the Holy See paid for the board and room of indigent bishops at Trent, which was twenty-five scudi each per month. No offer of money was made to du Ferrier at that time, however, because Mantua and Gualterio agreed that it would not be wise to attempt such a move; if it had not succeeded, as they seriously doubted it would, it would not have enhanced the pope's reputation, and it would have been of great disservice to the operation of the council. Mantua thought that Gualterio could continue to treat du Ferrier adroitly so that at a better time the pope might show him some favor without so much risk as would be incurred then.[34]

Before long Borromeo shifted his attention back to the theologians at the imperial court, exhorting the nuncio not to spare any expense to win them over, either all or some of them, because the pope would not fail to make good whatever Delfino might do or promise, believing that thus he was promoting the service of God in those difficult times.[35]

Bribery on a modest scale was practiced more successfully, however, by Cardinal Morone after he became president of the council in the spring of 1563. Before he visited the emperor at Innsbruck that April, Borromeo notified the nuncio at the imperial court that Morone had been ordered to pay two hundred gold scudi to Friedrich Staphylus, a lay theologian and counselor of the emperor, and to have him understand that the pope would not fail to grant him that amount every year. Borromeo added that he had advised Morone to discuss and decide with Delfino what could be done to win over George Drasković, bishop of Pécs (Fünfkirchen or Quinqueec-clesie), who represented Ferdinand as king of Hungary in the council and had proved to be a sharp thorn in the side of the Curia.[36] On the same day, in fact, the cardinal-nephew wrote to Morone that he should win Drasković over even if he had to promise him a cardinal's hat, for, he explained, "these are times not to spare anything to bring this business of the council to that good end which is necessary for the service of God and the salvation of the world."[37]

After Morone began his negotiations at Innsbruck, he reported to Bor-romeo that he had carried out his commission to Staphylus, but in the short

time that he had spent at Trent on his northward journey he could only begin
to caress Drasković and treat him sweetly, employing a mutual friend for
that purpose.[38] Later he wrote to Borromeo that he had given presents to the
imperial ministers, some in money and some in gold and silver objects. To
the vice-chancellor, Georg Sigmund Seld, who enjoyed the highest esteem of
the emperor, he had given a silver jug and basin or bowl worked in France
worth 150 gold scudi, and, he added, "it was a miracle that he accepted it."
He enumerated other gifts, even one hundred scudi to Peter Canisius as alms
for the Society of Jesus. The total of the expenses he incurred for all these
presents was approximately 820 gold scudi.[39]

Now that Seld was known to be willing to accept such gifts, Borromeo
sent him through the nuncio a box of solid gold weighing three hundred
scudi, in which was a chain with a little cross full of relics weighing two
hundred scudi more. He reminded Delfino that the latter, with his adroit-
ness, would "know how to extract that fruit which not only the quality of
the present but also the good, holy, and sincere intention of His Beatitude
deserve."[40] The papal agents were indeed successful in persuading the emperor to allow the closing of the council in a mutually agreeable manner.

Meanwhile Borromeo had reminded Morone in the pope's name to win
Drasković over to the Curia's side and for that purpose to promise him
whatever he judged good, even the cardinalate.[41] Later in May he renewed
the advice and included Anton Brus von Müglitz (Mohelnice), the archbishop of Prague and the emperor's other ecclesiastical ambassador to the
council, who had returned to Trent by then, as well as the bishop of
Calahora, Juan de Quiñones. The cardinal-nephew directed the legate to
promise them whatever would seem right, for the pope would not let him
deceive them even if he promised to make them cardinals.[42] He apparently
thought it so urgent to secure the support of these three ecclesiastics that he
repeated this directive to Morone a few days later, imploring him not to cease
to attempt all the ways and means possible.[43] It seems that Morone did not
deem it expedient to make use of this authorization; in any case, again in
August Borromeo exhorted him to strive to win over some of the important
participants in the council and not to hesitate to promise them whatever
might seem proper to him, either money or the cardinalate or anything else,
for the pope would not leave Morone's pledge unfulfilled, provided some
results became evident.[44] Morone, however, probably more out of prudence
than out of scrupulosity, never judged it opportune to make such promises.

In the summer of 1563 Borromeo also returned to the idea of buying the
good will of Arnaud du Ferrier, for the pope regarded him as a person who
could easily be won over. Accordingly, the papal nephew wrote to Morone
that if it seemed to him appropriate to give the French envoy with his own
hand five hundred or six hundred scudi in a handkerchief, Pius would rely
on Morone's good judgment, knowing that the chief legate would select the

opportune time and occasion. Borromeo reminded Morone that du Ferrier
was poor and that his expenses were not well paid; hence, he sometimes
found himself in need.[45] After Morone apparently indicated his willingness
to make the attempt, Borromeo expressed the pope's contentment and
assured the legate that he was authorized to give the French envoy four
hundred or five hundred scudi more than Borromeo had at first suggested;
the pope would like to know, he added, whether du Ferrier accepted the
money willingly and what he said; Pius also wanted Morone to try to win
over as many persons as he could in that way and in particular recommended
picking up the strands that he had already started to weave around Drasković.[46]

Following up on this scheme, Borromeo ordered that one thousand scudi
be entrusted to an unnamed friend of du Ferrier's; this person had assured the
pope and the pope's nephew that he would take the money and have it paid
out in Trent. Borromeo advised Morone, however, to pretend to know
nothing of this transaction and merely to wait to avail himself of du Ferrier's
co-operation whenever the need for it might arise and to deal with him in full
confidence, because he would find him very well disposed (amor-
evolissimo).[47] Later Borromeo had to admit that although the pope had
complete confidence in the person who took the thousand scudi, because it
was someone of great honor and integrity, he and Borromeo still did not
know whether du Ferrier was willing to accept them, because the intermediary had only told them that he hoped to have the envoy accept them, and
that he had written to him but had not received any answer, for which there
had not been enough time. Borromeo promised Morone that this money
would not prevent du Ferrier from receiving something greater from the
pope and that he would actually see it if he continued to behave well.[48]

Whether or not du Ferrier ever accepted the money is not clear; it is likely
that he did not, for he certainly did not sound like someone in the pope's
service when he spoke in the general congregation of 22 September 1563; on
that occasion he complained about the lack of serious reform in the council
and (ironically) demanded the abolition of many curial practices related to
money; he also asserted extravagant claims for the French crown in the
ecclesiastical sphere.[49] His unexpected tirade shocked Morone and convinced him that France intended to separate itself completely from the Holy
See as England had done.[50] After that harsh attack there was no longer any
question of buying du Ferrier's good will. In fact, after the council du Ferrier
went over to Calvinism.

Different tactics had been called for when Borromeo had had to assuage
the emperor's indignation at the pope's creation of two new cardinals who
were obviously unsuited for the dignity. One was Federico Gonzaga, son of
the late duke of Mantua, Federico, and the other was Ferdinando Medici, son
of the duke of Florence, Cosimo I. Borromeo explained to Delfino that

Gonzaga had the legitimate age, being already a mass priest, besides possessing good morals and learning. He added that Pius thought he was doing something pleasing to the emperor because of the latter's relationship to the house of Mantua (Federico being a brother of the reigning duke, Guglielmo, who was a son-in-law of Ferdinand I); moreover, the Gonzagas had importuned the pope, because Guglielmo thought that Cardinal Francesco, the son of Ferrante Gonzaga, count of Guastalla (a brother of Cardinal Ercole and of Duke Federico), who had been raised to the Sacred College early in 1561,[51] had taken the red hat away from his brother Federico, and both Guglielmo and Federico felt intense ill will against Francesco and Cesare Gonzaga (Borromeo's brother-in-law) and even against Ercole, the Cardinal of Mantua himself. As far as Ferdinando Medici was concerned, Borromeo argued that even if he was young, still he was sixteen years old, and that age was very close to the age required for ordination to the diaconate. (Borromeo was mistaken, for Ferdinando, it seems, was only thirteen and a half.) While he admitted that before the age of diaconate the cardinalate should not be conferred, still he claimed that the person of his father, Duke Cosimo, merited some difference and some respect, and the many misfortunes that had befallen him in a short time deserved some compassion and assuagement of his pain. (Cosimo's older son, Giovanni, who was a cardinal, had died in November 1562, and shortly afterward another son, Garcia, and then his wife Eleanore.) In the reform of the conclave decreed by Pius IV, furthermore, it was provided that no cardinal who was below the diaconal age could vote in a papal election. For all these reasons Borromeo thought that the nuncio had a broad enough field to defend the pope's action against anyone who would presume to slander it. "All rules," he stated, "must allow exceptions according to the cases, the times, and the persons; and you see well whether these are not times to give such princes this honorable satisfaction."[52] This last reason was the real motive of the pope, whose intention was to increase the security of his own temporal power by obligating the ruling Italian princes more heavily to himself.

This explanation did not satisfy the emperor, and Borromeo had to try again to rationalize in spiritual terms his uncle's political action. He pretended to be surprised that Delfino continued to write about Ferdinand's resentment, since the pope did not understand why this deed deserved to be criticized by anyone who wished to consider it dispassionately. He repeated that for many reasons they could not have failed to satisfy the two dukes whose importance in Italy Delfino recognized.[53] In spite of Borromeo's valiant efforts, the emperor shortly thereafter, in a confidential letter containing numerous complaints, reproved the pope for creating cardinals who in part were still lacking sound judgment because of their youth and in part were unlearned, so that they could not advise the pope in regard to the government of the church and would follow their "private passions" in a papal election and obstruct the votes of good and learned men.[54]

After the Cardinal of Mantua, who was bishop of that city, died in March 1563, the Gonzaga family insisted that his nephew, the new cardinal, Federico, be appointed his successor in the see although he was only twenty-three years old and thus lacked the age required by the reform decrees of this and earlier general councils.[55] Borromeo informed Morone that the imperial ambassador at Rome, Prospero d'Arco, had also requested this appointment in the name of Ferdinand I, father-in-law of Duke Guglielmo, who was Federico's brother. The emperor had intimated to Morone, however, during their conversations at Innsbruck, that he did not desire this favor "absolutely," because he did not expect to obtain from the pope something that was contrary to the decrees of the council. Morone concluded that Ferdinand would be more content with a refusal and reported that opinion to the cardinal-secretary.[56] Since the pope, nevertheless, was quite willing to gratify the house of Gonzaga and thought it convenient to cover his decision with the entreaties of Ferdinand's ambassador, Borromeo had to explain the papal policy to Morone, writing: ". . . it does not seem to be anything so unbecoming to give a bishopric to a cardinal of twenty-four years who is already a priest and has said many Masses and is not only of very rare life and morals but also a brother of the prince of that city, which things largely counterbalance the little that he could be said to be lacking in regard to age."[57] Accordingly, Federico was promoted to the see of Mantua in the consistory of 6 June. (He died less than two years later and was succeeded by Cardinal Francesco Gonzaga, who in turn died in less than one year—in the conclave following the death of Pius IV.)

Borromeo himself provided an object for criticism in the council, because he was then still a cardinal deacon and administrator of the archdiocese of Milan, as he had been for more than three years, although he had been ordained only to the subdiaconate. In the discussion of the abuses related to the sacrament of orders that took place at Trent in May 1563, the Cardinal of Lorraine advocated that no bishopric be given to a cardinal deacon and that no cardinal-priest be named administrator of a see. He declared it to be the greatest abuse that episcopal sees were conferred on cardinal deacons who sometimes were raised to the sacred purple in their twelfth year, when they should be at least thirty years old. He maintained that the cardinalate and the episcopate were incompatible, and he professed his readiness to resign his archbishopric of Rheims.[58] His shadow, Bishop Gualterio, reported to Borromeo in his usual rather familiar way: "He gave a great blow (remenata) to you cardinal deacons who have dioceses and do not promote yourselves [to higher sacred orders]." The archbishop of Granada, Pedro Guerrero, also blamed those cardinals who had to assist the pontiff personally and to discharge other duties and yet had the care of dioceses with so great peril to their souls.[59]

Shortly afterwards, on 4 June, Borromeo was elevated to the rank of cardinal priest. In that consistory Pius IV declared that after the death of Federico Borromeo, in whom he had placed all his hope of continuing the family, many other popes would perhaps have made his brother, who alone was left, pass over "to secular vows," as many others had already done, and they had not failed to acquire temporal states without harm to the Holy See. He added, however, that both he and Carlo intended that the nephew should remain in his clerical vocation and, therefore, he wished to raise him to be a cardinal priest.[60] Borromeo was ordained to the priesthood on 17 July. It appeared as though the council was promoting his reform instead of his promoting reform through the council.[61]

Still it took time for the conciliar fathers to become aware of the cardinal-nephew's gradual conversion. Taking advantage of the ambiguity, some of the curial cardinals who were opposed to the reform work of the council were so bold as to write to several bishops in Trent that Pius and Borromeo did not approve of the proposals being discussed, and they urged the bishops not to vote for such decrees. Alarmed by these machinations, Morone warned Borromeo in September that if the reform proposals were contested, not only would the council be lengthened, but the secular princes would demand even more stringent reforms, and the longer one temporized in the council, the more radical the demands for change became. The presiding legate lamented that from Rome, whence support ought to be expected, came obstruction through this pressure brought to bear on the bishops.[62] Borromeo replied that His Holiness was exceedingly amazed by the legates' report that letters had been sent from Rome to several of the fathers at the council asserting that the pope and the cardinal were not pleased with the rigor of the reform, and he added that Pius was no less amazed by the news that in the council this nonsense was believed, seeing that by then the pope had "with many signs openly declared the sincerity and candor of spirit" with which he had proceeded since the beginning and was still proceeding in this affair, in which he truly desired and willed that without regard to persons all the reforms deemed by the fathers honorable and appropriate for the service of God according to the needs of the times be enacted. The cardinal-secretary insisted that all these allegations were idle talk and foolish illusion invented by those who did not want the reform and that no faith be put in them.[63]

Such assurances notwithstanding, within two months of the close of the council Pius himself by his disposition of certain episcopal sees gave grounds for calling into doubt his devotion to reform. The legates reported to Borromeo in mid-October that certain letters received from Rome by several bishops in Trent had caused considerable murmuring because of some appointments said to have been made in the last consistory which were all contrary to the council's expectations; hence, it was being argued that the council could do nothing which would be binding.[64] The legates were alluding to the trafficking in residential sees that had taken place in the consistory of 8 October 1563. The bishop of Comacchio, Alfonso Rosetti, resigned his see and was appointed bishop of Ferrara, which had been vacated by the resignation of Cardinal Luigi d'Este; the latter had reserved to himself a Benedictine monastery in Embrun that he held *in commendam;* all the income of the episcopal *mensa* and the bestowal of benefices belonging to the bishop were also reserved to Cardinal d'Este, except a thousand gold [scudi?] granted to the new bishop, Rosetti. At the same time the consistory allowed the Cardinal of Ferrara, Ippolito d'Este, who had been legate in France, to resign the administration of the diocese of Auch, of which Cardinal Luigi d'Este was then appointed administrator; the income of the see was reserved to the Cardinal of Ferrara, except a thousand gold [scudi?] granted to the new administrator. Finally, the Cardinal of Ferrara was appointed bishop of Narbonne, which see was vacant through the resignation of the Cardinal of Pisa, Scipione Rebiba; the Cardinal of Ferrara retained the archiepiscopal see of Lyons for four months.[65] At the end of the consistory, speaking of the reform work, the pope declared his will that all the cardinals should go to their dioceses and that Borromeo should be the first; he also warned that if they did not obey him, he would deprive three or four of their sees to give an example to the rest.[66]

Once again Borromeo was obliged to rationalize his uncle's proceedings that contradicted the spirit of reform motivating the majority of the conciliar fathers. Writing to the legates, he remarked first that it ought to be sufficient to say that it had been the Cardinal of Lorraine who proposed all four appointments in the consistory and took upon himself the task of justifying them and of rendering an account of them in the council and wherever else it might be necessary. Borromeo went on to answer the objections that might be raised, adopting some of the arguments that the Cardinal of Lorraine had employed for the same purpose in the consistory. As far as the age of Cardinal Luigi d'Este, who was only twenty-four, was concerned, Borromeo asserted that since d'Este had already been allowed to hold the see of Ferrara and had done so for several years, he did not need any further dispensation on that score. As for being ordained bishop (since he was then only a deacon) and residing in his diocese, d'Este, according to Borromeo, had not requested and had even promised not to request an extension or dispensation, being resolved to fulfill both obligations within the time limit set by the council or to resign the see. Then in regard to the reservation of the income, as Luigi d'Este had done with respect to his old see of Ferrara and the Cardinal of Ferrara had done with respect to his old see of Auch,

Borromeo reminded the legates that the council had not yet passed any decree prohibiting the practice, and he added that the Cardinal of Lorraine had said that the council would decide that such reservations should be left to the judgment and discretion of the pope. Finally, taking up the question of the Cardinal of Ferrara's retention of two residential sees, Borromeo asserted that nothing new had been granted him, for formerly he had had Auch and now he had Narbonne, while the see of Lyons remained as it had been, and since that see had been returned to him by virtue of his *regressus*, it seemed that he had six months' time from the day of his taking possession of it to resign it, but he had not yet taken possession of it because of the Huguenots, nor was it known when he would be able to take possession of it. Borromeo assured the legates that Pius IV would not allow the Cardinal of Ferrara a day's delay either in disposing of the see or in receiving episcopal consecration or even in regard to residence. Hence, Borromeo concluded that the pope did not see what great error or scandal this had been, all the more so as he had expressly had it stated in the bull of appointment that this was in no way to be understood as a derogation of the Council of Trent, even though the council had not yet been confirmed.[67] It is doubtful whether the legates would have found such reasoning helpful in trying to convince bishops of the papacy's seriousness regarding reform, or whether the cardinal-nephew himself was satisfied with the logic of his apologia.

At the same time Borromeo boasted of the reforms of the Curia that his uncle had made even though he himself as well as the pope was financially hurt by some of them. He convinced visitors of his sincerity in this regard. Thus when the archbishop of Braga, Bartholomaeus de Martyribus, returned to Trent after his visit to Rome in the autumn of 1563, he spoke in the council about the pope's ardent desire for reform and likewise about that of Cardinal Borromeo, "who has moved and enkindled the hearts of all for this holy work."[68] It is not surprising, then, to read in the final report of the next Venetian ambassador to the pope, Giacomo Soranzo, that Borromeo was already an exceptional person:

> His life is most innocent and chaste. He says Mass every feast day, fasts very often, and in all things lives with such piety *(religione)* that he gives a unique example to everyone, so much so that one can reasonably say that he alone has more effect on the Court of Rome than all the decrees of the Council together, it being a thing rarely seen that a nephew of a pope and one very dear to him, in so young an age, in a court full of so many comforts, has overcome himself, the flesh, and the world.[69]

The obvious conclusion is that Borromeo contributed more to the cause of reform during these years by the example of his own increasingly purified way of life than by supporting the advocates of reform at the Council of Trent.

Notes

1. Eugenio Albèri, ed., *Le Relazioni degli Ambasciatori Veneti al Senato durante il secolo decimosesto,* vol. 10, ser. 2, bk. 4 (Florence, 1857), p. 74.

2. Josef Šusta, ed., *Die römische Curie und das Concil von Trient unter Pius IV. Actenstücke zur Geschichte des Concils von Trient* (Vienna, 1904–14), 1 : xxxiii–xxxiv.

3. Pio Paschini, "Il primo soggiorno di S. Carlo Borromeo a Roma, 1560–1565," in *Cinquecento Romano e Riforma Cattolica* ("Lateranum," n. s., vol. 24 [Rome, 1958], pp. 107–9.

4. Hubert Jedin, *Carlo Borromeo* ("Bibliotheca Biographica," 2 [Rome, 1971]), pp. 8–10; idem, *Geschichte des Konzils von Trient,* vol. 4: *Dritte Tagungsperiode und Abschluss;* pt. 1: *Frankreich und der neue Anfang in Trient bis zum Tode der Legaten Gonzaga und Seripando* (Freiburg, 1975), p. 78.

5. For a study of one aspect of this topic see Robert Trisco, "Reforming the Roman Curia: Emperor Ferdinand I and the Council of Trent," in *Reform and Authority in the Medieval and Reformation Church,* ed. Guy Fitch Lytle (Washington, D.C., 1981), pp. 143–337.

6. Ludwig von Pastor, *The History of the Popes from the Close of the Middle Ages* (St. Louis, 1891–1953), 15 : 244.

7. Borromeo to Simonetta, Rome, 1 (?) April, 1562, Šusta, 2 : 77, no. 26 annex.

8. Pastor, *History of the Popes* 15 : 279; Jedin, *Geschichte,* vol. 4, pt. 1, 134.

9. Borromeo to Simonetta, Rome, 11 May 1562, Šusta, 2 : 138, no. 40a.

10. Borromeo to the Cardinal of Mantua, Rome, 11 May 1562, ibid., pp. 139–141, no. 40b.

11. Borromeo to Simonetta, Rome, 11 May 1562, ibid., p. 137, no. 40a.

12. Same to same, 26 May 1562, ibid., p. 178.

13. Borromeo to the legates, 27 May 1562, ibid., p. 178, no. 49 annex.

14. The legates to Borromeo, Trent, 6 August 1562, ibid., p. 296, no. 79.

15. Borromeo to Simonetta, Rome, 14 November 1562, ibid., 3 : 79–80, no. 23a.

16. Borromeo to the legates, 12 May 1563, ibid., 4 : 5.

17. Calini to Cornaro, Trent, 5 November 1562, Alberto Marani, ed., *Muzio Calini. Lettere Conciliari (1561–1563)* (Brescia, 1963), p. 304.

18. Jedin, *Geschichte,* vol. 4, pt. 1, 174.

19. Borromeo to Visconti, 8 August 1562, Šusta, 2 : 309, no. 82 annex.

20. Borromeo to Crivello, Rome, 9 October 1562, ibid., 3 : 376–78, supplement 10.

21. Same to same, Rome, 15 December 1562, 27 January and 15 February 1563, ibid., pp. 465–68, 485, 497–99, supplements 34, 39, 41.

22. Jedin, *Geschichte,* vol. 4. pt. 1, 230–32, 237, 240, 243, 246.

23. Borromeo to Crivello, Rome, 15 February 1563, Šusta, 497–99, supplement 41. The nuncio had reported that Guerrero's deportment was disapproved at the Spanish court, and he transmitted Philip's solemn assurance of his readiness to protect the person of the pope and the Holy See with all his might, but the king could not effectively bridle his bishops without a permanent ambassador resident in Trent, and that had been hindered by the controversy over precedence between the French and Spanish ambassadors. Philip was also dissatisfied with the pope's management of the council. Crivello to Borromeo, Madrid, 27 November 1562, ibid., pp. 441–42, supplement 29.

24. Borromeo to Morone, Rome, 27 May 1563, G. Constant, *La Légation du Cardinal Morone près l'Empereur et le Concile de Trente, avril–décembre 1563*

("Bibliothèque de l'École des Hautes Études, Sciences historiques et philosophiques," fascicule 232 [Paris, 1922]), p. 157, no. 37B.

25. Borromeo to the Cardinal of Lorraine, 5 June 1563, ibid., p. 173, n. 3.

26. Morone to Borromeo, Trent, 31 May 1563, ibid., p. 162, no. 38.

27. Borromeo to Morone, Rome, 8 June 1563, ibid., p. 173, no. 43.

28. Morone to Borromeo, Trent, 7 June 1563, ibid., p. 169, no. 41.

29. Trisco, "Reforming the Roman Curia," pp. 169–77, 186–205.

30. Borromeo to Delfino, Rome, 11 July 1562, S. Steinherz, ed., *Nuntiaturberichte aus Deutschland nebst ergänzenden Actenstücken*, sec. 2: *1560–1572*, vol. 3: *Nuntius Delfino, 1562–1563* (Vienna, 1903), p. 92, no. 35.

31. Same to same, Rome, 22 August 1562, ibid., p. 110, no. 42.

32. Borromeo to the Cardinal of Mantua, Rome, 20 November 1562, Th. R. von Sickel, *Römische Berichte* ("Sitzungsberichte der Wiener Akademie der Wissenschaften," vols. 133, 135, 141, 143, 144 [Vienna, 1893–1901]), 3:86.

33. Borromeo to Mantua, Rome, 12 December 1562, Šusta, 3:116, no. 37.

34. Particular instruction of the Cardinal of Mantua for Visconti, Trent, 26 December 1562, ibid., pp. 127–28, no. 40a.

35. Borromeo to Delfino, Rome, 28 February 1563, Steinherz, 3:221, no. 77; see also same to same, Rome, 6 March 1563, ibid., p. 240, no. 82.

36. Same to same, Rome, 13 April 1563, ibid., p. 263, no. 91.

37. Borromeo to Morone, Rome, 13 April 1563, ibid., p. 264 (appendix).

38. Morone to Borromeo, Innsbruck, 23 April 1563, ibid., p. 269, no. 93.

39. Same to same, Trent, 17 May 1563, ibid., pp. 311–12, no. 99.

40. Borromeo to Delfino, Rome, 8 June 1563, ibid., pp. 331–32, no. 106.

41. Borromeo to Morone, Rome, 8–9 May 1563, Sickel, 2:134.

42. Same to same, Rome, 27 May 1563, Constant, pp. 157–58, no. 37.

43. Same to same, Rome, 2 June 1563, Šusta, 4:49–50.

44. Same to same, Rome, 21 August 1563, ibid., p. 209.

45. Same to same, Rome, 10 July 1563, ibid., p. 126, no. 27, and Constant, pp. 192–93, no. 53.

46. Same to same, Rome, 28 July 1563, Šusta, 4:157, no. 34a, and Constant, p. 207, no. 61.

47. Same to same, Rome, 4 August 1563, Šusta, 4:175, no. 38a, and Constant, p. 217, no. 64.

48. Same to same, Rome, 21 August 1563, Šusta, 4:209, and Constant, p. 234, no. 74.

49. "Expostulatio sive protestatio oratorum regis Christianissimi ad legatos & patres concilii Tridentini, adversus propositam reformationem principum," 22 September 1563, Judocus Le Plat, ed., *Monumentorum ad Historiam Concilii Tridentini potissimum illustrandum spectantium amplissima collectio*, vol. 6 (Louvain, 1786), pp. 233–37; the legates to Borromeo, Trent, 23 September 1563, Šusta, 4:268–69, no. 61.

50. Morone to Borromeo, Trent, 23 September 1563, Constant, pp. 272–73, no. 90.

51. On these relationships see Pompeo Litta, *Famiglie celebri italiane*, vol. 3 (Milan, 1820–56), "Gonzaga di Mantova," tables 5, 6, and 8.

52. Borromeo to Delfino, Rome, 6 February 1563, Steinherz, 3:176, no. 66.

53. Same to same, Rome, 21 February 1563, ibid., p. 214, no. 75.

54. Trisco, "Reforming the Roman Curia," p. 243.

55. In its seventh session (*de ref.*, cap. 1) on 3 March 1547, and again in its twenty-second session (*de ref.*, cap. 2) on 17 September 1562 (M. J. Schroeder, O.P., ed. and trans., *Canons and Decrees of the Council of Trent. Original Text with English*

Translation [St. Louis and London, 1941], pp. 333 and 425; English translation, pp. 55 and 153), the council had renewed the decree of the Third Lateran Council that prohibited anyone who had not completed his thirtieth year from being chosen as bishop (*Conciliorum Oecumenicorum Decreta*, ed. Giuseppe Alberigo et al., 3d ed. [Bologna, 1973], p. 212); the Fifth Lateran Council had prohibited dispensations for age to anyone below his twenty-seventh year (ibid., p. 615).

56. Morone to Borromeo, Trent, 17 May 1563, Steinherz, 3:305, no. 99.

57. Borromeo to Morone, Rome, 27 May 1563, Constant, pp. 155–56, no. 37.

58. "Acta," 14 May 1563, *Concilium Tridentinum*, ed. Societas Goerresiana (Freiburg im Breisgau), vol. 9: *Actorum Pars Sexta*, ed. Stephan Ehses (1924), pp. 492–93; and Calini to Cornaro, Trent, 17 May 1563, Marani, p. 447.

59. Gualterio to Borromeo, Trent, 16 May 1563, Hubert Jedin, ed., *Krisis und Wendepunkt des Trienter Konzils (1562/63). Die neuentdeckten Geheimberichte des Bischofs Gualterio von Viterbo an den heiligen Karl Borromäus* (Würzburg, 1941), pp. 239–40, no. 78. *Remenata* for *remata*, meaning a blow with an oar.

60. Consistorial *Acta* of Cardinal Francesco Gambara, 4 June 1563, Šusta, 4:68, n. 3.

61. Carlo's spiritual conversion had begun when his brother Federico died on 19 November 1562. See Jedin, *Geschichte*, vol. 4, pt. 1, 236.

62. Morone to Borromeo, Trent, 5 September 1563, Šusta, 4:227.

63. Borromeo to the legates, Rome, 15 September 1563, ibid., p. 252, no. 58.

64. The legates to Borromeo, Trent, 16 October 1563, ibid., p. 324, no. 72.

65. Cardinal Francesco Gambara, report on the consistory of 8 October 1563, Šusta, 4:573–75, supplement 31. Borromeo had consulted Morone in May about the proposed resignation of the see of Auch by the Cardinal of Ferrara, remarking that for many reasons the pope could hardly refuse to comply with this pressing request. (Borromeo to Morone, Rome, 27 May 1563, Šusta, 4:34, no. 6a; and Constant, p. 156, no. 39.) Morone had replied that it would be much better for Ippolito d'Este to remain in the government of his bishopric of Ferrara than to take a foreign-language bishopric in France and thus furnish the French bishops and ambassadors and others at the council grounds for hurling atrocious invectives and decrees "against us" at a time when the reform of the cardinals was being urged every day. (Morone to Borromeo, 3 June 1563, Constant, p. 156, n. 11.) Obviously, the pressure exerted on the pope by the d'Este family overrode Morone's caution.

66. Pier Luigi Fedele (Morone's agent in Rome) to Morone, 9 October 1563, Šusta, 4:575–76.

67. Borromeo to the legates, Rome, 23 October 1563, ibid., pp. 352–53, no. 79.

68. Calini to Cornaro, Trent, 4 November 1563, Marani, p. 559; cf. "Gabrielis Paleotti Acta concilii Tridentini annis MDLXII et MDLXIII," 3 November 1563, *Concilium Tridentinum*, vol. 3: *Diariorum Pars Tertia*, bk. 1, ed. Sebastian Merkle (1931), p. 744, and "Acta" of the general congregation of 3 November 1563, ibid., 9:916.

69. "Relazione di Roma di Giacomo Soranzo, 1565," Albèri, 10:133–34.

San Carlo Borromeo and the Implementation of the Council of Trent

JOHN B. TOMARO

Introduction

THIS BRIEF PRESENTATION WILL PORTRAY THE STYLE AND STRATEGY OF A reformer—San Carlo Borromeo (1538–84). It will touch on three important topics: (1) Borromeo's interpretation of the episcopal role in the Tridentine church; (2) the relationships between Borromeo and Rome, and between the stern cardinal-archbishop and the representatives of temporal authority; and (3) the image of Borromeo, and the significance of that image, in the half century after the reformer's death.

Borromeo was an austere, dedicated, humorless, and uncompromising personality. He was singularly motivated to carry out his episcopal duties in the fashion outlined by the council, as he understood it. Driven to fulfill his episcopal duties, he was perpetually conscious of their awesome demands. His convictions led him to prod others to follow and surpass his zealous example, and to counsel the pontiffs to accept his legislative recommendations. At times his advice and actions provoked tensions and sometimes breakdowns in the relations between himself and the popes, priests, and princes with whom he worked.

Cardinal-nephew during the last sessions of the council, Borromeo shared the fathers' emphasis on the importance of restoring and rebuilding the diocesan organization. Along with the fathers, Borromeo believed that the dioceses, led by the bishops, were the foundation on which the church rested. The decrees' emphasis on the meaning and importance of the sacraments and ecclesiastical discipline was not simply a calculated reaction to the Protestant threat. The council's concentration on pastoral themes was based on the conviction that priest and people should be firmly joined and the knowledge of the results achieved from the successful diocesan reorganizations carried out earlier in the century by several outstanding episcopal reformers.

Borromeo believed that the close of the Council of Trent in December

1563 was of little immediate significance. While the decrees approved by the fathers successfully harmonized discordant elements, they were open to many interpretations. Since the practice of the fathers was to write the disciplinary decrees in a fashion that would improve ecclesiastical order but not at the risk of alienating princes or prelates, topics were left undefined. Their meaning would only be revealed in the course of their application. The work of Borromeo in Milan gave one meaning to the decrees and new significance to the role of the *bishop* in the Tridentine church.

Borromeo and the "Bishop as Reformer"

In his work on the close of the Council of Trent, Jedin has written that combined in Borromeo were the spirit of Trent and the administrative ability to implement reform.[1] During his residency in Rome and his tenure in Milan, Borromeo was the force behind a great deal of the legislation composed and the actions taken by the pontiffs and his brother bishops. Immediately following his death he was heralded as the model bishop and held up for praise and emulation.

The opening months of 1563 were critical for both the church and the young Milanese. The Council of Trent, long desired but of dubious results, was about to debate again the question of episcopal residence. Borromeo had participated in the diplomatic negotiations surrounding the reopening of the council and was keenly aware of the importance of the issues under debate. He realized that those bishops, especially the Spaniards, who argued for episcopal residency *de iure divino* had a valid grievance, if not an acceptable remedy.

The crisis of the council corresponded with a personal crisis in Borromeo's life. He was recovering from the effects of the death of his brother, Federico, in November 1562. After considerable meditation and resisting pressure from his relatives to request laicization, Borromeo chose to be ordained. He turned to the Jesuit Padre Ribera for spiritual solace and instruction in the *Spiritual Exercises* and decided to make himself the model of the reformed prelate advocated by the fathers of the council.[2]

Borromeo reduced his household staff to the then quite modest level of eighty retainers.[3] He associated with men of the caliber of Guglielmo Sirleto who could instruct him in the meaning and spirit of the council and began to enact the conciliar decrees in Rome and his distant see of Milan.[4] Although very timid at first, Borromeo began to preach in those churches and monasteries of Rome with which he was associated. He was criticized for this action and for encouraging other prelates to follow his example. In spite of the criticism, Borromeo persisted.[5]

Borromeo was instrumental in proposing legislation that he hoped would produce a new moral climate in Rome. Since Pius IV had a special affection for his nephew, Borromeo had a relatively free hand in remaking the city. Giacomo Soranzo, the Venetian ambassador, reported in 1565 that Borromeo had incurred the wrath of the Roman Curia and claimed that his example had more influence on the atmosphere of the Roman court than all the decrees of the council. Annibale Caro, a retainer of Alessandro Cardinal Farnese and no friend of Borromeo, wrote in 1564 that Rome was no longer a place "one visited to enjoy oneself or to make a fortune. Carlo Borromeo has undertaken to remake the city from top to bottom," Caro claimed. He predicted that the young cardinal's ardor "would lead him to correct the rest of the world once he had finished with Rome."[6]

Borromeo remained in Rome from 1563 to 1565, gaining experience in government, diplomatic practice and the art of negotiating. He won prestige and adherents among a group of reform-minded prelates who would assist his pastoral work in Milan. During the same period, Borromeo completed his formation as a man of the newly reformed church and obtained some theological training to add to a culture that, until then, had been primarily juridical and literary. All the while Borromeo kept abreast of developments in the archdiocese of Milan and supervised its affairs from Rome.[7]

In 1564, even before he went to Milan to reside, the declared and closely followed intent of Borromeo was to secure the full and unqualified application of the disciplinary decrees of the Council of Trent. At the same time he worked to give life to those ecclesiastical institutions necessary for good pastoral government and recommended by the council—pastoral visits, diocesan synods, provincial councils, and seminaries.

In May of 1564 he appointed Niccolò Ormaneto, a man formed in the school of Giberti of Verona, as vicar-general and instructed him to proceed to Milan, to publish and execute the decrees of Trent, to establish a seminary, to convoke a diocesan synod, and to reform the religious houses. Aware of the fact that Milan had been without a resident bishop for eighty years, and that the diocese had fallen in the hands of vicars-general who were often inept and little concerned about "the welfare of souls," Borromeo chose Ormaneto as vicar-general because he had no ties with Milan and was committed to the restoration of ecclesiastical discipline according to the Tridentine norms.[8]

From the very first Borromeo sought to put the best available men to work in his diocese. Initially, he believed that administering an episcopal territory was no different from supervising his other patrimonial and ecclesiastical domains. In time, as he came to appreciate the significance of the issues debated at Trent, and to experience a new spiritual awareness, Borromeo felt it was imperative to make Milan in the image defined by the council and to reside in the diocese.

Milan was the largest archdiocese in Italy at the time. Within its ecclesiastical boundaries were more than two thousand churches, three thousand clergy, 110 monasteries, ninety convents, and over eight hundred thousand souls. Reports from the diocese in the year after Trent's close indicate that conditions were not ideal. Much work was needed to improve the quality of the clergy, the condition of church property, and the religious devotion of the people. Borromeo examined the Milanese situation carefully and concluded that a twofold action was necessary. Later called his *tecnica pastorale,* Borromeo's program of episcopal administration—never set forth in a formal treatise but manifested in the actions of the ascetic archbishop and his agents—mixed exhortation with intimidation, the promise of spiritual joy with the threat of corporal punishment. Borromeo's zeal for religious restoration was accompanied by a belief in the importance of ecclesiastical discipline. He directed his efforts in Milan not just to reconstructing an *ecclesia,* i.e., a community of faithful, but also to supporting an institution. Borromeo believed that the physical appearance of church property and the quality of lay and clerical devotional practices were expressions of an internal spiritual condition.

Borromeo set the pattern for his episcopal administration very soon after the close of the council. In July 1564 he sent Ormaneto twenty copies of the bull confirming the council along with instructions to circulate them among the suffragans of the archdiocese.[9] A short time later Ormaneto received a list containing the names of authors who had written treatises on the subject of celebrating diocesan synods.[10] In August the first Milanese diocesan synod was convened. Ormaneto read the bull confirming the Council of Trent, the decree prohibiting interpretations, and the decree authorizing the synod to take place. While in session the synod debated and, in spite of strong opposition, accepted two principal points of reform—residence for those who held benefices with *cura animarum* and the prohibition of the plurality of benefices.[11]

Borromeo was disturbed by his continuing residence in Rome and repeatedly petitioned Pius IV to allow him to go to Milan to conduct a provincial council and to take up residence. On 1 September 1565 Borromeo, named legate for all Italy, left Rome for Milan. On 23 September 1565 he entered the city dressed in pontificals, not vested in his cardinalatial regalia.[12] This act indicates the esteem with which he held the episcopal office and the importance he attached to tying bishops to their sees.

Eleven bishops and their retainers attended the first provincial council and examined all aspects of ecclesiastical life. From the content and execution of the liturgy to the administration of benefices, from the formation of the clergy to the extent of episcopal jurisdiction, all issues pertaining to the diocese came under discussion. There were strong differences of opinion on the subjects of residence, cloister, reorganization of the cathedral chapters, and the prohibition of mothers and sisters living in the parish house. In general, however, Borromeo's position on these issues—always the most austere and stringent interpretation—triumphed.[13]

Some in Rome and Milan complimented him for his stand on the reform decrees and for the example he provided;[14] others criticized him for the stern nature of his proposals. For example, Tolomeo Galli, an intimate of the pope, asked Borromeo to temper his ardor. Galli also reported that Cardinal Morone was disturbed by the rigorous fashion in which Borromeo was proceeding. Galli tried to soften the criticism by informing Borromeo that Morone's comment was a reasoned opinion, not a malicious assault.[15]

Borromeo's attitudes and practices during his first period of residence in Milan are indicative of his conduct during his entire tenure.[16] Like the fathers of the council, Borromeo repeatedly emphasized the importance of the episcopal office. In his estimation, the bishop in residence brought aid and comfort to his flock and provided an example for the universal church.[17] In fulfilling his function as the bishop of Milan, Borromeo believed that he was providing an example for the whole church. Bishops, he argued, have dynamic roles as heads of their dioceses and as solid pillars of the church.

Throughout his tenure he exalted the role of the bishop. In 1579, for example, Borromeo warmly thanked Cardinal Alciato for his efforts in support of the episcopal office and emphasized the point by signing his epistle as *bishop*—no other rank or title appears.[18] Borromeo also felt fully authorized to address the Congregation of the Council on the matter of episcopal authority and powers.[19] His commitment to episcopal residence also compelled him to resign those charges in Rome which required residence, and to surrender those titles and duties which were incompatible with his responsibilities as archbishop of Milan.[20] Borromeo had an exalted opinion of episcopal *auctoritas* and of the duty to exercise it. Like Cardinal Paleotti of Bologna, Borromeo held that diocesan reform worked through the bishop, and that the reform spirit was operational within him.[21] No activity in the diocese was outside the bishop's sacramental, juridical, or moral control. In analyzing the needs of the church, Borromeo concluded that bishops formed the organizational basis and the focus of spiritual concerns. The assistance of the religious orders, like the Jesuits, and the support of the popes were important factors in shaping reform, but their usefulness was conditioned by the bishop's effective action.[22]

The presence of Borromeo in Milan signaled the total reorganization of the archdiocese. Borromeo sought to establish a hierarchical structure that corresponded to his interpretation of the Tridentine precepts on episcopal authority. He suppressed those customs which, measured by the decrees of Trent, resulted in abuses and deviations from legitimate practice.[23] At the same time, Borromeo established fixed rules of conduct and had them supervised by archiepiscopal personnel.[24]

By rigorously enforcing the precepts of the council he gave not only substance to the conciliar decrees but stature to the episcopal office. Borromeo never forgot this dual aspect of his role. He made it equally clear to both the laity and the clergy that he conducted his office as ordinary according to the precepts of the council. Foremost among the council's charges to the shepherds were the directives (1) to visit the dioceses and (2) to convoke provincial and diocesan assemblies.[25]

Borromeo supported and encouraged episcopal visitations.[26] He made regular visitations of his own archdiocese and in 1575 and again in 1580 he was made an apostolic visitor by the pope. During his visits to Cremona, Novara, Lodi, Bergamo, and Brescia in 1575 and to Vercelli and Vigevano in 1580 he entered each diocese in pontificals rather than cardinalatial regalia. In this fashion he sought to restore powers that had been those of the metropolitan in antiquity.[27]

Similarly, Borromeo considered the celebration of provincial and diocesan councils of premier importance. The prescription of the Council of Trent on their frequency of convocation was more scrupulously adhered to by Borromeo than by any other bishop. During his residence in Milan he convoked eleven diocesan synods and six provincial councils.[28] In the diocesan synods Borromeo demonstrated his oneness with the clergy since he was always the first to submit himself to the strictures of the synods' edicts.[29] Borromeo believed that the reestablishment of discipline in the church was closely tied to the renewal of the practice of holding provincial councils. In Borromeo's estimation, provincial councils enabled bishops to come together to discuss common problems. At the same time, the assemblies made each bishop aware of his responsibilities to, and relationship with, other bishops and the metropolitan.[30]

Throughout his long and active tenure in Milan, Borromeo worked to refine and promote the Tridentine reform, which in his mind was the reorganization of the dioceses of Christendom under the guidance of the bishops. Borromeo was convinced that reformed dioceses would provide the building blocks of the new church structure. Bishops were the leaders of reform. Popes and princes were to provide inspiration, motivation, and support, but they were not to meddle in the activities of the bishops nor question the soundness of the shepherd's judgment.

Borromeo vis-à-vis Rome and Temporal Authority

There was a consistency in Borromeo's actions and a similarity in his dealings with the representatives of both the Spanish king and the tribunals of Rome. Both were taken to task when they interfered in the affairs of the episcopal administration. Borromeo's defense of the ecclesiastical jurisdiction has been traditionally viewed as an example of the effective action of a

resurgent papacy. In fact, Borromeo's opposition to temporal interference in
the ecclesiastical administration and his efforts to restore sovereignty to it
were no different from his efforts to resist Rome's interference in diocesan
operations, and they were prompted by the same motives. In no sense did
Borromeo minimize the importance of either the prince or the pontiff.
Cooperation between the bishop and the viceroy, as between the pope and
the prince, was an essential ingredient in Borromeo's plan to rebuild the
Roman Church. Still, Borromeo's first concern was to restore the authority
of, and respect for, the episcopal office. In his struggles against both temporal and ecclesiastical authorities Borromeo achieved only a qualified success. At his death the episcopal office had new stature, but the bishop's
authority was effectively harnessed and employed by Rome.

The often-recorded jurisdictional conflict between Borromeo and the
Spanish authority in Milan was not—I would suggest—an intentional and
unprovoked assault by the ecclesiastical authority on the temporal domain.
Borromeo's actions were a logical consequence of his definition of the
episcopal function.[31] His insistence on a completely autonomous ecclesiastical jurisdiction provoked an open and continuous conflict between him
and the government of Philip II and the Milanese municipal tribunals—
namely, the Senate.[32] Borromeo's challenge to the jurisdiction of the Senate
and the Spanish king in ecclesiastical matters was not anti-Spanish and was
not designed to weaken Spain's rule in Italy. He realized that the success of
the church's universal mission depended on Spanish arms. Spain was the lone
Catholic force capable of contesting the Protestant menace and turning back
the Ottoman tide.[33] Indeed, Borromeo looked toward the temporal forces
for support in his work of reform.

Borromeo considered his struggle with the temporal authority part of the
necessary action to define and document the particular laws and customs of
the archdiocese of Milan and as an attempt to resolve questions of temporal
and ecclesiastical relations pertinent to the whole church. The Spanish
governors, chief opponents in the jurisdictional confrontation, did not question the purity of Borromeo's motives. Still, as representatives of the Spanish
king, they argued that his acts and claims could have dangerous consequences, and all opposed changes in the ruling arrangement in Milan.
Milan was the key to northern Italy. If constitutional changes were permitted, or if constitutional pretensions went unopposed, all of Philip's realms
could be endangered. Don Luis de Zúñiga y Requesens and other Spanish
governors attempted to alert Borromeo to the potentially disastrous effect of
his claims; each unceasingly reminded him that "he was born a vassal and
subject of his majesty."[34]

Before Borromeo came to Milan in 1565 the archdiocese had been without
a resident bishop for more than eighty years. In the period of episcopal
nonresidence, civil magistrates had passed a series of laws designed to

regulate public morals and the observance of religious precepts. The legislation was particularly copious, if not well observed or enforced. Upon arrival
in Milan, Borromeo made his reform program known to the civil magistrates. Although he promised to call upon them for assistance and collaboration, he made it clear that the course of reform was to be directed by the
ecclesiastical authority—*alone*. He refused to request the civil authority's
approval of his synodal or conciliar decrees, and he promulgated them on his
own authority. Initially, the temporal magistrate adopted many of Borromeo's edicts and much of his legislation as its own. In time, Borromeo's
claims and actions, particularly those which occurred after the issuance of
the bull *In coena Domini* in 1568, prompted the temporal authority to reject
the archbishop's claims. The ensuing struggle between the archbishop and
the temporal magistrates continued with greater or lesser intensity
throughout the remainder of Borromeo's life.[35]

Throughout his tenure Borromeo pressed the popes to make some final
resolution on the subject of the controversy.[36] In this struggle he saw himself
as the model for proper episcopal action in the face of lay harassment and
interference, and as agent who could work with the pontiff to complete the
program of the "reform of the princes" left incomplete at Trent. Borromeo
viewed the contest as one to determine who defined the boundaries between
the ecclesiastical and temporal jurisdictions. He was annoyed, therefore,
when the popes hesitated to speak out and cautioned him to moderate his
enthusiasm.[37]

From Milan Borromeo tried to influence the pope and his brother
bishops. He was instrumental in prompting both to take certain actions but
was also criticized by pontiffs and bishops. Borromeo had a special devotion
to the Holy See and the popes had a high regard for the archbishop of Milan.
Yet this devotion was not abject obedience, nor was papal regard equivalent
to license. Borromeo honored the pope as the vicar of Christ and pastor of
the universal church. He always asked the pope's permission before leaving
his diocese. If special permission was needed in order to perform a certain
function, Borromeo was careful to solicit the pope's approval.

Still, Borromeo was determined to act according to the dictates of his
pastoral conscience. He would defend the rights of his church, eliminate
occasions of sin, and eradicate the abuses detrimental to the well-being of
souls in his care. He would tear away those obstacles which hindered the
progress of his reform program in Milan.[38] He objected, therefore, to
Rome's claims that he was shortsighted and to Rome's order to cool his ardor
and to postpone the application of his proposals.

The popes had a mixed reaction to Borromeo's forceful tactics. On the one
hand, Pius V and Gregory XIII were pleased to have in Borromeo a loyal
subordinate who could help the church reconquer the fullness of a jurisdiction she had once enjoyed.[39] On the other hand, the papacy recognized the

extent of its dependence on the Catholic princes, especially Philip II. The popes also understood that the practices Borromeo attacked had not been introduced by Philip but were characteristic of the domains he inherited and regarded as a sacred trust.[40] The popes sought a redefinition of the relationship between the temporal and ecclesiastical authorities, but neither wanted to endanger the fragile framework of cooperation between the papacy and the princes, a framework threatened by many of Borromeo's actions.

Rome did not hide its disapproval of Borromeo's rigor. His repeated requests for a prompt papal response went unanswered. In addition, time and again he was instructed not to innovate without first consulting the Holy Father. However, determined to produce a new moral climate in Milan, Borromeo was unable to overlook the smallest transgression, and he repeatedly punished offenders in spite of requests from Rome to "proceed slowly and with caution."[41]

Borromeo's clash with Rome over the wisdom of his conduct in the jurisdictional controversy was similar to his duel with the curialists on the question of the proper relationship between pontiff and bishop, and the nature of episcopal authority. While Borromeo was anxious to restore episcopal authority, he never failed to assure the pontiff of his undying loyalty. Still, in his estimation, the relationship between the pope and the bishops was neither simple nor unilateral.[42] Borromeo considered the pope an indispensable aide in helping the bishops carry out the work of reform, but he placed primary emphasis on the work conducted in the diocese by the bishops. Rome and the agencies of Rome were to help the bishops but not meddle in the operations of the diocese.

In the decade following the close of Trent, Borromeo was instrumental in establishing two curial commissions—the Congregation of the Council (1564) and the Congregation of Bishops (1573). These agencies were to work with the bishops to give meaning and structure to the decrees of Trent. In Borromeo's estimation, the vital work of reform could be done only at the diocesan level. Rome could not and should not attempt to shackle or harness the bishops. Only the pastor knew the problems of his flock, and only he was qualified to deal with them. Rome was obligated to see that good men were appointed, and to remind each of his duties; she was not, however, to interfere in diocesan operations.

The visitation of the dioceses and the legislation of the diocesan and provincial councils played an essential role in bringing the Tridentine reforms to the dioceses. These activities had the approval of the council and were to be carried out by the bishops. In Borromeo's estimation, the Congregation of the Council was to resolve ambiguities in the Tridentine decrees; the Congregation of the Bishops was to prod some bishops and to help others overcome the obstacles frustrating the successful implementation of the reform decrees. These congregations were to aid the bishop promptly, but neither was to interfere in the diocesan operations.[43]

In the early years of his tenure in Milan, these congregations gave whole-hearted support to the Borromean program. Initially, the congregations responded to the lead provided by Borromeo; later, they worked to control or at least question his interpretation of the meaning of reform. During the pontificate of Gregory XIII, Borromeo's conception of reform and episcopal authority was repeatedly challenged. His legislation was subjected to the scrutiny of the Congregation of the Council, and his episcopal actions were reviewed and questioned by the Congregation of Bishops.

Any number of incidents illustrate the shift in the manner in which Borromeo was regarded by Rome. For example, in 1569 and again in 1570 Borromeo sent copies of his provincial decrees to the Congregation of the Council, which promptly wrote to express its gratitude.[44] In 1576, during the pontificate of Gregory XIII, Borromeo sent the decrees of his Fourth Provincial Council to Rome. Still without a response from the congregation in 1579, he wrote a long letter to express his fury at the congregation's failure to respond promptly and supportively. Delay by the congregation only hampers the work of the bishops, he wrote. It is the bishop who best understands the needs of his diocese. Unless provincial decrees are contrary to the sacred canons and decrees, the congregation should not interfere.[45] Borromeo argued that the bishops were under no canonical obligation to send their decrees to Rome; they were bound only to celebrate the councils at the intervals prescribed by Trent. Borromeo indicated that his decrees were sent as an act of "obedience in every observance" [to the pope] and as an example to other bishops. He hoped Rome's endorsement would give added force to the decrees, but he did not consider himself obligated to secure Rome's approval, nor did he believe that Rome had the authority to censure, change, or alter his decrees.[46] When Borromeo convoked his Fifth Provincial Council in May of 1579, the Congregation of the Council had still not responded. Borromeo had to journey to Rome to ask Pope Gregory to endorse the decrees.

In 1581 Borromeo was again instructing his agent, Cesare Speciano, to ask Cardinal Carafa—who "spoke in the name of the whole Congregation [of the Council]"—why the membership had questioned the authority of the bishop of Bergamo to appoint a vicar to attend to the affairs of some nuns? How could the congregation question a faculty of the bishops confirmed by the Council of Trent.[47] Several months later Speciano wrote to report that Borromeo would have to change his methods of conducting provincial councils and diocesan synods. A loyal servant, Speciano praised the fruits of Borromeo's work but advised the cardinal-archbishop that he could expect to see revisions in the legislation of his future councils.[48]

By the time of his death in 1584 Borromeo was aware that his relationship with Rome had changed radically. Given a relatively free hand when he first went to Milan—his influence as the papal nephew cannot be denied—and repeatedly complimented for his diligence by popes and prelates, Borromeo was increasingly checked as to his actions and convictions in the pontificate of Gregory XIII. These actions and those of the Congregation of the Bishops well illustrate the attempts of Rome to harness and direct the activities of the Milanese reformer.[49] The actions of the Congregation of the Council also forecast the constitutional reorganization of the Roman Curia that occurred during the pontificate of Sixtus V (1585–90).

The Image of Borromeo

While he lived, Borromeo acknowledged his debt to bishops of his and an earlier age. At the same time, Borromeo's assistance was sought by church-men who wished to put the Tridentine norms into operation in their dio-ceses. Six thousand copies of the decrees of his first provincial council were printed. Countless prelates asked his advice on conducting various opera-tions of episcopal administration. His feverish activity brought reform not just to the Lombard plain, but to other dioceses as well—even Rome. Borromeo set an example on how to conduct the episcopal office, and he developed institutions that he hoped would produce clergy and laity of outstanding quality.[50]

Immediately after his death, Rome employed the figure of Borromeo to emphasize the importance of the episcopal office. But Rome interpreted Borromeo's work to show that he was a model bishop because he was a loyal servant of Rome. Borromeo's concept of the bishop as an intermediate and independent authority between Rome and the faithful was disregarded.

The actions of the Roman congregations, especially the Congregation of the Council and the Congregation of Bishops, well illustrate the interpreta-tion of Rome on the work of the reformer. While both congregations continued to praise Borromeo for his residence, his work in establishing the seminary and other schools, and his careful observance of the liturgy, he was described as an "agent" of Rome, acting on her orders and complying with her requests.[51]

This same trend is evident in the biographies of Borromeo and the commentaries on his work. Those appearing immediately after his death (e.g., Panigarola's funeral oration), praise Borromeo as the true example of the bishop and the executor of Trent. Those appearing in the first decade of the seventeenth century (e.g., Giampietro Giussano's biography) emphasize Borromeo's respect for the rank of cardinal. In addition, it is significant that the Congregation of Rites stipulated that the effigy of Borromeo be vested in cardinalatial regalia at the canonization liturgy and that all subsequent repre-sentations of the new saint were to depict him as a cardinal—not a bishop.[52]

Conclusion

Borromeo's development as a churchmen occurred in Milan, not in Rome. It is significant that he left the epicenter of the church to work at the periphery. Undoubtedly he was moved to implement the decrees of Trent as a pastor, an image that was of central importance to the fathers at Trent. As papal secretary during the last phase of Trent, Borromeo was conscious of the council's emphasis on episcopal authority and the mandate to convoke regular diocesan and provincial councils and to visit the diocese at regular intervals.

At the earliest opportunity Borromeo left Rome to go to Milan. He entered his diocese dressed as a bishop and he made the journey in order to hold a provincial council. Borromeo believed that Trent's prescription on the frequency of provincial and diocesan councils was based on the premise that there was a need to establish regular communication among the local councils, Rome, and the general assemblies.[53] It is noteworthy that Borromeo was the only bishop who regularly fulfilled the Tridentine precept on the frequency of convoking councils and synods.

His conflicts with papal and temporal authorities developed as he worked to eradicate abuses in his diocese that were condemned by the council, while he preserved those institutions, traditions, and practices in harmony with the spirit of Trent. He resisted interference from both quarters and opposed all efforts by Rome to establish a vertical, unilateral relationship between the dioceses and the Holy See.[54]

After his death, many of the practices he had developed or restored disappeared, and others, which he had resisted, triumphed. In the pontificate of Sixtus V, for example, Rome attempted to tie the dioceses more closely to the Holy See and sanctioned new instruments that sought to control diocesan operations in order to make them uniform. The apostolic visitation, the *ad limina* precept, the obligation to have recourse to the Roman congregations for approval of episcopal action, and the establishment of a formal system of nuncios, were sanctioned by papal bulls and developed to ensure Rome's primacy. The program of Borromeo, outlined in his *Acta ecclesiae Mediolanensis,* and the pleas of his associates who asked that bishops be allowed to continue to convoke local councils and to visit their dioceses on their own authority, were unenforced and unheeded.[55]

Borromeo was an administrative genius who worked to give substance to the Tridentine spirit. His actions did not always win approval, nor were his suggestions warmly received. However, no one ever doubted the sincerity and selflessness of his proposals.

Borromeo never doubted papal primacy, nor did he ever question the importance of Rome. Indeed, he was instrumental in directing the popes to enact certain reform measures. Borromeo did, however, hold certain reservations about the papal commitment to Trent and the willingness of the Roman hierarchy to transform itself into a reflection of Tridentine perfection. He questioned Rome's willingness to heed the voice of the bishops and to guarantee them the authority that the council delegated. He campaigned for the restoration of episcopal authority and for the development of an awareness, on the part of Rome, of the renewed importance of the reformed diocese.

To Borromeo, Milan was a particular diocese of Christendom whose unique traditions and customs were to be incorporated or revised according to the program of Trent. Milan was also the model for diocesan reform both in its internal organization and in its relationships with other dioceses and the papacy. Borromeo labored to bring the reforms of Trent to Milan, and to create institutions that could perpetuate their application and preserve their spirit. What he sought to establish in Milan, he longed to see in Rome and throughout the church.

Borromeo's interpretation of Trent would authorize the bishop to take the lead in defining the specific manner in which the disciplinary decrees would be applied. His view was based on two important but unstated assumptions: first, that all bishops held a common view of the importance of discipline and the form in which it should be expressed, and, second, that all bishops had Borromeo's energy. If these assumptions were valid, uniformity of diocesan administration would emerge along with a common understanding of Tridentine reform. Indeed, Borromeo's work in establishing schools, seminaries, and devotional practices was directed toward producing religious and lay individuals who would reflect his attitudes and energy.

While Borromeo and those who supported and succeeded him worked to secure and maintain an influential voice for the dioceses in the administration of the church, in no sense did he desire the democratization of the church. Neither Borromeo nor his disciples wanted the laity in positions of influence in the church. Restoration of the dioceses would, he thought, buttress the preeminence of Rome. The dangerous implications of his position were never apparent to Borromeo. In essence, he wanted to establish some form of federative church structure that, by definition, was antithetical to Roman centralism.

The disciplinary decrees of Trent were the touchstone of the Borromean reform, a movement built on the reforming energies of the bishop. In Borromeo's mind, Trent specified that the bishop was the agent of reform. It is a misconception to see reform in the immediate post-Tridentine period as directed and manipulated by Rome. Still, within Borromeo's lifetime Rome was claiming that the authority of the bishop, confirmed by the council, was exercised at the explicit direction and only with the approval of the pope.

Trent was a turning point because it gave direction and definition to those churchmen already committed to the cause of reform and initiative to those not yet committed. Papal centralism and authoritarianism were not the immediate by-products of Trent and the immediate postconciliar period. The council was an expression of the fathers' willingness to seek compromise rather than risk schism. The program of the council was not a simple restatement of the doctrine of the Middle Ages, nor an affirmation of papal absolutism, but a modification of the ecclesiastical constitution and the meaning of the pastoral ministry. The council itself was an outwardly modest act of self-examination and self-renewal by churchmen. The work of Borromeo is a direct reflection of the attitudes and objectives of the fathers of the Council of Trent. Borromeo remained unwaveringly consistent in the manner in which he conducted his responsibilities. His increasing difficulties with Rome suggest that changes in the meaning and direction of the Tridentine reform occurred at the center of the church, not the periphery, as a new Roman administration was developed and put in operation.

Notes

1. Hubert Jedin, *Der Abschluss des Trienter Konzils. 1562/63: Ein Rückblick nach vier Jahrhunderten*, Katholisches Leben und Kämpfen im Zeitalter des Glaubensspaltung, vol. 21 (Münster in Westfalen, 1963), p. 79. See also Paul Broutin and Hubert Jedin, *L'Evêque dans la tradition pastorale du XVIe siècle* (Paris, 1953).

2. Pio Paschini, *Il primo Soggiorno di San Carlo a Roma* (Turin, 1935), pp. 91–99. Hereinafter cited as Paschini, *Soggiorno di San Carlo*.

3. Antonio Sala and Aristide Sala, *Biografia e Documenti circa la vita e le gesta di San Carlo Borromeo* (Milan, 1857–61), 5:6. Hereinafter cited as Sala, *Biografia e Documenti di San Carlo*. See also Jean Delumeau, *Vie économique et sociale de Rome dans la seconde moitié du XVIe siècle*, Bibliothèque des Ecoles françaises d'Athenes et de Rome, 184 (Paris, 1957, 1959), 1:464. Hereinafter cited as Delumeau, *Vie économique de Rome.*

4. Pio Pecchiai, *Roma nel cinquecento*, vol. 13: *Storia di Roma* (Bologna, 1948), pp. 114–15. See also Paschini, *Soggiorno di San Carlo*, pp. 73–74.

5. Sala, *Biografia e Documenti di San Carlo* 1:13. See also André DeRoo, *Saint Charles Borromée: Cardinal Reformateur, Docteur de la Pastorale* (Paris, 1963), p. 195.

6. Annibal Caro, *Lettere del commendatore Annibal Caro, scritte a nome del Cardinale Alessandro Farnese* (Padua, 1765), 2:388. ". . . le ricordo che ci si viene ora per orare a non per pascere." Paschini, *Soggiorno di San Carlo*, pp. 62–63.

7. *Storia di Milano* (Milan, 1953–66), 10:127. Hereinafter cited as *Storia di Milano.*

8. Cuthbert Robinson, *Nicolo Ormaneto: A Papal Envoy in the Sixteenth Century* (London, 1920), p. 50. Orazio Maria Premoli, *Storia dei Barnabiti nel cinquecento* (Rome, 1913). Francesco Maria Carini, S.J., *Monsignor Niccolò Ormaneto veronese, vescovo di Padova, Nunzio apostolico all corte di Filippo II, Re di Spagna, 1572–1577* (Rome, 1849), pp. 7, 10. Carlo Bascapè, *Vita e opere di Carlo, archivescovo di Milano, Cardinale di Santa Prassede* (Milan, 1965), p. 47. From the Latin text of 1592. Carlo Bascapè, *De vita et rebus gestis Caroli S.R.E. cardinalis tituli S. Praxedis, archiepiscopi Mediolani* (Ingolstadt: ex officina typographica D. Sartorii, 1592). Hereinafter cited as Bascapè, *Vita di Carlo.*

9. Carlo Marcora, "Nicolò Ormaneto, vicario di San Carlo a Milano," *Memorie storiche della diocesi di Milano* 8(1961): 486. Hereinafter cited as Marcora, "Ormaneto, vicario." Borromeo to Ormaneto, 8 July 1564. "Nostro Signore . . . circa l'osservanza del Concilio che ha pubblicata una bolla amplissima della quale vi si mandan XX copie stampate . . ."

10. Ibid., p. 500. Borromeo to Ormaneto, 12 August 1564. "Quanto poi al modo di celebrare la Sinodo et della cose . . . Monsignor Paleotto data certa lista de' scrittori et luoghi che ne trattano me e parso di mandarvene copia."

11. Ibid., pp. 258, 261.

12. A. G. B., *Borromeo,* 1 : ff. 73–73*v.* "Feci l'entrata come arcivescovo col Piviale, et con la mitra, sopra il cavallo bianco: et non come legato, havenda sequitato in questo Paris di Grassis . . ."

13. *Storia di Milano,* 10 : 139. Marcora, "Ormaneto, vicario," p. 338.

14. B.A.V., *Vat. Lat.* 6183, ff. 15, 32. Bartolomeo, Conte di Portia to Sirleto, 10 October 1565. ". . . del mio travaglio del quale ho havuto unico rimedio l'accostarmi con ogni prestezza questo raro Signore, che con la sua dolcezza basta a temperare ogni amaritudine et con l'essempio della compositione d'animo indur gl'huomini a scordarsi di tutte l'afflitioni. . . ."

15. Antonio Monti, "Lettere inedite di Tolomeo Gallio cardinale di Como al Cardinal Carlo Borromeo," *Periodico della Società storica per la Provincia e antica diocesi di Como* (1889): 109–10. Hereinafter cited as Monti, "Gallio a Borromeo."

16. Cattaneo believes that the work of Gian Matteo Giberti in Verona influenced Borromeo's initial acts in Milan, as well as those which followed. Enrico Cattaneo, "Influenze veronesi nella legislazione de San Carlo Borromeo: Problemi de vita religiosa in Italia nel cinquecento," *Italia Sacra* 2 (1960): 123–38.

17. Carlo Marcora, "I primi anni dell'episcopato di San Carlo, 1566–1567," *Memorie storiche della diocesi di Milano* 10 November (1963): 533. Borromeo to Bonomi, 20 November 1566. "L'andata del prefato signore a la sua residenze non puo se non piacermi per ogni rispetto, perche stando a la sua chiesa particulare verra a servire anche a l'universale coll'esempio de le sue attioni."

18. A. G. B., *Borromeo,* 2 : ff. 255*v*–56. Borromeo to Alciato, 13 April 1579. "Degli amorevoli officii, che V.S. Ill.ma fa a favor de' vescovi, io come vescovo, et come quello che farsi ne godo la maggior parte. . . ."

19. A. G. B., *Borromeo,* 2 : ff. 230–31. Borromeo to Speciano, 12 October 1576. "Quanto al titolo di'vescovi. . . ." 4 December 1578. "Quanto ai titoli, pare a me ancora, che siano venuti a tal termine, che habbiamo bisogno di una buona riforma, ma il dar del Rev.mo asi vescovi, considerata le dignita dello stato loro, non mi par, che sia troppo."

20. A. G. B., *Borromeo,* 2 : ff. 11–11*v.* Borromeo to Speciano, 21 March 1571. "E molto tempo ch'io sento qualche inquiete d'animo per rispetto dell'Archip'brato di Santa Maria Maggiore, . . . come faccio col presente il mandato di procura ad resignandum in manibus S.tis Suae, all quale farete intendere questo mio desiderio. . . ."

21. Paolo Prodi, "San Carlo Borromeo e il card. Gabriele Paleotti: due vescovi della riforma cattolica," *Critica storica* 3(1964): 150–51.

22. *Storia di Milano,* 10 : 155.

23. Council of Trent: sess. 6, can. 3 de re.: sess. 6, can. 4, de ref.: sess. 23, can. 18, de ref.; sess. 24, canones 12 et 15, de ref.; sess. 25, can. 6, de ref. *Storia di Milano,* 10 : 174.

24. Before Borromeo resided in Milan the Ursuline Nuns, a new religious order,

wore religious habits but lived in their family homes. Borromeo put them into convents, prescribed a habit, and wrote a rule. *Storia di Milano*, 10:143, 191, 197.

25. Giovanni Pietro Giussano, *Vita di San Carlo Borromeo* (Rome: Stamperia della Camera Apostolica, 1610), p. 81. "Of the principal means of reform 'l'uno fu la celebratione de'concilii provinciali, et diocesani: et l'altro le frequentissima, anzi continua, visita della sua chiesa, ch'ei fece. . . .' "

26. Louis Thomassin, *Dictionnaire de Discipline ecclésiastique ou traité du gouvernement* (Paris: 1856), 2:1361–62.

27. Sala, *Biografia e Documenti di San Carlo*, 3:174–79. Borromeo was very conscious of the connection between rank in the social order and costume. He was deeply distressed to see the patriarch and clergy of Venice improperly vested at the time of his visit. In his estimation, proper external appearance reflected the internal commitment and provided a singularly forceful example of the clergy's worth in the diocese. A. G. B., *Borromeo*, 2:311*v.* Borromeo to Speciano, 1580, ". . . e una città libera, dove non e pur disciplina del clero. . . ."

28. For the dates of the councils, consult Sala, *Biografia e Documenti di San Carlo*, 1:28–30. *Storia di Milano*, 10:157. *Acta ecclesiae mediolanensis ab eius initiis usque ad nostram aetatem, opera et studio presb. Achillis Ratti* (Milan, 1890–97).

29. Paolo Prodi, "Charles Borromée archêveque de Milan et la papauté," *Revue d'histoire écclesiastique* 62(1967): 389. Hereinafter cited as Prodi, "Charles Borromée."

30. Ibid., pp. 387–88. *Storia di Milano*, 10:155–56.

31. Bascapè, *Vita di Carlo*, pp. 95, 99.

32. Paolo Prodi, "San Carlo Borromeo e la trattative tra Gregorio XIII e Filippo II sulla giurisdizione ecclesiastica," *Rivista di storia della Chiesa in Italia* 11(1957): 195, 198. Hereinafter cited as Prodi, "Borromeo e Gregorio XIII."

33. Federico Barbieri, "La riforma dell'eloquenza sacra in Lombardia operata da San Carlo Borromeo," *Archivio storico lombardo*, 15 (1911): 248. Eugenio Albèri, ed., *Le relazioni degli ambasciatori veneti al senato durante il secolo decimosesto*, 2, vol. 4, (Florence 1857), p. 230. (Tiepolo, 1576) The pope knew "di non essere più certo e più gagliardo difensore del Re Cattolico contro gli eretici e gli infedeli," and that it was necessary "amarlo, stimarlo ed aiutarlo."

34. Sala, *Biografia e Documenti di San Carlo*, 2:33 "Vassallo et suddito di Sua Maesta."

35. Alessandro Visconti, *La pubblica amministrazione nello stato milanese durante il predominio straniero (1541–1796)* (Rome, 1913), p. 499. Mario Bendiscioli, "L'inizie delle controversie giurisdizionali a Milano tra l'Arcivescovo Carlo Borromeo e il Senato milanese," *Archivio storico lombardo* 52 (1926): 242–43, 245, 249. Mario Bendiscioli, "La bolla *In coena Domini* e la sua pubblicazione a Milano nel 1568," *Archivio storico lombardo* 54 (1927): 385. Luigi Prosdocimi, "Il progetto di riforma dei principi al Concilio di Trento," *Aevum* 13 (1939): 3–64.

36. Sala, *Biografia e Documenti di San Carlo*, 3:469. Borromeo to Castelli, 29 October 1573. " . . . havera Nostra Santità bella occasione di risolvere una volta et terminare queste controversie tutte di giurisdizione et dare all chiesa il suo diritto."

37. A. G. B., *Borromeo*, 1:ff. 277–77*v.* Borromeo to Ormaneto, 18 January 1570. ". . . si fosse proceduto senza tante dilationi, et si fosse pubblicata la sentenza contra li senatori citati . . . si sarebbe facilmente estimata l'origine, et fonte d'onde successivamente sono poi scaturiti questi altri accidenti . . . et . . . havrebbe protato fine a queste controversie."

38. Prodi, "Borromeo e Gregorio XIII," p. 234.

39. Ibid., p. 233. Gaetano Catalano, *Controversie giurisdizionali tra Chiesa e*

Stato nell'età di Gregorio XIII e Filippo II, Atti della Accademia di scienze, lettere et arti di Palermo, vol. 14 (Palermo: Accademia di scienze, lettere, arti, 1955), p. 231. Hereinafter cited as Catalano, *Controversie giurisdizionali.*

40. Catalano, *Controversie giudizionali,* p. 230.

41. Monti, "Gallio a Borromeo," p. 28. 15 November 1578. Gallio asks that Borromeo "fugga ogni occasione di novità, ne dia causa alcuna di rottura contra di essa a li officiali del Re." See also letters of Gallio to Borromeo on pp. 27–28, 33.

42. Prodi, "Charles Borromée," pp. 386, 411.

43. Chap. 3 of John B. Tomaro, "The Implementation of the Council of Trent, 1564–1588" (Ph.D. diss., University of North Carolina, 1974).

44. A. G. B., *Borromeo,* 1 :ff. 355v–56. Borromeo to Ormaneto, 1 October 1570. Giuseppe Alberigo, "Studi e problemi relativi all'applicazione del Concilio di Trento in Italia," *Rivista storica italiana* 70(1958): 278–79.

45. A. G. B., *Borromeo* 2 :ff. 253v–54v. Borromeo to Speciano, 9 April 1579. "Quei SS.ri della Congregatione consumino molto tempo con poco frutto; et potrebbe anco esser causa di rallentar in questo la diligenza, et sollicitudine de' vescovi, poichè vedranno: che le ordinationi loro; senza alcuna necessità, ne ragione sono censurate di questa maniera, nelle cose minutissime, et che essi, che sono sul fatto, et sanno i costumi et bisogni particolari delle lor chiese, e conoscono esser necessarie, o utili per il buon governo di' suoi popoli. . . ."

46. A. G. B., *Borromeo,* 2 :ff. 252v–53v. See also Prodi, "Charles Borromée," p. 396.

47. A. G. B., *Borromeo,* 2 :f. 367. Borromeo to Speciano, 29 July 1581. "Desiderio che gli diciate confidentemente in nome mio, che io son restato maravigliato. che si metta pure in dubbio simule materia di questa deputationi di vicarii, le quali il Concilio di Trento, et tanto liberamente rimette al giudicio, et all'arbitrio de' vescovi."

48. A. G. B., *Borromeo,* 2 :ff. 368v–69. Speciano to Borromeo, 2 September 1581.

49. There may be grounds for arguing that the friction between the Congregation of the Council and Borromeo was exacerbated by the latent friction between the Carafa and Borromeo families. René Ancel, "Le procès et la disgrâce des Carafa," *Revue Benedictine* 22(1905): 525–35; 24(1907); 224–53, 479–509; 25(1908); 194–224; 26(1909); 52–80, 189–220, 301–24.

50. Prodi, "Charles Borromée," p. 401. Luigi Castano, *Gregorio XIV,* (Turin, 1957), pp. 88–91. *Storia di Milano,* 10:157. Julius Pogianus, *Epistolae et Orationes olim collectae ab Antonio Maria Cratiano nunc ab Hieronymo Lagomarsino e Societate Jesu adnotationes illustratae ac primum editae* (Rome: Generosus Salomonius, 1756–62), 2 :xv. Pogiano to Borromeo, 21 December 1566. "Non occorre che io dica altro a V.S. intorno all'stima che si fa della costitutioni sinodali, vedendo ognuno che la riforma romana e figliola della milanese. Il che di giorna in giorna si va cosi dilatanda che codesto membra entrera in molta maggior reputatione, poichè da quello, a un certo modo, ha preso esempio il capo."

51. Ramon Robres Llurch, "La Congregación del Concilio y san Carlos Borromeo en la problemática y curso de la controreforma," *Anthologica Annua* 14(1966): 105.

52. Marco Aurelio Grattarola, *Successi maravigliosi della veneratione de San Carlo* (Milan 1614), p. 174. ". . . poichè essendo stato determinato dalla Congregazione dei Sacri Riti, che si dovesse dipingere il Beato Carlo vestito da cardinale, e non da vescovo. . . ."

53. Paolo Prodi, "Note sul problema della genesi del Diritto nella Chiesa post-Tridentina dell'età moderna," unpublished manuscript, p. 14.

54. Ibid., p. 15.

55. Cesare Speciano, *Decreta provinciae mediolanensis sub Carolo Borromeo, cardinale archiepiscopo, Diversis temporibus in sex conciliis, totidemque, voluminibus edita . . . ad usum Ecclesiae Cremonensis in unum codicem collecta* (Brescia: apud Societates Brixiensem, 1591), pp. 1–2. In his first letter, Speciano calls on the clergy of Cremona to convoke provincial councils on a regular basis, as was the practice of "noster Borromaeus in coelo."

Archbishop Carlo Borromeo and the Ecclesiastical Policy of Philip II in the State of Milan

AGOSTINO BORROMEO

WHEN IN 1535 THE LAST SFORZA DUKE OF MILAN, FRANCESCO II, DIED without leaving a legitimate successor, the Sforza dynasty became extinct, and the duchy of Milan, in its capacity of imperial fief, reverted back to the emperor who at the time was Charles V, reigning potentate of Spain. Charles V on his part, eleven years later, invested with the duchy of Milan his firstborn son Philip, who would eventually in 1556 succeed to the Spanish throne as Philip II.[1]

Upon its entry into the Habsburg dominions, the duchy of Milan ceased to exist as an independent state. Coming under foreign rule changed specifically the international position of the former duchy but left the preexisting administrative structure totally intact. There was, however, one obvious change consisting in the fact that the new sovereign no longer lived among his subjects but governed the duchy from distant Spain by means of a governor who resided in Milan. Apart from this change, which was an immediate effect of the loss of autonomy, the bureaucratic apparatus remained that of the preceding Sforza administration. Maintenance of internal legislation, and of the institutions that had characterized the preexisting political entities, was moreover a policy pursued by the Spanish monarchy with regard to all its Italian possessions. Therefore, in Milan, under the authority of the Spanish governor, the same bureaucratic organs and the same magistracies that had been operating in the preceding age continued to function: in particular the "consiglio segreto" (secret council, i.e., the advisory body which assisted the duke in governing the duchy) and the "senato" (Senate) that was invested with supreme judicial and administrative authority.[2]

Thus, in the transition from the Sforza to the Spanish era, institutional continuity in Milan was maintained. And continuity in the internal workings of the duchy is also apparent in the relationship between secular and religious authority. The ecclesiastical policies of the Visconti and the Sforzas had

looked essentially toward a strengthening of civil powers at the expense of
the church, one principal objective being to exercise control over ecclesiastical nominations in the duchy, especially nominations to bishoprics, in
order to avoid appointment of persons hostile or politically unacceptable.[3]
In due time, these official policies had reached their objectives, so that under
the last Sforza duke almost no ecclesiastical nomination could be effected
without having previously received the ducal *placet*.[4] Under Duke Francesco
II, the interference of lay authority with religious life had come to extend
also into other sectors, e.g., into that of struggling against Protestant heresy
which at this time was beginning to infiltrate the duchy.[5] Moreover it became
evident that such lay interference with matters beyond its competence was
furthered precisely by the crisis that at this time was troubling the church, to
such a degree that by now many bishops were absent from their dioceses and
local religious authority was unable to deal with the lapse in discipline and
moral decline of the clergy.[6]

The Spanish king, in his ecclesiastical policy with regard to the duchy of
Milan, would be inclined to follow the same lines as those of the Visconti and
the Sforza administrations. Thus, under Charles V, we see the governors
keeping strict control with episcopal nominations in order to ensure, at a
tense moment in relations between France and the empire, that pro-French
elements were not placed in the dioceses of the state of Milan.[7] Not infre-
quently, it is the civil, and not the religious authority, that would try those
accused of heresy.[8] The same goes for reestablishing discipline in the convents, and for suppressing and sometimes punishing clerical abuses.[9] In fact,
a structure was created in which Milanese secular magistrates, with the
support of the Spanish crown, not only intervened in questions of a purely
religious nature but even violated ecclesiastical immunity, such as the fundamental principle of canon law according to which the clergy was subject only
to church authority and could be tried only by its own courts, in matters of
discipline as well as in civil and criminal cases.[10]

This state of affairs, notwithstanding some attempts of the papacy to
correct it, above all in the years after the opening of the Council of Trent,[11]
continued almost without change until the moment of the ultimate transferal
of Archbishop Carlo Borromeo to the diocese of Milan in the spring of 1566.
The fact that the young cardinal's activity was aimed at restoration of
episcopal functions to their fullest possible extent led inevitably, in the
course of his almost twenty years of personal, spiritual leadership, to some
moments of very real tension in his relationship with the secular authorities
of Milan and Madrid. Tension was not unique to Milan, and analogous
conflicts occurred also elsewhere in Italy after the Council of Trent,[12] but in
the Lombard capital the situation acquired a special significance due to the
firm and energetic determination with which Borromeo reassumed free
exercise of his archiepiscopal authority.

The following analysis does not aim at reconstructing the series of decisive events in the problematic relationship between secular and ecclesiastical authority during the episcopate of Borromeo.[13] It will tend, rather, to characterize their respective positions, ecclesiastical authority as represented by the archbishop, on the one hand, and secular power on its different levels of authority, Milanese and Spanish, on the other—in order to identify the fundamental points of contrast, but also the lines of convergence between the pastoral care of the archbishop and the ecclesiastical policy of Spain.

Carlo Borromeo was named administrator of the diocese of Milan in 1560.[14] Having received the full title of archbishop after episcopal consecration in 1563,[15] only in 1565 was he able to take personal possession of the diocese. In the autumn of that same year, in fact, he obtained from his uncle, Pope Pius IV, permission to absent himself briefly from Rome, where he was attending to his responsibilities as "Cardinal Nipote" (cardinal-nephew), in order to celebrate the First Provincial Synod of all the bishops in the ecclesiastical province of which Milan was the center.[16]

At the time of his arrival in Milan, the figure and the personality of the cardinal were already well known to the court of Madrid. Borromeo was known as a cardinal of intense spirituality and exemplary life, "one of the most exemplary clerics in the Church of God, who exercises a very positive influence on this Pontificate", as he was described in March 1565 by the Spanish Cardinal Francisco Pacheco, who at the time was entrusted with representing the interests of the Spanish crown at the papal court.[17] But, above all, it was perceived at Madrid that, even though the young cardinal was not openly pro-Spanish, he had still demonstrated some inclination in favor of royal Spanish interests. Therefore, when Philip II in November 1565 learned of Cardinal Borromeo's voyage to Milan, he instructed the duke of Alburquerque, governor of Milan, to do everything in his power to accommodate him and possibly win him even more effectively for the Spanish cause.[18] It is probable that Philip II's nomination of Borromeo, early in 1566, as cardinal-protector of the Spanish possessions in Flanders[19] was meant to serve the same end.

Thus, with the ultimate transferal of Borromeo to Milan, which occurred in April 1566[20] shortly after the death of Pope Pius IV and the election of Pius V, it seemed as if an era of close cooperation between the archbishop and Spanish secular authority in Milan was about to begin. Borromeo, also, upon his arrival in the archdiocese, had not failed to express his gratitude to the sovereign for such favors extended to him by the governor as well as by the Senate.[21]

Still, only two months after his installment as archbishop of Milan, Cardinal Borromeo found himself in open conflict with the duke of Alburquerque, on account of the latter's pretension of claiming precedence over the archbishop even in religious ceremonial—a presumption on the part of the governor that of course, Borromeo had firmly rejected[22] with the full support, also, of the Holy See.[23] However marginal and, furthermore, however promptly resolved as it proved to be,[24] this episode is still characteristic of the importance attached at this time to matters of honor and ceremony, and it reveals the effect of decades of spiritual neglect in the archdiocese: the head of the civil administration in Milan now considered himself superior to ecclesiastical hierarchy, even as far as outer ceremony was concerned.

But it was to be another matter, that of an opposition on the part of the Senate to the publication of some of the decrees of the First Provincial Synod, held the year before,[25] that was going to demonstrate effectively to the archbishop, shortly after his arrival, what kind of difficulty he was going to encounter in his future relationship with civil authority in the diocese. In spite of the fact that the deliberations of the synod had been in essence an implementation of the Council of Trent, and in spite of the fact that its decrees had already found the approval of the Holy See, civil administration in Milan now attempted to have the decrees modified before publication, finding some of their provisions detrimental to the prerogatives of lay authority, e.g., the decree obliging physicians and schoolmasters to profess Catholicism before being able to practice.[26]

These episodes, however, were to remain but episodes: in the first place because the governor eventually seems to have given up his claim;[27] in the second place, because the decrees of the provincial synod were published before Philip II had acted upon the Senate's protestations.[28] Especially the second of these clearly foreshadowed the difficulties that the two authorities were going to encounter in their mutual relations. To the archbishop, it demonstrated that the lay magistrates intended to continue their interference with ecclesiastical matters, in conformity with what had come to be the practice under his predecessors. To the representatives of secular authority, the decrees of the provincial synod, as well as their firm defense on Borromeo's part, were to bring out quite clearly that the archbishop had made it his primary and fundamental objective in exercising his pastoral obligations to proceed to a profound religious reform of the diocese and, generally, of the ecclesiastical province of Milan. In such work of reform, he intended to follow the lines laid down by the Council of Trent, making use of precisely those disciplinary and ecclesiastical institutions which this Council had been aspiring to revitalize. This would imply working out a series of particular rules for the diocese of Milan, adapting conciliar directives to local conditions, and stressing always the bishop's permanent obligation to ensure that such rules were observed. Borromeo was convinced that in order to attain fulfillment of his objectives, his own pastoral dedication, his constant exhortation, and his example were not enough. In comparison with other bishops of his generation, he would be more inclined to proceed when necessary with firmness and severity in order to eradicate bad habits and abuses that had come to be the order of the day, having recourse, eventually, also to punitive measures.[29] Consequently, from the earliest days of his spiritual leadership in the diocese of Milan, Borromeo turned his attention to ensuring full application of those coercive powers invested in his episcopacy, as based upon canon law, and as reformulated in the Tridentine decrees. To this purpose, upon his transferal to Milan and pursuant of directives that he himself had promulgated in the First Provincial Synod—directives which, incidentally, would be later elaborated in his subsequent synods—he reinstalled the civil and criminal tribunals of the archiepiscopal Curia in their previous functions, made provisions for the necessary attendant personnel, and reactivated the prisons subordinate to such courts of law.[30] Moreover, already at the end of 1566, he made use of the traditional prerogative of the archbishops of Milan to avail themselves of an independent executive force, the so-called *famiglia armata*, which was a corps of armed members of the archbishop's household placed under the command of their *bargello* to secure execution of the sentences of the ecclesiastical courts or reenforcement of such other measures for which the use of coercion would have to be envisaged.[31] This came to signify that ecclesiastical jurisdiction could function without calling upon the collaboration of lay authority—i.e., without having to invoke the secular arm—and even without having to inform lay authority of its action.

It goes without saying that such pretension on the part of the archbishop to an unrestricted use of his *famiglia armata* was hardly welcomed by the secular authority in Milan—even less so because such pretension was nothing else than the outer manifestation of a far wider claim, that of full restoration of archiepiscopal jurisdiction in Milan, which in its traditional sphere of competence was already far-reaching. In fact, according to canon law, the ecclesiastical judge had exclusive jurisdiction in all cases involving the clergy, which, in consequence of the principle of the *privilegium fori*, were in no way to be submitted to secular tribunals. Intrinsical parts of ecclesiastical jurisdiction were, furthermore, such matters involving laymen that had a bearing upon the salvation of the soul and thus pertained to the ecclesiastical *forum*, e.g., matrimony and heresy, not to speak of those cases which were objects of competing jurisdiction, i.e., where both *fora* could claim jurisdiction. This would be the case with offences that concerned morality, such as blasphemy, heresy, and sodomy, *delicta mixta* which could be punished either by ecclesiastical courts or by lay tribunals according to whichever jurisdiction took action first.[32]

However, Borromeo, in restoring full and uninhibited exercise of the jurisdictional rights invested in the archiepiscopal see, did not limit himself to such areas in which ecclesiastical jurisdiction was beyond dispute, but also reaffirmed rights that might be considered less certain. The ecclesiastical court operating under his authority heard civil cases between the clergy and the laity regardless of whether the clerical party was the plaintiff or the defendant: thus it deviated from the general canonical principle of *actor sequitur forum rei*, a principle deriving from the *jus commune* that would imply that cases where the defendant was a layman would belong exclusively to civil jurisdiction. Borromeo, in defending such legal action when it eventually came to be contested by the civil authority, referred himself to a particular Milanese *consuetudo trahendi laicos ad forum ecclesiasticum*, maintaining his right to hear any civil case involving institutions or individuals belonging to the clergy, while secular authority kept finding this *consuetudo* not sufficiently proved by the Milanese church.[33]

Such revendication on the part of the archbishop, from the very beginning of his episcopate, was inspired by his desire to make use of the most effective instruments possible to implement his program of religious and moral reform of the clergy and the people of Christ. He was convinced, in particular, that restoration of ecclesiastical discipline presupposed a total dependency of the clergy upon archiepiscopal authority, a dependency that could not be achieved if the clergy were to turn to civil tribunals to obtain their right in cases against laymen, or if in this context it was admitted that civil power could interfere with the action of ecclesiastical authority. Also in order to prevent any possible Spanish administrative interference with the legal activity of the archiepiscopal Curia, he came to use his *famiglia armata* ever more frequently against clerics as well as against the laity in cases where canon law or the particular usage in the church of Milan would call for such action.

In such a quasi-medieval conception of the relations between ecclesiastical and secular authority,[34] Borromeo would assign to the latter a subordinate part. This is brought out quite clearly in a letter written by Borromeo in 1581 to Philip II, a letter that, I believe, has not previously been known.[35] It dates from a period in which, as we shall see, the most acute conflicts had in some fashion been mitigated, even if the underlying problems had not been resolved. The letter presents two main lines of thought: first, that one of the obligations of secular authority is to offer to bishops in their pastoral activity all possible support and to refrain from any initiative that might impede attainment of the spiritual ends for which the episcopal activity is striving. The cardinal in this context stresses the fact that his own action had always had as its exclusive objective the "servizio di Dio," thereby making it clear that he was well aware that civil magistrates of Milan on more than one occasion (as we shall see later) had communicated to Madrid their conviction that the archbishop's revendication of jurisdictional rights for the church in fact served secondary purposes of building up his own temporal power. Borromeo at this point in his letter calls attention to the fact that his efforts to strengthen religious sentiment among the people would at the same time reinforce its feelings of loyalty to the crown. Making use of an ecclesiastical concept common to the age,[36] he points out that wherever religion and fear of God are diminishing, there also obedience to the crown and respect for the sovereign will be in decay, so that religious revival should in itself be seen as a phenomenon beneficial to political stability.

Borromeo's second point in his letter was that the bishop, especially if he had been living for many years among the souls entrusted to his care, was to decide exclusively, as his sole prerogative, the means to be considered most appropriate for promoting the spiritual growth of the people of Christ, taking into account always the time, the place, and the circumstances. The cardinal goes on to affirm his own constant consideration of precisely these factors, calling attention to the fact that his directives had always found ready acceptance on the part of the faithful, thereby also replying indirectly to accusations advanced against him at the Spanish court for being excessively severe.

Lay power in the cardinal's opinion, thus, ought not to interfere with the bishops' pastoral activity and should leave them free to exercise what jurisdictional rights were due them, always with a view to maintaining political stability in the territorial entities subject to such secular authority. In this respect, the cardinal's stance was precisely the opposite of the fundamental guidelines of Philip II's ecclesiastical policy, especially as far as his Italian dominions were concerned. Of course Philip II, motivated by his devout religious sentiments, was in favor of profound ecclesiastical reform, as is proved also by his efforts in the concluding phase of the Council of Trent.[37] In accordance with the centralist tendencies of his government in general, however, such religious and moral regeneration ought to be achieved without any expansion of the sphere of ecclesiastical jurisdiction and without prejudice to the prerogatives of the crown in the dominions of the Spanish monarchy. Control over religious life was a primary objective of the policy of the crown. Thus, in the realm of Naples, Spanish authorities would claim their right to ratify papal letters, give them the secular power's *assensus* (the *exequatur*), before they could be implemented. Here, there was also a revendication in favor of exclusively secular jurisdiction of matters that were elsewhere considered *delicta mixta,* on the ground that Neapolitan ecclesiastical usage ignored such categories of crimes: the ecclesiastical courts there could not even hear such cases in jurisdictional competition with secular jurisdiction.[38] Another even more important element of this policy was Philip II's stubborn defense of the so-called privilege of the *Legazia Apostolica* in Sicily (or *Monarchia Sicula*) on the basis of which the Spanish sovereign could exercise in Sicily the prerogatives pertaining to papal legates. Referring himself to this originally medieval privilege—whose validity, however, was contested by the Holy See—the Spanish king would reserve for himself exclusively the major part of ecclesiastical nominations in Sicily, as well as his right to submit pontifical commissions to his *exequatur* and supreme jurisdiction over verdicts of the Sicilian ecclesiastical courts, barring appeal to Rome.[39]

Specifically with regard to Milan, some initiatives taken by Madrid at the very beginning of Philip II's reign will illustrate quite clearly the orientation of Spanish ecclesiastical policy, first and foremost with regard to the powers of control over religious life. Having received, in 1560, information as to the excessive licence manifested by some nunneries in the state of Milan, in particular at Pavia, the king ordered the Senate to take the necessary steps to ensure, after hearing the diocesan bishops in question, that all convents and monasteries were reduced to ancient discipline and to full observation of the *clausura*.[40] This move shows clearly how Philip II considered himself supremely responsible for surveying, by means of the organs of the secular administration, the life of the religious orders.

Equally significant is the sovereign's attempt a couple of years later to introduce the Spanish Inquisition in the Lombard territory. In 1563, when Philip II was concerned with the growing infiltration of Protestant doctrine into the duchy, he obtained from Pius IV a bull authorizing him to replace the existing Courts of Papal Inquisition with new tribunals organized *ad instar Officii Inquisitionis regnorum Hispaniarum* and placed under the authority of a General Inquisitor for the state of Milan, to be nominated by the king.[41] Even if Philip II had in fact to give up his plans due to the amount of protest his initiative had created among his Milanese subjects, there can be no denying that his attempt to introduce the Spanish Inquisition in Milan testifies strongly to his desire to exercise control over the struggle against heresy conducted at this time by the ecclesiastical courts of the diocese.

Similar control, this time directly over Cardinal Borromeo's activity, even before the latter resided at Milan, was the objective of another step taken by Philip II. In keeping with Spanish practice, in October 1565, he ordered the Governor Alburquerque to nominate a royal representative to assist at the deliberations of the First Provincial Synod.[42] Philip's instructions to this effect, it must be admitted, were formulated at Madrid when it was not yet known there that the synod was already at work, so they were to have no direct bearing upon actual events.[43] But they do make it clear that the Spanish representative thus envisaged was not only to intervene if there arose obstacles to the orderly conduct of the synod's debates but was also to ensure that the decisions of the synod did not damage prerogatives and rights of the crown.

Secular control with ecclesiastical conditions in Milan, however, found its most important expression, since the days of Charles V and even earlier, in the fact that episcopal nominations in the state of Milan were to have the *placet* of secular authority.[44] When Philip II received notice of a papal nomination to an episcopal see in the duchy, unless the person nominated was already known to him, he would immediately instruct his governor to investigate whether he were "a person to be confided in for the matters of our service, or whether there would be anything to fear from him".[45] And if the information received did not contain sufficient evidence to the effect that the newly elected would be faithful to the crown, Philip did not hesitate to order refusal of the royal *placet* to the nomination. This was the case when Filippo Archinto was nominated archbishop of Milan by Paul IV in 1556. He died at Bergamo in 1558 without having been able to take possession of his diocese.[46] In the same way, Spain prevented in 1573 the transferal of Ferdinando Ferrero, bishop of Ivrea (in the duchy of Savoy) to the bishopric of Novara because he belonged to a notoriously pro-French family: this was enough to render him suspect in the eyes of Spanish authorities.[47]

That Philip II should not have been more hesitant to limit ecclesiastical freedom of action within his dominions may at first sight seem difficult to explain, since Philip virtually embodied the cause of Catholicism and, in his instructions to his viceroy and governors, constantly placed the defense and welfare of the Catholic faith above all other aspirations as well as setting all his strength to work in wars against infidels and heretics.[48] However, Philip II and his councillors saw the matter quite differently. A particular political and religious conception of the monarchy, which Philip had inherited from Spanish medieval tradition and which tended to enforce itself in the climate of the Counter-Reformation in which Philip II lived, implied that the "servicio de Dios", i.e., the implementation of the Divine Will, would be the first objective of all governmental action, so that attainment of every other political end would have to be subordinated to the needs of this primary effort.[49] This meant, to Philip II and his councillors, that those who opposed themselves to the objectives of Spanish policy were impeding the cause of Catholicism. Those who obstructed the sovereign's governmental action, whether by favoring the enemies of the Spanish monarchy or by damaging the rights and prerogatives of the crown, had to be fiercely opposed: this was necessary if Spain was to perform its mission in support of Catholicism. Consequently, Philip II considered himself entitled to take, even in confrontation with the supreme ecclesiastical hierarchy, all the steps he deemed appropriate to ensure that their action did not become an obstacle to Spanish policy. Such steps, as far as the clergy was concerned, might consist precisely in refusing the royal *placet* to prelates who were politically less acceptable or in stubborn opposition to the revendication of jurisdictional rights of the episcopacy in all the Spanish territories of Italy.

This was the line of action followed by Philip II and his governors with regard to Cardinal Borromeo's initiatives aiming at restoring episcopal jurisdiction to its maximum range. In their eyes, this was nothing but an infringement of royal prerogative, constituting an open usurpation of royal jurisdiction. As far as the Spanish administration was concerned, the archbishop's pretensions were legally unfounded: in particular, according to lay jurisprudence, the cardinal had failed to prove the right of the archiepiscopal Curia to avail itself of the *famiglia armata*, and he had failed to produce indisputable evidence that the famous *consuetudo trahendi laicos* in fact existed.[50] In lay opinion, these were innovations ("novedades") introduced by Borromeo.[51] This explains why Spanish authority, in the persistent controversies that were to begin in 1567, always based its case upon pure defense of the rights of the crown and depicted Borromeo as a prelate striving by all means to extend ecclesiastical jurisdiction at the cost of royal prerogative.[52]

There is evidence, however, that the cardinal's claims were not as unfounded as the Spaniards would maintain, especially with regard to the right to make use of the *famiglia armata*, which in fact the archbishops of Milan had been practicing ever since the era of the Visconti and the Sforzas without having ever been challenged in this respect.[53]

However, such stubborn resistance to the initiatives of Cardinal Borromeo as secular Spanish and Milanese authorities offered could not be explained without taking into consideration that these authorities thereby saw themselves deprived unlawfully of jurisdictional rights that were indisputably of their competence. Philip II and his governors were hardly disposed to abandon these rights, since, in the light of the principles that had inspired Spanish policy, such jurisdiction had always been exercised "for the Service of God, in the Interest of the Church and for the Common Weal".[54]

There is, however, one other factor that should be kept in mind when one judges the particular resolution with which Spanish authority opposed itself from the very beginning to the claims set forward by Cardinal Borromeo. This was the fear that an excessive expansion of the archbishop's competence might seriously endanger the stability of Spanish domination in Milan. The state of Milan, to the Spanish monarchy, was in fact of the utmost political and strategic importance, especially representing a territorial link between the two branches of Habsburg possessions and forming the passageway for the troops that were regularly sent from Spain to Flanders. Furthermore, ever since the days of Charles V, Milan had been considered the "key to Italy," in the sense that whoever controlled Milan would control the whole peninsula. Thus, losing Milan meant to the Spaniards strategically losing contact with Flanders and the empire and even exposing the whole Spanish dominion of southern Italy to serious danger.[55]

This is why the Spanish governors paid such close attention to the security of the state of Milan. Their attention was so much closer in view of the fact that its defense was entrusted to a military force of very modest number, not more than five thousand men, including the Spanish garrisons in Piedmont and Finale Ligure.[56] The merest indication of a potential revolt in Genoa produced by the French[57] or the very appearance in the state of Milan of a band of gipsies coming from the republic of Venice[58] was therefore enough to cause alarm to the governors. In this context of insecurity, further aggravated by serious Spanish mistrust of the loyalty of their Milanese subjects,[59] lay authority in Milan soon came to suspect that Borromeo, behind his program of religious reform, was in fact planning politically to overthrow the Spanish government in Milan. As Borromeo's work of reform proceeded—increasing his power and autonomy in confrontation with secular authority because of his far-reaching jurisdictional prerogatives over clergy and laity—the archbishop's authority and moral prestige were rapidly increasing. And because the archbishop had numerous adherents within and without the state of Milan, the result of his elevated social position and that of his family, the representatives of secular authority in Milan might easily fear that he intended to provoke a popular revolt in Milan, in order to chase out the Spaniards and take possession of the duchy himself. Already in 1569, Borromeo's activity was judged at Madrid as a potential disturbance of public peace,[60] while in 1573 Spanish suspicion toward him reached its peak. At this moment of acute tension between lay and ecclesiastical power, the Governor Luis de Requeséns suggested to Philip II that he use force to expel the archbishop from Milan, arguing that the latter was exercising "absolute patronage" over the state of Milan and defining him bluntly as "the most dangerous rebel that Your Majesty has ever had."[61] Philip II, however, rejected his suggestion,[62] perhaps because he realized immediately that the governor's accusations were exaggerated, but basically because he refused to take a measure that would inevitably have brought about a crisis in his relationship with the Holy See. He may even have shared the opinion of Requeséns' own brother, Don Juan de Zúñiga, the Spanish ambassador to Rome, who was strongly warning against such a drastic step. Don Juan called attention to the fact that the diocese of Milan extended beyond the boundary of the state of Milan and that Borromeo, if he so desired, could retire to a geographical position outside the reach of Spanish sovereignty and from there fulminate his censures against the secular authorities, so that ultimately it would be inadvisable to force the archbishop into exile.[63] Philip II, thus, did not take into consideration what Requeséns had proposed but gave instead his approval to another measure, that of ordering the delivery to the king of the fortress of Arona, which belonged to the private property of the cardinal, on the Lago Maggiore near the eastern borderlines of the Milanese state.[64]

Of course, the accusations of Requeséns and, later, those put forward by his successor, the marquess of Ayamonte,[65] were totally unfounded. Not only, as Philip II finally became convinced,[66] had Borromeo never worked for purposes other than those of the spiritual progress of the souls entrusted to his care, but he probably did not even wish for the expulsion of the Spaniards from Milan: in spite of the difficulties he kept encountering, he realized that ecclesiastical immunity was better safeguarded under the rule of the Spanish monarch than with the other princes of Italy.[67] Furthermore, Borromeo never failed to demonstrate his willingness to fulfill completely his obligations as the sovereign's loyal and faithful subject, provided that such fulfillment was not incompatible with the more solemn duties inherent in his pastoral office.[68] Illuminating, in this respect, is his attitude to the injunction concerning the fortress of Arona. No sooner had he received notice of this order issued by Requeséns than he gave instructions for the immediate surrender of the fortress into the hands of a representative of the governor, even though the order had not yet been officially presented to him.[69] In so doing, Borromeo intended to make it evident that while he was under obligation to fight with all means for the rights of his church, he would willingly sacrifice his private interests in order to fulfill the sovereign's will.

Perhaps this gesture of submission on Borromeo's part served to demonstrate to Philip II that the accusations for rebelliousness advanced against him lacked any justification. But it did not help to modify Madrid's negative judgment of the archbishop's action in defense of ecclesiastical jurisdiction. This could not be otherwise, either, because apart from the demonstrative value that Borromeo had attached to his gesture, the respective positions of civil and ecclesiastical authority remained difficult to reconcile. In fact, their lines of action were determined by directly contrasting principles. To Borromeo, it was a matter of applying to the diocese of Milan principles of moral and disciplinary reform that had been set up by the Council of Trent and in this context concentrating in the archbishop's hands the highest potential of coercion that canon law and particular Milanese ecclesiastical usage might allow him, thereby minimizing lay authority. To Philip II, his councillors, and his governors at Milan, on the contrary, religious life ought to develop in harmonious correspondence with the absolutist, and centralist, tendencies of the Spanish monarchy, under the direct control of the crown, in order to prevent local church action from becoming a threat to the maintenance of political stability. Apart from the objective difficulty in reconciling the respective parties' claims, in a phase of historical development in which the two powers had not yet been clearly defined in their various attributions of competence, the particular acuteness of the tension was due also to the firmness, even punctiliousness, with which the two parties respectively defended their prerogatives. The controversy over jurisdiction soon acquired an aspect of principle that contributed strongly to the stiffening of the two parties' positions. To Borromeo, giving in to civil authority on this point meant impairing from the very outset the effect of his work of reform and sanctioning the practice of secular interference in matters of ecclesiastical authority; to the Spanish governors, it would be a concession to the principle of ecclesiastical superiority over the lay authority, if they consented formally to abandon rights of which they had been in uncontested possession prior to the arrival of Borromeo in Milan. Such a renunciation would cause evident and immediate loss of prestige to the Spanish crown and for those who were its representatives in Milan.

It did not come immediately to such a hardening of the respective positions. In the initial phase of the controversies, shortly after the arrival of the cardinal in the diocese, opposition to his various claims was voiced exclusively by the Senate.[70] This was a body of lawyers and patricians that, since the era of Charles V, had been invested with the custody of Milanese regalist tradition. But the particular zeal with which the Senate from the very beginning opposed Cardinal Borromeo's ecclesiastical claims could not be totally explained by its obligation to safeguard the prerogatives of the crown; it was due also to the fact that in defending such rights, the supreme political body in Milan would also be defending the autonomy that it still was able to enjoy during the period of Spanish domination. The members of the Senate, furthermore, represented exactly the privileged strata of Milanese society that were to be the immediate victims of such Tridentine reform as the archbishop was setting in motion, given that the abuses, e.g., of accumulating ecclesiastical *beneficia* or assigning *prebendae* to minors, had always been favors bestowed upon younger sons of families belonging to the higher layers of Milanese society.[71]

This is the reason why, in the initial phase of the controversies, the governor of Alburquerque would lament to Madrid that the Senate without his knowledge had taken certain initiatives and expressed the suspicion that the Senate, in opposing the archiepiscopal court, was rather acting in the private interests of its members than striving to protect royal prerogatives.[72] What exactly the governor was referring to we are not allowed to know, but it is a fact that in July 1567, after a series of minor conflicts, the Senate had taken a particularly serious decision without informing Alburquerque. As a countermeasure to an arrest by the *famiglia armata* of a layman living illegitimately with a woman, the Senate had the commander of this archiepiscopal police force arrested and, after having publicly inflicted corporal punishment upon him, banished him from the state. Borromeo's reaction was immediate: he launched excommunication proceedings against the senators for having violated ecclesiastical immunity, and he informed the pope of the whole incident. The senators, on their part, also turned to the Holy See to appeal the archbishop's verdict; however Pius V not only approved the action of Borromeo but ordered three senators, including the president of that body, Gabriele Casati, to present themselves at Rome.[73]

Alburquerque's severe criticism of the Senate's incautious proceedings thus caused Philip II to intervene: while he ordered the Senate not to take any important initiatives without having previously obtained the approval of the governor,[74] he also applied to the pope for the suspension of the three

senators' summons to Rome, until there could arrive a Spanish plenipotenti-
ary, the marquess of Cerralbo.[75]

From this moment onward, the Milanese controversies became the object
of diplomatic negotiation, in conjunction with the numerous other problems
inherent in the rivalry between Spain and the Holy See, especially those
concerning conflicts over jurisdiction in the Spanish dominions of Italy. But
neither the negotiations held by Cerralbo at Rome from the beginning of
1568 nor the mission of Vincenzo Giustiniani, general of the Dominican
Order, to Philip II around the turn of the year 1569/70 succeeded in bringing
about any result worthy of notice. The same was true of a Spanish legation in
1571 of Michele Bonelli, cardinal nephew of Pius V.[76] Such negotiations
failed, not because the Holy See reduced its commitment—indeed rather, the
pope energetically defended ecclesiastical positions—but because the Spanish party hesitated to conclude negotiations in which the crown would be
bound sooner or later to make concessions to its counterpart. The Spanish
authorities therefore preferred to contest concretely, *in loco*, i.e., in a factual
context, what action the ecclesiastical authority had been taking, thereby
trying to maintain its position of bargaining and leaving the crucial legal
questions unsolved. In this way, they avoided exposing themselves to the
cardinal point of the negotiations, that of proving the legal foundation of
those assertions of the secular power which the ecclesiastical party rejected.

In the first series of Milanese controversies, the questions of the *famiglia
armata* and those regarding ecclesiastical tribunals in their jurisdiction over
laymen had been the essential ones, but, after a period of relative calm, in
1573, under the governorship of Luis de Requeséns,[77] a new matter of
dispute presented itself.

Having arrived the year before from Rome where, in his position of
Spanish ambassador, Requeséns had been able to follow closely the development of the Milanese conflicts, he did not hesitate to confront the still
unresolved questions of the *famiglia armata* and the jurisdiction over
laymen. On notifying the archiepiscopal court of an order by Philip II to
limit the number of the ecclesiastical police force and to set up restrictions
with regard to the types of arms it was allowed to bear, Requeséns received
from Cardinal Borromeo a reaction of unexpected gravity, i.e., his own
immediate excommunication. It was in a state of profound consternation
over this ruling that Requeséns made his previously mentioned proposal to
Philip II that the archbishop be expelled from the state of Milan, based on
the governor's suspicion that Borromeo was acting with the ultimate intention of subverting public order in the state, while Requeséns on his own part
prepared himself to take possession of the fortress of Arona.[78] Furthermore,
the governor made use of the pretext that the approximately twenty thousand members of the religious fraternities, during the time that the ecclesiastical authority, entrusted with their spiritual guidance, proved hostile to

the crown, might represent a serious threat to the security of the state. He obtained approval from Philip II of orders he would issue to prohibit fraternities from assembling without the presence of a royal representative nominated by secular authority and also, for motives of security, to forbid their members to participate in processions with their faces covered by their traditional hoods.[79]

This was indubitably a measure of retaliation against Borromeo's excommunication of the governor, since neither in Requeséns's nor in his predecessors' correspondence can there be found any indication of episodes that might raise suspicion that members of religious fraternities had ever engaged in activity that could be interpreted as subversive. Nonetheless, soon after, on his leaving Milan to assume the governorship of Flanders, Requeséns obtained papal absolution[80] without having to recall his edict as Borromeo had stipulated, and so his provisions to this effect remained in force and were to be reissued by his successors.[81]

Such edicts did not directly touch upon ecclesiastical jurisdiction in the sense that religious fraternities still remained under the spiritual authority of the archbishop, but they certainly represented a step forward in the policy of reinforcement of the crown's powers of control over religious life in the state of Milan. Within the activity of Spanish civil authority, this is perhaps the only instance that could not be interpreted in terms of purely defensive reaction against the initiatives on the part of ecclesiastical authority, but which constitutes a new claim to a prerogative that had never before been exercised or requested.[82]

This initiative, however, remained an isolated phenomenon, due also to the fact that, even if it had been approved by Philip II,[83] in essence it had matured in a climate of particular tension and under the effect of personal resentment. Under Requeséns's successor, the marquess of Ayamonte, who held the governorship from 1573 to 1580, secular authority returned to its traditional lines of opposition to the "innovations" being gradually introduced by Cardinal Borromeo. To the old points of conflict, the *famiglia armata* and the scope of ecclesiastical jurisdiction, there came to be added new ones, in some way connected with the former, such as whether ecclesiastical authority had visitation rights over pious institutions governed by laymen, or the right to inspect their financial registers;[84] or matters concerning the problem of whether ecclesiastical immunity implied that clergymen and their tenants, for motives of public utility,[85] were exempt from the secular authority's orders concerning watering and the sowing of rice.

Other tensions arose from elements of Borromeo's specific reform work regarding ecclesiastical discipline and usage. This was the case with an archiepiscopal edict of 7 March 1579, which, under penalty of excommunication, prohibited tournaments and stage plays on church holidays, at the very moment when civil authority, in accordance with a local tradition, was making preparations for a particular festivity on the first Sunday of Lent. To the marquess of Ayamonte, this edict caused all the more annoyance because it coincided with two other archiepiscopal decrees of which he disapproved. According to the first of them, the seat of honour in the churches reserved for the king's representative was by order of the archbishop to be moved outside the altar parapet, in compliance with the Tridentine decrees, which reserved the chancel for the clergy exclusively. With his other order, the archbishop forbade the governor to avail himself of musicians and chanters from the chapel of the court for profane occasions, in order to prevent the abuse and disorder that inevitably occurred in such events.[86]

To the new controversies over the jurisdictional prerogatives of ecclesiastical authority—whether it were the right of visitation of pious institutions or the question of whether the clergy were exempt from lay authority regarding such orders as lay authority issued in the name of public utility—now were added further sources of contention. It was no longer just the archbishop's sphere of competence that was disputed, but also the very measures of his work of religious reform, and the methods with which they were applied, that were being contested. This further rigidified the position of lay authority at Milan that consequently once more accused the archbishop, at Madrid as well as at Rome, of proceeding with excessive severity, of introducing unfounded new orders, and of disturbing public peace.[87]

Such aggravation of tension in Milan, and the contemporary suspending of official diplomatic negotiations between Spain and the Holy See, which went on in Rome from October 1578,[88] nourished in Borromeo the conviction that it would be useless to hope for a settlement of the conflicts based upon a theoretical delineation of the two powers' respective spheres of jurisdiction. Instead, he came to find it necessary to reach a *de facto* agreement with the authorities at Madrid, in this way deliberately bypassing the administrative organs of Milan. To this end, in August 1580, shortly after the death of the Governor Ayamonte (the preceding 20 April),[89] Borromeo entrusted his close collaborator, the Barnabite Carlo Bascapè, with a secret mission to the Spanish court, charging him with reassuring Philip II of the archbishop's absolute loyalty towards Spain and convincing him that all his efforts pointed to one sole purpose, that of saving the souls entrusted to his care. This move had a conclusive effect; even if it did not succeed in eradicating from the sovereign's mind the conviction that Borromeo was proceeding in his reform work with an excess of zeal, Bascapè's mission did remove the king's political concern about the true intentions of the cardinal, by convincing him that the latter was only working for the spiritual and moral progress of the people of Christ.[90] Thus, opposition to ecclesiastical reform in Milan lost its support at the court at Madrid, and Borromeo was able, consequently, to proceed in his efforts without encountering notable resistance on the part of civil authority,[91] even if, at the time of the cardinal's death on 3 November 1584, all the jurisdictional controversies of the previous twenty years remained unresolved.

As has been demonstrated above, the relations between Cardinal Borromeo and the Spanish authorities were characterized by continuous tension, deriving from the opposition that the latter presented to any extension of ecclesiastical jurisdiction. The fact that the jurisdictional controversies have become perhaps the most studied theme of Borromeo's episcopacy may have created an image of a period of acute conflict between lay and ecclesiastical authority,[98] thus eventually obscuring the fact that such controversies were but the most obvious appearance of the relations in question. The controversies did not and could not preclude extensive cooperation between the two authorities.

It has been noted[93] that Philip II, as Catholic sovereign, was determined in his favoring religious and moral regeneration in his dominions and that consequently he intended to support any application of Tridentine Reform measures, preferably by means most compatible with his overall political orientation. Consequently, when prerogatives of the crown were not at stake, the sovereign proved always ready, at Milan as well as elsewhere, to sustain the bishops in their pastoral activity. Borromeo had had occasion to assure himself of this fact when, in 1569, the chapter of the Santa Maria della Scala in its capacity of royal patronage and on the basis of a papal privilege— which, incidentially, had never acquired absolute validity—declared itself exempt from visitation by their diocesan bishop. Given that such pretension was without any juridical foundation, Borromeo did not hesitate nonetheless to order visitation; but in the morning of 30 August 1569, he was rejected on the threshold of the church by the armed canons themselves, and they even went as far as to declare the archbishop under excommunication for having violated a papal privilege.[94] But the royal support that the canons were counting upon did not come about; instead, when Philip II was informed of the incident, he declared the conduct of the canons inadmissible and placed himself on the side of the archbishop. Expressing, nonetheless, his reservations concerning Borromeo's proceedings, which in his opinion were too precipitous, he instructed the governor to render all necessary assistance to the archbishop in order to carry out visitation and punish the guilty parties.[95]

But convergence of interest between the two authorities, lay and ecclesiastical, also manifested itself outside the diocese of Milan, in that Borromeo's intensive spiritual reform action in the Swiss regions[96] was performed in collaboration with the Spanish authorities. It is not possible, in the present context, to examine fully Spain's attitudes to Cardinal Borromeo's activity in Switzerland, because such attitudes, even if connected with the ecclesiastical policy of Philip II in the state of Milan, should be

interpreted within the far wider framework of the general objectives of
Spanish foreign policy. It may suffice, at present, to note that Switzerland
was a territory in which Borromeo's religious initiatives and Spanish political
aspirations combined to produce effective cooperation.[97]

In the measures taken against the phenomenon of heresy, however, the
policy of the Catholic crown of Spain could not but concern itself with the
initiatives taken by the archbishop. The dedication with which Borromeo,
during the twenty years of his episcopacy, fought constantly to prevent the
dispersion of heretical doctrine, is well known—in particular his severe
control of the press and the diffusion of books—as is his repression, by
means of the archiepiscopal tribunal, of every form of heterodoxy.[98]

Such substantial elimination of all heretical ferment that Borromeo encountered, is an accomplishment which could not be interpreted correctly
without consideration of the fact that, in this respect, his intentions were
facilitated by parallel action on the part of the civil government. It is true that
in its struggle against heresy, Spain was driven by political motivation, i.e.,
by the conviction that dissemination of Protestant doctrine in the state of
Milan would lead inevitably to the population's rebellion against Spanish
domination.[99] But it is just as true that defense of the Catholic faith,
wherever it was threatened, was perceived by Philip II as one of the primary
obligations of a Catholic prince.[100]

Hence the particular support furnished by the civil authority to the
tribunals of papal Inquisition in Milan, especially after the Spanish Inquisition failed to be introduced into the duchy. Such assistance might consist in
measures taken to prevent foreign heretics from entering into the state or to
hinder the importation there of forbidden books,[101] but it might also consist
in occasional financial support to the Holy Office, as in 1568 when the
sovereign donated four hundred scudi to the Tribunal of Papal Inquisition in
Milan.[102] On their part, the governors exercised continuous surveillance and
furnished the inquisitor and Borromeo with all information at their disposal,
also handing over to them persons suspect of heresy who had fallen into the
hands of local civil authority.[103] Incidentally, in 1573, the Roman Congregation of the Inquisition itself recognized that the representatives of
Philip II at Milan had always, when so requested, proved willing to assign to
the congregation persons under their own indictment.[104]

Therefore, in substance, in spite of occasional conflict between inquisitors
and local magistrates,[105] civil government, in questions related to the suppression of heresy, followed a line of action directly opposite to that which it
assumed when prerogatives of the crown were at stake. In these cases, the
governors and the Senate did not hesitate to claim their jurisdiction over the
laity and to interfere with the activity of ecclesiastical tribunals, while in
matters of surveying the orthodoxy of the population, civil authorities
offered their unrestricted collaboration, abstaining from any interference

with ecclesiastical jurisdiction, whether it were that of the Holy Office or that of the diocesan bishop. This is due, however, not only to the obligation of the representatives of the Catholic king to fight against heresy. Such apparent contradiction is to be explained also by the delineation recognized between the two spheres of jurisdiction. While civil power judged itself entitled to defend the rights presumably rightfully attributed to it, there was never any doubt that in the matter of suppression of heresy, a purely religious crime, ecclesiastical authority would have exclusive jurisdiction, and civil authority could not make any rightful claim.[106]

To conclude the present rapid and summary analysis of the positions taken by Archbishop Carlo Borromeo and Philip II in his ecclesiastical policy at Milan, some evaluation of their lines of action may be due. On the one hand we see the archbishop arriving in the diocese inspired by his firm decision to initiate an application of the Tridentine decrees and trying, in order to achieve these objectives, to avail himself of a maximum of coercive power attributed to him by canon law and by particular usage of the Milanese church. On the other hand, Philip II and his agents, while favoring in general religious and moral regeneration of the population along the lines indicated by the Council of Trent, remained still firm in their intention that such reform should be brought about without any extension of the sphere of ecclesiastical jurisdiction, and furthermore under strict control of the crown. Such policy, contrary to what historians—among them especially Ludwig von Pastor—have in the past maintained, is deprived of cæsaropapist and jurisdictionalist tendencies and is, therefore, clearly to be interpreted otherwise. It ought to be recognized that the ecclesiastical policy of Philip II in its development, at least with regard to the state of Milan, is in complete conformity with fundamental principles in theological and canonist theory of the age regarding the relationship between church and state. What was contested during these controversies was never ecclesiastical liberty or the immunity of the church as such, but solely the practical scope of such principles. Likewise, supreme authority of the Holy See never came to be contested; rather, Spain in its diplomatic negotiations with Rome submitted itself, eventually, to a papal decision with regard to its claims at Milan. Thus, the positions taken by Philip II bear no resemblance to those adopted by the Venetian Republic at the beginning of the following century, positions of rupture with the papacy which led to the Interdict of Venice by Pope Paul V.[107]

Even in their most acute phases, the controversies took place in an environment of unrestricted recognition on the part of Spain of the pope's supreme authority over the church. This allowed also for considerable collaboration between the two powers at Milan, especially in the struggle against heresy. Thus, while differing in intentions and in methods as well as in instruments, the ecclesiastical policy of Philip II at Milan and Carlo

Borromeo's activity there pointed essentially to the same end: that of the triumph of the cause of Catholicism.

Notes

I am grateful to my Danish colleague, Dr. Kai Hørby of the University of Copenhagen, for his generous assistance in rendering my Italian text into English.

1. M. Formentini, *La dominazione spagnola in Lombardia* (Milan, 1881), pp. 43ff.; F. Chabod, *L'epoca di Carlo V* in *Storia di Milano*, 9 (Rome, 1961); idem, *Storia di Milano nell'epoca di Carlo V* (Turin, 1971), pp. 5ff.; D. Sella, *Sotto il dominio della Spagna* in D. Sella and C. Capra, *Il ducato di Milano dal 1535 al 1796* (Storia d'Italia diretta da G. Galasso, 11), (Turin, 1984), pp. 3ff.

2. F. Chabod, *Storia di Milano*, pp. 412ff; idem, *Lo Stato di Milano e l'impero di Carlo V* in idem, *Lo Stato e la vita religiosa a Milano nell'epoca di Carlo V* (Turin, 1971), pp. 143ff. Cf. also A. Visconti, *La pubblica amministrazione nello Stato milanese durante il predominio straniero (1541–1796)* (Rome, 1913), pp. 167ff.; U. Petronio, *Il Senato di Milano. Istituzioni giuridiche ed esercizio del potere nel ducato di Milano da Carlo V a Giuseppe II*, 1 (Milan, 1972), pp. 62ff.; D. Sella, *Sotto il dominio della Spagna*, pp. 21–27.

3. L. Prosdocimi, *Il diritto ecclesiastico dello Stato di Milano dall'inizio della Signoria Viscontea al periodo Tridentino* (1941; reprinted, Milan, 1973), pp. 59ff.; still worth consulting is L. Fumi, "Chiesa e Stato nel dominio di Francesco I Sforza," *Archivio Storico Lombardo* 51 (1924): 1–74, esp. pp. 4ff.; Gian. Biscaro, "Le relazioni dei Visconti con la Chiesa," *Archivio Storico Lombardo* 46 (1919): 84–229; 47 (1920): 193–271; 54 (1927): 44–95, 201–36, Ger. Biscar., "Le relazioni dei Visconti di Milano con la Chiesa," ibid., 55 (1928): 1–96.

4. A. Galante, *Il diritto di placitazione e l'economato dei benefici vacanti in Lombardia. Studio storico-giuridico sulle relazioni fra lo Stato e la Chiesa* (Milan, 1894), pp. 71–73.

5. A. Borromeo, "Contributo allo studio dell'inquisizione e dei suoi rapporti con il potere episcopale nell'Italia spagnola del Cinquecento," *Annuario dell'Istituto Storico Italiano per l'età moderna e contemporanea* 29–30 (1977–78): 219–76, esp. 239–40.

6. For the ecclesiastical situation in Milan in the first half of the sixteenth century cf. C. Marcora, "Il cardinal Ippolito d'Este, arcivescovo di Milano (1497–1519)," *Memorie Storiche della Diocesi di Milano* 5 (1958): 325–520; idem, "Ippolito II, arcivescovo di Milano. I periodo (1519–1550)," ibid., 6 (1959): 305–521; idem, "La Chiesa milanese nel decennio 1550–1560," ibid., 7 (1960): 254–501; E. Cattaneo, *Istituzioni ecclesiastiche milanesi*, in *Storia di Milano*, 9:531ff.; for a synoptic view of the condition of Italian dioceses, see G. Penco, *Storia della Chiesa in Italia*, 1 (Milan, 1978), pp. 591ff.

7. F. Chabod, *Per la storia religiosa dello Stato di Milano durante il dominio di Carlo V. Note e documenti*, in idem, *Lo Stato*, pp. 280–83.

8. For examples, cf. L. Fumi, "L'inquisizione romana e lo Stato di Milano," *Archivio Storico Lombardo* 37 (1910): 32, 351; P. Paschini, *Venezia e l'inquisizione romana da Giulio III a Pio IV*, Padua, 1959 (*Italia Sacra*, 1), pp. 74–75.

9. F. Chabod, *Per la storia religiosa*, pp. 259–60, 274–77.

10. Thus for example, it happens that in 1560 the tribunal of the captain of justice was conducting a trial for homicide against the archpriest of the collegiate church of

Santa Maria della Scala at Milan (C. Marcora, "La Chiesa milanese," p. 353). Cf. also F. Chabod, *Per la storia religiosa*, pp. 288–96 L. Prosdocimi, *Il diritto ecclesiastico*, pp. 300–301.

11. C. Marcora, "Ippolito II," pp. 497–99; idem, "La Chiesa milanese," pp. 301–2.

12. For the relevant bibliography, see A. Borromeo, "Le controversie giurisdizionali tra potere laico e potere ecclesiastico nella Milano spagnola sul finire del Cinquecento," in *Atti dell'Accademia di San Carlo. Inaugurazione del IV anno accademico* (Milan, 1981), pp. 43–89, esp. p. 44, n.3.

13. More detailed studies of the controversy, or of some of its aspects, may be found in F. Bertani, *San Carlo Borromeo, la bolla "Coena" e la giurisdizione ecclesiastica in Lombardia* (Milan, 1888); *Correspondencia diplomática entre España y la Santa Sede durante el pontificado de S. Pio V*, ed. L. Serrano, O.S.B., 4 vols. (Madrid, 1914), 3 : v–xl; M. Bendiscioli, "L'inizio della controversia giurisdizionale a Milano tra l'arcivescovo Carlo Borromeo ed il Senato milanese," *Archivio Storico Lombardo* 53 (1926): 241–80, 409–62; idem, "La bolla in Coena Domini e la sua pubblicazione a Milano," ibid., 54 (1927): 381–99; L. Prosdocimi, "Controriforma e politica spagnola a Milano," in *Echi di San Carlo Borromeo* (Milan, 1937–38), pp. 501–4, 536–43; J. M. March S.J., *El Comendador Mayor de Castilla don Luis de Requeséns en el gobierno de Milán, 1571–1573* (Madrid, 1943), pp. 185–308; G. Catalano, "Controversie giurisdizionali fra Chiesa e Stato nell'età di Gregorio XIII e Filippo II," *Atti dell'Accademia di Scienze, Lettere ed Arti di Palermo* 15, 2 (1954–55): 5–306; P. Prodi, "San Carlo Borromeo e le trattative tra Gregorio XIII e Filippo II sulla giurisdizione ecclesiastica," *Rivista di Storia della Chiesa in Italia* 11 (1957): 195–240; M. Bendiscioli. "Politica, amministrazione e religione nell'età dei Borromei" in *Storia di Milano*, (Rome, 1957), pp. 200–255; D. Maselli, "San Carlo nelle relazioni dei governatori di Milano," in *Accademia di San Carlo. Inaugurazione del 2° anno accademico* (Milan, 1979), pp. 11–37.

14. C. Marcora, "La Chiesa milanese," pp. 337–38.

15. C. Marcora, "La Chiesa milanese," pp. 387–88.

16. P. Paschini, "Il primo soggiorno di San Carlo Borromeo a Roma, 1560–1565," in idem, *Cinquecento romano e riforma cattolica*, special publication of *Lateranum* 24 (1958): 174–76.

17. Archivo General de Simancas (hereinafter referred to as AGS), E leg. 899 n. 45: Pacheco to Philip II, Rome, 9 March 1565.

18. AGS, E leg. 1218 n. 93: Philip II to Gabriel de la Cueva, duke of Alburquerque, n.d., but evidently November 1565. Cf. also ibid., leg. 1221 n. 109: Alburquerque to Philip II, Milan, 29 September 1565 (publ. also in D. Maselli, "San Carlo," p. 25).

19. Archivio Segreto Vaticano (hereinafter referred to as ASV), *S.S., Spagna*. 2, fols. 5*r–v:* Borromeo to Philip II, Milan, 7 April 1566.

20. The cardinal arrived in Milan on 5 April 1566 (Biblioteca Ambrosiana, Milano, hereinafter referred to as BAM, Pl inf., fol. 59*r–v:* Borromeo to Cardinal Guglielmo Sirleto, Milan, 9 April 1566; in this draft the date is erroneously given as 9 March).

21. ASV, *S.S., Spagna*, 2 fols. 5*r–v:* Borromeo to Philip II, Milan, 7 April 1566; cf. also BAM, F 184 inf., fols. 31*r–v* and 38*r:* Borromeo to Giovanni Francesco Bonomi, Milan, 30 July 1566.

22. ASV, *S.S. Spagna*, 2 *fols. 11r–12r:* Borromeo to the nuncio Giovanni Battista Castagna, Milan, 8 May 1566.

23. ASV, *S.S. Spagna*, 1, f. 542*r:* the cardinal-nephew of Pius V, Michele Bonelli,

to Castagna, Rome, 19 April 1566; fols. 552r–v and 561r: Bonelli to Castagna, Rome, 22 May 1566; fols. 554r–v and 559r–v: Bonelli to Castagna, Rome, 25 June 1566 (these last two letters in *Correspondencia diplomática*, 1 : 242–43, 266–67).

24. Cf. infra, n. 27.

25. C. Marcora, "Nicolò Ormaneto, vicario di San Carlo (giugno 1564–giugno 1566)," *Memorie Storiche della Diocesi di Milano* 8 (1961): 209–590, esp. 338–442; E. Cattaneo, "Il primo concilio provinciale milanese (a.1565)," in *Il Concilio di Trento e la riforma tridentina. Atti del convegno storico internazionale, Trento 2–6 settembre 1963*, 1 (Rome, 1965), pp. 215–75.

26. E. Cattaneo, "Gli ostacoli posti dal Senato milanese alla pubblicazione del I Concilio Provinciale (a. 1565)" in *La Sacra Congregazione del Concilio. Quarto centenario della fondazione (1564–1964). Studi e ricerche*, (Vatican City, 1964), pp. 599–615. Cf. also M. Bendiscioli, *Politica, amministrazione e religione*, pp. 202–4; C. Marcora, "I primi anni dell'episcopato di San Carlo (1566–1567)," *Memorie Storiche della Diocesi di Milano* 10 (1963): 517–617, esp. 572–73.

27. Indeed the outcome was that the governor accepted a position inferior to that occupied by Borromeo (ASV, *S.S. Spagna*, 3, fol. 31r: Cardinal Francesco Alciati to Castagna, Rome, 16 September 1566).

28. AGS, *Secr. Prov.* lib. 1156, fols. 210v–212r: Philip II to Alburquerque, Madrid, 30 November 1566.

29. M. Bendiscioli, *S. Carlo Borromeo e la Riforma Cattolica*, in idem, *Dalla Riforma alla Controriforma* (Bologna, 1974), p. 117. For a comparison of Borromeo's position with that of another distinguished bishop of the period, see P. Prodi, "San Carlo Borromeo e il cardinale Gabriele Paleotti: due vescovi della Riforma Cattolica," *Critica Storica* 3 (1964): 135–51, esp. 138–39.

30. M. Bendiscioli, *S. Carlo Borromeo*, p. 117. Cf. also *Acta Ecclesiae Mediolanensis ab eius initiis ad nostram aetatem*, ed. A. Ratti, 2, Mediolani, 1890, cols. 84–88 (1 Provincial Council); cols. 274–78 (3 Provincial Council); 688–98 (5 Provincial Council).

31. M. Bendiscioli, *Politica, amministrazione e religione*, p. 204.

32. Cf. L. Prosdocimi, *Il diritto ecclesiastico*, pp. 290–92.

33. L. Prosdocimi, "Controriforma e politica spagnola," p. 536; idem, *Il diritto ecclesiastico*, pp. 310–12.

34. This judgment is given by H. Jedin, *Carlo Borromeo* (Rome, 1971), (*Bibliotheca Biographica*, 2), p. 32.

35. AGS, E leg. 962 n. 136: Borromeo to Philip II, Milan, 10 May 1581.

36. This argument recurs frequently in the diplomatic correspondence of the Holy See during these years: for example, cf. the letter of Bonelli to Castagna, Rome, 29 October 1567, in ASV, *S.S. Spagna*, 1, fols. 299r–v and 310r–311r (publ. in *Correspondencia diplomática*, 2 : 245–48).

37. B. Llorca, "Participación de España en el Concilio de Trento" in *Historia de la Iglesia en España*, 3 : 1 (Madrid, 1980), pp. 453–503. Cf. also R. Garcia Villoslada, *Felipe II y la Contrarreforma Católica*, ibid., 3 : 2 (Madrid, 1980), pp. 5–106.

38. G. Catalano, "Controversie giurisdizionali," pp. 40ff.; for a specific instance during these years, see P. Villani, "Una visita apostolica nel Regno di Napoli (1566–1568): conflitti giurisdizionali e condizioni del clero," in *Studi in onore di Riccardo Filangieri*, 2 (Napoli, 1959), pp. 433–46.

39. G. Catalano, "Controversie giurisdizionali," pp. 125ff.; H. G. Koenigsberger, *The Practice of Empire. Emended edition of the Government of Sicily under Philip II of Spain* (Ithaca, N.Y., 1969), pp. 144–49.

40. AGS, *Secr. Prov.* lib. 1155, 1, fol. 47*v:* Philip II to the Senate, Toledo, 26 August 1560.

41. E. Verga, "Il Municipio di Milano e l'inquisizione di Spagna 1563," *Archivio Storico Lombardo* 24 (1897): 86–127; cf. also M. Formentini, *La dominazione spagnola,* pp. 150–54, 435–48; H. C. Lea, *The Inquisition in the Spanish Dependencies* (New York, 1908), pp. 125–29; L. von Pastor, *Storia dei papi dalla fine del Medio Evo,* 7 (Rome, 1950), pp. 502–5.

42. AGS, *Secr. Prov.* lib. 1156, fols. 92*r*–93*v:* Philip II to Alburquerque, Aranjuez, 10 October 1565; fols. 94*r*–96*r: Orden de lo que . . .* [space left blank for the name of the person nominated as royal representative] *que por orden y en nombre de Su M.*d *haveis de asistir en el concilio provincial que se celebra en esta ciudad de Milan . . . ,* same date. For the presence of royal representatives at the provincial councils of Spain, cf. J. L. Santos Diez, *Política conciliar postridentina en España. El concilio provincial de Toledo de 1565. Planteamiento jurídico canónico,* Rome 1969 (*Publicaciones del Instituto Español de Historia Ecclesiástica Monografías,* 13).

43. The First Provincial Council took place between 10 October and 3 November, 1565 (E. Cattaneo, "Il primo concilio provinciale, p. 244); while we do not know when the letter of the king reached its destination (a missive took over a month to go from Madrid to Milan), from a subsequent letter we learn, however, that the orders of 10 October arrived when the synod had already ended (AGS, *Secr. Prov.* lib. 1156, fols. 129*r*–32*r:* Philip II to Alburquerque, Madrid, 18 January 1566).

44. Cf. supra, n. 4.

45. AGS, *Secr. Prov.* lib. 1157, fol. 493*r:* Philip II to the governor, Antonio de Guzman, marquis of Ayamonte, El Pardo, 12 February 1577; fol. 493*v:* Philip II to Ayamonte, San Lorenzo del Escurial, 24 February 1577.

46. G. P. Giussano, *Vita dell'Illustrissimo et Reverendissimo Monsignor Filippo Archinto . . . ,* (Como, 1611), pp. 161–80; C. Morcora, "La Chiesa milanese," pp. 321 ff.; G. Alberigo, Filippo Archinto in *Dizionario Biografico degli Italiani,* 3 (Rome, 1961), pp. 761–64. The conceding of the *placet* to Archinto was delayed because of the current war between Philip II and the Holy See; although, on 15 January 1558, Philip II had ordered the *placet* to be conceded, this was not effected because of the opposition that Archinto encountered in some Milanese contexts.

47. AGS, *Secr. Prov.* lib. 1157, fol. 284*v:* Philip II to Ayamonte, Madrid, 30 October 1573; fol. 306*v:* Philip II to Ayamonte, Aranjuez, 4 February 1574.

48. H. G. Koenigsberger, "The Statecraft of Philip II," *European Studies Review* 1 (1971): 1–21, esp. pp. 12ff.

49. Cf. A. Borromeo, "Il cardinale Cesare Baronio e la Corona spagnola," in *Baronio storico e la Controriforma. Atti del convegno internazionale di studi. Sora 6–10 ottobre 1979,* ed. R. De Maio, L. Guilla, A. Mazzacane (Sora, 1982), pp. 57–166, esp. 62–63.

50. Borromeo to Ormaneto, Milan, 27 November 1566 in C. Marcora, "I primi anni," pp. 577–79; L. Prosdocimi, "Controriforma e politica spagnola," p. 536.

51. See for example the memorandum of the Council of Italy, summer 1577, in which are referred to the sovereign "las novedades que el cardenal Borromeo intenta cada dia en prejuizio de la jurisdiction real" (AGS, *Secr. Prov.* leg. 1793 n. 134, n.d., bearing the approval of the king affixed at Toledo, 3 July 1577).

52. For example, one may cite the letter sent by Philip to the ambassador at the Holy See, Don Juan de Zúñiga, in October 1573, in which the king emphasizes how, on the part of the lay Milanese authority, "no se ha hecho . . . ninguna novedad, sino continuado la possession tan antigua en que hasta aqui havemos estado." Consequently, it falls to the lot of the pope to give orders to the clergy so that "no pasen

adelante en las novedades que hasta aqui han hecho contra nuestra jurisdiccion" (AGS, *Secr. Prov.* lib. 1157, fols. 276v–77r: Philip II to Zúñiga, El Pardo, 1 October 1573; analogous concepts are found expressed ibid., fols. 505r–06r: Philip II to Ayamonte, San Lorenzo del Escurial, 15 July 1577).

53. L. Prosdocimi, *Il diritto ecclesiastico,* pp. 312–14.

54. The expression is contained in an instruction of Philip II to Luis de Requeséns, at that time Spanish ambassador to the Holy See, Madrid, 31 July 1568, published in *Correspondencia diplomática* 3 : 2–19; the phrase cited in the text is found on p. 9.

55. L. Prosdocimi, "Controriforma e politica spagnola," p. 501; F. Chabod, *Lo Stato di Milano,* pp. 16–18; idem, *L'epoca di Carlo V,* pp. 5–7; D. Sella, *Sotto il dominio della Spagna,* pp. 3–8.

56. In 1571, the total military force assigned to the collective defense of the state of Milan, Piedmont and Finale Ligure amounted to 5359 men (AGS, E Leg. 1232 n. 94: *Relaçion de la gente de guerra, assi de a pié como de a cavallo, que ay al presente en este excercito de Su Mag.*d *en Piemonte y Lombardia y donde esta aloxada en 14 de noviembre 1571*).

57. AGS, E leg. 1236 n. 159: Luis de Requeséns—since the preceding year governor of Milan—to Philip II, Milan, 12 August 1573.

58. AGS, E leg. 1244 n. 34: Ayamonte to Philip II, Milan, 28 April 1576.

59. In 1572, the governor Requeséns averred: "De los vassallos deste Estado no se aun la confiança que se puede hazer, porque en fin muchos dellos son de opinion françesa" (AGS, E leg. 1234 n. 8: Requeséns to Philip II, Milan, 17 April 1572). This lack of trust in the Milanese subjects was also shared in Madrid: some of the closest agents of Philip II would express the fear on more than one occasion that since it had occurred in Flanders so also in Milan a revolt might well take place (Cf. G. Parker, *The Army of Flanders and the Spanish Road, 1567–1659* [Cambridge, 1972], p. 128, n. 1).

60. M. Bendiscioli, *Politica, amministrazione e religione,* pp. 223–24.

61. AGS, E leg. 1236 n. 194: Requeséns to Philip II, Milan, 31 August 1573; n. 202: Requeséns to Philip II, Milan, 19 September 1573; n. 213: Requeséns to Philip II, Milan, 4 October 1573. This last letter, which contains the phrase cited in the text, is published with the incorrect date of 3 October, in D. Maselli, "San Carlo," pp. 25–26. On Requeséns—the Spanish governor with whom Borromeo had the most difficult relations—see: J. M. March, *El Comendador Mayor de Castilla don Luis de Requeséns en el gobierno de Milán, 1571–1573* (Madrid, 1943); F. Arese, "Le supreme cariche del ducato di Milano da Francesco II Sforza a Filippo V," *Archivio Storico Lombardo* 97 (1970): 21; A. W. Lovett, "The Governorship of don Luis de Requesens, 1573–1576. A Spanish View," *European Studies Review* 2 (1972): 187–99.

62. AGS, *Secr. Prov.* lib. 1157, ff. 275v–76r: Philip II to Ayamonte, who in the meanwhile had succeeded to Requeséns, Pardo, 1 October 1573.

63. Zúñiga to Philip II, Rome, 6 November 1573 in *Coleccion de documentos ineditos para la historia de Espana* (Madrid, 1842–95), 102 : 342–44.

64. AGS, *Secr. Prov.* lib. 1157, fols. 275v–76r: Philip II to Ayamonte, Pardo, 1 October 1573.

65. AGS, E leg. 1244 n. 110: Ayamonte to Philip II, Milan, 28 September 1576.

66. ASV, *S.S. Spagna,* 8, fols. 37r–38r: the nuncio in Spain, Nicolò Ormaneto to the intimate secretary of Gregory XIII, Cardinal Tolomeo Gallio, Madrid, 23 January 1574.

67. BAM, F 53 inf., fols. 135r–39r: the archbishop's agent at Rome, Monsignor Cesare Speciano to Borromeo, Rome, 13 December 1578; fol. 109r: Borromeo to Speciano, Milan, 24 December 1578.

68. ASV, *S.S. Spagna*, 3, fols. 421*r*–23*r*: Borromeo to Castagna, Milan, 23 February 1568. See also BAM, F 183 inf. n. 9: Borromeo to Philip II, Milan, 17 July 1567; AGS, E leg. 962 n. 136: Borromeo to Philip II, Milan, 10 May 1581.

69. Borromeo to Giovanni Battista Castelli, Milan 17 August 1573 in A. Sala, *Documenti circa la vita e le gesta di S. Carlo Borromeo*, 3 vols. (Milan, 1857–61), 3 : 473–75; Borromeo to Philip II, Milan, 19 August 1573 (ibid., pp. 479–80).

70. L. Prosdocimi, "Controriforma e politica spagnola," pp. 536–37.

71. M. Bendiscioli, *Politica, amministrazione e religione*, pp. 200–201; E. Cattaneo, "Gli ostacoli posti dal Senato," pp. 601–2.

72. British Library, London (hereinafter referred to as BLL), ms. Add. 28390, fols. 92*r*–93*r*: Alburquerque to Philip II, Milan, 2 September 1567. Similar ideas are found expressed in an earlier letter: ibid., fols. 61*r*–62*v*: Alburquerque to Philip II, Milan, 20 July 1567.

73. C. Sylvain, *Histoire de Saint Charles Borromée, cardinal archevêque de Milan*. (Lille, 1884), 1 : 379ff.; M. Bendiscioli, "L'inizio delle controversie," pp. 409ff.: idem, *Politica, amministrazione e religione*, pp. 212ff. On president Casati and on his conduct during the jurisdictional controversy, cf. A. Borromeo, *Gabriele Casati* in *Dizionario Biografico degli Italiani*, 21 (Rome, 1978), pp. 242–44.

74. AGS, *Secr. Prov.* lib. 1156, fol. 272*v*: Philip II to the Senate, Madrid, 19 September 1567.

75. AGS, *Secr. Prov.* lib. 1156, fol. 295*v*: Philip II to Pius V, Madrid, 12 October 1567 (publ. in *Correspondencia diplomática* 2 : 220); the instructions to Cerralbo are found in AGS, *Secr. Prov.* lib. 1156, fols. 290*v*–94*v*: *Instruction de lo que vos el Marques de Cerralvo, nuestro pariente, haveis de hazer en este viaje de Roma adonde os enviamos*, Madrid, 12 October 1567.

76. For details on these tracts, see *Correspondencia diplomática*, 3 : xvi–xxii, xxxvii, lxi–lxviii; G. Catalano, "Controversie giurisdizionali," pp. 23–94.

77. On Requeséns, cf. supra, n. 61.

78. Beyond what has already been presented in the preceding notes 61ff., see, for the controversies occurring during the governorship of Requeséns, the ample documentation published in A. Sala, *Documenti* 3 : 448–536. Cf. also J. M. March, *El Comendador Mayor*, pp. 209–308; M. Bendiscioli, *Politica, amministrazioine e religione*, pp. 230–33.

79. AGS, E leg. 1236, n. 171: edict of the Governor Requeséns, Milan, 21 August 1573 (in print); a subsequent edict specified that the guidelines contained in the first edict did not apply to the School of Christian Doctrine (ibid., n. 174: edict of 25 August 1573). The exact number of the members of the Milan's religious confraternity is not known: according to Requeséns, there were, in 1573, twenty thousand in all the state of Milan (ibid., E leg. 1236 n. 119: Requeséns to Philip II, Milan, 26 May 1573), of whom six thousand were at Milan (ibid., E leg. 1236 n. 166: Requeséns to Philip II, Milan, 16 August 1573). According to Governor Ayamonte, three years later, there were thirty thousand in the diocese of Milan alone (ibid., E leg. 1244 n. 56: Ayamonte to Philip II, Milan, 8 July 1576). Only for one city of the state, Alessandria, have we the exact numbers: 1,874 in the city itself, 1,435 for the environs (ibid., E leg. 1238 n. 33: Francisco de Sesse, governor of Alessandria, to Ayamonte, Alessandria, 29 September 1573).

80. AGS, E leg. 1236 n. 204: Gregory XIII to Requesens, Rome, 26 September 1573 (copy); Cardinal Gallio to Borromeo, Rome, same date (publ. in A. Sala, *Documenti* 3 : 516).

81. A. Borromeo, "Le controversie giurisdizionali," p. 68 n. 77.

82. L. Prosdocimi, "Controriforma e politica spagnola," p. 538.

83. AGS, *Secr. Prov.* lib. 1157, fols. 285r–v: Philipp II to Ayamonte, Madrid, 12 November 1573.

84. A. Noto, "L'ingerenza ecclesiastica negli istituti milanesi di beneficenza elemosiniera," *Archivio Storico Lombardo* 65 (1938): 430–38; A. G. Ghezzi, "Conflitti giurisdizionali nella Milano di Carlo Borromeo: la visita apostolica di Gerolamo Ragazzoni nel 1575–1576," ibid., 108–9 (1982–1983): 193–237, esp. 221ff.

85. Whereas concerning the problem of water and specifically whether or not ecclesiastics have the obligation to contribute to the expense of cleaning the canals, the discussions dragged on at length (P. Prodi, "San Carlo Borromeo," pp. 207–8; 228–29), concerning the cultivation of rice Borromeo succeeded without great difficulty in forwarding the ecclesiastical viewpoint, namely that possible prohibitions of seeding that might conflict with the clergy could come only from the archbishop. (Archivio Spirituale della Curia Arcivescovile, Milan, sect. 14, vol. 114 bis, fasc. 4: Ayamonte to Borromeo, Milan, 17 April 1576; ibid., vol. 110, fasc. 2: Borromeo to Ayamonte, Milan, 27 April 1576). Only under the successors of Borromeo would this question yield to conflicts between lay and clerical power (A. Borromeo, "Le controversie giurisdizionali," pp. 65ff.).

86. Cf. *Instruttione sopra il luogo dei magistrati di Milano mandata al nuntio in Spagna*, Milan, 24 September 1578, and the letter of Borromeo to the nuncio in Spain, Filippo Sega, written from Milan, 3 April 1579, publ. in F. Molinari, "Il card. Filippo Sega, vescovo di Piacenza, e san Carlo Borromeo (1574–1584)", *Archivio Ambrosiano* 31 (1976): 199–201, 204–6; also see C. Sylvain, *Histoire* 2:205–7, 215–20; P. Prodi, "San Carlo Borromeo," pp. 213–14.

87. C. Sylvain, *Histoire*, 2:207 ff.; M. Bendiscioli, *Politica, amministrazione e religione*, p. 250.

88. G. Catalano, Controversie giurisdizionali," pp. 96ff.; P. Prodi, "San Carlo Borromeo," pp. 198ff.

89. F. Arese, "Le supreme cariche," p. 77.

90. On Bascapè's mission, besides the ample narration that he himself has left (C. Bascapè, *De vita et rebus gestis Caroli S.R.E. cardinalis* . . . , Latin and Italian edition by A. Majo [Milan, 1983], pp. 510–36), see A. Sala, *Documenti* 2:70–94; C. Sylvain, *Histoire* 2:281–300 G. Guariglia, "La corrispondenza di Carlo Bascapè e san Carlo Borromeo nella collezione della Biblioteca Ambrosiana, *Aevum* 10 (1936): 282–337; P. Prodi, "San Carlo Borromeo," pp. 224–27.

91. P. Prodi, "San Carlo Borromeo," p. 227; H. Jedin, *Carlo Borromeo*, pp. 37–38.

92. In this respect it is interesting to note that in the more recent work on Spanish Milan, the longest paragraph of the chapter dedicated to the ecclesiastical and religious life is that which considers the jurisdictional conflicts: cf. D. Sella, *Sotto il dominio della Spagna*, pp. 68–69.

93. Cf. supra, nn. 37ff.

94. C. Sylvain, *Histoire* 2:1–16, 35–42; M. Bendiscioli, *Politica, amministrazione e religione*, pp. 222–25.

95. AGS, *Secr. Prov.* lib. 1156, fols. 413r–15r: Philip II to Alburquerque, Madrid, 27 November 1569; fol. 461r: Philip II to Borromeo, same date: fols 416v–17v: Philip II to Zúñiga, same date. However, it is noteworthy that the favorable conduct toward the cardinal assumed by Philip II had also been determined by the fact that in the meantime, on 26 October, Borromeo was saved from an attempt on his life organized by some rebel members of the order of the Umiliati (the letter to the governor cited earlier makes explicit reference to it). Evidently, the king sought to escape the accusation of having indirectly fomented the rebellion and delinquency

among the more undisciplined elements of the clergy by presenting obstacles to the exercise of the episcopal jurisdiction.

96. C. Sylvain, *Histoire* 3 : 1–24, 157–97; C. Camenisch, *Carlo Borromeo und die Gegenreformation im Veltlin mit besonderer Berücksichtigung der Landesschule in Sondrio* (Chur, 1901); E. Wymann, *Der heilige Karl Borromeo und die Schweizer Eidgenossenschaft* (Stans, 1903); P. d'Alessandri, *Atti di San Carlo riguardanti la Svizzera ed i suoi territori* (Locarno, 1909); E. Wymann, *Kardinal Karl Borromeo in seinen Beziehungen zur alten Eidgenossenschaft* (Stans, 1910).

97. P. Prodi, "San Carlo Borromeo," p. 222.

98. A. Borromeo, "L'opposizione all'eresia," in *Il grande Borromeo tra storia e fede* (Milan, 1984), pp. 225–51: contrary to what might be suggested by the title—which has been imposed by the editor—this essay deals with the activity taken by Borromeo during his episcopacy to prevent and repress heresy; refer to it for the relevant bibliography.

99. Few phrases could better render this identification of heretic and of rebel than that written by Requeséns in a letter to Philip II: according to the governor, the heretics ought to be considered "rebeldes de V. Mag.ᵈ pues lo son a Dios" (AGS, E leg. 1233 n. 153: Requeséns to Philip II, Milan, 12 December; duplicated in leg. 1234 n. 56).

100. H. G. Koenigsberger, "The Statecraft of Philip II," pp. 12–17.

101. L. Fumi, "L'inquisizione romana," p. 374.

102. AGS, *Secr. Prov.* lib. 1156, fol. 320r: Philip II to Alburquerque, Madrid, 7 March 1568; ibid., E 1223 n. 67: fra' Angelo, inquisitor of Milan, to Philip II, Milan, 9 April 1568.

103. BLL, ms. Add. 28390, fols. 336r–v: Philip II to Alburquerque, n.d. but in fact 1568; ibid., ms. Add. 28405, fol. 37r–v: Zúñiga to Alburquerque, Rome, 13 January 1570; AGS, E leg. 1236 n. 119: Requeséns to Philip II, Milan, 26 May 1573.

104. BAM, F 83 bis inf., fol. 480r: Cardinal Scipione Rebiba to Borromeo, Rome, 3 October 1571.

105. The conflicts turned especially upon confiscations of the property of those accused and condemned by the Inquisition: L. Fumi, "L'inquisizione romana," pp. 400–401.

106. The prohibition directed at the civil authority for meddling in the judgment of cases of heresy had been confirmed with Julius III's bull *Licet a diversis* of 15 February 1551. Cf. A. Borromeo, "Le controversie giurisdizionali," p. 45 n. 5.

107. L. Prosdocimi, "Controriforma e politica spagnola," pp. 538–39; A. Borromeo, "Le controversie giurisdizionali," pp. 87–89.

Clerics and Laymen in the Work of Carlo Borromeo

ADRIANO PROSPERI

IT HAS BEEN SAID THAT THERE ARE TWO WAYS TO AVOID COMING TO GRIPS
with the person and with the work of Carlo Borromeo: by isolating them in
the splendidly exceptional nature of the saint or else by confounding them in
the indistinct grayness of the austere Counter-Reformation church.[1] In short
the tendency to stereotype Borromeo as the unsurpassed model or as the
example followed by a host of followers has militated against analysis of the
work carried out by Borromeo. This helps us also to understand why, since
the biographies written by contemporaries and conceived as instruments for
realizing the work started by San Carlo, no one else has attempted a
complete and analytical portrait of the man and of his work; proof of this
omission is the fate of the immense body of correspondence, always the
object of incursions in the interest of particular research projects, that has
never been exhaustively read, nor has an edition been projected and brought
to fulfillment. It is certainly not the magnitude of the enterprise that has
discouraged possible projects, because indeed other editorial monuments
have been raised for extolling the pastoral activity and asceticism of San
Carlo—that is, those acts and attitudes which most clearly bespeak his
exemplary nature. The present centennial anniversary does not seem destined to change the situation. One ought therefore to start from this knot of
his exemplariness, tightened by the canonization of 1610, and attempt to
understand the work of Borromeo in the context afforded by his epoch.
Proposed as a model for the bishop, this exemplariness has been interpreted
up to now as capacity for continually exhibiting to the Christian people a
practice of daily asceticism of the type that the medieval church had reserved
to monks. It is understandable that this model, with contours of individual
holiness cut in such a way as to make them proposable whenever and to
whomever,[2] resists every attempt at concrete definition.

In the meantime the fact ought nevertheless to be emphasized that the
interpretation of the bishop's person and the duties constituted a response—
indeed, the official response of the Catholic church—to the principal prob-

lem discussed during the entire sixteenth century: what ought to be the image of the bishop. All the projects for reform of the church in that epoch have in the bishop a point of common reference: from Luther to Gasparo Contarini, from Erasmus to the *Consilium de emendanda Ecclesia,* all lamented the nonresidence of bishops among their "sheep," and all proposed more or less explicitly ecclesiastical models in which the function of the bishop was emphasized. The church to which this thinking addressed itself was above all a church of bishops: this can be measured by the contemporary discrediting of the monastic world and the monastic ideal of perfection and the resultant modifications in the tripartite model of the society inherited from the preceding age. In this context matured the decrees of the Council of Trent and, later, Carlo Borromeo's own decision to exercise his episcopal ministry in a certain way. The crisis of the monastic ideals imposed a redefining of the whole relationship between clerics and laity and a discovery of new, positive proposals. But when Carlo Borromeo took the decision to reside in his diocese, the seething phase of the crisis had passed, and the framework within which he would operate was sufficiently clear. Far distant now were the years in which Luther had attacked the walls that divided clerics from the laity; there was already developing an inversion of that tendency toward the progressive blurring of the ecclesiastical estate's distinctive features that had characterized early sixteenth-century society. In Catholic countries around the middle of the century, a vigorous restoration of the dignity and functions of the clergy occurred. The generation of Carlo Borromeo had nothing to invent in this regard: vestments, morality, training—in short, all the distinctive features of the ecclesiastical estate as they had thus been defined in the course of the long history of the church—had recently been recalled into force by the Council of Trent; besides contemporary attitudes tended strongly to emphasize clerical-lay differences and more clearly to demarcate the two groups for the purpose of exalting the dignity of the clergy over the laity. But neither these ancient usages nor these attitudinal tendencies of the epoch need have made of Carlo Borromeo alone that zealous executor which the hagiography of admirers and the malevolence of adversaries have generally described for us. To the extent that one considers the relationship between laypeople and ecclesiastics, the problem has been one of defining the appropriate median between the separation of the sacred from the profane and the necessary contact for the exercise of the functions of guide and of spiritual direction. Perhaps no creation of this epoch sums up the question more eloquently than the confessional, this construction that is made for separating and at the same time for permitting a contact which powerfully brings the parties together again. The question that seems to be posed, then, is how the choices wrought by Carlo Borromeo affected the workings of tradition and whether they tended to close down or open up the ecclesiastical world for laity.

First of all it is worth remembering that the ecclesiastical world was extremely diverse, with very strong internal differences in terms of power and of social level. The harshness of the sudden attack of the Lutheran reform worked to accentuate its unity and compactness, restraining, therefore, and reducing the differences by making conspicuous instead the supreme papal authority. Therefore, in this respect one must emphasize an original aspect of the work of Borromeo and of the conception of the church that took shape therein: his insistence upon the ecclesiastical province as an intermediate institutional dimension between the diocese and the papal see. Well known are the decisive importance the provincial councils had for him and how much of his work was dedicated to making effective their regulations and to substantiating the nominal authority of the archbishop over the bishops of the Milanese province. It was by this means that there came to be trained a body of bishops bound to the model offered by Borromeo and guided by him in the application, see by see, of the firm measures taken by the provincial councils in enforcing the Tridentine decrees. The sharp tones in which Borromeo appealed in order to make the relationship of subordination to the archiepiscopal Milanese see respected and in order to convince the reluctant are a proof of how much he held to this institutional articulation of the life of the church. In its time this effort would appear anachronistic: by now the archiepiscopal title had been conceded in too many cases to reward the political fortunes of a city or of a dynasty for it to evoke any recollection of its other meanings. Moreover the generalized nonresidence of bishops had particularly affected the rest, for a see of Milan's importance had left inactive those links articulating its ecclesiastical province. Carlo Borromeo, on the contrary, reactivated them with an energy that to some appeared as an obvious ingredient of the character of a man habituated to command, while on the other hand it is an index of the importance that the resumption of the functioning of this institution held for him. As Borromeo himself repeated many times in the inaugural discourses of the provincial council, the province filled the desert between that undiscussed papal authority and the entire ecclesiastical body which, abandoned to itself and deprived of control by intermediate authority, appeared to him to have fallen into a terribly flaccid state. Borromeo's plan failed to be realized: the provincial councils fell into disuse after his time, and the establishment of a new province in central northern Italy under the administration of Bologna had no success.[3]

* * *

With the functioning of an organ of intermediate control, committed by Borromeo to the ecclesiastical province, a precise idea of the church emerges. We see his conception of the duties of a bishop. In this regard indications are certainly not lacking in the writings and in the sermons of

Borromeo, which rather are in good part specifically dedicated to a recognition of episcopal duties and imply a strict examination of the relationship between progress made and that which remains to be made in order to conform to the model established in advance. Still, rather than starting from the myriad of minute references to episcopal duties, it is better to begin with a text where the dimension and the function of the bishop receive a high and solemn definition. In a sermon of 29 September 1569, Borromeo presented to his hearers the organic design of the ecclesiastical hierarchy. He selected the well known and traditionally invoked text of Pseudo-Dionysius on the angelic hierarchy: the illustration made of it by Borromeo started from the premise that the celestial order ought to find an earthly reflection in the hierarchy and in the internal functioning of the church militant. This intense hierarchical emphasis focused on the present; it is not intended as a casual reference to tradition. Therefore, because of the correspondence established by Borromeo between celestial and terrestrial hierarchies, the bishops correspond to the first order of angels, which includes seraphim, cherubim, and thrones; to these falls the duty to manifest by their words, to show by their example *(manifestare verbo, monstrare exemplo)* the revelation of God; under them stand abbots and rectors of churches who ought to transmit in the same way the revelation to the third order, that of the common people *(plebei)*, that is, of those who ought neither to administer sacraments nor teach, for in the order are included "virgins, the chaste, and the married" *(virgines, continentes et coniugati)*. If each will stand to his post and will obey his superiors, the church of God will then be without blemish.[4] To this therefore the image of the church's reform has been reduced; to the attainment of the "summa tranquilitas" of a system where everybody respects the superior authority and transmits its will to inferiors. It is a proposition that risks appearing settled, given also the traditional vehicle of the sermon in which it is presented. But if one reflects on the medieval precedents of generally similar design, one discovers that the church has been made narrower and more uniform, reduced as it is to a structure of control for the mass of the faithful and obligated to a daily asceticism that is no longer the prerogative of the monks. The bishop's function as the supreme regulator of social relations involved a very high sense of his dignity and a dynamic and combative interpretation of his presence in the city. This ideal bishop can be seen when the archbishop of Milan proposes again to his audience the model dearest to him, that of Saint Ambrose. The most significant sermon regarding this proposal was that given on 7 December 1567. The first "pastoral rule," according to this sermon, is that of "not calculating one's life when it concerns the spiritual benefit of one's flock." Carlo Borromeo illustrates this with an episode that shrewdly suggests his intentions regarding the nonecclesiastical authority of his city: "This glorious saint"—he said—"confronts with his clergy in his own church the soldiers of Count Stilicho, in having given asylum to a poor fugitive in the most evident peril for his life, by means of ecclesiastical immunity."[5] It is easy to translate the Ambrosian model into the Milanese reality of these years when points of contention accumulated between the archbishop and the political authority; one might also impute to Borromeo a preconceived will for giving battle to the political authority in order to restore an anachronistic image of the clergy's authority. Indeed the "sea of new things" introduced by the provincal council was not passed, as the same archbishop had foreseen, without great difficulty.[6] Disputes with and resistance from the political arm fed a climate of engagement from which Borromeo did not withdraw: but his motivation did not so much involve any preconceived desire to enlarge the sphere of honors and powers of the ecclesiastical body as it involved the substance of the measures taken in the provincial council, indeed the very substance of what we are able to define as the "reform" of Borromeo. Therefore if the first rule drawn from the model of Saint Ambrose was that of putting at risk one's own life for the welfare of the "flock," it becomes evident that Carlo Borromeo himself was not in the habit of perceiving occasions of risk only at extreme distances—as indeed did many candidates to martyrdom attracted to the "Indies"—but saw them directly in front of himself, in the principals of political power delegated by the "most Catholic" Spanish monarchy.

The second pastoral power derived from the Ambrosian model and formulated by the evangelical phrase "I know my sheep" *(ego cognosco oves meas)* permitted Carlo Borromeo to refocus attention upon the entirety of religious rules, ceremonies, and acts that constituted, in his words, "the splendor of the Church of Milan." Here, then, in the institutional system by means of which the clergy knew and governed the laity, stood the substance of pastoral work. It involved daily, hard, unremitting work, done in order to nourish without interruption a relationship exposed to infinite risks. It concerned also a work not belonging exclusively to the bishop nor even to the clergy but properly to all those who disposed of any authority. Carlo Borromeo affirmed it very clearly:

> Great titles are those of good Pastor, of worthy Pontiff; great however are the toil, the sweat, the vigils, the bloodshed with which they are acquired . . . and we pastors and priests, you magistrates, fathers and mothers of families: all you that in whatever way have responsibility and government of others . . . by providing that subjects, children, servants may live with good skills, acquire good learning, grow in the fear of God.[7]

We will turn now to this intensive interpretation of "pastoral" functions and responsibility. At the outset, it is worth the trouble to emphasize the preeminence of this positive, constructive component in the Borromean manner of understanding the functions and the duties of the bishop compared to that negative one of struggle and repression of heretical dissent. In the delineation of the rules for the good pastor, we find in the third of these something that approaches the sphere of antiheretical warfare; but let us see how. The third rule consists in the obligation of inducing other "sheep" *(adducere alias oves)* to constrain the one who is outside the sheepfold to enter therein. Saint Ambrose offered to Borromeo the model of his own struggle against Arianism, but more than the conflict with the heretics is emphasized here: the point of "compel them to enter" *(compelle intrare),* of the obligation imposed on all to use their authority in order to bring within the unique sheepfold any who stand outside. Once again we are sent back to the concrete characteristics that identified the church of Borromeo. In speaking of present heresies, while ignoring their actual content yet implying a common denominator many times affirmed by Catholic controversialists, Carlo Borromeo dwelt upon the characteristic that struck him most: the idea of an invisible church. This point, around which the polemic against the Anabaptists had furiously raged up to then, was for him the supreme deception that the enemy of the human race had found and which made most dangerous the complex of doctrinal aberrations of his time. The Church, unique and true, was quite visible and concrete, identifiable in an institutional network of precise hierarchical structure: "head and principal pastor Christ, and his vicar the pontiff, subordinates, all the other particular pastors."[8] It was the interior of this structure that he should affect in order to restore to it a fervor of religious life that had become tepid. Only after this was it possible to confront the problem of those outside, the heretics:

> Having placated the wrath of God on account of our sins and removed our scandals, great opportunity and aid will be given to regain many lambs from the hands of heresiarchic wolves who now stay outside the sheepfold and like vagabonds go about concocting for themselves this invisible church.[9]

Here it is not to be denied that San Carlo might have underestimated the problem of internal religious dissent or that of the formation of new churches, different from the Roman one; we know that he did not overlook it in practice. The indications of activity turned against the heretics that emerge from the letters of Borromeo, documents remaining from an inquisitorial work no further documentable, are rather numerous and permit one to affirm that the archbishop of Milan had a way of testing directly the problems of the struggle with heresy. As result especially of the studies of Domenico Maselli, we know that around 1568 Borromeo carried out personally rather delicate missions, like that to Mantua and that relative to the heresy of Siculo in the Cassinese congregation of the Benedictine order. Still it is quite significant that, while the mission to Mantua was in full swing, on

3 April 1568—that is, on the day before they were to proceed in the public square with fifteen abjurations and twelve executions for contumacy—Borromeo would write to the Cardinal of Pisa earnestly requesting permission for the heretics' being returned to Milan: "From [Milan]," writes Maselli, "he is afraid of the case having been removed by reasons of jurisdictional conflict then present and attempts to diminish the importance of the Mantuan heretical phenomenon."[10] We have the opportunity here to discover the complete correspondence between the hierarchy of pastoral duties affirmed in the sermon of 1567 and practical behavior verifiable in a precise situation: more than the struggle against heretical nests in the vicinity of Mantua, Borromeo was pressed to pursue to the fullest the exacting jurisdictional question that at Milan held suspended the application of episcopal decrees. Thus the praises we encounter in the homilies of Borromeo for the anti-heretical work of illustrious bishops—his predecessors or models—seem always rather distracted. There is, for example, that one dedicated to San Simpliciano in a sermon which in this respect had as its explicit aim to nourish the cult of that saint's memory for the episcopal tradition of the Milanese church. In only one case does it seem to me possible to distinguish a different tone and a dramatic accentuation of an emergency situation however much it relates to the heretical engulfment of the Church. In a late sermon (1583) San Carlo turned directly to Saint Ambrose—"O Most holy Ambrose now is the moment that I shall turn myself to you" (O Ambrosi Sanctissime, iam tempus est ut ad te me convertam)—in order to ask him to illuminate his successor with his example and to instruct him how it might be possible to clean the heretical "putredo" from the community of the faithful.[11] But there is an explanation for such unaccustomed stress on the heretical danger: the audience that heard the sermon was that of Bellinzona. In short, it was on the border of the Milanese archdiocese where pressed the menace of a world in which the heretics had become the winners. It was a world so near that, as the archbishop of Milan noted, a day's journey sufficed to get there.[12] Yet we seek in vain in the pages of San Carlo Borromeo anything similar to the tone of extreme exasperation regarding the imminence of the heretical danger that is easily found in so many documents of late sixteenth-century Catholicism, especially in the sermons of the friars. Certainly even the writings of Borromeo contain darkly pessimistic references to the church and the world, as does almost all post-Tridentine ecclesiastical literature, harshly marked with suspicion and fear. But the pessimism of Carlo Borromeo seems to be fed by traditional ascetic themes rather than by the fear of heretical encirclement. The state of the "respublica christiana," thus, as he represented it in a sermon of 12 August 1568, appeared to him painful and miserable because of the moral corruption of Christians; only on a secondary level figures the danger of the heretics and the Turks. The faltering bark of Saint Peter presents itself in the background

of an appeal to all for asceticism and penitence.[13] The daily struggle against evil as the internal enemy for every Christian characterizes Borromeo's own sense of life and distinguishes it by a more modern tonality as compared to that of so many of his contemporaries who continued to insist on the dangers of oppression from outside—namely the heretics and the Turks—and on apocalyptic themes.

Therefore the model of bishop that San Carlo had in view did not resemble the combatant-martyr of the struggle against heresy, of which even the sources offered so many examples, but reflected rather the figure of a magistrate preoccupied with the failings and vices of his people and determined to have his authority respected against all transgressions. If Saint Ambrose is exalted for his firmness in resisting Stilicho, if Saint Basil and Saint Ambrose are cited for their defense of *ecclesiastica libertas*[14] or the firmness of Saint Bernard is exalted in his conflict with William, Count of Aquitaine, if finally is recorded the courage with which the exemplary bishop prevented access to the emperor[15] even up to the choir, this is always done not only to sustain with illustrious examples the justification for a present battle but also because of a precise conception of what the bishop ought to be. It is a duty to be hard and exacting: few bishops, Borromeo records, citing Saint John Chrysostom,[16] shall be saved because of the sins of the people committed to them. Moreover the negative model for excellence, that of Judas, is properly ascribed to those who hang on to the weighty charge of the ecclesiastical ministry through desire of gain and of vainglory without considering the associated duties.[17]

For whatever such evidentiary materials may be worth, testimony from a literary genre as formalized as that of the homily, a singular fact nevertheless becomes evident: the names selected by Borromeo as points of reference lead far away to heroic times and personages, but they do not help us to decipher within what context and according to what contemporary models he means to move. The names of contemporaries are absent: not only are these not present in the sermons—where it is understandable that he might have preferred to make reference to canonical texts, to canonized bishops, and even to figures who might have belonged to an undisputed tradition long since incorporated into the liturgy—but singular reticence on this matter also runs through the correspondence of Borromeo. Take the more obvious case, also more exaggerated by hagiographers and scholars, namely the model of episcopal action represented through the Tridentine generation by the bishop of Verona, Gian Matteo Giberti. All scholars who have attempted to associate the personage of Borromeo with past precedents have had to refer to the historic model of that *Gibertalis disciplina* which in the first half of the sixteenth century had represented a strident rupture with the practices of nonresident bishops and had given expression to new needs. Carlo Bascapè in his biography of Borromeo appeals to the model of Giberti, this "princeps" of the "*ecclesiasticae disciplinae restitutio,*" and records how a most direct connection between the two was indeed constituted by an apprentice of Giberti's having become collaborator of Borromeo: this was Niccolò Ormaneto who, having also been collaborator of Cardinal Pole in the work of Catholic restoration in England, constituted a living deposit of the pastoral heritage of the first half of the century. Close to Ormaneto we find also another Veronese trained in the school of Giberti, Alberto Lino, whom Borromeo engaged in the reform of convents. Moreover Enrico Cattaneo's research has gathered many other indications which sufficiently demonstrate how Borromeo would not have been able to miss an encounter with Giberti and from how many sources that model would have been suggested to him.[18] Particularly insistent and patriotically motivated was in this respect Agostino Valier, successor of Bernardo Navagero in the see of Verona; Valier was to send to Borromeo a portrait of Giberti with the implicit suggestion that he imitate his example.[19] Borromeo, who does not seem to have requested such a present, was nevertheless grateful to him for it and allotted, according to Bascapè, a place for that portrait in his private gallery of exemplary bishops. The reason I emphasize this is that here was, it seems, a true and original gallery of portraits of bishops which Borromeo acquired for himself "so that," writes Bascapè, "he might preserve for imitation, having gathered together for review, the living memory of episcopal virtue" *(ut ob oculos collocata, vivam virtutis episcopalis memoriam, ad imitationis studium in eo conservaret).*[20] According to Bascapè there were in this gallery portraits of Saint Ambrose, for which no further explanation is needed, of Giberti, and of John Fisher, the bishop-martyr of the Anglican schism. This information is confirmed only in part by the inventory of Borromeo's property, which mentions only those of Saint Ambrose and of John Fisher. The inventory appears more credible as testimony than the biographer, too preoccupied in constituting his gallery made up of precursors and disposed to superimpose the categories of antecedents and of models. It is evident that the high sense of ecclesiastical dignity and of his duties which had led Fisher to resist his sovereign might vividly have represented for Carlo Borromeo that ideal model of bishop which we have seen to emerge from his sermons. But in the case of Giberti the elements of resemblance that impress the historian were not sufficient to maintain admiration and religious service on the part of Borromeo. Some of the resemblances belong not to the biographical curriculum but to the instruments and forms of diocesan administration. But the fulfillment of residential duties and the forsaking of Roman political responsibilities were not heroic acts to stimulate the admiration of one like Borromeo who had effected detachment from Rome on conditions pertaining to the very peak of power quite different from that which Giberti had enjoyed after the sack of Rome. Regarding then the concrete moments of diocesan administration, the institutions and instruments of which Giberti had made use, there is no doubt that Borromeo took over no small number of them; indeed several points of concordance have been pointed out between Gibertine constitutions and Borromean statutes of Councils. But from this point of view the historical continuity between the two experiences, which certainly exists, does not remove their existing differences for composing a hagiographical model of the good bishop.[21]

Although thus coming near to being able to communicate through the mediation of men who would in different instances work for each, Giberti and Borromeo were separated by that decisive turning point which was the Council of Trent. After it things yoke very differently: the charming halo of expectations and of hopes belonging to the first half of the century gave way to the hard relations between forces and well-defined institutions. The religiosity of the *spirituali* gathered about Giberti had provoked not a few suspicions. The same men who then came to collaborate with Borromeo would not be exempt from it. Alberto Lino, for example, had roused the interests of Lutherans and Anabaptists in Verona with his sermons, and only toward 1555 was there a clarification and separation. That all this had ended was in small part a consequence of the conclusion of the Council of Trent. But on the actual terrain of the forms of diocesan administration, where the Gibertine constitutions had marked an important stage, the conclusion of the council had changed completely the rules of the game. This is best expressed in Carlo Borromeo's own words in responding to Alberto Lino, who counseled him in a given case to have recourse to excommunication and appealed to the model of the Gibertine constitutions. Thus he replied:

> The example of Bishop Giberto(!) is quite near to me and I do not doubt that that rare prelate was moved thus by just cause. But then it had not yet been ruled by the Council which warns us to proceed in a reserved fashion and to use the knife of excommunication sparingly.[22]

Giberti and his work are understood for what use they had in the decrees of the Council of Trent. To these then it is necessary to refer. This involves an exact indication of the historical distance between the two periods. It is a distance that even revises all the other initiatives of renewal of pastoral care of the first half of the sixteenth century yet does not prevent these initiatives from being matched with those related to Borromeo's work, comprised in some fashion within the same idea of the religious life. In short, one may speak of a single well-defined line of reform inspired as a standard for the episcopal administration of the religious life.

Carlo Borromeo did not write treatises, nor did he elaborate general schemes of reform. He who would approach this personality has to pursue its realizations in the sphere of social relations and to reconstruct the network of personal interventions through which this man succeeded in modifying reality—that of his own archdiocese and that of the Catholic Tridentine church in general. This does not mean that there was no general plan of reform, nor that we wish to reduce Carlo Borromeo to the role of the most active organizer and realizer of others' projects. However, in no text drawn up by Borromeo can one pretend to find consigned the general plan of his activity as bishop or even the general definition, valid for him, of that term which traverses in various ways the entire century, "reform." A rapid and casual sounding in his writings yields, it is true, some interesting results regarding the use of terms. The obvious result is that while his interlocutors speak of "Milanese reform," alluding to the complex of measures taken by the archbishop, he prefers rather to remain on the level of a more concrete and less ambitious description. Thus we see Carlo Borromeo described during the first provincial council as one who "attends most diligently to the reform;[23] when the decrees of the council itself subsequently arrive in Rome, the enthusiastic comment of Giulio Poggiano is that "the Roman reform is daughter of the Milanese."[24] Instead Carlo Borromeo seems to hesitate to make use of such a compelling term. When he does, however, he relates it to rules and decrees, distinguishing implicitly between the instruments of reform and the reform itself. In short the term conserves in his texts the significance of a profound interior alteration of the individual that manifests itself in his mode of living; this alteration is induced by the example and by the laws of whoever governs but needs to be continually encouraged and controlled. The reform is therefore an interior process whose rules and decrees are alone able to create the conditions, but it is not reduced to a single fact, to a pure and simple movement of penitence and conversion to individuals. Nor on the other hand does the function of who governs stop at the conservation of an existing order or with the tranquil administration of a complex of rules. Carlo Borromeo's mode of seeing things properly appears much more agitated and dramatic; his sermon opens with the affirmation that two great kings contend with each other for the dominion of the world, "God and the Devil" (Deus et Daemon).[25] It is a revealing image of the dynamic and aggressive mode in which he interpreted the function of the church in the world. The clergy, to whom belonged the task of governing the fortunes of the battle on the side of God, ought to invest all their energies in a work of conquest for whose result they entirely bore the responsibility. This impulse to the conquest of the soul is not a sentimental or mystical burst of ardor but demands to be organized and structured according to precise rules whose better model is that original one of the apostolic church: "Ecclesiastical discipline must be renewed" (ecclesiastica est renovanda disciplina), San Carlo Borromeo will declare.[26] But even in appeals of this type there are always included precise proposals relative to rules, customs, and forms of well-defined religious life, not of vaporous aspirations for general renovation. In short we are far from the programs and desires of general renewal of church and society that nourished the religious ideas of the early sixteenth century. The "reform" of which San Carlo thinks is above all a declaration of war, the selection of a battleground in the struggle that invests all men; when he turned to the Milanese after the plague with his celebrated *Memoriale,* it was in order to propose to them "this prime reform above all the others, this public profession of making enmity with the world."[27] "To make enmity" does not mean to abandon the world. It is true that the same San Carlo in his sermons to nuns allowed himself to imagine what might be the effects of the hypothetical victory of his appeals to distrust the world: cities deserted, plazas reduced to pastures for animals, convents packed with women finally secure from the dangers of the world.[28] But San Carlo was not the man for withdrawing into a monastery, awaiting the fulfillment of that monastic utopia; the battle that he had in mind was something uninterrupted, destined to be continually reproposed with alternating vicissitudes that depended on the zeal of the combatants. It was a struggle in which the clergy was opposed by a powerful lay world attached to its own values and culture. Borromeo, product of noble birth, used terms of profound indignation against the nobles devoted to worldly amusements like hunting—"to breed hounds and train horses and beasts"—and against the lettered who, "delighting in gentility and with amusements that were formerly pagan, renew the names, the memories and the costumes of the people that did not know God."[29] Against the revival of ancient paganism, the plan of Borromeo's reform is naturally embattled: "I see the renewal, the memory, the imitation of so much profaneness and trappings of paganism. . . . Indeed Satan himself now triumphs."[30] An opposition thus clearly between Christian reform and pagan revival does not produce a static position of abstract values but rather a plan ably and constantly pursued for the Christianization of society. Gone are the mystic and prophetic tones of the religiosity of the early sixteenth century, absent the climate of curiosity and theological uncertainty that had then nourished so many discussions; the question now is only that of the conquest of a society, living and acting in a pagan fashion, by the values of Christian reform, the values of penitence and mortification. The instrument and fundamental point of reference in this encounter is, as has already been stated, the clergy.

✳   ✳   ✳

The question of the reform of the clergy and of the relations between clerics and the laity had been for some time the capital question of the church. The contribution of Carlo Borromeo had been generally considered exemplary in the sense that he should have furnished the most authoritative and in some ways definitive interpretation for the decrees of the Council of Trent: in short the post-Tridentine turn given to the relations between clergy and laity would be accomplished according to the Milanese model by Carlo Borromeo, its point of reference. But in reality there are important differences that distinguish the work of Borromeo either from the antecedents of the early sixteenth century or from the epoch following him. It may be said summarily that the dominant preoccupation in the pre-Tridentine age had been that of reacting to a process of secularization that tended to cancel the distinction between clerics and layfolk; in the church of the succeeding period there is in some ways an inverse process, one of domination according to clerical models and values by an ecclesiastical body preoccupied with the defense specifically of its dignity and generally of its elevated social status. It has been justly emphasized how this preoccupation may have led to the isolation and the closing of the ecclesiastical body. Indeed Carlo Borromeo's cousin, Cardinal Federico, invited the clergy to preserve "their proper dignity by appearing seldom in public and by standing apart from others."[31] Between these two poles the model offered by Carlo Borromeo is quite distinct because he conceived the relationship between clergy and layfolk as an active relationship of penetration and of conquest in which the clergy had continuously to win its prestige like a commander in the course of a battle.

The clergy at the center of Borromeo's preoccupation is the secular, established in the diocese. This is the fundamental point from which one ought to start reconstructing his relations with the diverse reality of the ecclesiastical world. In the encounters with all the other institutional forms in which that world was articulated, Borromeo's attitude was determined by the possibility of utilizing the clergy in the framework of his program of reform. The range of the relations thus set in motion varied from collaboration for well-defined areas and precincts to true and open hostility. The necessity for collaboration was made evident to the archbishop by the dramatic reality of the existing disproportion between the needs of the diocese and the disposable parochial clergy. That of Milan was, as Borromeo wrote to his agent in Rome, Cesare Speciano, on 16 February 1578, "a diocese quite large . . . where there are many a number up to fifty, seventy, one hundred parishes vacant . . . and so many souls."[32] To deal with a situation of dearth such as this—and it had been even graver at the beginning of his administration—he did not want to retravel the road of substitution, entrusted to the religious orders; rather he intended to increase as much as possible the training of an adequate clergy and to block to anyone entering the ecclesiastical body the most traditional route, which led to the orders and congregations. By this approach how many had been initiated up to then who had refused the comfortable arrangement of an ecclesiastical benefice in order to dedicate themselves instead to a most severe type of clerical life? The congregation of clerks regular of which the first half of the century had been full was the terminus of roads of this type. Thus all those bishops who had wanted to offer models to their own clergy and to accelerate the time for the reform of the diocesan structure inevitably turned to Jesuits, Theatines, and Barnabites. Even San Carlo asked the Jesuits to send him teachers for his seminary; but he insured himself with a special brief that prohibited the clerics of his seminary from abandoning the route undertaken by entering the Society of Jesus. The brief conceded to him by Pius V on 28 July 1570 was subsequently reiterated,[33] given the insistance with which Carlo Borromeo continued to perceive the risk that the Jesuit teachers' charm exerted upon their clerics of his seminary. In the encounter with the Jesuits therefore as with the other orders and congregations Borromeo nevertheless did not nourish only the fears of an undue competition; other and more specific were the reasons for his diffidence. These emerge actually from the way in which the seminary was organized: the rules given by Borromeo insisted more on complex education, from moral and disciplinary control to that of physical deportment, rather than on literary and cultural preparation in general. As he himself had said to Speciano in a moment of friction with the Society of Jesus, the Jesuits instead were too interested in culture whereby they ended in favoring those "who have some talent for letters."[34] The other motive for the diffidence of Borromeo was bound to the question that for centuries had placed bishops and regulars in opposition: the independence of the latter from the former, the hierarchical structure of the religious orders that withdrew them from any confrontation with the ordinary clergy. The question presented itself on several occasions and under different aspects during the entire episcopate of Borromeo; it is exemplified in a symbolic instance, that of the relation between San Carlo and the Oratorians of St. Philip Neri. The group of Oratorians summoned to Milan in 1575 was quickly recalled to Rome because of the discords stemming from their use. Carlo Borromeo, who intended to use them as his auxiliaries in the reform of the diocesan clergy, did not tolerate any who might consider themselves independent of him: "I desire that all be obedient to my will," he wrote with a phrase that requires no comment.[35] In the attitude of Borromeo were combined therefore these two elements fast bound together: the desire that nothing should escape his authority and the strong pastoral impulse to the clergy. It includes elements already present at the moment he began his diocesan administration but that will be accentuated in the course of years.

It is possible that in this matter there may have still weighed on him the experiences accumulated from the deterioration of certain forms of religious life withdrawn from his control. Many examples might be given, but at least two are especially significant: that of the Cassinese congregation of the Benedictine order and that associated with the binomial Ludovica Torelli-Paola Antonia Negri. In the confrontation with the Cassinese congregation Borromeo would have had to commit himself in a decisive as well as discreet action that would purge from the congregation without too much publicity the conspicuous infiltrations of heretical ideas. It is an episode whose contours remain unknown even now; because of the privileges that the order enjoyed, the trials were held within the congregation and they have never been made accessible to us. Nevertheless, that it would have involved a sufficiently relevant question is established by the fact that among the suspected, besides several abbots, there was even the president of the Cassinese congregation, Andrea da Asola. The wave of trials that then occurred led some accused laymen, like the doctor Francesco Severi, to die on the gallows, while the fate of the Benedictines remains unknown; Andrea da Asola, arrested and deprived of office, extricated himself with light punishment. The heretical ideas imputed to them derived from the ex-Benedictine, Giorgio Siculo, sentenced to death at Ferrara in 1550. They were an assemblage of visionary expectations and of radical criticism of the doctrine and religious practices of the Catholic church.[36] One of those arrested, Don Giulio da Brescia, declared at the time that the group "took delight in living *in spiritu libertatis*" and that assembled "in some removed place . . . they practiced certain communions with pieces of Milanese sausage."[37] One derives from this at least an idea of what ought to have struck the archbishop of Milan, then engaged in an inquisitorial proceeding: the spontaneous tendency of a religious order in the search for perfection, summed up in the fascination of a Nicodemite like Siculo who had theorized about the division between the perfect and all the others; he had himself believed that persons placed in the superior offices of an important religious order might distance themselves from several of the doctrines and the practices of Catholicism even by maintaining an exterior appearance beyond suspicion. The division between a religion for the few—the perfected, the illuminated, or however they might be termed—and a religion for the majority, superstitious according to the foremost, had been a scattered tendency in the elite of the early sixteenth century. The reaffirmed importance of the cure of souls *(cura animarum)*, placed at the center of the Tridentine decrees, went in an opposite direction, constraining the clergy to make uniform doctrine and comportment in the compelling work of pastoral government. To these indications of the council Borromeo was sensible in a particular way, as noted.

The other case to which reference has been made closely touches a congregation of clerks regular who had direct relations with San Carlo: that of the Barnabites. In the initial history of this congregation it is known how large a part the ideas of the Dominican friar Battista da Crema and the personality of two ladies, Countess Ludovica Torelli and the Angelic Paola Antonia Negri, had had.[38] In this case also Carlo Borromeo found a situation already notorious as a result of previous inquisitorial condemnations. Nevertheless just at Milan the question came to be entangled with the controversy arisen over the printing of the *Lettere spirituale* of Negri and with the renewed activity of the Countess Torelli, founder at Milan of a college for noble daughters. The archbishop of Milan was then the point of reference for many—from Alessandro Saule to Gian Pietro Besozzi—meaning to close accounts with the mystic and "illuminated" religiosity of aristocrats and to cut ties with the female side of the congregation. The concrete initiatives were many: newly founded colleges, revision of the constitution, collaboration in the formation and in the control of the clergy. In the meantime the feminine congregation of the Angelics was subjected to the obligation of seclusion. Consequently Torelli, in order to protest against the line of action taken by Borromeo, placed her new institution under the patronage of the king of Spain and under the administration of Milanese nobles who were able to guarantee to her the exemption of the college from the obligations of seclusion. A rigid conception of moral practices and of doctrinal terms operated within the congregation, expressive of a religion founded, as Besozzi wrote in 1576, upon ecstasies, prophecies and revelations of women."[39] Even from this point of view therefore Borromeo reaped the results of experiences from the first half of the century that in the changed historical condition appeared remote and finished. Their significance could be that of further reinforcing the line of pastoral activity where the clergy, remaining quite distinct from laymen, found nevertheless, in their constant responsibility of government and of model, a useful corrective against all degenerations into sects of "perfect ones" and into quietistic practices. The conviction that this route ought to be pursued was certainly not limited to Borromeo. Also some like the Barnabite Father Gian Pietro Besozzi, who participated with complete conviction in the religious climate of the Italian spiritual groups of the first half of the century, were now prompt to make amends and to declare candidly: "Now I realize what I was not seeing and therefore I speak in a different fashion than I once spoke." In short if a provisional conclusion may be drawn from cases such as these, the reform of the church presented itself at the beginning of the second half of the century in a pastoral and diocesan aspect; Carlo Borromeo was the most significant exponent of a tendency that had already achieved expression.

Turning to the question of the relations with the great orders and congregations, one ought to distinguish another difference in Borromeo's behavior regarding what had preceded him on the path of pastoral reform—or, to state it differently, the path of the revitalization of the cadres of diocesan administration. On this road, for example, the bishop of Verona, Gian Matteo Giberti, had proceeded, making his way with the title of "delegate of the Apostolic See" thanks to which he had been able to pass over privileges and exemptions. Borromeo also, as noted, enjoyed powers of the same type, in fact even more ample, having had the powers of apostolic legate for all Italy. The sum of these powers was such that there were some who defined him as being another pope.[40] Nevertheless on more than one occasion he wanted to emphasize how his authority as bishop was to be considered fundamental and the legatine powers as accessory. It will suffice to record the ceremonial of his "Entries," that of 1565 in Milan and that ten years later as visitor, and the importance which was then attached not only to the rituals in general but to those of the Entries in particular is well known. Moved by the high sense of his own authority Borromeo decided in a particularly delicate and difficult moment to open a new conflict and, in addition, with a powerful order, the Society of Jesus.

The society had been the traditional reservoir of forces for bishops who had wanted to start a work of transformation on their own clergy; even at Milan, as it has been said, recourse was had to the Jesuits, although with significant and unwonted circumspection, for the organization of the seminary. But in 1579 at the peak of the conflict with the governor, Carlo Borromeo asked for the impeachment and removal of the Jesuit Giulio Mazzarino, who in his sermons had spoken in the cathedral and at Brera "against the dispositions which are made for the reform and good spiritual government of this people."[41] The moment was particularly difficult and the front opened the more sensitive, if account is taken of the fact that in the preceding years the governor, knowing well how difficult were the relations between archbishop and the religious orders, had collected the complaints of the regulars and had transmitted them to Rome.[42] That did not prevent Borromeo from energetically attacking the question of Mazzarino. In his letters to Speciano of that period, exhumed not by accident in the epoch of the suppression of the Society of Jesus, he expresses with great clarity his reservations regarding the entire company, which concerned the importance, excessive in his view, that was given thus to cultural preparation to the detriment of pastoral activity. Years earlier Borromeo had criticized the most ample concession made in general to the religious orders by Pius V.[43] But in the case of Mazzarino it was to his own episcopal authority and to the text of the Tridentine decrees that he appealed: "There is left to me—he wrote to Speciano on 16 April 1579—"the authority that I have as bishop from the Council of Trent of not allowing to preach in my diocese what I do not judge well to be preached."[44]

Thus in this case also, as previously in that relating to the Oratorians, the apologetic scheme that envisions holy bishops and religious orders operating compatibly within the framework of Catholic reform does not correspond to reality. Yet Carlo Borromeo was not capable only of attacking decisively the Company of Jesus at a critical moment and did not seek only to twist the regular clergy to the exigencies of his own work as bishop. On this terrain the disproportion between the capacity of the parochial clergy and the tasks to which it was directed was met by creating an instrument whose originality has not been sufficiently emphasized: the congregation of Oblates. This body, created *"ad Dei gloriam et animarum salutem"* with the special tie of obedience to the bishop of Milan, was a replication in certain respects, on the local and diocesan scale, of the Company of Jesus.[45] But from the limitation of this sphere of action descended a series of differences not to be neglected: rooted in a well-defined place, directed to the training of the clergy, but still to all the most urgent pastoral tasks for which there was need of persons well prepared and completely dedicated to the religious life of the diocese, the Oblates resolved the perennial problem in the relation between religious orders and bishops. In short they were able to furnish a more decisive action and a better preparation of the average without escaping from the obedience of the bishop. But in outlining the tasks of the Oblates, Carlo Borromeo showed how the problem of the training of the clergy was for him of instrumental and not final nature; that is, it was subordinated to the basic problem, which was that of offering a model Christian life. In the congregation were admitted clerks and laymen; and if a particular preparation was required of the clerks for preaching and for the education of the clergy, from the laymen were required activities commensurate with their social condition. Even in this case the task of instruction figured as the foremost one. In short it was necessary to attack and resolve all those problems which prevented a positive practice of Christian life. The Oblates had to act positively in order to resolve those problems by simultaneously offering a model of the morality desired by Carlo Borromeo.

The function of example associated with the Oblates characterized, or was intended to characterize, the entire clergy, as has been emphasized many times. A simple reading of the legislative work of Carlo Borromeo suffices to reveal this. The attention to physical appearance, to the mode of clothing and of movement not only during the sacred rites but at all moments, the insistence on dignity, gravity, order, and on all those qualities which ought to become attributes of the ecclesiastic are not meant to exalt one component of society over others in order to separate it but so that the others might draw an example from it. The comportment of the ecclesiastical is constantly designed from the eye of the laymen in the sense that Carlo Borromeo anticipates every possible criticism from that side. Moreover the virtues that he wants to be practiced by his clergy are not clerical virtues in the strict sense but something that all could and should repeat. Thus, for example, since the first provincial council it is ordained that the clergy go to hear the sermons as a means of stimulating the laity to do so.[46] And the admonition that precedes the *Monitiones* to the clergy of the fourth council insists again: "Appropriate this virtue, so that others may see your holiness to shine forth as some sort of lamp" *(eam vos virtutem inducite, ut videant alii quasi lumen aliquod vestram sanctitatem elucere).*[47] The clerical condition is symbolized therefore as a heroic condition, where it is always necessary to strain to surpass human limitations. The personal temperament of Carlo Borromeo, as had already been made evident in his youthful admiration for the manual of Epictetus, is completely tied up with his religious convictions. The vocation or sacerdotal lease is a choice of the battleground that divides the world: "You are clerics . . . the Lord is your part" *(Clerici estis . . . Dominus pars vestra)*.[48] The rules of subordination and the principle of obedience count functionally as a warlike conception of the Church Militant. Successive imitators and reechoers would isolate the themes of the dignity and the superiority of the clergy from that of its function of stimulus and model: the society of the Counter-Reformation would frequently know only one version of the work of Borromeo emptied of its principal promoters.

*   *   *

We come ultimately to the attitude of Borromeo toward the religious life of laymen. For this, as has been seen, a great part of the Borromean construction relative to the clergy is prearranged, in the sense that the ecclesiastical structure set in motion has as its principal function that of "reforming" and keeping alive the religious practice of laymen. One must therefore examine in broad outline the physiognomy of the layman who emerges from the initiatives and ideas of Borromeo. The accusation that was raised against him during the controversy with the Spanish authority was that he wanted "to make the clerics suspicious of laymen."[49] This was then considered in terms of political cohesion of the state and the accusation was turned to make him suspect by Philip II. Nevertheless it must be kept in mind because a thread of suspicion toward the lay world exists in the disposition of Borromeo; it could be said that everything ought to be done for the laity but nothing ought to occur through their initiative. Their function was subordinate, that of obedience; the duty of the pastor was like that of the general toward his soldiers or the pilot to his ship, as Carlo Borromeo said in his discourse before the first provincial council: "This duty of pastor, this office of leader, these are the functions of a governor. . . . *(Hoc munus pastoris, hoc ducis officium, hae gubernatoris partes sunt.)*. . . .[50] The function of the laity was to obey; moreover the obligation of obedience ran through all of Christian society with a precise scheme of subordination that assigned to each one of the points of reference and of authority whom to obey. On the ladder of the medieval "ordines" with their diverse grades of perfection a network of authority was superimposed as we shall see. Meanwhile it will be worth the trouble to record how Borromeo concerned himself with the complete exclusion from the chancel, according to the model of Saint Ambrose, not only of the highest political authorities of the city but also of all those laymen who in any way exercised offices withdrawn from clerics: the very detailed decree of the fourth provincial council established, for example, that wherever a layman might have the function of guarding, opening or closing a church, ringing the bells or other things of this type, he ought to be replaced as soon as possible by a cleric.[51] Still more uncompromising was the order to withdraw from laymen all direct relation with sacred things when it involved, for example, blessings like those given in confraternities.[52] The most severe exclusion, however, concerned the possibility that a layman might preach or be entrusted with the explanation of the Bible. In all these points is measurable the great distance that separates the latter world from the former, chronologically not distant from the first half of the century. Quite different had been the case of the diocesan "exemplaries" of Verona where, according to the sarcastic judgment of Ercole Gonzaga, "the common people went about preaching on predestination and screaming through the country with the crucifix in hand 'Christ! Christ!' "[53]

Certain experiences were no longer possible. But let us see better in what ways and within what boundaries the religious life of laymen is predisposed. What fundamentally is the parish? It involves a dimension of well-defined territorial boundaries; even more to this purpose it is worth the trouble to cite a decree of Borromeo that illuminates how this dimension had been made to prevail over all others. Among the constitutions of the second provincial council is studied and examined a way of distinguishing the parishes not by means of territorial limits but by means of families: a mobile distinction, of a personal type that appealed to the family cell. Borromeo enjoined that it be abolished within six months:[54] the measure was justified by the necessity for a clear distinction of zones for parish priests who had to administer the sacraments. Certainly the rigid organization of sacramental practice in the Tridentine parishes did not easily permit a subordination to the movements of families. Nevertheless it is probable that this decree also attests to the slight confidence that the post-Tridentine church placed in the family, as John Bossy has noted.[55] How then the parish views with suspicion that which happens in the family emerges from the dispositions on baptism. This sacrament can be administered in the home but only in the case of imminent danger for the newborn. There will be an ecclesiastic present or, if he is absent, a cleric, or, next in order, a male, or—only as last resort—a woman for discharging the rites that will nevertheless have to be repeated in the parish church as soon as possible, "where [in the church] if there shall have been ascertained that the right form of baptism has been provided, to such a degree may the rites and ceremonies of baptism be applied to the infant."[56] On the question of godparents the rule intervenes eliminating all those traditions which made of godparenthood a form of "Christian friendship," as Bossy has also written. The godparents have a residual religious significance as vice-parents, ready to succeed to the parents, if necessity requires, in order to impart the religious education that is the sole task of the family.

In the presentation of these tendencies in the work of Borromeo, one must naturally never forget the number of concrete forces, the incessant fatigue, and the obstacles that might be interposed to his initiatives. Even more important is the fact that his tendency to reduce the initiative of laymen and to insist on the characteristics of instruments of control and of government of the parish was in accord with a more general tendency of Italian society of the period for the strengthening of the links of subordination. No matter if the reproaches directed at him by contemporaries cast doubt upon his will to repress and to control and maintained that he had diminished the dignity of the ecclesiastical body. The governor of Milan, Requeséns, for example, insinuated that Borromeo "did not show himself to be sufficiently warm in diligently pursuing the heretics that are in Milan."[57] This can only astonish anyone who reads the minute prescriptions for the control of orthodoxy with which the first provincial council was opened and anyone who continually returns to the legislative work of Borromeo. This same first council found at Rome those who accused its author of having wanted to introduce a dangerous "reformation" and of tending "to remove all the splendor in the prelates of the ecclesiastical hierarchy" *(auferre omnem splendorem in praesidibus ecclesiasticae hierarchiae)*.[58] Confronting these voices, Borromeo brought a truly remarkable vigor that affirmed the dignity of the clergy in his own pastoral activity and opened a line of conflict with the ethic of the nobility. There is no doubt, for example, that he possessed a very clear vision of the emergence of aristocratic values in the society of his day; in his sermons recurs the example of the various social categories whose sole aspiration is that of ascent to the nobility: "The merchant, why does he willingly expose himself to so many dangers, why does he manipulate illicit contracts, why does he daily devise new business deals, unless so that made wealthy he may be able to be preferred to others and to take his seat among the nobility?" *(Mercator, cur tot periculis sponte se obiicit, cur illicitos contractus exercet, cur nova quotidie commercia excogitat, nisi ut ditatus ceteris praeferri possit ac cum nobilioribus considere)*.[59] This makes all the more significant the fact that he had explicitly declared a preference for the "simple and the lowly" to the nobles who "stand always on points of honor and of worldly nobility":[60] yet it would be a distortion to see in this a type of alliance of classes between the post-Tridentine church and the world of the common people.[61] In this direction Borromeo's contribution consists, as Alessandro Manzoni apprehended, in strengthening to such a point the sense of ecclesiastical dignity as to make the clergy capable of standing up to the ruling class—at least in the cases in which it did not consider allying itself with them more opportune.

The temporary suspension in the confrontations with the popular world as world of underprivileged did not signify, however, an opening toward the culture of the popular classes nor toward the forms of association in which that culture expressed itself. It is sufficient to glance at the *Acta ecclesiae mediolanensis* to find negative evaluations explicitly connected with the people's culture and mode of thinking: that of the "populace" is "an empty opinion" to which is counterposed what proceeds from an elevated and severe culture *(docte et graviter)*.[62] "Popular utterances" *(populares voces)* are expressions of inveterate customs to be expunged, of insensible resistance quite unmoved to the changes that the decrees want to introduce.[63] But if it is not possible here to go over in its many aspects the relationship between Carlo Borromeo and the forms of life and of organization of the laity, there is at least one point that must be recorded for its importance and for the reflections it renders: it involves the lay confraternities.

In the study of religious history the confraternities have not had the attention they deserve. The reasons for this lack of attention are many and in good part attributable to the affirmation of those relations of hierarchical subordination; by verticalizing, so to speak, the religious life within the institutions of the Catholic Church, these relations have placed in an awkward position forms of association and of piety of a different sort. The result is that we know little about the profound modifications that this type of organism underwent in the age of which we are now speaking. It is to be noted, however, that the relation between the resident bishops and reformers of that epoch and the confraternities was not one of the easiest: the documents are full of complaints and accusations about the forms of social life of the confraternities. The interventions of the ordinary ecclesiastical authority of this epoch were generally characterized as suspect and scarcely appreciated. The original creations on this level were those confraternities which in reality did not live independently from the parish. Rather they were conceived as instruments in the hands of the parish priest for all the tasks beyond his own resources or else at the most for guaranteeing automatic transmission of Tridentine forms of devotion and of elaborate ritual among the layfolk. Even Carlo Borromeo approached the matter thus: his principal cares will go to the confraternities of the Holy Sacrament and to the Schools of Christian Doctrine, while in the encounters with those more ancient ones of the Disciplinati he limited himself to fixing rules of a restrictive type that led them back under the strict control of the ordinary ecclesiastical authority and prevented possible conflicts with the parishes.

The fixed regulation established especially for the Schools of Christian Doctrine had an exemplary worth not only for Milan; on the other hand, even before Borromeo's coming to Milan, the Milanese company had encountered circumstances that had led to major modifications concerning the autonomy of the laity. The original name itself, which entitled the schools to "Christian reformation," had been omitted for fear that someone might hear in it the echoes of another and less tolerable reform. But there are at least two direct interventions of Carlo Borromeo concerning the confraternities that reward examination. One of these that all biographers record is that relative to the confraternity of San Giovanni Decollato, called "of the red establish-

ments." It involves a confraternity that in this epoch enjoyed great wealth
not limited to Milan and underwent in general a process of ennoblement.
Consequently, Borromeo, newly arrived in Milan, interested himself in it,
moved, as his biographers often tell, by their compassion for the high
number of those condemned to death who were the institutional object of
that confraternity's solicitude. The intervention of the archbishop pointed
above all in the direction of a vigorous revamping of the work of this
institution; instead, however, a subsequent intervention of the governor of
Milan (1589) led to a stricter tie of that confraternity with the urban political
authority and to a regulation of a fixed presence of noble brethren.[64] In
short, matters of penal justice belonged to the state and even the legitimate
powers that the confraternities were then justifiably assuming everywhere,
to a modest degree, now could not be exercised without political control.

The other intervention of Borromeo took an opposite tack from that
frequented by the civil authority; it concerned the company of the Disciplinati. For reasons of political control the governor had forbidden their
masked processions and had imposed particular restrictions for their assemblies (1574). But on the occasion of the plague in Milan the archbishop sent a
long and impassioned letter to the governor in which he lamented that the
public forms of mercy and penitence customarily furnished by the Disciplinati had been forbidden at a time like this, when it was more than ever
necessary to encourage the population with active and visible signs of self-
mortification and penitence.[65] Once more, in short, the archbishop did not
find himself in accord with prevailing attitudes and allowed himself to be
guided solely by concern with the salvation of souls.

*   *   *

These summary observations cannot exhaustively resolve the problems
posed by an activity of diocesan administration that was, if not long,
certainly of exceptional intensity and most broadly influential in a decisive
phase for the interpretation and implementation of the Tridentine decrees.
Regarding this activity we have sought to collect the positive aspects of the
matter, neglecting those signs of repression pertaining to alternative movements and tendencies, internal and external, which were present in Catholicism: these aspects were there, even if a diffuse ecumenicism makes it bad
taste to speak of them. Yet here one can record that the conquered or
minority tendencies of the religious world of the epoch would find in Carlo
Borromeo an adversary all the more decisive because of the strength of his
obsession with unity and discipline linked with his fear of the diabolic
presence in the world. These fears and these obsessions remained associated
with his name, above all after the tragic experience of the plague, which
contributed to make still darker the tones of his religious proposal. On
account of this it seems an empty terminological exercise to use for his work

that term, "reform," by which is suggested the tendencies of the first half of the century toward the general renewal of religion and of social life. Perhaps nothing of Borromeo's general proposals concerning religious life better reveals his predominant preoccupation with the looming menace of evils than that he proposes to escape the danger not by instituting a new complex model of church but rather by affirming a hard, daily asceticism: it is a rule that is applied as much to the clergy as to the laity. The pessimistic anthropology of Borromeo does not make exception of anyone: "Our nature, already wasted by sin, by itself is only bent to evil, which easily we allow and we are lost to doing right;[66] this warning pertains to "every condition of persons." Hence the obligation of ruling all daily acts under the general norm of self control and of asceticism: "Keep guard upon your heart. . . . When it promotes in you some vicious passion or evil thought, seek from the beginning to resist it. . . . Similarly be careful with your eyes . . . bridle your tongue, not saying all that comes into your mouth. . . . Remember that continually we are tempted and surrounded by demons."[67]

On this level nothing differentiates the ecclesiastical from the lay person; the admonitions turned upon the laity of the Milanese archdiocese are not different from those directed to the princes of the church.[68] Certainly this hard daily asceticism is not of the same sort as that which struck Max Weber in Calvinism, although it would not be difficult to find analogies between the two, for example, in the obsessive attention to the use of time and in the abolition of every playful or carnivalesque moment. From the general principle of the corruption of human nature, Carlo Borromeo obtained justification for the importance of the clergy as a select body of overseers for remedying the weakness of the faithful: "We have need of aids and stimuli for living well and against him who continually distracts us from it."[69] The hierarchy of Christian society, so frayed and motley colored in the pre-Tridentine age, had its own remote justification in the selection of diverse conditions of life as the attainment of a major or minor Christian perfection. In the interpretation of Carlo Borromeo the obligation for asceticism includes all the members of the church, lay and ecclesiastic, but the latter are indispensable as dogs are necessary if the flock is not to be dispersed. For the rest, if we remove the distinctions from the levels of authority, the differences are lost. Here and there along the fence that divides the laity from the ecclesiastics there are only individuals daily committed to the hard toil of the salvation of the soul—a toil in which they are dependent on any sort of help that may allow them to escape the principal danger: the freedom to decide for themselves.

Notes

1. P. Prodi, "Note sulla genesi del diritto nella Chiesa post-tridentina," in *Legge e Vangelo* (Brescia, 1972), p. 214.

2. On this passage from the image of Borromeo as model for bishops to model of individual asceticism and sanctity valid for all, cf. G. Alberigo, "Carlo Borromeo come modello di vescovo," *Rivista storica italiana* 74 (1967): 1031–52 and A. Turchini, *La fabbrica di un santo. Il processo di canonizzazione di Carlo Borromeo e la Controriforma* (Casale Monferrato, 1984).

3. Cf. P. Prodi, "Charles Borromée, Archevêque de Milan, et la Papauté," *Revue d'histoire ecclésiastique* 62 (1967): 379–411.

4. *S. Caroli Borromaei Homiliae nunc primum in lucem productae,* ed. J. A. Saxius (Milan; apud Marellum, 1747–48), 1:77.

5. *Homilae* 1:20; *Omelie e discorsi vari di S. Carlo Borromeo* (Milan, 1842), 4:241.

6. Letter to Niccolò Ormaneto, 3 February 1565, cited by Mario Bendiscoli, "Politica, amministrazione e religione nell'età dei Borromei," *Storia di Milano,* vol. 10 (Milan: Treccani, 1957), p. 202.

7. *Homiliae* 1:24.

8. *Homiliae* 1:28.

9. Ibid.

10. D. Maselli, *Saggi di storia ereticale lombarda al tempo di S. Carlo* (Naples 1979), p. 46.

11. "Utinam viveres! non hic Luterana putredo, non hic Zuvingliana pestis . . ." (*Homiliae* 3:115f.).

12. "Quam parum (haeretici) a nobis distant! Vix iter diei conficere possumus ac statim in speluncas incidimus rapacium luporum" (*Homiliae* 4:167).

13. . . . Ut a submersione eam (Christus) dignetur conservare, cum tot et tantis fluctibus agitetur" (*Homiliae* 1:53).

14. *Homiliae* 3:271.

15. *Homiliae* 3:121 (the Italian text in *Omelie e discorsi vari* 4:241). On Borromeo as preacher, see F. Barbieri, "La riforma dell'eloquenza sacra in Lombardia operata da s. Carlo Borromeo," *Archivio storico lombardo,* ser. 4, 15, (1911): 231–62 and to the studies mentioned by H. Jedin, *Carlo Borromeo* (Rome, 1971). On the relation between Carlo Borromeo and his episcopal models, cf. A. Dallaj, *Carlo Borromeo e il tema iconografico dei santi arcivescovi,* in *Culto dei santi, istituzioni e classi sociali in età preindustriale,* ed. S. Poesch Gajano and L. Sebastiani (L'Aquila and Rome, 1984), pp. 649–80.

16. *Homiliae* 2:313.

17. *Homiliae* 1:12.

18. E. Cattaneo, "Influenze veronesi nella legislazione di s. Carlo Borromeo," in *Problemi di vita religiosa in Italia nel Cinquecento* (Padua, 1960), pp. 123–66.

19. The letter of Valier to Borromeo of 1 May 1566 and Borromeo's reply have been published by L. Tacchella, *San Carlo Borromeo ed il card. Agostino Valier* (Verona, 1972), pp. 57, 94.

20. Carlo Bascapè, *Vita e opere di Carlo, Arcivescovo di Milano, Cardinale di S. Prassede* (Milan, 1965), lib. 7, cap. 17.

21. I refer to this proposal in my study on G. M. Giberti (*Tra evangelismo e controriforma, G. M. Giberti 1495–1543,* Rome, 1969).

22. Cattaneo, *Influenze veronesi,* p. 128 (letter of 18 August 1565).

23. Letter of T. Ferri to Sirleto, Milan, 17 October 1565, published by A. Sala, *Documenti circa la vita e le gesta di s. Carlo Borromeo,* vol. 1 (Milan, 1857), p. 576.

24. Letter of G. Poggiani to Carlo Borromeo, 21 December 1566, published ibid., p. 578.

25. *Homiliae* 2:170.

26. *Homiliae* 1:85.

27. *Memoriale ad milanesi di Carlo Borromeo,* ed. Giordano (Milan, 1965), p. 153.

28. "Desertae redderentur civitates, ac loca ubi homines simul conveniunt animalium pascua redderentur . . . et mulieribus plena essent monasteria" (*Homiliae* 2:56).

29. *Memoriale,* pp. 10–11.

30. Ibid., p. 150.

31. Cited by P. Prodi, "Nel quarto centenario della nascita di Federico Borromeo. Note biografiche e bibliografiche," *Convivium* 33 (1965): 349.

32. Letter of 16 February 1578 (*Aggiunta di una nuova raccolta di lettere del glorioso arcivescovo di Milano s. Carlo Borromeo cardinale di s. Prassede* [Lugano, per gli Agnelli, 1762] pp. 14–15).

33. Cf. Sala, *Documenti* 1:245 and *Aggiunta di una nuova raccolta di lettere,* pp. 14–15.

34. Letter to Cesare Speciano, 16 April 1579 (*Lettere del glorioso arcivescovo di Milano S. Carlo Borromeo cardinale di s. Prassede,* [Lugano, per gli Agnelli, 1762] p. 34).

35. "These want," wrote Borromeo to his agent, Cesare Speciano, "that their congregation depends on themselves and I desire that all stands at my will, wanting to create a fellowship of men ready at my every nod" (letter of 7 September 1577 to Cesare Speciano: the document was brought to my attention by Professor Marcocchi, whom I cordially thank).

36. Cf. D. Maselli, *Saggi di storia ereticale lombarda al tempo di s. Carlo* (Naples, 1979), pp. 106ff.

37. Constitution of don Giulio da Brescia of 18 November 1568 (Archivio di Stato di Siena Notarile antico, f. 2777). The evidence of the Brescian Benedictine, for which I owe the reference to Silvana Seidel Menchi, pertains to the group that assembled around Luciano degli Ottoni in the Benedictine monastery of Saint Benedetto Po di Mantova. On the religious ideas of this group, see my study, "Opere inedite o sconosciute di Giorgio Siculo," *La Bibliofilia* 1 (1985): 137–57.

38. Cf. O. Premoli, *Storia dei Barnabiti nel Cinquecento* (Rome, 1913); G. Zarri, "Le sante vive. Per una tipologia della pietà femminile nel primo Cinquecento," *Annali dell'Istituto storico italo-germanico in Trento* 6 (1980): 444f.

39. This and the phrase quoted above are taken from the manuscript of Besozzi, conserved in the archive of the Barnabites (cf. the heading "G. P. Besozzi," *Dizionario Biografico degli italiani* [1967], 9:680–84).

40. Prodi, "Charles Borromée," p. 383.

41. *Lettere del glorioso arcivescovo,* p. 10.

42. Gio. Pietro Giussano, *Vita di s. Carlo Borromeo,* (Milan: Motta, 1821), pp. 406–8.

43. Prodi, "Charles Borromée," p. 383.

44. *Lettere del glorioso arcivescovo,* p. 34.

45. ". . . Praecipuum . . . huius congregationis fundamentum, in exquisita ac plane perfecta erga ipsos Archiepiscopos ecclesiae Mediolanensis obedientia positum esse debet, ad Dei gloriam et animarum eiusdem ecclesiae salutem impense procurandam, adiuvandamque et promovendam" (*Acta Ecclesiae Mediolanensis a Carolo Card. S. Praxedis Archiepiscopo condita,* (Milan: apud Pontium, 1599), p. 828; to this edition of the *Acta* is prefaced a dedication of the congregation of the Oblates to Federico Borromeo).

46. *Acta Ecclesiae Mediolanensis,* p. 4.

47. *Acta Ecclesiae Mediolanensis,* p. 373.

48. *Acta Ecclesiae Mediolanensis,* p. 379.

49. P. Prodi, "San Carlo Borromeo e le trattative tra Gregorio XIII e Filippo II sulla giurisdizione ecclesiastica," *Rivista di storia della chiesa in Italia* 11 (1957): 201.

50. *Acta Ecclesiae Mediolanensis,* p. 57.

51. *Acta Ecclesiae Mediolanensis,* p. 141.

52. *Acta Ecclesiae Mediolanensis,* p. 142.

53. Letter of Cardinal Ercole Gonzaga to G. M. Giberti of 13 November 1537 (Bibl. Apostolica Vaticana, Barb. Lat. 5789, cc. 75r–78v; partially published in M. Firpo and D. Marcatto, *Il processo inquisitoriale del cardinal Giovanni Morone,* vol. 2, part I (Rome, 1984), p. 298.

54. *Acta Ecclesiae Mediolanensis,* p. 6.

55. John Bossy, "The Counter-Reformation and the People of Catholic Europe," *Past and Present* 47 (1970): 51–70.

56. *Acta Ecclesiae Mediolanensis,* p. 7. (". . . ubi (in ecclesia) si rectam baptismi formam servatam esse constiterit, ei (infanti) tantum ritus ac caeremoniae baptismi adhibeantur.")

57. Sala, *Documenti* 2:26.

58. Sala, *Documenti* 1:25.

59. *Homiliae* 3:201.

60. *Memoriale ai milanesi,* p. 10.

61. Cf. Danilo Zardin, *Riforma cattolica e resistenze nobiliari nella diocesi di Carlo Borromeo* (Milan, 1984).

62. *Acta Ecclesiae Mediolanensis,* p. 4.

63. *Acta Ecclesiae Mediolanensis,* p. 79.

64. Cf. on this institution the study of Serafino Biffi, *Sulle antiche carceri di Milano e del ducato milanese e sui sodalizi che vi assistevano i prigionieri ed i condannati a morte* (Milan, 1884); reprinted as "Politica, amministrazione e religione nell'età dei Borromei," *Storia di Milano,* vol. 10 (Milan: Treccani, 1957), p. 233; idem, "Vita sociale e culturale," Ibid., pp. 400f.

65. Sala, *Documenti,* 2:92; 3:662.

66. *Ricordi di Monsign. Illustriss. Borromeo, Cardinale di Santa Prassede, et Arcivescovo di Milano. Per il vivere christiano ad ogni stato di persone,* (Rome: Domenico Piolato, 1580), p. 3.

67. *Ricordi,* pp. 11–12.

68. Compare the *Ricordi* cited above with the *Epistola Caroli Cardinalis Boromei ad Andream Cardinalem Battoreum, de instituenda vitae ratione Principi Ecclesiastico convenienti* (Rome: Bart. Bonfadini, 1590).

69. *Ricordi,* p. 3.

Saint Charles Borromeo and the *Praecipuum Episcoporum Munus:* His Place in the History of Preaching

JOHN W. O'MALLEY, S.J.

SCHOLARS HAVE LONG RECOGNIZED CHARLES BORROMEO'S IMPORTANCE IN the history of preaching.[1] We possess ample documentation about his activity in the pulpit, about his insistence upon preaching as, in the words of the Council of Trent, the *praecipuum munus* of bishops and pastors, about his authorship of an important instruction concerning it, and about his encouragement of the publication and diffusion of several influential treatises on "ecclesiastical rhetoric." The careful studies of texts of Saint Charles related to preaching by Carlo Marcora and other contemporary scholars confirm his intense involvement in the enterprise. Of the fact, therefore, there is no doubt.

What has been lacking until quite recently, however, have been close analyses of the distinctive character of his contribution and a location of it in the more general history of sacred eloquence. Statements to the effect that he revived or reformed preaching and gave a new impetus to it in the post-Tridentine era, while true and often repeated, fail to indicate either the particular emphases that he promoted or the peculiar junction in the history of preaching in which his activities took place. The history of rhetoric in the postclassical period is, in fact, a relatively new discipline, and the history of sacred rhetoric even newer.[2] Along with the partisanship that has long characterized Counter-Reformation studies, this fact helps explain the generally eulogistic and uncritical nature of many of the assessments of Saint Charles and their detachment from a broader perspective.[3]

Three contemporary scholars have begun, however, to rectify this situation—Peter Bayley,[4] Frederick McGinness,[5] and Marc Fumaroli.[6] Fumaroli, in his massive and erudite study entitled *L'âge de l'éloquence* (1980), has especially inserted Saint Charles into the revival of enthusiasm for eloquence that began in the Italian Renaissance but was transformed and reached a certain culmination in the late sixteenth and the seventeenth centuries, particularly in Italy, Spain, and France. My present study of Saint Charles is profoundly indebted to Fumaroli's book, although originally begun independent of it. On the other hand, I approach Saint Charles with somewhat different concerns and, hence, will be able from another viewpoint to confirm many of Fumaroli's judgments, amplify upon a few of them, and in some instances make them even more emphatic. My particular focus will be the history of treatises on how to preach, the relationship between Saint Charles's theory and practice concerning the *praecipuum munus*, and, in general, the convergence of factors that assured for Saint Charles his unique position in this area of pastoral ministry, the public presentation of the Christian message.

First of all, then, a brief review of the history of treatises or instructions on how to preach.[7] Apart from Saint Augustine's *De doctrina christiana*, there were at the beginning of the sixteenth century no treatises in print on this subject besides the scholastic *Artes praedicandi*. Dissatisfaction with these manuals was, however, already widespread, and alternatives to their prescriptions in the actual practice of preaching have been substantially documented. Forms of the patristic or monastic homily had never died out and were in some quarters experiencing a revival. Moreover, especially in Italy, the principles of classical rhetoric were being applied to sacred eloquence in a way and to a degree hitherto unknown, even in Christian antiquity.[8]

In the early decades of the century, some attempts were made to theorize about new forms for the sermon, notably by Johann Reuchlin, Philipp Melanchthon, and a few others. Without any doubt, however, the great turning point in this development was Erasmus's *Ecclesiastes sive De ratione concionandi* of 1535.[9] That immense treatise, Erasmus's last major work and his longest, for the first time reviewed the whole history of Christian preaching and placed before contemporaries the biblical, patristic, and classical alternatives to the "thematic sermon" of the scholastics and the so-called penitential sermons of the mendicants. The importance of the work was immediately recognized, and within a decade it ran through ten editions, some authorized and some pirated.

But almost as immediately, the *Ecclesiastes* began to run into difficulties. Within a few years after its first appearance, it was criticized with some justification as "diffuse, prolix, and confused."[10] Something better organized, something indeed more practical was needed, but it would take a while for Erasmus to be digested and for alternatives to begin to appear. Only in the 1550s did Protestants like Andreas Hyperius (Gerard d'Ypres) (1553),[11] Niels Hemmingsen (1555),[12] and Niels Palladius (1556)[13] produce their treatises that set off the "golden age" of such works in the Protestant sector—more dependent perhaps upon Melanchthon than upon Erasmus.

Catholics were notably slower to produce effective and widely accepted alternatives to the *Ecclesiastes*. However, the placing of that work on the

"Index of Forbidden Books" in 1559 and the especially rigorous enforcement of the prohibition in Spain now made alternatives to Erasmus imperative. The scholastic method of preaching was by this time as emphatically rejected by Catholic theorists as by Protestant, despite the notable revival of scholastic theology during these years. It was thus that the 1570s came to mark the "golden age" of Roman Catholic treatises on the subject, the crucial decade that coincided with the central years of Charles Borromeo's activities as archbishop of Milan. These treatises symbolize the new and universally diffused enthusiasm for the ministry of the Word that would be a hallmark of the Counter-Reformation.

Now let me review a few well known facts about Saint Charles pertinent to this issue. In the first place, he had no formal theological training and therefore would not have been committed ahead of time to a scholastic theory of preaching that he would have been exposed to "in the schools." Indeed, his background was to a large extent humanistic (literature and law), and we can presume he shared the prejudice against scholastic preaching that was widespread in that environment and even beyond it. Moreover, the circle that he helped form as a young prelate in Rome, the *Noctes Vaticanae*, read and imitated classical and patristic authors, and during this period he underwent a religious conversion somehow related to the *Enchiridion* of Epictetus.[14]

During the sessions of the *Noctes*, various issues of Stoic philosophy were discussed. Also discussed and debated were the uses of the three classical *genera* of oratory—judicial, deliberative, and demonstrative, with a preference seemingly given to the deliberative because of its relationship to prudence and to other moral virtues.[15] This preference coincided in a general way with Erasmus's theory and, in part because of his influence, with that of some other theorists. The only oration certainly by Saint Charles to survive from this circle is in Italian and deals with the so-called Fourth Beatitude, "Blessed are they who hunger and thirst for justice."[16] Loosely demonstrative in its form, the oration is a panegyric of the virtue of justice in its several meanings and is moral rather than theological in its content. He does not deal, significantly enough, with the Pauline concept of "justitia."

Saint Charles was profoundly influenced by the Tridentine legislation pertaining to the episcopal office once he took up residence in Milan, and he gave special attention to its determination of preaching as the *praecipuum munus* of its ideal bishop.[17] That phrase was often on his lips and animated his various efforts to reduce the ideal to effective practice in himself and in other pastors of souls with whom he had contact.[18] It has escaped the notice of scholars, with the exception of McGinness, that among the few lines specifically devoted to the content of preaching in the Tridentine decree of 17 June 1546, is found a paraphrase of chapter 9 of the "Second Rule" of Saint Francis of Assisi, viz., that preaching concerns "virtues and vices, punish-

ment and reward."[19] This specification thus confirmed a moralistic emphasis
that characterized much preaching of the late Middle Ages and would help
extend it into the new era just beginning.[20]

The first, second, and fourth Provincial Synods of Milan under the presidency of Saint Charles touched on preaching in their various decrees, but
only after the fourth, 1576, did Borromeo issue in his own name his famous
and widely diffused "Instructiones praedicationis verbi Dei."[21] This was the
first, longest, and most influential of a series of such statements composed or
authorized at about the same time by other reforming bishops like Gabriele
Paleotti of Bologna[22] and Cornelio Musso of Bitonto, himself an important
preacher and a member of the commission at Trent that drafted the decree on
preaching.[23] Both these bishops quote the Franciscan Rule—not a surprise
from the Franciscan, Musso—and Paleotti actually structures his document
around it.

In his "Instructiones" Saint Charles quotes neither the "Rule" nor Trent's
paraphrase of it, but the content he proposes for sermons corresponds to it
in a generic way: sins, occasions of sin, virtues, and, finally, the sacraments
and other holy usages of the church.[24] His assessment of the situation of the
Christian audience as souls needing constant recall to the "way of the Lord,"
living as they do under incessant assault by the world and the devil, corresponds to his prescriptions about content.[25] This moralistic, vaguely Stoical,
framework stands in contrast to the doctrinal content concerning works-
faith, Law-Gospel, wrath-grace that Lutheran treatises insisted upon, and
also the more generally doctrinal and affective emphasis in preaching even in
other sectors of Catholicism, especially earlier in the sixteenth century.[26]

The moralistic viewpoint extends into the long section of the "Instructiones" that deals with the virtues and knowledge which are prerequisites for
the preacher of the Word of God.[27] The preacher must be convinced of the
truths he propounds and live according to them. Erasmus had given impetus
to such traditional considerations in the long first book of the *Ecclesiastes*.
Like that of Erasmus and others, Saint Charles's treatment of this issue can
be assessed as a slightly baptized version of the ethos that classical Roman
treatises on rhetoric insisted upon for the genuinely successful orator—"vir
bonus, dicendi peritus."

Admirable though that definition is from many viewpoints, it lacks an
important component. What is missing in Saint Charles, as well as in many
others who addressed the issue in the sixteenth century, is any developed
"theology of the Word" or "theology of the minister of the Word." We know
of Saint Charles's reverence for the Bible, and we know that he often read it
on his knees,[28] but indications of the suprahuman efficacy of the Word, or
suggestions that the task of the Christian preacher is therefore substantively
different from the task of the merely secular orator, receive scant attention in
his "Instructiones."[29]

He does prescribe a life-style for the preacher that sets him off from the laity, and he even advises him to eschew their ordinary company.[30] One might argue that in this fact recognition is given to the special character of the ministry and minister of the Word. But most obviously indicated here is rather a special, even narrow, ecclesiastical culture, segregated from general culture and thus presumably immune to its contaminations. A higher and distinctive level of virtue is required of the preacher, but the relationship of that virtue to the special energies inherent in the Word of God is only rarely suggested. Perhaps such considerations sounded too Lutheran; perhaps they were considered inappropriate in a document that was, after all, only an instruction, not a treatise; or, more likely, they never occurred to somebody with such a meager theological training, just as they seem to have been ignored even by theorists who had a better background in sacred learning.

Nonetheless, for all its limitations, the "Instructiones" alone would establish for Saint Charles a significant place in the history of post-Tridentine ministry. But that document is only the first such monument, supported by similar legislation he initiated for seminarians and for his Oblates of Saint Ambrose.[31] The second monument is the example he provided his contemporaries of a bishop indefatigable in the *praecipuum munus*. In this he resembled and followed the lead of his colleague, Paleotti of Bologna.

Despite a natural aversion for public speaking and despite a weak voice and a slurred speech pattern that often made him difficult to understand, Saint Charles eventually overcame his hesitancies and sometimes preached as often as three or four times a day, composing a new sermon for each occasion at those times.[32] No representative segment of his sermons was published until the eighteenth century, but the fact of his activity was well known to contemporaries and later generations and was incorporated into the canon of the post-Tridentine ideal of the bishop and conscientious pastor.[33]

Unlike his contemporaries, we are in a position to examine those sermons, principally from the last two years of his life, which have come down to us more or less intact and have been published. Hence, we can ask how his practice conformed to his instructions, and where his sermons were as spiritually and theologically barren as his directives to others suggest. As we read the sermons, we in fact experience a pleasant surprise.

There are, to be sure, some passages in the sermons that are drearily and disconcertingly moralistic in their exaggerated alarm over sometimes innocent pleasures. On 3 July 1583, for instance, he excoriates parents at length for allowing their children to spend so much time playing games; in their games they learn cupidity, the root of all evil, they learn to blaspheme, they waste time and neglect their religious duties.[34] In other sermons he decried what may have been more genuine problems, like indecent plays and obscene literature in circulation in Milan, but one is forced to wonder how objective his judgment was in such matters.[35] Everlasting torment in hell was the penalty for breaking the Lenten fast.[36] Moreover, he preached so consistently the respect due the clergy and the evil of any criticism of the church that we immediately perceive how an insistence on ecclesiastical order extirpated any impulse to prophetic criticism.[37] Finally, he gave special prominence to certain issues controverted by Protestants and explicitly reaffirmed by the Council of Trent, such as the necessity of good works, the superiority of virginity to marriage, the utility of indulgences, and the veneration of relics. In the history of Catholic preaching, an important shift in emphasis was beginning to take place.

Nonetheless, despite a pervasive moralism, the published sermons are relatively inspirational in their language and content, and they rest on a broad basis of the doctrines of Creation and Redemption. This positive teaching finds verification in his so-called "collations" to religious women. Along with a bleak picture of the dangers of the world coexists a presentation of the joys of religious life and of the especially intimate and satisfying relationship with the Lord that it provides.[38]

Even the sermons to general audiences, however, manifest an optimistic view of the spiritual capabilities of humankind, created by God and redeemed by Christ. The workings of grace in the redeemed are described sometimes as a process of deification and its results in peace and joy. Surely somewhat influenced by Trent's pronouncement on this issue, Saint Charles emphasized the role of human cooperation, but rather successfully avoided formulations that sound Pelagian or Semi-Pelagian.[39] In an impressive peroration on the feast of Saint Michael, 1583, he speaks of the dignity of human nature, redeemed and "kissed" by Christ, without any previous merits, and thus raised in excellence above even the angels.[40]

A word that he frequently employs to describe the contents of his sermons is *mysterium*. He thereby intimates the surpassing excellence as well as the transcendence of the message he propounds. Theological elucidations of the *mysteria* are few, it is true. Somewhat like the sacred orators of the papal court during the Renaissance, he contents himself with basic statements about doctrines like Creation and Redemption and then amplifies these by speaking about their significance for Christian behavior, attitudes, and affect. Saint Francis de Sales observed that Borromeo's theological knowledge was meager, but that it was sufficient for effective preaching.[41] The sermons I have examined would, in fact, tend to substantiate both aspects of that judgment.

A related feature of these sermons is their often liturgical starting point.[42] The feast of the day provides the context of the *mysterium,* and some parts of its liturgy provide its content. This means that the sermons tend as much to be as church related as Bible centered. It also sometimes means that Saint Charles begins with certain visual elements immediately perceived by his audience. A dramatic instance of this phenomenon occurs in his sermon in

Milan on the occasion of the death of the queen of Spain, for which he had an immense catafalque erected in the cathedral from which his eulogy took its exordium.[43]

The biblical texts of the liturgy, however, generally provide the starting point and the framework of the discourse. This raises the question of the rhetorical genre into which his sermons fall—a question not easily answered. We know from his activities in Rome, from the works of Cicero in his library, and from his contact with authors of "ecclesiastical rhetorics" that he was not isolated from this issue.[44] In a general way, many of the sermons can be described as homilies in that they are loose commentaries on a verse or passage from Scripture. They do, however, often evince features of "oratory" in the stricter sense, with clear exordia and perorations, and they are certainly marked with the effects of "secondary rhetoric" in their style and literary techniques. Fumaroli is correct in seeing the impact in these sermons of an anti-Ciceronianism, of a "severe ideal," deriving partly from Spanish theorists on preaching, and a desire to return to the simpler style of the Fathers, where the force of the sermon would derive more from its serious content (the *res*) than from elaborate and studied rhetorical techniques (the *verba*).[45] Nonetheless, they are quite different from sermons related to the scholastic and mendicant traditions and must be described, rather, as classicizing. Saint Charles explicitly legislated for his seminarians, in fact, that the lectures for them on sacred Scripture not be done "scholastico more," but according to a more humanistic or patristic methodology, "tamquam theologia positiva."[46] In his sermons the more directly scriptural and affective homily is often admixed with elements from the moralistic *genus deliberativum*, and even with the congratulatory *genus demonstrativum* (panegyric). Without being "masterpieces of pulpit eloquence," the sermons of Saint Charles are intelligent, straightforward, and appropriate for his audiences.

We thus finally arrive at a consideration of the theorists about preaching with whom Saint Charles had contact and whose works he promoted. His activity in this regard constitutes the third monument that established his position in the history of preaching. It came at a crucial and unprecedented moment, as I indicated earlier, and helped set Catholic preaching on a course that would have influence for centuries.

The first Catholic to react to Erasmus was the Spanish cleric Alfonso Zorrilla. He published in Rome in 1543 his *De sacris concionibus recte formandis formula* as a counterpiece to the *Ecclesiastes*.[47] The work had only one printing. It was an act of successful and outrageous plagiarism, principally from Lutheran authors like Melanchthon. Certainly influential in introducing some of Melanchthon's ideas into the Catholic tradition, it was sometimes cited later by orthodox authors. But, perhaps because of its radical nature, it did not inaugurate a trend.

The same can be said of four other works written in Italy in the 1560s that in one way or another dealt with pulpit eloquence: Cornelio Musso's *Discorso intorno all'artificio delle prediche* (1557),[48] Marcantonio Natta's *De christianorum eloquentia* (1562),[49] Luca Baglione's *L'arte del predicare* (1562),[50] and Benedetto Palmio's "De excellentia praedicationis evangelica."[51] The last work, it should be noted, was not published until 1969 but was intended for the eyes of Borromeo and is found in manuscript among his papers. None of these writings was theoretically comprehensive; none attracted wide readership.

It is from Spain, in fact, that books on "ecclesiastical rhetoric" in the strict sense really first derive.[52] After the early publication in 1541 of a book on rhetoric in Spanish for preachers by Miguel de Salinas,[53] the next to be published, in 1563, was the *De formandis sacris concionibus* by the Augustinian friar, Lorenzo de Villavicencio.[54] This work is heavily indebted to the treatise with the same title by the Lutheran, Hyperius. The problem has seemingly escaped the notice of some modern authors but was actually detected in Spain a few years after its publication.[55] The book did, however, have several subsequent printings. For whatever reasons, it did not attract the support of Saint Charles, and its influence was limited.

Besides the two short works on the subject of Andrés Sempere and Alonso de Orozco,[56] the next work of the genre, *De methodo concionandi*, was published at Alcalá (1570) by Alfonso Garciá Matamoros. Written expressly to supply contemporaries with a treatise on the subject of which the suppression of the *Ecclesiastes* had deprived them,[57] it is uncompromisingly dependent on the oratorical precepts of Cicero and Quintilian. This quality perhaps accounts for its limited circulation and the lack of interest Saint Charles showed in it. In 1573 Juan de Segovia published at Alcalá his *De praedicatione evangelica*, a work that also attracted little attention.[58]

This was the situation that prevailed during Saint Charles's first years in Milan. Trent had determined preaching as the *praecipuum munus* of bishops, and by extension, of all pastors, yet there was no received body of literature in existence corresponding to the *Artes praedicandi* produced by the medieval scholastics that told them how to go about it in a way which would satisfy the aesthetic and religious tastes of the day. In this context Saint Charles's importunities to his friend and fellow bishop, Agostino Valier (Valerio) of Verona, to produce a work on "ecclesiastical rhetoric" take on their immense significance. The treatise would be, for all practical purposes, a "first," dependent though it might be on the works that preceded it.

Valier's *De rhetorica ecclesiastica* was published in 1574 and reprinted some twenty-three times thereafter. This book must be immediately conjoined with the similar treatises published just two years later by the Spanish practitioners and theorists, Luis de Granada, a Dominican, and Diego de

Estella, a Franciscan.[59] These three books were characterized by their comprehensiveness, their easy intelligibility, their organizational clarity, and their grasp of both the classical and patristic traditions. In a different way, but along with Erasmus's *Ecclesiastes,* they mark a great watershed not only for the sixteenth century but for the entire history of preaching in the Roman Catholic Church. Like Valier's work, the two works from the Iberian peninsula ran through many editions, published on an international basis. The three together in effect determined the models for the great tradition of treatises on the subject that would mark the seventeenth century, but this fact does not detract from their importance in their own right.

Valier always maintained that he undertook his work only at the insistence of the archbishop of Milan and that Saint Charles was almost a coauthor of it.[60] Given the exaggerations of which the sixteenth century was capable, we might be inclined to dismiss these protestations as flattering, even obsequious, hyperbole. The evidence from the correspondence of Borromeo and his collaborators, however, only confirms Valier's assertions and gives them substance.

Beginning in 1572 the correspondence of Saint Charles with Valier is filled with comments on the drafts of the *Rhetoric* and suggestions for it.[61] He reviewed drafts himself and enlisted others like Pietro Galesino and the two Jesuits—Emmanuale Alvaro and Francesco Adorno—to make emendations. An important letter of Adorno to Valier survives that treats specifically of the book in its formative stages and communicates suggestions from Borromeo.[62] Even before the book was printed, Saint Charles had put a draft of it into use in his seminary.

When Diego de Estella and Luis de Granada published their rhetorics in 1576, Saint Charles was eager to receive copies. He incorporated verbatim a short section of Estella's work in his "Instructiones," and the Venice edition of the rhetoric (1584) was dedicated to him.[63] Saint Charles was even fonder of Luis de Granada, whose published sermons he had been reading for some time and eventually published in Milan for the use of his clergy. He was in personal contact with him through correspondence and through friends in the Iberian peninsula. In a letter of 10 July 1576, Saint Charles requested of a friend in Lisbon that he send him a copy of Granada's book as soon as possible.[64] It is surely due directly or indirectly to Saint Charles that the next year in Rome and the following year in Venice it was published in a single volume together with Valier's treatise.

The first attraction these Spanish texts had for Saint Charles was simply that they existed, filling a gap that had long been recognized. But their content and approach also would commend them. Estella's work was thoroughly Franciscan in the moral purpose it assigned to preaching, with chapter 9 of the "Second Rule" its obvious inspiration. Moreover, it proposed the patristic homily as the appropriate form for preaching, which by this time surely appealed immensely to Borromeo and corresponded in a general way to his own preaching style.[65] Granada's work was more oratorical, favoring the moralistic genus deliberativum, but was still "severe" and measured.[66] Moreover, from Granada's other works Saint Charles had already come to esteem and appropriate his theological learning. The pervasive Stoic undercurrent in Granada correlated with similar strains in Borromeo.[67]

Saint Charles's patronage in this sphere went even further. I have already mentioned the work on preaching by Palmio. In 1585, the year after Borromeo's death, Giovanni Botero, another of his collaborators, published his De praedicatore verbi Dei.[68] This effort to construct a "fully Christian rhetoric" explicitly owes its origins to Saint Charles's urgings and inspiration.[69] Not nearly so influential as the works of Valier, Granada, and Estella—it had only one printing—the De praedicatore is, nonetheless, another significant document in a tradition of "ecclesiastical rhetorics" that can justly be called "Borromean."

The final monument establishing Saint Charles's importance for preaching is his effort to bring to his archdiocese effective preachers for protracted periods of time and the example he thus set for other bishops.[70] The most famous of these was the Franciscan preacher and theorist, Francesco Panigarola, who preached the eulogy of Saint Charles at his funeral[71] and whom Tiraboschi describes in unqualified fashion as "il più eloquente predicatore che sia vissuta in quel secolo."[72] Saint Charles's efforts to bring Panigarola to Milan began as early as 1575, but they did not succeed until 1581, when Panigarola preached for a short while in the cathedral with great success.[73] In 1582 Panigarola returned to Milan after Lent, where he remained off and on even for several years after the death of Saint Charles on 4 November 1584. On 25 August of that year, he had sent to him a copy of his recently published Modo di comporre una predica.

In 1579 Saint Charles called Alfonso Lobo, another distinguished Franciscan, to his diocese.[74] Lobo is sometimes considered one of Panigarola's few contemporaries to rival his effectiveness in the pulpit. The Jesuit preachers Benedetto Palmio and Francesco Adorno also responded to Saint Charles's invitation to preach in the cathedral, and the saint's correspondence often indicates his other efforts to bring good preachers into his archdiocese.[75]

* * *

This brief review of Saint Charles's activities regarding various aspects of the ministry of the Word has only touched on issues and personages that deserve more ample study. Much more could be said, for example, about his relationship with the Oratorians and Barnabites in this regard. It is no exaggeration to affirm that a full volume on the subject could easily and profitably be written and that it would illuminate an aspect of the Counter-Reformation and general European culture that until now has received woefully inadequate study. I trust, however, that enough has been indicated here to establish with some detail as well as comprehensiveness his special place in the history of preaching. Fumaroli speaks of the Borromean "atelier" for preaching established at Milan.[76] If anything, that judgment is, in my opinion, too modest. It would be more adequate to the reality to speak of a huge "industry."

This industry consisted of at least four parts, any one of which would point to Saint Charles's importance: first, his "Instructiones" and the related documents; secondly, his example as a bishop who sought indefatigably to reduce the *praecipuum munus* of pastors to practice in his own direct ministry; thirdly, his encouragement of the publication of "ecclesiastical rhetorics" during the crucial years of that new literary genre; fourthly, his efforts to bring to Milan the best preachers of the day and thus share with them some of his already immense prestige.

It is true that other bishops of the period set a good example by their frequent preaching and by promoting in other ways good preaching in their dioceses—notably Gabriele Paleotti of Bologna, with whom Saint Charles was in close contact.[77] But none of these enjoyed the contemporary and posthumous fame of Borromeo. None of these was canonized. Moreover, not even around Paleotti did so many factors converge in such an eminent degree as they did around Saint Charles.

In the history of Christian preaching there have been some critical turning points. There was first of all the long patristic and monastic period, with the homilies of Origen and the *De doctrina christiana* as the most important documents. That tradition was not really challenged until the thirteenth century by the sermons of the scholastics and mendicants along with their correlative *Artes praedicandi*. The humanistic revival of classical oratory and patristic homiletics was in part a reaction to the scholastics and had a long gestation period. Erasmus's *Ecclesiastes* of 1535, along with his other works that dealt indirectly or in passing with preaching, signaled that another great change was in the making—a change which at first would touch only refined and well-educated circles, but that touched off a development which within a century would begin to reach down to more popular audiences. These impulses and scattered efforts were not marshaled, in other words, until the late sixteenth century. Many people collaborated in organizing these impulses and efforts into an effective and more or less coherent program. The new religious orders would be especially important. But without any doubt Saint Charles is a figure who centered these impulses and efforts. No matter what aspect of this phenomenon one investigates, the saint's name appears at every critical juncture. He is a major figure and a chief promotor of that extraordinary enthusiasm for the ministry of the Word in the sixteenth century which, as I said earlier, was just as characteristic of Catholicism as it was of Protestantism, although often not recognized as such.

To be sure, Borromeo's activities in this regard suffer from limitations, and any assessment of them that fails to take these limitations into account would be unbalanced. Although in his own preaching the strongly moralistic tendencies that he explicitly espoused were tempered by a message with a doctrinal and devotional base, he doubtless promoted such tendencies, which were already strong and even canonized by Trent in its decree of 17 June 1546. He thus reflected and helped confirm the assumption, not shared by many Protestants, that preaching was largely moralistic and behavioristic in its aims.

His own culture was broad, but his espousal of a special clerical culture, distinct from general culture and even inimical to it, doubtless worked harm on future generations that did not enjoy the benefits of good family and broad personal contacts as he did. He often focused on ecclesiastical traditions in his preaching, without much historical or even theological perspective on them, and his insistence on church order suppressed an important and traditional aspect of preaching.

These and other limitations are serious. They tarnish the luster of his achievements. Nonetheless, there is no doubt that Charles Borromeo enjoys a place in this critical period in the history of preaching that no other single figure—Catholic or Protestant—enjoys. For the reasons I have adduced, his place is unique and pivotal.

In closing, I can do no better than quote Fumaroli's summary of the achievement of Saint Charles and his generation: ". . . [after the close of the Council of Trent], a veritable 'rhetoric workshop' opened in Spain and Italy, more productive than any of the schools of the ancient Sophists or any humanist Academy. . . . One can also rest assured that no humanist orator, not even the Chancellors of the Florentine Republic, had either the authority or the immediate audience of a Charles Borromeo, heir and imitator of Ambrose in the archiepiscopal see of Milan."[78]

Notes

1. See Herman J. Heuser, "Saint Charles Borromeo as a Preacher," *The American Ecclesiastical Review* 7 (1892): 332–40; Joseph M. Connors, "Saint Charles Borromeo in the Homiletic Tradition," ibid. 138 (1958): 9–23; Federico Barbieri, "La riforma dell'eloquenza sacra in Lombardia operata da San Carlo Borromeo," *Archivio Storico Lombardo*, ser. 4, 15 (1911): 231–62; Angelo Novelli, "S. Carlo Borromeo, oratore sacro," *La Scuola Cattolica* 38 (1910): 108–36; 63 (1935): 313–22; Germano Carboni, "S. Carlo e l'eloquenza sacra," ibid. 57 (1929): 270–90; Balthasar Fisher, "Predigtgrundsätze des hl. Carl Borromäus," *Trierer theologische Zeitschrift* 61 (1952): 213–21; Roger Mols, "Saint Charles Borromée, pionnier de la pastorale moderne," *Nouvelle Revue Théologique* 79 (1957): 600–622, 715–47, esp. 728–34; Carlo Marcora, "La 'Sylva pastoralis' di S. Carlo Borromeo," *Memorie Storiche della*

Diocesi di Milano 12 (1965): 13–98, and Marcora, ed., *Arbores de Paschate* (Milan: Biblioteca Ambrosiana, 1984). Saint Charles is often treated, however, in more general works on preaching in a cursory fashion. See, e.g., Yngve Brilioth, *A Brief History of Preaching,* trans. Karl E. Mattson (Philadelphia: Fortress Press, 1965), p. 143; Emilio Santini, *L'eloquenza italiana dal Concilio Tridentino ai nostri giorni* (Milan: R. Sandron, 1923–28), 1:30; Ernesto Vercesi and Emilio Santini, *L'eloquenza dal sec. XVII ai nostri giorni* (Milan: F. Vallardi, 1938), pp. 14–16; Johann Baptist Schneyer, *Geschichte der katholischen Predigt* (Freiburg: Seelsorge, 1969), pp. 249–50; Werner Schütz, *Geschichte der christlichen Predigt* (Berlin: W. de Gruyter, 1972), pp. 111–12.

2. See, e.g., the comments by James J. Murphy, "One Thousand Neglected Authors: The Scope and Importance of Renaissance Eloquence," in *Renaissance Eloquence,* ed. James J. Murphy (Berkeley and Los Angeles: University of California Press, 1983), pp. 20–36, and my own "Content and Rhetorical Forms in Sixteenth-Century Treatises on Preaching," ibid., pp. 238–52. See also my "Erasmus and the History of Sacred Rhetoric: The *Ecclesiastes* of 1535," *Erasmus of Rotterdam Society Yearbook* 5 (1985): 1–29, and "Luther the Preacher" in *The Martin Luther Quincentennial,* ed. G. Dünnhaupt (Detroit, Mich.: Wayne State University Press, 1984), pp. 3–16.

3. On the present state of Counter-Reformation studies, see my "Catholic Reform," in *Reformation Europe: A Guide to Research,* ed. Steven Ozment (Saint Louis: Center for Reformation Research, 1982), pp. 297–319, and especially the volume under my editorship, *Catholicism in Early Modern History: A Guide to Research* (St. Louis, 1987).

4. See his "Les Sermons de Jean-Pierre Camus et l'esthétique borroméenne," in *Critique et création litteraire en France au XVIIᵉ siècle,* ed. Marc Fumaroli (Paris: CNRS, 1977), pp. 93–98; *French Pulpit Oratory, 1598–1650* (Cambridge: Cambridge University Press, 1980); *Selected Sermons of the French Baroque (1600–1650)* (New York: Garland Publishing Company, 1983).

5. See his *Rhetoric and Counter-Reformation Rome: Sacred Oratory and the Construction of the Catholic World View, 1563–1621* (Ann Arbor, Mich.: University Microfilms International, 1982); "Preaching Ideals and Practice in Counter-Reformation Rome," *The Sixteenth Century Journal* 11, no. 2 (1980): 109–27; "The Rhetoric of Praise and the New Rome of the Counter Reformation," in *Rome in the Renaissance: The City and the Myth,* ed. P. A. Ramsey (Binghamton, N.Y.: Center for Medieval and Early Renaissance Studies, 1982), pp. 355–70.

6. See especially his *L'âge de l'éloquence: Rhétorique et "res literaria" de la Renaissance au seuil de l'époque classique* (Geneva: Droz, 1980).

7. See my studies cited above in note 2.

8. See, e.g., my *Praise and Blame in Renaissance Rome: Rhetoric, Doctrine, and Reform in the Sacred Orators of the Papal Court, c. 1450–1521* (Durham, N.C.: Duke University Press, 1979), and the articles by John M. McManamon, "The Ideal Renaissance Pope: Funeral Oratory from the Papal Court," *Archivum Historiae Pontificiae* 14 (1976): 9–70; "Renaissance Preaching: Theory and Practice. A Holy Thursday Sermon of Aurelio Brandolini," *Viator* 10 (1979): 355–73; "Innovation in Early Humanistic Rhetoric: The Oratory of Pier Paolo Vergerio the Elder," *Rinascimento* 22 (1982): 3–32.

9. See especially my "Erasmus and the History of Rhetoric."

10. This criticism came from the Spanish cleric Alfonso Zorrilla in 1543. On his curious book, see my "Lutheranism in Rome, 1542–43: The Treatise by Alfonso

Zorrilla," *Thought* 54 (1979): 262–73, now reprinted in my *Rome and the Renaissance: Studies in Culture and Religion* (London: Variorum Reprints, 1981), 10.

11. *De formandis concionibus sacris* (Marburg: A. Colbius, 1553). On him, see John S. Chamberlin, *Increase and Multiply: Arts-of-Discourse Procedures in the Preaching of Donne* (Chapel Hill: University of North Carolina Press, 1976).

12. *De methodis libri duo . . . posterior Ecclesiastes, sive methodum theologicam interpretandi concionandique continet* (Rostock, 155); I consulted a subsequent edition (Wittenberg: J. Crato, 1559).

13. *Concionator, seu Regulae quaedam utiles ac necessariae concionatoribus observandae* (Copenhagen, 1556).

14. See, especially, *Noctes Vaticanae, seu Sermones habiti in Academia a s. Carlo Borromeo*, ed. Giuseppe Antonio Sassi (Milan: Bibliotheca Ambrosiana, 1748), and Luigi F. Berra, *L'Accademia delle Notti Vaticanae fondata da San Carlo Borromeo* (Rome: M. Bretschneider, 1915).

15. See, Biblioteca Apostolica Vaticana, cod. Ottob. lat. 2429, pt. 1, fols. 3–7, "Della causa deliberativa."

16. Published in Sassi, *Noctes Vaticanae*, pp. 74–116.

17. On the episcopal ideal, see especially Hubert Jedin, *Il tipo ideale di vescovo secondo la riforma cattolica* (Brescia: Morcelliana, 1950); Giuseppe Alberigo, "Carlo Borromeo come modello di vescovo nella Chiesa post-tridentina," *Rivista Storica Italiana* 79 (1967): 1031–52; Massimo Petrocchi, "L''ideal del vescovo' nel Panigarola," *Rivista di Storia della Chiesa in Italia* 8 (1954): 93–95. As background, see also M. Piton, "L'idéal épiscopale selon les prédicateurs français de la fin du XVe siècle et du debut du XVIe," *Revue d'Histoire Ecclésiastique* 61 (1966): 77–118, 393–423.

18. See, e.g., the solemn exordium to his "Instructiones praedicationis verbi Dei," in *Acta Ecclesiae Mediolanensis*, ed. Achille Ratti (Milan: Typographia Pontificia Sancti Josephi, 1890–97), 2:1207; decrees of First Provincial Synod, 1565, ibid., col. 32; *Homiliae nunc primum e mss. codicibus Bibliothecae Ambrosianae in lucem productae*, ed. Giuseppe Antonio Sassi (Milan: Bibliothecae Ambrosiana, 1747–48), 1:106, 238.

19. See *Conciliorum Oecumenicorum Decreta*, ed. Giuseppe Alberigo, et al., 2d ed. (Freiburg im Breisgau: Herder, 1962), p. 645: ". . . annuntiando eis cum brevitate et facilitate sermonis vitia, quae eos declinare, et virtutes, quas sectari oporteat, ut poenam aeternam evadere et coelestem gloriam consequi valeant." The quotation conforms verbatim to the "Rule" in the earlier version of the decree, 13 April 1546. Cf. the "Rule" in *Seraphicae Legislationis Textus Originales* (Quaracchi: Collegium S. Bonaventurae, 1897), p. 44: ". . . annuntiando eis vitia et virtutes, poenam et gloriam, cum brevitate sermonis, ..." The relationship to the "Rule" is noted and given its due importance by McGinness, *Rhetoric and Counter-Reformation Rome*, p. 164, but barely suggested by Arsenio d'Ascoli, *La predicazione dei Cappuccini nel Cinquecento in Italia* (Loreto: Libreria "S. Francesco d'Assisi," 1956), p. 66. On the decree, see also the following authors, who do not mention this Franciscan element: Johann Ev. Rainer, "Entstehungsgeschichte des Trienter Predigtreformdekrets," *Zeitschrift für katholische Theologie* 39 (1915): 256–317, 465–523; A. Larios, "La reforma de la predicación en Trento (Historia y contenido de un decreto)," *Communio* 6 (1973): 223–83; Hubert Jedin, *A History of the Council of Trent*, trans. Ernest Graf (London: Thomas Nelson and Sons, 1957–61), 2:99–124. We can infer, although there seems to be no direct evidence for it, that Cornelio Musso was the person most responsible for this element in the decree. Authors who have studied him do not mention this possibility: Hubert Jedin, "Der Franziskaner Cornelio

Musso, Bischof von Bitonto," *Römische Quartalschrift* 41 (1933): 207–75; G. Cantini, "Cornelio Musso, O.F.M., Conv., predicatore, scrittore e teologo al Concilio di Trento," *Miscellanea Francescana* 41 (1941): 146–74, 424–63; Roger J. Bartman, "Cornelio Musso, Tridentine Theologian and Orator," *Franciscan Studies* 5 (1945): 247–76; Giovanni Odoardi, "Fra Cornelio Musso, O.F.M., Conv., padre, oratore et teologo al Concilio di Trento," *Miscellanea Francescana* 48 (1948): 223–42, 450–78; 49 (1949): 36–71.

20. See, e.g., the thoughtful article by Zelinda Zafarana, "Bernardino nella storia della predicazione popolare," in *Bernardino predicatore nella società del suo tempo*, Convegni del Centro di Studi sulla Spiritualità Medievale, no. 16 (Todi: Accademia Tuderina, 1976), pp. 41–70.

21. The Instruction is found in *Acta Ecclesiae Mediolanensis* 2:1205–48. It was reprinted many times after its first publication.

22. *Istruttione di Monsig. Illustrissimo et Reverendissimo Card. Paleotti* (Bologna: A. Benacci, 1586), first published in 1578. On Paleotti, see Paolo Prodi, *Il cardinale Gabriele Paleotti (1522–1597)* (Rome: Edizioni di Storia e Letteratura, 1959–67), especially 2:75–136.

23. The section on preaching comes towards the end of *Synodus Bituntina Rmi. Patris F. Cornelii Mussi Episcopi Bituntini, totam fere ecclesiasticam disciplinam . . . complectens* (Venice: apud Iolitos, 1579). See n. 18 above for bibliography on Musso.

24. See "Instructiones," cols. 1230–43; *Homiliae* 2:48–49, 418; decrees of First Provincial Synod, 1565, *Acta Ecclesiae Mediolanensis* 2:35; decrees of Fourth Provincial Synod, 1576, ibid., 336.

25. See "Instructiones," col. 1215: ". . . videbit [concionator] diligenter, quanta, et quam summa difficultate ei proponitur, qui in tanta, tamquam perpetua et mundi et Satanae oppugnatione fidelium animas ad viam Domini revocare contendit." See also *Homiliae* 2:15, ". . . ut homines beluarum more vitam ducentes, ad Evangelicam vitam tam numerose converteret. . . ."

26. See, e.g., my *Praise and Blame*, pp. 123–64.

27. See "Instructiones," cols. 1207–15.

28. See, e.g., Agostino Valier, *Vita Caroli Borromei* (Verona: H. Discipulus, 1586), p. 48.

29. There is a suggestion of such a theology, "Instructiones," col. 1215: "Deinde se, qui praedicationis munus aggreditur, ministrum esse, per quem verbum Dei ab ipso divini Spiritus fonte ducitur ad fidelium animas divinitus irrigandas." See also ibid., col. 1217. See also *Homiliae* 1:108–9; 2:23–24, 70; decrees of Fifth Provincial Synod, 1579, *Acta Ecclesiae Mediolanensis* 2:523–24.

30. See "Instructiones," especially cols. 1217, 1228–29; *Homiliae* 2:159, ". . . ut Deo tantum [clerici] vacantes cum Deo loquantur, cum sanctis versentur, in Ecclesiis permaneant, sacris lectionibus et studiis tempus consumant; . . . ideo nec a vobis [laicis] sunt importune perturbandi"; *Discorsi inediti di S. Carlo Borromeo*, ed. Carlo Marcora (Milan: Pro Istituto pei Figli della Providenza, 1965), pp. 101–10. See also Enrico Cattaneo, "La santità sacerdotale vissuta da San Carlo," *La Scuola Cattolica* 93 (1965): 405–26, and Giovanni Moioli, "Temi di spiritualità episcopale e sacerdotale in S. Carlo Borromeo," ibid., pp. 459–88.

31. See "Institutionum ad oblatos Sancti Ambrosii pertinentium epitome," in *Acta Ecclesiae Mediolanensis* 3:49–90, and "Institutiones ad universum seminarii regimen pertinentes," ibid., cols. 93–146.

32. His contemporaries frequently speak of these problems and of his hesitancies. See, e.g., Valier, *Vita*, pp. 10, 29; Carlo Bascapè, *De vita et rebus gestis Caroli S. R. E. cardinalis* (Ingolstadt: D. Sartorius, 1592), pp. 329, 333; Giovan Battista

Possevino, *Discorsi della vita et attioni di Carlo Borromeo* (Rome: J. Tornerius, 1591), pp. 45–46; Giovanni Botero, *De praedicatore verbi Dei* (Paris: G. Chaudière, 1585), sig. a ii; Francesco Panigarola, *Il predicatore* (Venice: B. Giunti, G. B. Ciotti, 1609), 1:39.

33. The first major collection of his sermons to be published was *Sermoni familiari di s. Carlo Borromeo*, ed. Gaetano Volpi (Padua: G. Comino, 1720), followed by the five volumes by Sassi, *Homiliae* (1747–48). Other major collections of his sermons, orations, and other religious discourses are: *Discorsi inediti*, ed. Marcora; *Ammaestramenti di S. Carlo Borromeo alle persone religiose* (Milan: Arte Sacra, 1902); *Vingt discours de saint Charles Borromée à des religieuses* (Roulers: J. de Meester, 1910); *Saint Charles Borromée: Homélies, Sermons et Entretiens*, ed. J. B. Gaï (Namur: Soleil Levant, 1961); *Sancti Caroli Borromaei Orationes XII*, ed. Angelo Paredi (Rome and Milan: G. Campi, 1963). The contents of these collections overlap; those edited by Sassi and Marcora are fundamental. Ten volumes of autograph sketches or outlines of sermons survive, principally in the Biblioteca Ambrosiana; see Marcora, *Discorsi*, pp. 9–11.

34. See *Homiliae* 1:392–94. See also ibid. 2:7.

35. See, e.g., ibid. 2:101, 151. See also Carlo Borromeo, *Veri sentimenti di san Carlo Borromeo intorno al teatro* (Rome: G. Zempel, 1753), and idem, *Opusculum de choreis et spectaculis in festis diebus non exhibendis* (Rome: Fratres Palearinos, 1753).

36. See *Homiliae* 2:315–16.

37. See, e.g., ibid. 1:53–54, 88–89, 303; 3:151–52; *Discorsi inediti*, pp. 101–10.

38. The basic collection is still in Sassi, *Homiliae* 5:191–350, in Italian. See also ibid. 2:121–34; 3:58–70.

39. See, e.g., *Homiliae* 1:74–79, 108–16, 239; 2:250; 3:450; *Discorsi inediti*, pp. 55–63, 127–34, 185–89.

40. See *Homiliae* 3:17–19.

41. See his letter to André Frémyot, 5 October 1604, in *Oeuvres de saint François de Sales* (Annecy: J. Niérat [etc.], 1892–1932), 12:301: "Quant a la doctrine, il faut qu'elle soit suffisante, et n'est pas requis qu'elle soit excellente. . . . et en nostre aage, le bienheureux Cardinal Borromee n'avoit de science que bien fort mediocrement: toutefois il faisoit merveilles." This letter is sometimes designated Saint Francis's "Traitté de la prédication." See also his letter to Antoine de Revol, 3 June 1603, ibid., p. 189: "Ayés, je vous prie, Grenade tout entier, et que ce soit vostre second breviaire; le Cardinal Borromee n'avoit point d'autre theologie pour prescher que cella la, et neanmoins il preschoit tres bien." On the relationship between Saint Charles and Saint Francis, see Paul Broutin, "Les deux grands évêques de la réforme catholique," *Nouvelle Revue Théologique* 85 (1953): 282–99, 380–98. Jean-Pierre Camus described Saint Charles as "un pauvre prédicateur selon le jugement ordinaire du monde," in *Homélies panégiriques de sainct [sic] Charles Borromée* (Paris: C. Chappelet, 1623), p. 142.

42. See decrees of Third Provincial Synod, 1573, *Acta Ecclesiae Mediolanensis* 2:235–36, and Fisher, "Predigtgrundsätze," pp. 216–17.

43. "Concio in funere regina[e] Hispaniarum [Anne of Austria]," 6 September 1581, in *Acta Ecclesiae Mediolanensis* 3:825–40. For a description of the event, see Giovanni Pietro Giussano (Glussianus), *De vita et rebus gestis sancti Caroli Borromei* (Milan: Bibliotheca Ambrosiana, 1751), cols. 591–92.

44. See Orazio Premoli, "S. Carlo Borromeo e la cultura classica," *La Scuola Cattolica* 45 (1917): 427–40.

45. *L'âge de l'éloquence*, especially pp. 116–52.

46. See "Institutiones ad universum seminarii regimen pertinentes," in *Acta Ecclesiae Mediolanensis* 3:100.

47. See n. 10 above.

48. (Venice: Aldus, 1557).

49. (Venice: Aldus, 1562), not really a treatise on preaching.

50. (Venice: A. Trevisano, 1562).

51. Published by Carlo Marcora, "S. Carlo e il gesuita Benedetto Palmio," *Memorie Storiche della Diocesi di Milano* 16 (1969): 7–53. On this edition, see Mario Scaduto, *L'epoca di Giacomo Lainez* (Rome: Edizioni "La Civiltà Cattolica," 1964–74), 2:514–15, n. 3.

52. The most complete and systematic treatment of this phenomenon is by Antoni Cañizares Llovera, "La predicación española en el siglo XVI," in *Repertorio de Historia de las Ciencias Eclesiásticas en España (Siglos I–XVI)*, vol. 6 (Salamanca: Instituto de Historia de la Theologia Española, 1977), pp. 189–266, with bibliography. See also Melquiades Andrés, "Humanismo español y ciencias eclesiásticas (1450–1565)," ibid., pp. 111–42. Also important are José Rico Verdu, *La retórica española de los siglos XVI y XVII* (Madrid: Consejo Superior de Investigaciones Científicas, 1973); Antonio M. Martí, "La retórica sacra en el Siglo de Oro," *Hispanic Review* 38 (1970): 264–98; Felix G. Olmeda, ed., *Fray Dionisio Vázquez, O.S.A. (1479–1539): Sermones* (Madrid: Espasa-Calpe, 1943), especially the "Prólogo."

53. On Salinas, see Martí, "Retórica sacra," pp. 280–81, and Verdu, *Retórica española*, pp. 195–99.

54. The edition I consulted was (Cologne: A. Birckmannus, 1575).

55. Bayley states that Villavicencio's work is an "adaptation" of Hyperius, *French Oratory*, p. 61. The problem is not noted by Fumaroli, *L'âge de l'éloquence*, pp. 127–28, or by David Gutiérrez, "De fratribus Laurentio de Villavicentio et Bartholomaeo de los Rios curriculum et documenta," *Analecta Augustiniana* 23 (1953–54): 102–21. The possibility that Lorenzo copied his *De studio theologico* from Hyperius is peremptorily and uncritically rejected by Segundo Folgada Flórez, "Fray Lorenzo de Villavicencio y los estudios teologicos," *La Ciudad de Dios* 177 (1964): 335–44. H. Hurter notes that Lorenzo's *De studio* is copied for the most part from Hyperius, *Nomenclator Literarius Theologiae Catholicae*, 3d ed. (Innsbruck: Libraria Academica Wagneriana, 1907), 3:61n.

56. Sempere, *Methodus oratoria, item de sacra ratione concionandi libellus* (Valencia, 1568), and Orozco, "Epistola X para un religioso predicator," in *Segunda parte de las Obras* (Alcalá, 1570). Orozco also wrote a "Methodus praedicationis" that was never published but is found in manuscript at Valladolid; see Llovera, "Predicación española," pp. 201–2. On Sempere, see Adrián Miró, *El humanista Andrés Sempere: Vida y obra* (Alcoy: La Victoria, 1968), especially pp. 95–100.

57. See his *Opera omnia* (Madrid: A Ramírez, 1769), pp. 436–37. See also my "Content and Rhetorical Forms," pp. 250–51. Also to be noted is Benito Arias Montano, *Rhetoricorum libri III* (Antwerp: C. Plantinus, 1569), written in verse, intended to some extent for preachers. See Martí, "Retórica sacra," pp. 283–85, and Verdu, *Retórica española*, pp. 80–86.

58. See Llovera, "Predicación española," pp. 203–4.

59. Granada, *Ecclesiasticae rhetoricae, sive De ratione concionandi* (Lisbon: A. Riberius, 1576); de Estella, *Modo de predicar y Modus concionandi: Estudio doctrinal y edicion critica*, ed. Pio Sagües Azcona (Madrid: Instituto M. de Cervantes, 1951), done for the most part from the first edition Salamanca, 1576. On these figures, see Llovera, "Predicación española," pp. 199–201, 204–7; Fumaroli,

L'âge de l'éloquence, pp. 143–48; E. Allison Peers, *Studies of the Spanish Mystics* (London: S.P.C.K., 1951–60), 1:25–61, 2:171–94; the pertinent articles ("Estella," "Louis de Grenade") in the *Dictionnaire de spiritualité,* with bibliography.

60. See, e.g., his comments in *Praelectiones tres ab Augustino Valerio,* ed. Giovanni Antonio Possevino (Verona, 1574), sig. B4: "Filii, hoc opus cum erit perfectum, si Cardinalis Borromei opus esse existimabitis; . . . si meum putabitis, quid illud delineaverim, ex patris vestri industria et labore aliquot fructus percipietis."

61. See especially the collection of letters edited by Lorenzo Tacchella, *San Carlo Borromeo ed il Card. Agostino Valier (carteggio)* (Verona: Istituo per gli Studi Storici Veronese, 1972). Valier also wrote a "synopsis" of the book and then, at Saint Charles's insistence, composed a homilary.

62. See *Lettera del padre Francesco Adorno . . . a monsignore Agostino Valiero,* ed. Pietro Bettio (Venice: G. Picotti, 1829), dated 4 May 1572. Valier's undated reply is also printed in this edition.

63. See Azcona's comments in his edition, *Modo de predicar* 1:259.

64. See Alvaro Huerga, "Fray Luis de Granada y San Carlos Borromeo: Una amistad al servicio de la Restauración Católica," *Hispania Sacra* 11 (1958): 299–347, especially p. 344 for the letter of 10 July 1576. See also Ramon Robres Luch, "San Carlos Borromeo y sus relaciones con el episcopado iberico posttridentino, especialmente a través de Fray Luis de Granada y san Juan de Ribera," *Anthologia Annua* 8 (1960): 83–141, and, on a more general level, Benedetto Croce, *I predicatori italiani del Seicento e il gusto spagnuolo* (Naples: Pierro e Veraldi, 1899).

65. See my "Content and Rhetorical Forms," pp. 248–49.

66. See ibid., p. 249; Tacchella, *Borromeo e Valier,* p. 104; Fumaroli, *L'âge de l'éloquence,* pp. 137–40, 143–48.

67. On this issue, see, e.g., M.-J. González-Haba, "Séneca en la espiritualidad española de los siglos XVI y XVII," *Revista de Filosofía* 11 (1952): 287–302; Julien Eymard d'Angers, "Les citations de Sénèque dans les sermons de Luis de Grenade," *Revue d'Ascetique et Mystique* 37 (1961): 31–46; Marcel Bataillon, "De Savonarole à Luis de Granada," *Revue de Litterature Comparée* 16 (1936): 23–39. For more general studies, see Michel Spanneut, *Le permanence du Stoïcisme, De Zénon à Malraux* (Gembloux: Duclot, 1973); Leontine Zanta, *La renaissance du Stoïcisme au XVIᵉ siècle* (Paris: H. Champion, 1914); Antoine Adam, *Sur le problème religieux dans la première moitié du XVIIᵉ siècle* (Oxford: Clarendon Press, 1959); William J. Bouwsma, "The Two Faces of Humanism: Stoicism and Augustinianism in Renaissance Thought," in *Itinerarium Italicum: The Profile of the Italian Renaissance in the Mirror of its European Transformations,* ed. Heiko A. Oberman with Thomas A. Brady, Jr. (Leiden: E. J. Brill, 1975), pp. 3–60; Alphonse Dupront, "D'un 'humanisme chrétien' en Italie à la fin du XVIᵉ siècle," *Revue Historique* 175 (1935): 296–307.

68. (Paris: G. Chaudière, 1585).

69. See the dedicatory letter to Vincentius Laurus, ibid.

70. See his letter to Paleotti on this subject, transcribed by Prodi, *Paleotti* 2:91–93.

71. *Oratione di Fr. Francesco Panigarola in morte e sopra il corpo dell'Ill.mo. Carlo Borromeo* (Venice: De Imberti, 1585), many times reprinted.

72. Girolamo Tiraboschi, *Storia della letteratura italiana,* (Milan: N. Bettoni, 1833), 4:322.

73. See Paolo-Maria Sevesi, "S. Carlo Borromeo ed il P. Francesco Panigarola,

O.F.M.," *Archivum Franciscanum Historicum* 40 (1947): 143–207. See also Bascapè, *Vita,* p. 64.

74. On Lobo (Lupus), see *Annales Minorum seu Trium Ordinum a S. Francisco Institutorum,* ed. Stanislaus Melchiorri de Cerreto, 2d ed. (Quaracchi: Collegium S. Bonaventura, 1934), vol. 23 (1591–1600), pp. 198–203. On his relationship to Saint Charles, see Federico Borromeo, *De sacris nostrorum temporum oratoribus* (Milan: n., 1632), pp. 49–69.

75. See, e.g., Tacchella, *Borromeo e Valier,* pp. 128, 130–33. Valier says of him, *Vita,* p. 29: "In concionatoribus deligendis mirum studium adhibebat."

76. *L'âge de l'éloquence,* p. 142.

77. See Prodi, *Paleotti* 2 : 75–136.

78. *L'âge de l'éloquence,* pp. 138, 141: ". . . s'ouvrit en Italie et en Espagne un véritable 'atelier' de rhétorique, plus prolifique qu'aucune école de sophistes antiques ou qu'aucune Académic humaniste. . . . On peut aussi être assuré que nul orateur humaniste, pas meme les Chanceliers de la République florentine, n'eut l'autorité, ni l'audience directe d'un Charles Borromée, héritier et imitateur d'Ambroise sur le siège archiépiscopal de Milan."

Borromeo and the Schools of Christian Doctrine

PAUL F. GRENDLER

DURING THE ERA OF THE CATHOLIC REFORMATION, NUMEROUS INDIVIDUALS and groups in Italy tried to relieve human misery, and save their own souls, by performing works of charity.[1] One favored effort was to teach the principles of religion and some elementary education to poor children. Several initiatives were attempted in northern Italy, including Milan, in the last years of the fifteenth and the first three decades of the sixteenth century.[2] None endured until Castellino da Castello tried. Born at Menaggio on Lake Como, about forty miles north of Milan, between 1470 and 1480, Castellino may have come from an artisan family. He was ordained a priest and became a chaplain at a Milanese church. This is all that is known about Castellino until 1536.[3]

In the fall of that year, Castellino and several lay associates founded the first School of Christian Doctrine. According to the standard account, on the feast of Saint Andrew (30 November), one of the numerous holidays on which work was suspended, one of Castellino's lay colleagues went out into the streets of Milan with a large sack of apples. He began to toss them to boys who were roaming the streets. With the apples he persuaded them to follow him to a church. There he and Father Castellino began to speak to the boys about salvation: they offered to teach them how to make the sign of the cross, promising an apple to the one who learned it first. When they had finished their instruction, they promised the boys more apples if they would return on the next holiday. Combining fervor and imagination, Castellino and his lay colleagues soon established holiday Schools of Christian Doctrine across the city.[4]

Castellino founded a lay confraternity in 1539 to carry on the work of the schools. In the next twenty to twenty-five years, the movement achieved remarkable success in bringing the schools to numerous cities and towns and, to a limited extent, to the countryside of northern Italy. Lay confraternities under various names ran and staffed the schools.[5]

The Schools of Christian Doctrine movement produced three genres of books from which come most of what we know about the internal workings of the schools. First were the *Regole (Rules)*, books that laid down the procedures and regulations for the confraternities and the operation of the schools. The *Regola* provided the calendar. According to it, the schools met throughout the year on Sundays and religious holidays (Epiphany, the Annunciation, numerous saints' days, etc.) for a total of eighty to eighty-five days a year.[6] The schools met in churches; boys went to one church, girls to another. Men taught boys, and women taught girls. The pupils ranged in age from five or six to fourteen or fifteen, usually divided into three or more levels of difficulty. But one can assume that the schools enrolled more younger than older pupils. Books were provided for those too poor to purchase their own. Once in the church, the children were divided into small groups. Several rules stressed that a teacher should instruct only eight to ten pupils. The large number of teachers involved suggests that this admonition was heeded. The schools usually lasted two to three hours, divided into shorter periods for different kinds of instruction. According to a Milanese document, a series of signs in the church might direct the children to where they could learn the alphabet, read the *Summario*, read and memorize the *Interrogatorio*, learn to write and count, learn about Holy Communion, and dispute, i.e., engage in competitive question-and-answer sessions before the whole school.[7]

The guidelines always stressed that the schools should be joyful. Singing, processions, contests, and prizes were used to make the learning experience pleasurable. Nor should teachers be severe; all the rules forbade the use of force against pupils. Instead, the teacher might embarrass the miscreant by ordering him or her to kneel in the middle of the school and kiss the floor. At the end, the students were dismissed "two by two in silence." Dismissal by pairs not only evoked Christ sending his disciples out into the world but also discouraged screams and scuffles on a Sunday afternoon.

The Schools of Christian Doctrine taught reading and writing as well as religion, according to most sixteenth-century rules. For example, the earliest surviving *regola*, that of Milan (1555), listed three teachers for each school: the prior who taught the children to say from memory the commandments of God, etc.: a second teacher who taught reading; and a third who taught writing.[8]

The first book used in the catechism schools was a short compilation of basic prayers, commandments, beliefs, and admonitions, called a *libretto* or, more commonly, *Summario*.[9] The title page, which is also the first page of the text, begins with IESUS in capital letters. Next come the alphabet and words of the sign of the cross: "In nomine Patris, et Filij, et Spiritus Sancti. Amen." Crosses, signifying the sign of the cross, precede the three lines of the alphabet and words of the sign of the cross. Then comes the Pater Noster in Latin: "Pater noster, qui es in caelis. . . ." Page two presents the Ave

Maria, Credo, and Salve Regina in Latin. Then the *Summario* switches to Italian. In the following pages are given the baptismal promises, the Ten Commandments, and the two precepts of the law of grace (which are "Love one God alone with all our heart, with all our spirit, with our whole mind, and with all our force, and our neighbor as ourselves"). Then come two precepts of the natural law ("Do not do to others what you do not wish them to do to you, and do unto others what you reasonably wish for yourself"). Next come lists of the four cardinal virtues, seven gifts of the Holy Spirit, seven spiritual works of mercy, seven corporal works of mercy, seven capital sins, the opposite seven virtues, the three powers of the spirit (which are "memory, intellect, and will"), the five senses of the body, seven sacraments of the church, and ten commandments of the church. The medieval fascination with numbers (seven of this, three of that, etc.) has been inherited and continued.

So far, the contents of the *Summario* are simply prayers, precepts, and factual information to be memorized. There is no explanation or justification. Just as letters of the alphabet served as the building blocks of reading, so these rudiments were the bricks of Catholicism.

The rest of the *Summario* provides more of the same, with a minimum of instruction. It continues with a list of what the Christian must do to keep holy the sabbath: abstain from sin and servile work, be contrite for your sins, adore God, give thanks for benefits received, and spend the day attending mass, listening to the sermon; do not pass the day playing, dancing, wandering about the piazza, or in debauchery and nonsense. Next follow the list of the eight beatitudes, grace before meals (in Latin, the first use of Latin since the opening two pages), the four fruits of confession, the twelve fruits of Holy Communion, and hymns. The contents of the *Summarii* were traditional, for they repeated and expanded material that had been grouped together before. Fifteenth-century manuscripts entitled "Trattati della dottrina cristiana" presented much of the same material.[10]

The second, more advanced book used was the *Interrogatorio,* a question-and-answer catechism of two hundred to three hundred pages in a small format.[11] It is divided into three parts of more or less rising levels of difficulty. Part one begins with the basic principle which is repeated throughout: the fear of God is the beginning of wisdom. Fear of God induces us to learn what is necessary for good spiritual health, to do good, to flee evil, and to attain salvation. With the fear of God in him, the Christian conquers the world, the flesh, and the devil and attains eternal reward.

The *Interrogatorio* also emphasizes works very strongly and throughout: one's good works demonstrate that one fears God. It is not enough just to believe that God exists. The Turks and Jews, even the demons, believe that God exists, but they are not saved. Moreover, there are many false Christians who have the name of Christian but do not do the works of him who sees. One must love God with one's whole heart, keep his commandments, and do good works for his love. In a discussion of the seven corporal works of mercy, the question is posed: are we all obligated to do these works? Answer: for those who lack the means, it is enough to do them in desire. But it is a grave sin for those who possess the means to fail to do them. Question: where does it say this? Answer: the Gospel proves this, because the Lord threatens with damnation the man who does not do the works of mercy for the poor.

The *Interrogatorio* might have emphasized strongly the love of God or the importance of sanctifying grace acquired through frequent reception of the sacraments. But there is little stress laid on the sacraments and not much emphasis on the mass as a channel of grace. Purgatory and devotions to Mary are mentioned but not underscored. The great amount of time devoted to learning prayers, however, demonstrates that prayer does matter.

The dominant theme is a struggle to do good works, a combat against sin and the devil, with the rewards being peace and even success in this world and salvation in the next. This attitude or spirit is typical of a prominent strain in Catholic Reformation devotional literature, that of spiritual struggle. Lorenzo Scupolo's *Combattimento spirituale* (first published in 1589, followed by innumerable reprints) is an example. The theme of spiritual struggle also seems to be an offshoot of the whole Catholic Reformation emphasis on activity: doing good in the world by building orphanages, providing shelter for the homeless, teaching the catechism, aiding the sick, and performing other charitable functions.

Overall, this is a catechism that presents the basic elements of Catholicism in an uncomplicated way to the lay person whose goal was to do good, avoid evil, and get to heaven. The *Interrogatorio* presents Christianity to the layperson engaged in secular affairs who lacks great interest in the intellectual origins and justification of his or her faith. The *Interrogatorio* is not for the person with a professional religious commitment, the boy or girl who wishes to become a priest, monk, nun, or theologian. The books of the Schools of Christian Doctrine set out to instruct uneducated, or minimally educated, layfolk in the rudiments of the faith in order that they might live a good life and achieve salvation. They seem well designed to accomplish this purpose.

The Schools of Christian Doctrine flourished in Milan and elsewhere. In 1563 the Milanese Company had more than two hundred members, thirty-three schools, and over two thousand children in attendance.[12] The Spanish viceroy and the Milanese Senate approved, to the point of threatening to punish anyone who might impede the Company's work.

Enter Carlo Borromeo. The Borromean tradition leaves the misleading impression that, while others had founded the movement, it had accomplished little before Borromeo took charge. Carlo Bascapè (1550–1615), Borromeo's collaborator and disciple, published in 1592 his biography of

Borromeo. Bascapè wrote that "a good layman" had founded the movement, but Borromeo had done a great deal more.[13] Gian Pietro Giussani (1540–1615), a Milanese noble and priest, published his comprehensive biography of Borromeo in 1610. He claimed to have known Borromeo intimately since youth.[14] Giussani wrote that "some good priests had already founded about fifteen Schools [of Christian Doctrine]," but Borromeo and Cardinal Federico Borromeo had vastly expanded the schools.[15]

Modern biographers have not altered this view very much. Cesare Orsenigo in his life of Borromeo (first published in installments between 1908 and 1910) put it this way:

> For some decades the custom already existed in Milan, introduced by Blessed Angelo Porro and Father Castellino da Castello, of gathering the children for instruction in the primary elements of knowledge and especially in Christian doctrine. St. Charles rejoiced in this wise beginning, but with a vaster genius he understood that the religious instruction of the people must take on much larger proportions and not be limited to the children. And thus arose the grand and simple organization of the School of Christian Doctrine. . . .[16]

After presenting a brief summary of the organization of the company, Orsenigo remarks: "This was St. Charles' ingenious plan for the instruction of the people in Christian doctrine." And in conclusion, Orsenigo states: "The neighboring dioceses soon followed the example of Milan."[17]

Bascapè, Giussani, and Orsenigo greatly misrepresented the facts. The early biographers eliminated any mention of Castellino. All biographers failed to mention the strength of the movement and that it had already spread across northern Italy before Borromeo arrived in Milan. They also gave Borromeo too much credit for his reorganization of the company and the schools, because he changed very little. One cannot easily uncover the reasons for the deception from a distance of nearly four hundred years; the historian can only surmise. Bascapè and Giussani, in their admiration and zeal to create the image of the reforming bishop who single-handedly transformed Milanese life, may have gotten carried away. If not excusable, it is understandable. But they followed Borromeo's lead: he consistently suppressed both the name of Castellino and the early history of the Schools of Christian Doctrine.

The facts seem to be the following. In 1564, the Milanese company found itself the object of accusations, specifically that it was inappropriate that lay persons should teach doctrine and that they were doing it badly. They were mixing "heretical lies" into "the simplicities of laymen."[18] The Milanese Company wrote to Borromeo in Rome asking him for help in securing papal approval. Prominent nobles and political figures of Milan added their signatures to the letter. Borromeo, who had been named archbishop of Milan in

1560, but had not yet begun to reside in his see, asked his vicar, Nicolò Ormaneto, to investigate the Company. Although Ormaneto's report was very favorable, Borromeo did not respond to the Company's petition nor, so far as is known, did he make any effort on its behalf.[19]

Borromeo entered Milan in September 1565 and soon began to promote the Schools of Christian Doctrine. Yet his attitude toward his predecessors did not change. Castellino, ill for years, died on 21 September 1566. Teachers and pupils from the Milanese Schools of Christian Doctrine, and others, accompanied the body to the *Duomo* where Castellino was interred. But Borromeo was not present.[20] The pattern continued. When Borromeo promulgated a new rule for the Company and a revised *Interrogatorio* in 1568, these books failed to mention Castellino. Finally, as Carlo Marcora pointed out, Borromeo made no effort to initiate beatification proceedings for Castellino.[21]

Borromeo's hostility to Castellino and his associates is hard to understand. Had heresy tainted them, Borromeo would have prosecuted quickly and vigorously. But Ormaneto exonerated them, and nothing has come to light since. Indeed, the doctrinal matter in the *Summario* and *Interrogatorio* is so simple that it is difficult to see how it might have been interpreted as heresy.

Possibly the fundamental problem was Borromeo's opposition to lay involvement in what he considered to be the proper sphere of the clergy. In his view, the clergy taught and the laity learned; the clergy led and the laity followed. He saw nothing but trouble when layfolk stepped over the line he drew, whether it was viceroy and Senate infringing on ecclesiastical jurisdiction, or lay persons teaching the catechism. Further, Borromeo completely lacked understanding or sympathy for popular life.[22] A festival meant an irreligious abuse to Borromeo. Of course, carnival celebrations often had anticlerical elements, but rather than ignoring them, Borromeo tried to transform carnival into a spiritual celebration.[23] He attempted to fill Sundays with so much religious observance that laypersons would spend the larger part of the day in church. He also instituted fairly strict controls over lay confraternities.[24] From this perspective, Borromeo naturally viewed the Company of Christian Doctrine with suspicion. That he did accept it and did permit laypersons to teach the catechism shows his ability to transcend his prejudices for a good cause.

Borromeo approved the Company and the Schools of Christian Doctrine in 1566. He promulgated rules in a series of provincial councils and diocesan synods, especially in his second provincial council of 1569.[25] Borromeo followed Castellino's outline but added more organization and brought the schools under clerical direction. Every urban and rural parish should have at least one School of Christian Doctrine and its Company. Territorial congregations led by a "protector," a priest appointed by the archbishop, guided the whole.[26]

The parish priest was expected to assume local leadership. He must exhort, preach, and teach the members of the Company; he should try to keep them away from dances, masques, games of chance, inns, taverns, and other occasions of sin.[27] Borromeo insisted on comprehensive record keeping and frequent visitation of individual schools. He ordered parish priests to compile a list of all children between the ages of five and fourteen with a view to ensuring that they attended catechism school.[28] Each pastor was expected to send quarterly reports on the schools in his parish to the archbishop.[29] And historians often credit Borromeo with the introduction of the "fishermen," although it is not clear who started the practice. Members of the Company carrying a rod walked the streets encouraging children to attend the catechism schools. In Rome, two members of the Company accompanied by two children walked through a neighborhood ringing a little bell and calling out: "Fathers and mothers, send your children to learn Christian doctrine. Otherwise, you will have to render a strict accounting to God on Judgment Day!"[30]

Yet Borromeo did not alter the internal structure of the schools, their pedagogical methods, or the content of instruction. The schools continued to teach Christian doctrine, reading, and writing, with the same combination of recitation, disputation, prayer, and song.[31] In 1567 Borromeo appointed a commission to revise the *Interrogatorio*. The first printing of the revision appeared in Milan, 1568, with many to follow.[32] The contents were nearly identical to part one of the text published in Venice, 1560, with the changes making it slightly more theological and ecclesiastical in orientation. For example, the 1560 version had omitted the Trinity, but the Milanese version mentioned it, although without explanation. The Milanese version placed slightly more emphasis on church rules and ceremonies, such as observing feast day regulations and hearing mass with reverence. The image of the striving Christian who does good works was slightly softened in favor of the pious Christian who prays, but the difference was one of nuance rather than substance.

Given his predilections, Borromeo exercised great restraint. He might have bent the *Interrogatorio* completely to his own views. He had stern ideas on how to make laypersons more virtuous, including a long list of penances to be imposed on sinners: up to ten days' fasting on bread and water for talking in church, up to seven years' penance for the single man committing fornication with a married woman, and five years' for her adultery.[33] But none of this appeared in his revised *Interrogatorio*. Indeed, Borromeo did not alter the teaching of the Schools of Christian Doctrine.

Under Borromeo, enrollment in the Milanese catechism schools grew. There were thirty-three schools, and the Company numbered more than two hundred members, in 1563, before Borromeo arrived. In 1578, there were fifty-three schools for boys and fifty-eight for girls.[34] In 1581, the company had 1,230 members.[35] At his death in 1584, the diocese of Milan as a whole had 740 Schools of Christian Doctrine, almost one for each parish. Three thousand members of the Company taught about forty thousand pupils, impressive statistics for a diocese of about 560,000 souls.[36] The schools continued to flourish after Borromeo's death. A census of 1599 (for Milan only) listed a Company of 7,700 members who taught 20,500 pupils.[37]

Borromeo and other prelates brought the Schools of Christian Doctrine under the authority of the bishop. The move was jurisdictionally easy because Castellino had formed a lay confraternity instead of a religious order. The Council of Trent and popes Pius V and Gregory XIII endorsed the teaching of the catechism.[38] Bishops such as Borromeo, Gabriele Paleotti of Bologna, Domenico Bollani of Brescia, and Patriarch Lorenzo Priuli of Venice threw their support behind the Schools of Christian Doctrine.[39] Now *regole* and catechisms carried episcopal approbation. The hierarchy's direction undoubtedly strengthened the schools. But their action was also part of a general move to use education as a vehicle for teaching doctrine and good morals. Bishops insisted that school teachers teach the catechism in addition to the Latin classics or commercial arithmetic; sometimes they directed teachers to set aside one day a week for that purpose. Textbooks now might include elementary religious matter. And as a result of the papal bull *In sacrosancta beati Petri* of 13 November 1564, bishops demanded professions of faith from all teachers.[40]

The Schools of Christian Doctrine offer some insight into the problems of bridging the social gap in order to teach religion. They began as an attempt by some members of the middle and working classes to teach poorer and less educated members of the same classes. When bishops made the schools part of the church's teaching mission, the social gap possibly widened. The Schools of Christian Doctrine tried to become a mission from the elite to the lowly. Or, possibly, social differences inherent in the movement surfaced with the hierarchy and a few well-educated, upper-class men and women involved themselves in the catechism schools.

One sees this in the comments of the upper-class observers who knew the schools well. Ludovico Carbone (ca. 1545–97 or later) received a degree in theology, taught at Perugia and Venice, and wrote a book on sacred eloquence. He may have been a Jesuit at one time but was a layman in Venice in 1596 when he published a book on the catechism schools. He had taught in them and warmly defended the schools. He promised that catechetical instruction would provide social and moral benefits to society. Civil rulers should favor the Schools of Christian Doctrine in order to have a strong, devout, and well-ordered state, he wrote. A populace well instructed in Christian doctrine is peaceable, obedient, just, constant, and faithful in the defense of the *patria*. Pastors who support the work of the catechism schools will have an obedient, faithful, and devout flock who will fill the church, confess, and receive Holy Communion. But parents who do not send their offspring to the catechism schools will have restless, immodest, disobedient, and dissipated children who will become disturbers of the peace.[41] *Regole* printed at the end of the sixteenth and in the early seventeenth century also occasionally made promises of this sort, but in milder tones.[42]

Carbone also promised that the catechism schools would eradicate among the *rudes* and *idiote* (the "rough" and "ignorant," as he called them) such popular errors as the following: fasting is required only of members of religious orders; one may work to earn a living on holy days; the devil is not so ugly or hell so awful as pictured, because such descriptions are intended to frighten the crowd; it is not such a great calamity to go to hell because the majority of people including the great and noble are there; it is permitted to the young to have a good time so that they will not age so quickly; fornication is only the lightest of venial sins; one may take an oath and testify falsely in order to save not just a comrade but anyone; to forgive an injury is the mark of a coward *(animo vile);* the first sign of madness is to give away one's goods for the love of God. These beliefs were the irreligious, hedonistic traditions of some members of the lower classes. They manifested an earthy skepticism toward authority. Carbone, who knew those he was trying to improve, resisted the temptation, to which some clergymen succumbed, to label these beliefs heresy. He called them "abominable blasphemies."[43]

Since some people in the late sixteenth century viewed the catechism schools as a mission from the high to the low, proponents held up for emulation members of the nobility who participated. Don Ferdinando of Toledo, an illustrious and rich cavalier, declined the cardinal's hat in order to devote himself to teaching Christian doctrine, according to Carbone. In Brescia, many gentlemen, including the "leading ones," taught Christian doctrine in the city and countryside; gentlemen of Milan and Naples did the same. Highborn ladies joined in the work. Leonora of Austria, the duchess of Mantua, founded a teacher-training institute to prepare ninety girls to teach in the Schools of Christian Doctrine. She visited the catechism schools of Mantua, exhorting the gentlewomen who accompanied her to support this Christian exercise. Noblewomen of Milan, Brescia, Parma, Piacenza, Venice, and Naples acted similarly, according to Carbone.[44] Such examples demonstrate that some of the highest of society embraced the Schools of Christian Doctrine as a charitable mission to the lowly. But one wonders how, in such a quasi-feudal society as that of Italy at the end of the sixteenth century, the relationship between noble teacher and commoner pupil could have been anything other than that of master and servant.

Despite such examples, it is doubtful that very many members of the upper classes participated in teaching the poor. In 1609, Giussani, the biographer of Borromeo, published an open letter urging nobles to teach Christian doctrine. He lamented that few nobles participated in this "glorious enterprise." He noted the objections voiced by members of the upper classes: that it was not appropriate for nobles to join in where only the "lower classes" *(gente bassa)* assembled, and that the schools were "a low and plebian thing" *(cosa vile & da plebeo)*. Giussani presented the example of Christ who taught the lowly; he even resurrected in these aristocratic times the fifteenth-century Renaissance argument that true nobility was based on virtue, not rank or birth. One might demonstrate virtue by helping in the Schools of Christian Doctrine, he argued.[45]

But it does not appear that many nobles heeded his appeal. Carbone observed that he had many times seen laymen and artisans who, after having worked all day in their shops, spent two or three hours on feast days teaching Catholic doctrine in the churches without any priest or ecclesiastical person joining them.[46] The catechism schools probably recruited the bulk of the large number of adults needed to operate the schools from much the same middle- and working-class ranks that provided the pupils. Indeed, the practical operation of the schools took this into account.

The clearest sign that the catechism school movement did not bridge the social division is that noble children did not attend. A few nobles might teach in the schools, but they did not often send their children to learn in them. Carbone lamented that some noble parents would not send their offspring to the catechism schools because they did not want them to mix with boys of "inferior class" *(bassa conditione)*.[47]

But why should noble children attend? They learned to read and write, and learned the catechism as well, because they were fortunate enough to attend ordinary schools. In the 1570s and 1580s, Borromeo had ordered all teachers to teach the catechism as part of the regular curriculum. Attending the Schools of Christian Doctrine would have been redundant, as well as socially undesirable.

In short, the Schools of Christian Doctrine filled an important religious and social need for part of the population. They provided elementary literacy and religious instruction for poor boys and girls who, otherwise, would have gone without. Castellino and his associates met a real need with imagination, organization, energy, and charity. The Schools of Christian Doctrine were one of the most appealing efforts of the Catholic Reformation. But they could not do more. Bishops and others who, with laudable motives, wanted to make the movement into a vehicle for catechizing the entire populace expected too much. They were trying to do something that ran counter to the social foundation of the movement.

Despite the efforts of Borromeo and others to co-opt the movement into their own upper-class and ecclesiastical universe, the Company of Christian Doctrine probably remained part of the little world of commoners. Perhaps a typical catechism teacher was Giambattista Casale (d. after 1629), a Milanese layman who had had Father Castellino as his confessor, and who worked devotedly in the company for decades. He served as an underprior in one school, a prior in another, and then as a visitor to numerous schools. His wife and two sons also served in the Milanese Company. From 1554 through 1598, he kept a diary of notable events in the city and of the activities of his beloved Company of Christian Doctrine. More than once, Casale explained why he labored in the catechism schools: "for the honor of God, the salvation of souls, and the common good." He joyfully recorded how his fifteen-year-old son helped him establish a new school. His son then acquitted himself extremely well in the first *disputa*, the question-and-answer competition held in the new school that was conducted by the proud father.[49] Casale was an unsophisticated man who deeply loved his church and its archbishops. In his diary, Carlo and Federico Borromeo are revered leaders who can do no wrong. Their presence at events and their gestures of approval were deeply appreciated, despite the wide social and ecclesiastical gap that separated bishop from flock.

There was no reason in the world for Borromeo initially to have feared such people as Giambattista Casale. Indeed, Borromeo did learn to trust members of the Company to carry on their duties without his constantly peering over their shoulders. And the anecdotes that were part of the tradition of the Schools of Christian Doctrine began to attach themselves to Borromeo. For example, according to the tradition, Borromeo went to teach Christian doctrine carrying a sack of red apples to reward the children.[50] If the story is true, Borromeo unbent as much as he ever did in the catechism schools.

Despite Borromeo's suspicions and the inevitable social distinctions that the Schools of Christian Doctrine could not overcome, Castellino and Borromeo shared a basic aim. Each wanted to reform the people according to Catholic doctrine; each believed that an organized, highly structured approach would do it. The rules of the Company of Christian Doctrine, written long before Borromeo appeared on the scene, had some of the same spirit of rigid direction to be found in Borromeo's synodal decrees in which he told bishops, regular clergy, parish priests, and laypersons exactly what was expected of them. The mentality of the times endorsed this approach.

Perhaps the best way to understand this rigidly structured reform mentality is to compare it with a utopian work, because utopias presented in imaginary form the goals of reformers. Ludovico Agostini (1536–1612), lawyer and civil servant of Pesaro, wrote between 1585 and 1590 a utopia that breathed Catholic reform zeal.[51] In Agostini's utopia, parallel civil and religious authorities closely supervised the physical and spiritual lives of the people in order to make them good. Bishop and priests exercised close supervision to ensure that the populace heard mass and sermons, performed good works, and avoided frivolity that diverted men from virtue. A similar civic supervision eliminated the extremes of wealth. Authoritarian direction produced a virtuous populace and a good society along Catholic reform lines.

Both Castellino and Borromeo tried to make a real Catholic utopia of Milan. The members of the Company of Christian Doctrine taught a simple faith accompanied by strong moral exhortation in order to make men good. Borromeo gave authoritarian direction to priests and people for the same purpose. Inevitably they would join forces because they had the same ends in view. Together they tried to transform a utopian dream into reality.

Notes

1. The Schools of Christian Doctrine are the focus of one part of my monograph in preparation on primary and secondary education in the Italian Renaissance. Before discussing the relationship between Borromeo and the Schools, I am restating briefly some points from another paper but without full documentation. Please see "The Schools of Christian Doctrine in Sixteenth-Century Italy," *Church History* 53 (1984): 319–31. A Guggenheim Memorial Fellowship made possible research in Italy during 1978–79, and a fellowship from the Woodrow Wilson International Center for Scholars gave me the opportunity to write in a stimulating environment during the winter of 1982–83. I also thank John O'Malley for providing me with photocopies.

2. Alessandro Tamborini, *La compagnia e le scuole della dottrina cristiana* (Milan, 1939), 28–45. Despite its uncritical viewpoint and occasionally careless documentation, it is fundamental. Also see Giambatista Castiglione, *Istoria delle scuole della Dottrina Christiana fondate in Milano e da Milano nell'Italia ed altrove propagate. Parte Prima* (Milan, Cesare Orena nella Stamperia Malatesta, 1800); and the splendid study of Miriam Turrini, " 'Riformare il mondo a vera vita christiana': le scuole di catechismo nell'Italia del Cinquecento," *Annali dell'Istituto storico italo-germanico in Trento* 8 (1982): 407–89.

3. L. Cajani, "Castellino da Castello," *Dizionario biografico degli italiani* 21 (1978): 786–87.

4. Tamborini, *La Compagnia e le scuole*, 50–52.

5. For the details, see Castiglione, *Istoria delle scuole*, and Tamborini, *La Compagnia e le scuole*.

6. For example, a Roman rule listed eighty-two days on which the schools would function: *Regole della Compagnia della Dottrina Christiana di Roma (In Roma, Appresso li Stampatori Camerali*, 1598), sigs. C3v–C4v. For a list of *regole*, see Grendler, "Schools of Christian Doctrine," 322, n. 11; and Turrini " 'Riformare il mondo,' ", 468–72.

7. Tamborini, *La compagnia e le scuole*, 76–77.

8. The earliest surviving *regola*, *La regola della compagni delli servi dei puttini in carita* (Milan, 1555), is reprinted in Carlo Marcora, "La Chiesa Milanese nel decennio 1550–1560," *Memorie storiche della Diocesi di Milano* 7 (1960): 470–81, reference to p. 479. The identical words are found in *Regola della Compagnia delli Servi de i puttini in carità* (In Milano, 1566), sigs. A viiv–A viiir.

9. This is based on a typical *Summario: Summario della vita Christiana, qual s'insegna alli fanciulli di Cremona* (Colophon: In Milano per Vincenzo Girardoni, ad

instantia de Mattheo da Besozzo, 1567). For others, see Grendler, "Schools of Christian Doctrine," 325, n. 21.

10. See, for example, Florence, Biblioteca Riccardiana, Ms 1657, ff. 80–81 (dated 1410), and MS 1716.

11. *Modo breve et facile, utile et necessario, in forma di dialogo, di amaestrare i figliuoli mascoli, & femine, & quelli che non sanno, nelle divotioni, & buoni costumi del viver Christiano* (In Vinegia appresso Gabriel Giolito de' Ferrari, 1560). Although not the earliest surviving *Interrogatorio*, it became the basic text to be copied or improved. For a listing of various editions and a discussion of the relationship between them, see Grendler, "Schools of Christian Doctrine," 328 and n. 27. Turrini, " 'Riformare il mondo,' " also lists numerous catechisms.

12. Tamborini, *La compagnia e le scuole*, 185.

13. Carlo Bascapè, *Vita e opere di Carlo arcivescovo di Milano, Cardinale di S. Prassede*, Latin and Italian ed. (Milan, 1965), bk. 7, ch. 41, p. 869.

14. I cite the revised 1612 edition: *Vita di S. Carlo Borromeo . . . scritta dal Dottore Gio. Pietro Giussano . . . novamente dall'istesso autore revista & purgata d'alcuni errori che sono nell' editione Romana* (In Brescia, Per Bartolomeo Fontana, 1612), sig. t3r.

15. "E trovando che alcuni buoni Sacerdoti n'havevano già erette circa quindici Scuole. . . ." Giussano, *Vita di S. Carlo Borromeo*, 372–76, quoted on p. 372.

16. Cesare Orsenigo, *Life of St. Charles Borromeo*, trans. Rudolph Kraus (St. Louis and London, 1947), 96.

17. Orsenigo, *Life of Borromeo*, 97. Adolfo Rivolta is fairer but still undervalues the importance of Castellino and his associates: *San Carlo Borromeo: Note biografiche. Studio sulle sue lettere e suoi documenti* (Milan, 1938), 218–33.

18. Tamborini, *La compagnia e le scuole*, 192.

19. Tamborini, *La compagnia e le scuole*, 186–196.

20. Carlo Marcora, "Il Diario di Giambattista Casale (1554–1598)," *Memorie storiche della Diocesi di Milano* 12 (1965): 240–42. Given his worshipful respect for Borromeo, Casale would have rejoiced in Borromeo's presence, if he had been there. Of course, Borromeo could have been unavoidably absent from the city.

21. Marcora, "La Chiesa Milanese nel decennio 1550–1560," 285.

22. Roger Mols, *S. Carlo Borromeo iniziatore della pastorale moderna*. Supplemento ad Ambrosius n. 5 (Milan, 1961), 47, an Italian translation of "Saint Charles Borromée, pionnier de la pastorale moderne," *Nouvelle revue théologique* 79 (1957): 600–622, 715–47.

23. Marcora, "Diario di Casale," 243–44.

24. Antonio Rimoldi, "I laici nelle regole delle confraternite di S. Carlo Borromeo," in *Miscellanea Carlo Figini* (Milan, 1964), 282–303.

25. The 1569 rules are found in *Acta Ecclesiae Mediolanensis* (Hereafter *AEM*), ed. Carlo Cajetano (Milan, 1846), 2:1029–1131, and are summarized in Rimoldi, "I laici," 282–87.

26. *AEM* 2:1100.

27. *AEM* 2:1043–44, 1047.

28. *Interrogatorio del maestro al discipulo per instruere li fanciulli & quelli che non sano nella via di Dio. Visto & corretto dal R. P. Inquisitore generale nel Stato di Milano . . . et di novo ristampato con certi agionti d'ordine dell'Illust . . . Cardinal Borromeo. . . .* (Colophon: In Milano per Vicenzo Girardoni, ad instanza de M. Mattheo da Besozzo, al segno della Stella, nell'anno 1568), 2.

29. *AEM* 2:1044.

30. *Regole della Compagnia della Dottrina Christiana di Roma* (Rome, 1598),

26r–v. Also see Tamborini, *La compagnia e le scuole* 213; and Turrini, " 'Riformare il mondo,' " 450–51.

31. *AEM* 2:1053, 1055, 1060, 1108.
32. See n. 28 for the citation.
33. Mario Bendiscioli, "Politica, amministrazione e religione nell'età dei Borromei," in *Storia di Milano* (Milan, 1957), 10:197.
34. Marcora, "Diario di Casale," 329–33.
35. Marcora, "Diario di Casale," 349–51.
36. Rimoldi, "I laici," 297.
37. Tamborini, *La compagnia e le scuole*, 323–25.
38. Tamborini, *La compagnia e le scuole*, 167–72. A small printed pamphlet to be found in the Biblioteca Apostolica Vaticana, Stamp. Ferraioli V. 8011 int. 1, reproduces in Italian translation the letters of Pius V and Gregory XIII: *Breve col quale nostro S. Pio Papa V essorta gli ordinarij . . . si debbano ammaestrare i fanciulli nella Dottrina Christiana. . . .* (In Brescia, Appresso Vincenzo Sabbio, 1593. Ad instanza di Pietro Gennaro).
39. Tamborini, *La compagnia e le scuole*, 210–21; Paolo Prodi, *Il Cardinale Gabriele Paleotti (1522–1597)* (Rome, 1967), 2:182–87; Turrini, " 'Riformare il mondo,' " 458–63; Castiglione, *Istoria delle scuole*, 202–4.
40. Grendler, "What Zuanne Read in School: Vernacular Texts in Sixteenth Century Venetian Schools," *Sixteenth Century Journal* 13 (1982): 41; Hubert Jedin, *Storia del Concilio di Trento*, trans. G. Cecchi and Giorgio Beari (Brescia, 1981), vol. 4, part 2, pp. 347–48.
41. Lodovico Carbone, *Dello ammaestramento de' figliuoli nella dottrina Christiana* (In Venetia, appresso Giovanni Guerigli, 1596), 114–16, 118, 104, 110.
42. For example, see *Constitutioni della ven. Archiconfraternità della Dottrina Christiana di Roma* (In Roma, nella Stamperia della Cam. Apost., 1611), 22.
43. Carbone, *Dello ammaestramento*, 33–34.
44. Carbone, *Dello ammaestramento*, 129–132; also see Agostino Cabrini, *Ordini con li quali devono essere regolate le scole della Santissima Dottrina Christiana* (In Venetia, 1685, Per Francesco Basetto), sigs. A3v–A5v.
45. *Lettera scritta dal Signor Gio. Pietro Giussani Patritio, & Sacerdote Milanese ad una persona nobile per animarla al perseverare nell'insegnar la Dottrina Christiana* (In Milano, Appresso Gio. Battista Alzato, 1609; Colophon: Appresso Bernardino Lantoni), 85, 90–91.
46. Carbone, *Dello ammaestramento*, 231.
47. Carbone, *Dello ammaestramento*, 112–13.
48. "Perché io Ioan Batista insegnava dico a scrivere gratis: et amore Dei. . . . Et tutto questo a honore de Dio, a salute de le anime: et al ben comune." Marcora, "Diario di Casale," 220–21; also see 250.
49. Marcora, "Diario di Casale," 382.
50. Tamborini, *La compagnia e le scuole*, 214–15; also see Marcora, "Diario di Casale," 382.
51. Ludovico Agostini, *La repubblica immaginaria*, ed. Luigi Firpo (Turin, 1957): Luigi Firpo, *Lo stato ideale della Controriforma. Ludovico Agostini* (Bari, 1957), 272–306.

Borromeo's Influence on
Sacred Art and Architecture

E. CECILIA VOELKER

THE CLOSURE AND PROMULGATION OF THE CHURCH COUNCIL AT TRENT IN December 1563 and the ratification of its canons and decrees by Pope Pius IV in June of the following year mark a significant moment in the history of ecclesiastical art and architecture. With the distribution of the published Tridentine norms and statutes, diocesan bishops were held responsible for their implementation, accepting more or less seriously the fact that these statutes were now law.[1] Trent did not dictate the process of reform or its extent, nor did it delineate an order of preferences. What it did do, in most cases, was to encourage episcopal leadership, and, with approximately 287 Italian dioceses and an equal number of pastoral and administrative personalities, diversified and unpredictable reactions ensued.[2] This paper focuses upon one such early post-Tridentine personality, Cardinal Carlo Borromeo, archbishop of Milan from 1563 to 1584.

In 1565, upon the death of his maternal uncle, Pope Pius IV, twenty-seven-year-old Carlo Borromeo was relieved of his Vatican obligations, and he returned to Milan prepared to give full attention to ecclesiastical responsibilities. Confronted with the task of overseeing reform in so large an area, his initial resolve was to name assistants who either undertook preliminary visits to parishes or supervised the application of his directives.[3]

The results of the first cycle of visits appear in the decrees of the Third Provincial Council of 1573.[4] Borromeo and selected churchmen of the archdiocese had reviewed problems relative to ecclesiastical architecture such as maintenance, furnishing, decoration, and general good order, stipulating that only bishops might judge departure from the rules that they were about to codify. In seeking to restore an atmosphere of dignity and functionality, these men promised a forthcoming set of instructions that would serve as guidelines in this area of Catholic reform.[5]

The provincial council of 1576 also refers to a publication of architectural norms, and, this same year, Gerolamo Ragazzoni, Bishop of Famagosta, was appointed apostolic visitor (papal inspector) to the Milan diocese.[6] A more sophisticated system of visitation was devised. Borromeo sectioned off city zones according to city gates and assigned a visitor to each district. The visitors formed a committee headed by the prefect of buildings, and their responsibility was to implement the *Instructiones*.[7] The first *Prefectus Fabricae* was Ludovico Moneta, and there is evidence that Moneta wrote chapters 32 and 33, instructions for monastic churches and monasteries, respectively. A letter of 18 July 1577 from the priest Galesino to Borromeo mentions that the book of the *Instructiones* is advancing, and that soon he will need to have the chapters from Monsignor Moneta, especially those on the monastery of nuns, since these chapters come at the end of the first book.[8]

The first printing of instructions for ecclesiastical buildings and furnishings appeared as a small single volume with the following title page: *Instructionum fabricae et supellectilis ecclesiasticae libri II. Caroli S.R.E. Cardinalis tituli s. Praxedis, Archiepiscopi iussu, ex provinciali Decreto editi ad provinciae Mediolanensis usum. Mediolani, Apud Pacificum Pontium, Typographym Illustri[ss]. Cardinalis S. Praxedis Archiepiscopi 1577* (fig. 1). (There were 213numbered leaves and 8 leaves unnumbered, signatures: A–S[12]T[6], 14cm.)

The first book of instructions is arranged in thirty-three chapters of varying lengths dealing with topics basic to spatial arrangements. Borromeo's concern with the specificity of space will become increasingly obvious as the chapters are outlined in this paper.[9] (Chapter headings are shown in capitals hereinafter: subheadings are divided by slashes.)

Book 1. Building Instructions

1. SITE OF THE BUILDING/other ecclesiastical buildings on the same site/ location of the church/size and site of the church.

   Moreover, the size of the church ought to be large enough to accommodate not only the number of people inhabiting the locality where the parochial, collegiate, or cathedral church is to be constructed, but also to hold the numbers of people flocking there on holy days. Consideration ought to be given to the provision of a space of one cubit and eight ounces [58.19cm] square for each person, in addition to the space occupied by columns, pillars, and walls.[10]

2. PLAN OF A CHURCH/cruciform. "As far as round edifices are concerned, this type of plan was used for pagan temples and is less customary among Christian people." From these words, taken out of context, it has been stated that Borromeo banned the central plan. This misinterpretation is disproved not only by the remaining text, but by extant Borromean structures.[11]

3. EXTERNAL WALLS AND FACADE

   In the upper part of the main doorway . . . there should be painted or carved . . . the image of the most blessed Virgin Mary holding her son Jesus in her arms; on the right side, an effigy of the saint to whom the church is dedicated, while on the left . . . a saint to whom the people of that parish are particularly devoted.[12]

4. ATRIUM, NARTHEX PORCH, AND COVERED ENTRANCE. This chapter allows for various possibilities, dependent upon site and finances.

5. ROOF

6. PAVEMENT. "Church pavement should not consist of bricks set edgewise, nor of tiles, nor of any kind of brickwork, unless glazed. . . . regardless

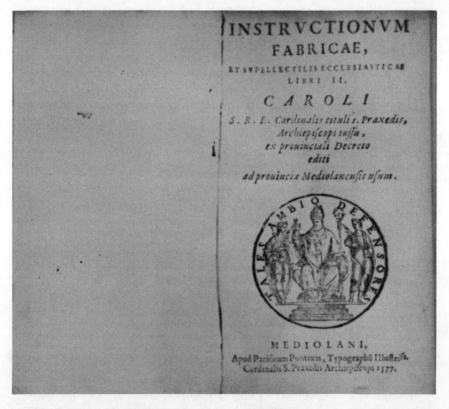

Figure 1. Title page: *Instructiones Fabricae et Supellectilis Ecclesiasticae*, 1577, Carlo Borromeo. (*Courtesy of Biblioteca Ambrosiana, Milan.*)

of what material is used, no cross, no sacred image should be represented."

7. DOORWAYS

> . . . should not be arches as city gates, but square as in ancient basilicas. If it [church] consists of only a single nave then it should have the necessary three doorways . . . to maintain a separation between men and women.[13] The middle doorway must be distinguished by its width and ornamented with sculptures of lions . . . to represent the Temple of Solomon and the vigilance of bishops.

It is explicitly written that no public doors are to be at the back or sides of the church.

8. WINDOWS

9. STAIRS AND STEPS OF A CHURCH

10. MAIN CHAPEL

> . . . /the main chapel/ should be constructed toward the west, as in accordance with the ancient rite of the Church. The Holy Sacrifice of the Mass is celebrated by the priest facing the people.

Measurements given for the height of the altar platform differ in the main chapels of parochial, collegiate, and cathedral churches.

11. MAIN ALTAR/steps of the main altar/location of the image of the crucifix.

> If there is sufficient space at the sides and in front of the altar, three steps should be prepared; that is, one consisting of the predella itself, and two others lower than this predella. The two lower steps ought to be made of marble or of solid stone, or, if this is not possible, of brick. . . . The third step, however, which consists of the predella itself, is to be made of wooden boards.[14]

12. CHOIR

> As is obvious from ancient buildings and also from church discipline, the location of the choir should be separate from the standing place of the people. [It should be] enclosed by rails and be situated near the main altar, whether the choir surround it in the front (following ancient tradition) or whether it be in the back owing to either the site of the church, or the position of the altar. . . . it should correspond accurately in size and proper ornamentation with the importance of the church and the number of its clergy.[15]

13. TABERNACLE OF THE MOST HOLY EUCHARIST. "It is proper that some instruction on the subject of the tabernacle should be given, since a provincial decree has made it obligatory to put the tabernacle on the main altar."

14. MINOR CHAPELS AND ALTARS. The material covered in this chapter relates to the place of minor altars in various locations throughout the church, but with clearly defined spatial and directional requirements. All main altars are to stand free, minor altars are attached to, or at least brought up to, the back wall. No altars may be erected under an organ or choir loft.

15. DETAILS COMMON TO BOTH MAJOR AND MINOR CHAPELS OR ALTARS/ cruet niche/iron peg to hang up the beretta/altar bell/railings of chapels and altars/wooden molding of the altar/cloth frame of the altar/wooden gradines on the back of an altar/the main altar table/the niche of the holy relics for the consecration of an altar/the altar table and waxed cloth/ stone of portable altars.[16]

16. SHRINES, VASES, OR CASES IN WHICH HOLY RELICS ARE KEPT/first form of shrine/second form of shrine/third form of shrine/vases and cases for holy relics which are placed in the shrines prescribed above.

Two poles should be made of ebony, Brazilian wood as it is called, or some similar kind of hard wood. These should be three cubits [1.30m] long and should be finished with a top of silver plate having two small hooks from which the faithful may suspend their rosaries in order to touch the sacred relics, or rather the vases in which they are enclosed.

17. SACRED IMAGES AND PICTURES/what is to be avoided and observed in sacred images/the dignity of sacred images/the symbols of the saints/ places unsuitable for sacred pictures/the ceremony of blessing images/ occasional inscription of saints' names/accessories and additions for ornamentation/votive tablets.

Now, with regard to the pious and religious representation of sacred images, not only must the bishop be attentive to the decree of the Council of Trent and the Provincial Constitutions, but also a heavy punishment or fine has been set for painters and sculptors so that their works do not depart from the prescribed rules. Penalties have also been determined in regard to pastors, who, contrary to the prescribed rules of the Tridentine decree, have permitted an unusual and offensive image to be painted or placed in their churches.

This important chapter is a veritable manifesto against artistic license. In 1573, at the Third Provincial Council, Borromeo warned that those who did not conform to his reform measures regarding painting and sculpture would be punished, clergy as well as artists. The warning was repeated in 1576, and a new rule was added that forbade animal figures unless they were based on biblical or hagiographic themes. Borromeo also advised that, "in order that bishops might more easily execute these and other like prescriptions of the Council of Trent, let them call together the painters and sculptors of their dioceses and inform all equally about things to be observed in producing sacred images."[17]

At the Biblioteca Ambrosiana, there is a letter from Bishop Paleotti of Bologna to Borromeo that alerts us to the fact that both men were familiar with the book of Johannes Molanus whose treatise on religious art is the first which can be identified as a direct result of Trent.[18] Paleotti's letter is dated 22 April 1579. In it, he informs Borromeo that he has found a copy of the Molanus volume, and he requests to be kept informed of future religious art regulations issued for the Milan archdiocese.[19] Paleotti, at this time, was preparing a five-volume work, *Discorso intorno alle immagini sacre e profane,* of which two volumes were published in 1582,[20] and during this period young Federico Borromeo was studying at Bologna under his guardianship. The moralistic and didactic reflections expressed by the Bolognese bishop later appear in Federico's treatise on sacred art published in Milan in 1624 as *De pictura sacra.*[21]

The tremendous program of renovating and constructing churches during Carlo Borromeo's period required artistic decorations that called for painters, sculptors, stucco workers, wood workers, and craftsmen. This means that one must look beyond the time of Saint Charles's life to estimate the effect of his norms on the figurative arts, simply because the decorative process had to follow the phase of construction.[22]

18. LAMPS AND LAMPADARIUM/form of the lamps/form of the lampadarium/ number of lamps/place of the lampadarium.

> The form of the lamps may be as diverse as the fashion of the times. None, indeed, are forbidden, provided that they are in conformity with Church usage. . . . The lampadarium is a circular arrangement from which a particular number of hanging lamps are suspended.

Borromeo merely records the established methods of lighting with no recourse to religious symbolism.

19. BAPTISTRY/the place and form of the baptistry chapel/altar of the baptistry chapel/location of the baptistry when it is not possible to erect it separate from the church/distinction between a Roman and Ambrosian

baptistry/site and form of the Roman baptistry/silver shell/site and form of the Ambrosian baptistry/details common to Roman and Ambrosian baptistries/ciborium/table/site of each kind of baptistry/colonnade/canopy/ambry for the holy chrism, etc./small kind of baptistry/another form of chapel and site for the purpose of both Roman and Ambrosian baptistries/placing a baptistry on the right side/second form of baptistry according to the Roman manner/the other vase/second form of baptistry in the Ambrosian manner/sacrarium/details common to the second form of both kinds of baptistry/ciborium and ambry/another form of ciborium/door panels of the ciborium/third form of baptistry for Roman use only.

The ideal baptistry was a separate structure, similar to those of the cathedral complexes at Pisa, Parma, Cremona, and Florence. As the Christian population increased, a permanent baptistry was designed for a specific chapel within the parish church. The acceptable location, according to the norms, was the first chapel to the left, upon entry. Additional requirements, recommendations, and alternatives found in the instructions remained in existence until Vatican II. An identical treatment of baptistries is found in early ecclesiastical structures throughout the Americas.

20. SACRARIUM/first form of sacrarium/second form of sacrarium.

21. HOLY WATER VASE

It should not be put outside, but rather inside the church, accessible to those who enter and at their right hand, if possible. One font should be placed on the side where the men enter and another . . . where the women enter. These [vases] should not be near the wall but distant from it in proportion to the space that is there. They should be supported . . . on a small column, pillar, or some type of base on which nothing profane appears.

There should be a sprinkler on a small metal chain hanging from the rim [of the font] . . . it should not terminate with a sponge but with bristles. It may terminate with a sponge only if it is enclosed in a silver, tin, or brass perforated knob that has bristles attached on the outside.

Borromeo maintained that within the door of every parochial church there was to be a stone holy water font accessible to the people. Fonts outside of the churches were to be removed. Holy water was to be changed every week, and this was to be done before mass with the priest dressed in a surplice and stole.[23] The "bristles" replace the branches of hyssop (Ps. 50: "Sprinkle me with hyssop and I shall be cleansed; wash me and I shall be made whiter than snow"). Although no longer attached to the holy water font, these sprinklers with "bristles" are still used in the Ambrosian rite.

22. AMBONES AND PULPIT/two ambones/one ambo/site of the ambones/ pulpit.

Liturgists of the sixteenth century showed a renewed interest in the early Christian tradition of ambones. These elaborate platforms were used singly or in pairs for the reading of the Gospels, Epistles, and Divine Office.

23. CONFESSIONAL/number of confessionals/form of the confessional/dais of the confessional/seat for the confessor/height of the confessional/rail for the confessor to lean upon/kneeler for the penitent/kneeler/the intermediate opening/representation of the crucifix/what is to be attached to different sides of the confessional/that alms boxes are not to be erected in a confessional/where confessionals are to be placed/the position of both the confessor and the penitent.

> . . . in a cathedral church as many confessionals should be built as are . . . necessary. . . . In every parish church there should be two confessionals so that men do not find themselves intermingled or crowded together with women when large numbers are gathered together. . . . as in most of the churches in this province a special place for each confessional has already been established.

The confessional made its appearance around 1545, prior to the first sessions of Trent. In 1565 Borromeo issued what appears to be the first precise measurements and explicit directives for the construction and spatial arrangement of a standard confession booth. During the next nineteen years he wrote repeatedly about the sacramental rite, underscoring the fact that the use of a booth was of recent vintage. The most important documents describing the new practice are found in the 1565 Constitutions.[24]

24. THE WOODEN PARTITION USED TO DIVIDE A CHURCH

> Because it is an ancient . . . custom attested to by blessed Chrysostom, and one in use throughout most of this province, that in church men should be separate from women, the following is the method . . . of how this division may be realized. . . . There should be a partition down the nave from the entrance door to the [rails of the high altar].

Borromeo goes on to describe a wooden partition that can be adjusted in height from three to almost seven feet by raising and lowering wooden panels.[25]

25. BENCHES FOR WOMEN

> In churches where bishops have allowed the use of benches, these benches should be designed according to the following norms and they should be placed on the women's side to serve for either sitting or kneeling.
>
> With the exception of churches where, on account of the site, or where the bishop judges otherwise, the women's side should be on the north.
>
> [Benches] should be made in sets of three so that they can be moved when it becomes necessary to avoid obstructions. As many of these benches suitable for the size of the church should be placed on [the women's side] along the length of the wall. . . . On the side of the church reserved for men, there should be no benches to kneel upon. However, if any seats are permitted, these too, should be made of planks . . . and have no back rests . . .

The so-called benches (predelle, bradelle), were less than ten inches off the floor, conducive perhaps for kneeling, but that women who were aged, pregnant, or ill might have been meant to sit upon this squatting board is incomprehensible.

26. BELL TOWER AND BELLS/floors/windows/stairs/spire/doorway/site of the campanile/number of bells/clock/another form of campanile/brick piers to serve as a bell tower/blessing of the bells and what is to be avoided in their ornamentation.

At first churches had but one bell; later other bells were added to distinguish different services and to identify the hierarchy of a church. With the use of several bells came the study of tintinnalogia: the art of ringing bells, and also the problem of tuning them. Borromeo added nothing new to the construction of bell towers; thus, what is found in the norms is essentially a persistence of tradition.

The spire, writes Borromeo, should be circular or pyramidal. At the top of it, in accordance with symbolism, there should be the figure of a cock and a cross used as a weathervane. The cock takes on a double meaning, that of the vacillating Peter and that of "the ever watchful cock, who even in the depth of the night gives notice of how the hours pass."[26] As regards the clock, he writes: "In this tower it is proper to place a clock, tastefully made and in harmony with the style of the building. This is so that the fractions of each hour may be known: inside, by the sound of the bell, and outside by means of the symbol of a star moving around a circle that has been put in a conspicuous place."[27]

27. SEPULCHERS AND CEMETERIES/double cover of a place of entombment/
ring for the tomb/cemeteries/ossuary place/cemetery doorways/.

"Since bishops, priests and other ecclesiastics are permitted by law to be
interred inside the church, it is essential to set down some instruction in
regard to their places of burial." The bishop's site of entombment is located
in front of the choir entrance. To its right Borromeo assigns space for the
canons and cathedral chapter members; on the left, a similar space is prescribed for other priests, clergy, and ecclesiastical ministers of the cathedral.

> In collegiate churches there should be three sepulchers in front of
> the choir. . . . The middle tomb should be for provosts, archbishops,
> or rectors of that church. The second tomb, for canons, and the third
> for other priests, clergy, and ecclesiastical ministers.
> In every parish church there should be two sepulchers, the first
> reserved for the parish priest or rector, the other for the clergy.
> . . . Tombs should be vaulted, and this vaulting should not in any
> way project or rise above the church floor. It must be exactly level.
> To avoid their becoming malodorous, sepulchers should be closed
> with a double cover which should be solid stone, square in shape, or
> of any shape proportioned to the site. A certain space should be left
> between the two covers. The lower one should be rough stone while
> the upper one should be polished stone that is level with the church
> pavement. Moreover, a ring should be inserted in the center of the
> upper cover for the purpose of raising it. This should fit so well that
> nothing protrudes above the level of the pavement. [An area] should
> be cut out from the cover in order to hold the thickness of the ring.

Borromeo takes up a discussion of cemeteries, advocating their placement
on the north side of a church. He recommends that at the top of the main
entrance gate there should be a crucifix "with the image of a head or the skull
of a dead man attached to its base. No vines, fruit bearing trees, no hay nor
fire-wood is to be allowed within the cemetery precincts."[28]

28. SACRISTY/position of the sacristy and its windows/sacristy pavement/
sacristy door/place for the sacred picture and the sacristy altar/oratory
or sacristy altar/prayer tablet/lavabo/cabinet for the sacred vestments/
stands used to hang the sacred vestments/the book ambry/vestry/closet
for the canons' vestments.

29. THE PLACE WHERE BIERS AND OTHER SIMILAR OBJECTS SHOULD BE KEPT

> Close to the sacristy or at least close to the cemetery, another place
> should be constructed in every parochial and collegiate church. In this

[place] should be stored the biers, the large iron candlesticks, the cenotaphs, the oil vases, poles, ladder, brooms, pick-axes, shovels, stands for crosses, also various articles that serve the purpose of cleaning and other similar things. This is so that not only the church but also the sacristy will be completely free from unnecessary obstacles.

The entrance to this place should be well secured with door panels, a latch, and lock.

* * *

Two main classifications of ecclesiastical building types in existence during Borromeo's time were the church and the oratory. The church (thus far discussed) with its major and minor chapels, baptistry, confessionals, and sacristy had precise architectural definitions and a distinct possibility for some architectural variations. The second ecclesiastical type, the oratory, as a fundamentally single rectangular or square room had limited possibilities for spatial variations.

Oratories were hierarchically categorized as public, semiprivate, and those where mass was rarely celebrated, known generally as "wayside shrines."

30. ORATORY IN WHICH THE HOLY SACRIFICE OF THE MASS IS OCCASIONALLY OFFERED

Public oratories were canonically erected for the purpose of religious services. Their architectural plan called for a single nave with the main chapel separated visually from the nave by a single raised step. A short distance ahead was the altar, raised on a two-step platform. The windows of the oratory "should be constructed so high up that one standing outside cannot look in."

Semiprivate oratories were erected in such places as hospitals, orphanages, and schools. They were also found in private residences, usually a priority of the wealthier class.

31. ORATORIES IN WHICH MASS IS NOT CELEBRATED

Oratories in which Mass is not offered and which are likely to be erected along the wayside, should not be constructed in the middle of fields, but on the public road. . . . The site . . . chosen [should be] on a somewhat higher part of the road and a little more distant from the path of carriages so that it will be protected from mud or muddy water.

These oratories may be either square or round . . . in an ornamental manner, well roofed so as to keep the holy images inside completely safe from rain. . . . They should have no altar whatsoever.

Borromeo's meticulous instructions for female monasteries are apparent when one scans the considerations listed below in chapters 32 and 33. One of the primary concerns regarding nuns was that of enclosure, and the Council of Trent reaffirmed this, decreeing that bishops were "under the threat of eternal malediction" if they were careless in their duties toward female monasteries.

> . . . No nun shall after her profession be permitted to go out of the monastery, even for a brief period under any pretext whatever, except for a lawful reason to be approved by the bishop. Neither shall anyone, of whatever birth or condition, sex or age, be permitted, under penalty of excommunication to be incurred *ipso facto*, to enter the enclosure of a monastery without the written permission of the bishop or the superior. . . .[29]

32. A MONASTIC CHURCH FOR NUNS/the main altar/the window to be constructed over the main altar/opening used for setting out the sacred vestments/the opening used for administering Holy Communion/the window for holy relics/opening for holy oils for the sick/the altar steps/ the sacristy/chapels/altar window/the interior church/the bell tower.

When discussing the monastic church, Borromeo describes a large rectangular room divided by a high wall that serves to partition off two distinct spaces: one for the nuns, the other for laymen or visitors. The altar abuts the wall on the side known as the outer church. An opening or grille, as long as the altar, is to be set into the wall above the altar, so that the nuns in the inner church may see and hear Holy Mass.[30]

> The bell tower should be joined to the nuns' inner church: neither its door nor its window, nor even the slightest crack should allow any sight into the outer church.
> The structure of the first floor should be that of a solid vault, within which, or in some side of, may be fashioned a small narrow doorway, through which, when necessary, access to the upper tower is provided. This is to be the only means of access. However, small holes should be bored through the vaulting for the ropes to ring the bells.
> The small doorway mentioned above should be so tightly made that it can be kept closed and furnished for this purpose with two bolts and two locks having two different keys. . . .

33. A MONASTERY FOR NUNS/chapter hall/refectory and wine cellar/kitchen/ place for washing hands/warming room/workroom/porticos/parlors/ locutory window/doors/rotae/bakehouse/laundry/tonsorium/administrative office/food dispensary/pharmacy/upper quarters of a monastery: the dormitory/latrines/site of the novitiate school/wardrobe/ granaries/infirmary/site for the education of young girls/monastery gar-

dens/prison and place of retreat/place for hearing confession/confessor's
lodging/concerning lodging outside the enclosure for farmers and servants who occasionally come to the monastery/dwelling of the lay
sisters/regarding certain precautions to be taken in the general construction of a monastery.

The various, independent parts of the monastery are as follows,
distinguished with respect of their functions. The areas on the ground
floor consist of: the chapter hall, the dining room, the wine cellar, the
kitchen, the warming room, the place to wash hands, the workroom,
the porticos, the interior and exterior parlors, the doors, the rotae or
turn tables, the bake house, laundry, tonsorium, administrative office,
food dispensary, and the pharmacy.

The areas on the upper floor consist of the dormitory or dormitory
cells, the novitiate school, the wardrobe, and the granary or loft.

The separate areas of the monastery include: the infirmary, the
school of young girls, the garden and kitchen garden, the prison and
place of retreat, the interior and exterior place for Confession, the
external accommodation for outside workers, and the accommodation
for the priest-confession.

. . . The diningroom should be adequately large so as to accommodate all the nuns seated along the walls. . . . in the middle of one wall
there should be a raised platform from which spiritual reading can be
heard distinctly . . . A wine cellar should be built under the refec-
tory . . .

The interior and exterior parlor should not be in a remote or
concealed place, but rather situated in a place that is public, visible,
and in proximity to the monastery's entrance. The windows of the
inner room should receive light from the inside of the monastery, and
those of the outer room from the outside. Care must be taken that
beyond the one or more openings used for conversation, no additional aperture be made in the walls between both rooms.

The instructions set down in this chapter are very explicit, and to explore
them is to go beyond the confines of this paper, in that they concern the
fusing of monastic discipline to architectural design. Suffice it to say that
each subheading is treated concisely and thoroughly.

The distinct austerity of future plans, the special character of the buildings
incorporated into the monastic complex, and the effort of Borromeo to
institute and define an architectural vocabulary that would lend itself to the
spiritual and practical aspects of the life-style contained therein eventually
established a pattern that continued for four hundred years.

Then came Vatican II.

Book 2. Instructions for Ecclesiastical Furnishings

Carlo Borromeo prefaced the second book of the *Instructiones* with the
following introduction:

In the first book we explained the size and form of the exterior and interior of ecclesiastical buildings. Now another book follows in which we will talk about ecclesiastical furnishings.

First, we have arranged, in an overall view, the basic furnishings appropriate to the sacred functions and to the parts of each church. This, according to the number of its ministers and its rank.

Then, because it is necessary for those sacred furnishings to be more numerous, various, different in colors, and more elegant on certain established days, it was important, after defining rules, to show also which of these ecclesiastical furnishings should be doubled, trebled, quadrupled, quintupled, and even more, to allow changes for washing.

Finally, we wanted to give some examples of all the furnishings listed so that the material may be both appropriate to the purpose of the solemnities and the rules for the rite, and, in so far as possible, fitting in every respect in every church.

All of book 2 is a catalog of minute descriptions for each and every liturgical vestment, object, and furnishing. There are norms for processional crosses, lengths for capes, descriptions for vestments, recommendations for altar linens, measurements for hand towels, and prescriptions for priests' handkerchiefs. The two books were intended to help create an ecclesiastical ambience that, in Borromeo's consideration, would lead the congregant to an interior equilibrium fundamental to a predisposition for prayer.[31] The value of the *Instructiones* is still to be plumbed as it continues to present researchers with a thorough and reliable font of liturgical traditions otherwise obscure or alien to contemporary society.[32]

Notes

This paper is indebted in part to research funds from Clemson University, S. C.; the American Council of Learned Societies; and the Istituto per la Storia dell'Arte Lombarda, Milan, Italy.

1. H. Jedin, *Crisis and Closure of the Council of Trent* (London, 1964); idem, *Geschichte des Konzils von Trient* (Freiburg, 1949–75), 4, pt. 2, 785–89.

2. P. Prodi, *Il Cardinale Gabriele Paleotti* (1522–1597) (Rome, 1959–67), 1:193–232; *Il Concilio di Trento e la Riforma Tridentina, Atti del Convegno . . . Trento . . . 1963* (Rome, 1965); C. Black, "Perugia and Post-Tridentine Church Reform," *Journal of Ecclesiastical History* 35 (1984): 429–51. M. Bendiscoli, "Carlo Borromeo cardinale nepote arcivescovo di Milano e la riforma della Chiesa milanese," *Storia di Milano* (Milan, 1957), 10:119–99; also E. Cattaneo, "Le religione a Milano dall'età della Controriforma," ibid. 12:294–98.

3. A. Palestra, "Le visite pastorali di S. Carlo," *Ambrosius*, supplement to 3 (1966): 43, 901, lists a chronology and description of procedures for visitations. See also R. Mols. "San Carlo Borromeo iniziatore delle pastorale moderna," *Ambrosius*, suppl. to 5 (1961): 9–88.

4. *Acta Ecclesiae Mediolanensis*, ed. A. Ratti (Milan, 1890), cols. 265–67. Hereafter cited as *AEM*.

5. *AEM*, col. 265.

6. Archivio Curia Arcivescovile di Milano, section 10, *Visite Pastorali, Pievi Diverse,* xvi.

7. *AEM,* col. 905, Decretum 46, "Visitatio a Praefectis urbis et Vicariis Foraneis obeunda et alia quaedam;" also col. 1640, "De Visitatoribus."

8. C. Marcora, "Monsignor Ludovico Moneta, collaboratore di San Carlo, in una biografia coeva," *Memorie storiche della Diocesi di Milano* 10 (1963): 445–94.

9. E. Voelker, "Charles Borromeo's 'Instructiones fabricae et supellectilis ecclesiasticae, 1577.' A translation with commentary and analysis" (Ph.D. diss., Syracuse University, 1977), 46.

10. The allotted space per person was calculated for a church where there were no benches. Borromeo used the Milanese ecclesiastical *cubito* = 0.426 m. A narrow foldout *cubito* was bound into each copy of the *Instructiones.*

11. Voelker, "Charles Borromeo's 'Instructiones,' " 56–75.

12. The vital friendship between St. Philip Neri and St. Charles Borromeo cannot be ignored. In 1575, when Gregory XIII officially recognized the importance of the apostolic work of St. Philip and his community, their church of S. Maria in Vallicella, Rome, was begun. Although the facade was not completed until 1605, the architect Rughesi followed St. Philip's iconographic program, which reads identically with that of Borromeo's third chapter. Since the facade plans dated ca. 1574 and the Borromeo norms date 1577, speculation links Borromeo's inspiration with that of the church norms of St. Philip Neri.

13. Gian Possevino, a Milanese contemporary of Borromeo, discusses the return to the old practice of separating the sexes. Two clerics were assigned posts in front of the *Duomo* doors and if any male crossed to the female side, causing confusion, the constables were to take him to prison. See G. B. Possevino, *Discorsi della vita et attioni di Carlo Borromeo* (Rome, 1591), 55 and 90.

14. In June 1883, the Sacred Congregation of Rites in decree 2576, canon 1, incorporated Borromeo's norm stating that if the last or top step of an altar dais were of marble, it was to have a strong wooden insert as long as the altar table. The priest must celebrate with his feet on the wooden section, although rugs may be used to cover these steps. (Long before the Borromean norm was incorporated into law, wooden inserts appeared in early American churches.)

15. Borromeo was drawing on a disciplinary recommendation of Trent. In November 1563, after the twenty-fourth session, directives were issued regarding communal prayer. The recommendation was that "all shall be obliged to perform the divine offices in person and not by substitutes; also to assist and serve the bishop when celebrating or exercising other pontifical functions and, in the choir instituted for psalmody, to praise the name of God reverently, distinctly, and devoutly in hymns and canticles. . . . With regard to matters that pertain to the proper manner of conducting the divine offices, the proper way of singing . . . the definite rule for assembling and remaining in choir . . . the provincial synod shall prescribe [these things] for each province." H. Schroeder, ed., *Canons and Decrees of the Council of Trent* (New York, 1941), 93.

All the Milan Provincial Councils during Borromeo's time refer to the need to distinguish the choir space from that of the nave, i.e., the laity from the clergy, during a liturgical function, *AEM,* col. 1121.

16. Voelker, "Charles Borromeo's" Instructiones,' " 187–206.

17. *AEM,* col. 37.

18. Johannes Molanus, *De Picturis et Imaginibus Sacris, Liber unus, tractans de vitandis circa eas abusibus ac de earundem significationibus* (Louvain, 1570).

19. P. Prodi, in "Ricerche sulla teorica delle arti figurative nella riforma cattolica," *Archivio Italiano per la storia della pietà* 4 (1965): 137, 144.

20. These may be found in Paola Barrochi's *Trattati d'Arte del Cinquecento fra Manierismo e Controriforma* (Bari, 1961), 2:117–509. For informative material on Paleotti's influence on art and artists, see Günther Heinz, "Carlo Dolci, Studien zur religiösen Malerei im 17. Jahrhundert," *Jahrbuch der kunsthistorischen Sammlungen in Wien* 56 (1960): 197–234.

21. A. Diamond, "Cardinal Federico Borromeo as a Patron and Critic of the Arts and His MVSAEVM of 1625" (Ph.D. diss., University of California, 1974).

22. For further studies on the extended impact of the norms upon art, see Prodi, "Ricerche," 123–212.

23. *AEM*, col. 1958.

24. *AEM*, col. 52; Voelker, "Charles Borromeo's 'Instructiones,'" 297–304.

25. Ambrosiana Library, Milan, MS Gian Battista Casali, fol. 51.

26. J. Neale and B. Webb, eds., *Rationale Divinorum Officiorum of William Durandus* (London, 1893) 1:23.

27. Voelker, "Charles Borromeo's 'Instructiones,'" 328–98.

28. *AEM*, cols. 111–112, 323, 325, 1189. *Cum primum Apostolatus* (1 April 1566), a bull promulgated by Pope Pius V, ordered that sarcophagi above the ground, modest or elaborate, were to be removed from all churches. On Borromeo and the removal of the monumental Bernabo Visconti tomb, see Archivio Arcivescovile di Milano, sec. 10, *S. Alessandro* 4:2.

29. Schroeder, *Canons and Decrees of the Council of Trent*, 220–21.

30. The window or grating of the main altar had been discussed in the First Provincial Council of 1565. Borromeo cautioned that all windows and grilles through which the nuns could look into the church (with the exception of the small opening through which they received communion) were to be covered with a linen cloth that was to be removed only at the moment of elevating the Eucharist during Mass. The arrangement of this window was to be such that the priest could not see the nuns. *AEM*, 141. By 1576 Borromeo's recommendation is even more restrictive: "In the event that the grille is located in such a position that the nuns can see into the outer church, a brick wall is to be built to block their view." *AEM*, col. 479.

31. M. L. Gatti Perer, "Progetto e destino dell'edificio sacro dopo S. Carlo," in *San Carlo e il suo tempo*, vol. 1 (Rome, 1986).

32. Lucia A. Ciapponi and I are jointly preparing a complete translation of book 2 of the *Instructiones* and a revision of book 1. Both translations will be supported by commentary and analysis.

The Borromean Ideal
and the Spanish Church

A. D. WRIGHT

WHEN IN 1796 POPE PIUS VI BEATIFIED JUAN DE RIBERA, THE UNFORTUNATE
pontiff contrasted the revolutionary tribulations of the church, where false
prophets appeared in sheep's clothing but were ravaging wolves, with the
exemplary virtues of the patriarch of Antioch, archbishop of Valencia from
1569 to his death in 1611.[1] Saint Charles Borromeo, archbishop of Milan
from the end of the Council of Trent to his own death in 1584, had been
canonized as early as 1610, so that Ribera's successor, Fray Isidro Aliaga, in
reporting to Rome on the rich devotional life of Valencia which Ribera had
fostered, mentioned, among the confraternities, one dedicated to Saint
Charles, conspicuous for its Holy Week flagellant procession. This point in
Aliaga's *ad limina* report of 1617 was substantially repeated in 1622, and the
subordination of this confraternity to archiepiscopal authority, in the approved Borromean tradition, made a particularly dramatic contrast with the
excesses of an unauthorized popular cult that grew up in the city, diocese,
and province of Valencia, following the death in 1612, of a local priest,
Simon, reputedly in the odor of sanctity. The attempts of Archbishop
Aliaga, and even more remarkably of the Spanish Inquisition, to repress this
cult had barely succeeded by 1622, against a popular tumult in the city, in
1619, and open-air Masses in honor of the dead priest celebrated, as Aliaga
lamented in 1617, amid the irreverence of crowds of men, women, mules,
horses, and carts. Such extraordinary devotional licence, in the face of even
Inquisitorial authority in Spain, might at first seem to suggest that the legacy
of Ribera was far from the closely ordered piety of the Milanese church
directed by Charles Borromeo.[2] Yet a closer examination of both men,
equally inspired by Luis de Granada for example, will reveal striking similarities, as well as obvious contrasts stemming from personal background
and political situation, rather than from differing ecclesiastical ideals.

During his own, shorter archiepiscopate, Charles Borromeo admired
Ribera's work, and an exchange of synodal decrees was suggested.[3] Contemporary appreciation of the achievements of the archbishop of Milan, ex-

pressed for example by Gregory Martin and Agostino Valier, established Borromeo as the ideal post-Tridentine bishop. This tradition has of course been traced, by modern scholars such as Jedin and Broutin, among conscious imitators of his episcopal activity, in sixteenth-, seventeenth-, and even eighteenth-century France and Italy. However, practical concern to emulate the diocesan legislation and administration of Charles Borromeo, as well as enthusiasm for his cult—as officially established from the early seventeenth century—can be found in other areas, such as Poland and Spain, on the evidence of the correspondence of Federico Borromeo, cousin of Charles and himself archbishop of Milan from 1595 to 1631. Moreover the different length of their episcopates, Charles Borromeo's at Milan and Ribera's at Valencia, does not alter the extent of their similar concerns, nor can the apparent collapse of some of Ribera's enterprises, in the chaos that followed the expulsion of the Valencian Moriscos and his own death, be simply contrasted with a Borromean achievement at Milan established securely on Charles's death. For much of what Charles Borromeo had effected there, against real opposition—clerical and lay, local and Spanish—to post-Tridentine Catholic reforms, was seriously challenged or even briefly overturned under his unfortunate successor, Gaspare Visconti. Only the long archiepiscopate of Federico Borromeo, beginning in 1595 and thus overlapping in part with the last stage of Ribera's episcopate, succeeded in reasserting eventually the Caroline standards of ecclesiastical and religious life at Milan. Even then there remained much real opposition, not least from Spanish secular authority, particularly in the first years of his episcopate.

The origins of the extraordinary eminence and potential powers of Charles Borromeo, as a papal nephew, obviously determined to a large degree his relations as archbishop with the papacy. Although these relations were not as totally free of strain or conflict as is sometimes supposed, nevertheless it could be said that Charles imposed obedience to Rome on others, while asserting the legitimate rights of the Milanese church. Ribera's personal status as patriarch of Antioch, as well as archbishop of Valencia by royal nomination, indicated a link with the papacy unusual among Spanish episcopal appointments after the Council of Trent. For the independent action of Pius V in bestowing the patriarchal title and pallium on the young bishop of Badajoz was the occasion for papal praise both of the defence of papal rights by the deceased Spanish prelate who had held the title and of the pastoral example set by Ribera's personal administration of the sacraments to other Spanish diocesans.[4] On Ribera's translation to the archbishopric of Valencia, his double title as patriarch and archbishop was always meticulously observed in government correspondence; but the archbishop of Valencia was also *ex officio* chancellor of the university of that city, distinguished among the Iberian universities at that date for its unusual defence of papal rather than royal legal rights, as well as for its precocious—even by Spanish standards—promotion of the doctrine of the Immaculate Conception.[5] Unlike his predecessor, Ribera held no provincial, as opposed to diocesan synod, despite the urging of Charles Borromeo; yet the latter recognized the reasons behind this, the royal insistence on the presence of royal representatives, as at the Spanish provincial councils of 1565, and the limitations on ecclesiastical freedom that this represented, as Quiroga was still to find at Toledo in 1582.[6] Ribera never succeeded in paying an *ad limina* visit to Rome in person, despite setting out on one occasion, which was more than most post-Tridentine Spanish bishops were prepared to do, as the papacy and the nuncios in Spain often lamented.[7] But his *ad limina* report of 1597, presented by proctor, did not hesitate to point out those areas, in the attempted regulation of Morisco life or the provision of worthy parish priests with adequate incomes, where curial practices or the action of nuncios was hampering archiepiscopal efforts. Indeed Ribera's personal control of licensing confessors and preachers, issuing to priests their *celebret*, examining those presented from whatever source for benefices, and reviewing, with legal experts, the sentences of his diocesan judicial officials, was truly in the style of Borromeo, as were personal visitation of the diocese and continuous personal residence. Regulation of the cathedral chapter and services, which Borromeo similarly made a personal priority, was to a degree made possible for Ribera by the peculiarity at Valencia that the archbishop was the formal head of the chapter, which required his presence or his vicar's to meet or act.[8]

The detailed legislation of Borromeo, in the matter of church furnishings as well as the conduct of ceremonies, was indeed notorious even among his contemporaries. While he revived and defended the distinct Ambrosian liturgical and musical use at Milan, he elsewhere imposed the postconciliar standard of the Roman rite against all opposition. Similarly Ribera, as a young bishop at Badajoz, at the time of the Compostellan provincial council that followed that of Trent, had already demonstrated a concern to end abuses connected with the saying of Mass in Spain, in a way admittedly comparable to the concern of other Spanish diocesans then and into the seventeenth century. He subsequently became conspicuous for establishing liturgical and devotional standards that may still be observed at Valencia.[9] While his care of such matters at the cathedral, possibly limited by the financial complications of providing adequate clerical service,[10] most noticeably resulted in the performance on Saturday evenings of the Marian *Salve*, the Counter-Reformation devotion to the Reserved Sacrament was not lacking there. It found its full expression in his purpose-built chapel at his foundation of the college of Corpus Christi. There the ceremonies of the Mass and the other services were regulated with an exquisite detail worthy of Borromeo, and the concern to ensure grandeur, against the background of much Spanish malpractice, was enshrined in the minimum timings laid down for the saying of Mass and the singing of offices. Only in the climax of the liturgical celebrations of the feast of Corpus Christi itself did the founder perhaps depart from the canon of Borromean austerity: he originally intended that the four stations of the procession, at the four corners of the cloister of his college, should be marked not only by the arts of music and painting, but also by the dances of *seises*, as remembered from his own boyhood amid Seville's splendors.[11]

The other most conspicuous similarity of the concerns of Ribera to those of Borromeo was arguably the provision of clerical education in the form of a seminary conducted on explicitly Tridentine lines. Here the foundation of the patriarchal college of Corpus Christi was an even more outstanding achievement, in Spain, than was Borromeo's lead in establishing diocesan seminaries in Italy. For the establishment of true seminaries after the Council of Trent, and even until the suppression of the Jesuits in the eighteenth century, was notoriously a failure in Spain—despite eventual successes at Burgos or pious intentions, such as those of Quiroga in 1582—with all too few honorable exceptions.[12] The quality of the secular clergy for the diocese of Valencia was of particular importance, given the local privileges, periodically defended, of excluding non-natives from benefices, in a way comparable to conditions in many other parts of the post-Tridentine church.[13] Ribera's concern to control his own foundation, his search for royal patronage of the college, and his decision to appoint seculars, not Jesuits, as the staff of the foundation should not be assumed to mark serious divergence from the Tridentine norm. For Borromeo's experiences, in the creation of a diocesan seminary, led him to replace Jesuit direction by his own specially created diocesan elite of clergy, the Oblates of St. Ambrose; the work of the diocesan seminary was complemented by the education provided for those of the requisite qualities at the Collegio Borromeo at Pavia, under Borromean rather than Milanese control. Borromeo's relations with the Jesuits at Milan remained indeed correct rather than conspicuously warm, even to the extent that their church there was, unusually, erected under the direction of the archbishop rather than of the society. Ribera's relations with the Jesuits, on the other hand, were excellent from the start, even when he was still bishop of Badajoz and appreciating their pastoral efforts in rural Spain, at a time, not indeed brief, when the society was viewed with grave suspicion in royal, episcopal, and inquisitorial circles there. It was in effect Ribera's defence of Jesuit claims to enter the educational arena in Valencia—the cause of conflict between the society and university authorities not only in Spain but throughout Catholic Europe after the Council of Trent—that led to his first major crisis as archbishop: the conflict with those of his cathedral canons who were defending the claims of the university.

But this early conflict of his archiepiscopate also involved a swift realization that his relations with the Inquisition, whose authority had also been touched on in the case, were not to be easy.[14] After the defeat of any proposals to introduce at Milan the presence or procedure of the distinct Spanish Inquisition, Charles Borromeo was able with little difficulty to establish his dominance over the local tribunal of the Holy Office. Problems relating to Milanese contacts with the heretics of Alpine or trans-Alpine Europe arose rather in terms of the political considerations necessary for Spanish government in northern Italy. But, by Charles's death, not only was Lombardy essentially free of heresy, but he had even carried the campaign against Protestantism into the Alps, by his visitation, as apostolic visitor, of certain valleys and his concern to train priests to work in such areas. Ribera, on the other hand, as the son of a Spanish viceroy of Naples, could hardly be suspected of using archiepiscopal authority to arouse native unrest or assert noble independence, as the Spanish government at times accused Borromeo of doing. It was obviously impossible that Borromeo should have acted even as interim governor of Milan, despite the later periods of interim viceregal administration in Sicily by the archbishop of Palermo, Cardinal Doria. Ribera's brief period of office as viceroy as well as archbishop at Valencia was more naturally in the tradition of those cardinals in Spanish service who at times served as viceroys at Naples, distinct from the Italian cardinal archbishops of that city. But even this period of viceregal office on Ribera's part ended abruptly with the *Corts* of Valencia directed by Lerma. The attempts of the archbishop to repress clerical participation in violent crime in the kingdom, despite the support obtained eventually from papal authority, led to local conflict with secular and clerical representatives, even if not on the dramatic scale of Borromeo's defence of his right of a private police force for the imposition of clerical order, against secular opposition both local and royal.[15] It is in the light of such considerations that Ribera's momentous shift of opinion, on the problem of the Valencian Moriscos, can perhaps best be viewed. While he had certainly contemplated the possibility of an eventual expulsion as early as 1591, his agreement with the outlines, if not the detail, of the final governmental decision is well known. But he alone, as opposed to other clerical and lay supposed contributors, had made real financial provision, under royal orders, for the successive plans to provide adequate religious instruction for the Moriscos, until the expulsion. Such attempts at true conversion, continued into the seventeenth century, also revealed that his good relations with new or reformed religious orders were more in line with Borromean concerns than were his own uneasy relations with the other diocesan bishops of the Valencian province in their far from rich sees.[16] Ribera's eventual decision that expulsion, not further attempts at conversion, was necessary may indeed have turned as much on a genuine belief that an armed conspiracy against Catholic Spain was at hand, as on a growing disillusionment with attempts at catechizing the Morisco population. He was unsuccessful in his own attempts to forestall the likely consequences of the expulsion in economic terms, for the work of the archiepiscopal see met with little royal encouragement; the continued attempts, after his death, to recover for the needs of his seminary foundation those episcopal revenues originally diverted, at royal orders, to the education of Morisco boys and girls, failed in the face of Inquisitorial determination to regain some of the economic ground lost to the tribunal from its most obvious source of income previously, from whatever funds existed. Yet the foundation, and even the founder's collection of religious art, comparable in miniature to the Milanese institution of the Ambrosiana, by Federico Borromeo, survived this crisis.[17] The economic consequences of the expulsion for archiepiscopal authority were perhaps more severely compounded by the selection of a friar, Aliaga, to succeed the noble Ribera. Thus the remarkable repetition of incidents akin to those of Ribera's own early episcopate, with the posting of pasquinades against Aliaga on the door of the cathedral and the suspected complicity of those canons with whom the archbishop was in dispute, should not be taken as simple evidence that Ribera had achieved nothing in the end: the circumstances of the Valencian church after the expulsion were too distinct to allow such a ready inference. The conflict at the cathedral was, moreover, in part at least over the determination of Aliaga to continue Ribera's imposition of the Roman rite in every detail.[18] Even well before, in the preparations made for Quiroga's provincial council of 1582 at Toledo, advice, from a cathedral canon there as well as from a Jesuit, included points worthy of emulation not only from Borromeo's provincial synods of Milan, but also from diocesan synodal decrees of Ribera at Valencia.[19]

In an area that shared some of the peculiar problems of the Valencian province, that of Granada, a tradition of vigorous episcopal activity and independence asserted where necessary against papal or even royal authority, expressed in governmental or Inquisitorial form, had existed since at least the later stages of the Council of Trent. At the end of the sixteenth century, the independence of Archbishop Pedro de Castro was certainly marked in such spheres, even if his determination to establish a cult of the "relics" he believed to have been discovered on the Sacro Monte of Granada proved more troublesome to the papacy than the less problematic translations of proper saints and embellishment of their cults that took place in sixteenth-century Spain in Toledo, Valencia, and Cordoba, for example, as much as in Borromean Milan.[20] The legislation of Charles Borromeo's councils was however explicitly cited by Archbishop de Castro in his *ad limina* report to Rome of 1596, in his search for papal support of true archiepiscopal control over the hearing of confessions by regular clergy and over the testing of real vocation in girls entered by their parents and family for conventual life. In the case of Granada, as of Valencia, then, the example of Charles Borromeo was valued for the assertion of independent episcopal authority, as restored potentially by the decrees of the Council of Trent, not as a jurisdictional end in itself, but as the means of imposing true standards of ecclesiastical reform and religious life.[21] The investigation of such active Spanish prelates, or of those whose activity was eventually obstructed by royal intervention, as in the case of Quiroga's unpublished provincial decrees from the Toledo council of 1582, certainly heightens the contrast with conditions after the Council of Trent in those Spanish dioceses, Avila for example or Calahorra, where bishops and chapters became locked in jurisdictional battles of ever greater legal complexity, with apparently little pastoral advantage to be shown in the end.[22] From such initial comparisons of the variety of Spanish conditions after the Council of Trent with those in the exemplary, if certainly not typical, case of Milan under the Borromeo archbishops in Italy, an impression is perhaps gained of the real efforts made by many Spanish bishops to enforce Tridentine standards: the decrees of diocesan synods of the late sixteenth and early seventeenth century repeat orders not only for clerical decency of dress and behavior, administration of the sacraments and saying of Mass, but also for preaching and catechizing, the regulation of lay devotion and popular piety, the enforcement of postconciliar standards of morality and the application of charitable legacies. But an impression is perhaps also confirmed of the very real obstacles to such attempted reform by Spanish prelates, epitomized by the royal objections to certain of the 1582 proposed Toledan provincial decrees, intended to apply Tridentine norms to local needs, precisely on the grounds that such proposals represented innovation in Spanish traditions and as such were unacceptable. Amid such difficulties and the peculiar problems of the kingdom of Valencia with its essentially non-Catholic Morisco population, the achievements of San Juan de Ribera, even by the exacting standards of Charles Borromeo, arguably appear all the more remarkable.

Other Spanish prelates, after the Council of Trent, could also be compared favorably with Borromeo, however. Cardinal Zapata's main claim to eminence, like that of so many Iberian bishops, was essentially that of political service to the crown, even in the face, when necessary, of Roman disapprobation. Yet before he became archbishop of Burgos—a see including remote mountain areas where poverty and clerical inadequacy were so endemic as to defeat even his efforts—his heroic charitable provision for the faithful at Pamplona during a plague epidemic was such as to prompt subsequent comparison with that of Borromeo at Milan.[23] The special plague regulations of Charles Borromeo, directed to his diocesan clergy, were not in the end incorporated, in the 1582 provincial council decrees of Quiroga's Toledan synod, for eventual use in Spain: objection from the royal court that the plague instructions were hardly part of normal provincial legislation was accepted. But Quiroga's own charitable provision at Toledo, in social emergencies as well as more generally, was on the Borromean scale.[24] So too in Portugal, where the personal action of Archbishop Bragança at Evora to relieve distress in similar circumstances was interrupted only by the necessity of his temporary absence from his see, following the Spanish annexation of the kingdom.[25] The Portuguese inspiration to Borromeo himself, from the published work of Archbishop de Martyribus of Braga,—itself another link with Ribera—indeed predated even the Spanish admiration for the Caroline *Acta* of the Milanese church as published within Charles's own lifetime.

The variety of practical application of Borromean standards, found after all in Italy itself in the critical enthusiasm of Bollani as well as of Paleotti and Valier, was also exemplified in Portugal, in later archiepiscopates at the primatial see of Braga, after the retirement of de Martyribus on the advent of the Spanish monarch.[26] The distinction of the Rite of Braga, falling like the Ambrosian Rite within the degree of antiquity that the new Tridentine liturgical norms allowed to be preserved, was carefully maintained in the Mass and Office at the cathedral, even if its use was displaced by the Roman Rite in other churches of the diocese where it had remained.[27] In Spain, however, objection was explicit from the royal court, at the time of Quiroga's provincial council and the monarch's preoccupation with Portuguese affairs, to the Borromean application of post-Tridentine papal rules for the attendance of medical practitioners on those who were in danger of neglecting their religious duties: such rigor was not to be imitated in Spain, just as, in fact, it created problems in Venetian-ruled Padua. Yet although the matter was left to the conscience of individual bishops of the Toledan ecclesiastical province and not incorporated in those parts of the conciliar acts which were originally intended to be published as formal provincial decrees, subsequent application in Spain at the level of diocesan synodal legislation can be found.[28] Quiroga's own aim of establishing greater liturgical uniformity in his ecclesiastical province, by means of his revised ritual, was clear at this time and equally in line with the metropolitan directives of Borromeo. The Borromean aims of separating male and female worshippers in parish churches and of prohibiting disruptive begging during church services were also reproduced in the decrees of post-Tridentine Spanish bishops, as was the concern to prevent unlicensed or unsuitable statues and decorations in churches, and the placing of crosses or statues in places where they might be treated with casual disrespect. The ideal of using confraternities to eradicate popular blasphemy as well as to foster devotion to the Reserved Sacrament, alongside the encouragement of systematic catechetical instruction of both children and adults, was another reflection in Spanish episcopal legislation, after Trent, of Borromean priorities. So also were attempts to guard the faithful from spurious indulgences, whether or not related to the activity of mendicants, and to regulate both proprietary

seating and funerary display within churches: Spanish bishops shared Borromeo's concerns. The attempt to exclude the laity from the chancels of
churches that led to celebrated Milanese conflict over the placing of the
governor's throne in the cathedral, with repercussions in the contested
legatine role of the viceroy in Sicily and appeals at Milan to the disposition of
choir stalls in Toledo cathedral, met in Spain itself with greater obstruction.
Objection at the royal court to the likely exclusion of lay patrons, male or
even female, from the choirs of parish churches followed the general defence
of patrons' rights immediately after the Council of Trent itself and was
specifically asserted at the time of Quiroga's 1582 provincial council, despite
the continued efforts of some bishops subsequently.[29]

Indeed the immediately post-Tridentine royal orders to guard against
innovation in such matters, as in royal rights and lay privileges more generally, were issued with reference to the first provincial councils in Spain, held
in 1565–66, but also to any such councils that should meet in Milan, as well
as in Naples or Sicily. The special status of the conciliar decrees nevertheless
issued at Milan, in the eyes of Spanish episcopal reformers, was thus all the
more strikingly evident, in the use made of Borromean legislation, in the
preparation of draft decrees for Quiroga's 1582 council. It was also particularly noted, moreover, that Ribera's diocesan synodal decrees represented a worthy source of detailed inspiration, as did the decrees of the
Valencian provincial council held, under a predecessor of Ribera's as archbishop, immediately after the Council of Trent. The relative success, in
Spain, of the Valencian example in matching Italian standards and Iberian
limitations was demonstrated in relation to the vexed question of the Tridentine provision for provincial regulation of the required qualities in newly
appointed bishops, given the royal rights of patronage in such appointments
in fact. It was also demonstrated in the delicate wording of published
descriptions of provincial conciliar authority, given Roman sensitivity to any
implied independence of papal supremacy and royal determination, in 1582
as much as in 1565, to control provincial councils in Spain. In the light of
these constraints, the relative success of the Castilian episcopate—at least in
the Toledan province—in pursuing Tridentine ideals despite the eventual
failure to publish Quiroga's provincial decrees, even after papal approval,
compares favorably with the Valencian experience.[30] Elsewhere in the crown
of Aragon, however, for all the efforts of the archbishops of Tarragona and of
certain other diocesan bishops, standards clearly remained lower: whether in
terms of a lack of liturgical uniformity, or with reference to the education and
morals of the clergy, the maintenance of cathedrals and their liturgical
standards, or the behavior of monks, canons regular, and mendicants.[31] In
both Castile and Aragon, however, the episcopal attempt to enforce strict
enclosure and ascetic life in female convents, and to regulate popular devotion in confraternities, pilgrimage, and vigils, maintained a Borromean en-

ergy. These were indeed areas where even Charles Borromeo had not been assured of success, as the history of the Ursulines of Varese and Novara, for example, demonstrated. Yet, as nuncios as well as bishops in post-Tridentine Spain knew, there were peculiar problems present in Spain, over and above those encountered in Italy, not least royal defence of the traditions of social intercourse between noble laywomen and wellborn nuns and the pervasive social phenomenon of the unenclosed *beatas*.[32]

If the extraordinary detail of ceremonial protocol enshrined in Spanish episcopal agreements with cathedral chapters—designed to settle some of the persistent discords after Trent still between prelates and canons in the Iberian kingdoms—thus reflects the legal training of so many of the higher clergy of the peninsula and indeed the legal careers of many appointed in old age to bishoprics of Philip II and his successors, a wider concern for standards of public devotion can also on occasion be found. The origin of the Herreran *lonja* in Seville, in a desire to exclude commercial business from the grandiose spaces of the cathedral, was in line with Borromeo's determination to close the great passages of Milan cathedral to secular thoroughfare. The severity of Borromean attitudes to popular festivity on Sundays or holy days, in the form of dancing or comedies, as with his restrictive positions on usurious interest as well as on carnival licence, were all reflected in post-Tridentine Spanish episcopal activity, even if not with certain success.[33] At the level of more positive provision of pastoral care, Ribera was far from unusual in his attention to personal visitation of parishes, involving preaching and confirming, as well as communicating the faithful. Instances of bishops hearing confessions in person were indeed rare in Spain, although episcopal visitation of the sick or poor in their own homes was not unknown.[34] Still occasionally found, following Tridentine provision, was episcopal direction of confessors in cases of conscience, by means of periodic instruction or meeting of confessors, at least as far as regulars did not escape from episcopal control in Spain. More frequent was the reordering of diocesan administration in order to subject rural deans and archdeacons more truly to episcopal supervision. Similarly, attempts to improve the standing and force of church courts, by means of salaried judicial officials and closer regulation of lawyers and fees in episcopal tribunals, betrayed a relatively frequent following of Borromean standards. The Tridentine ideal of restoring the efficacy of excommunication and spiritual censures, by their more restricted, clerical use, proved more difficult to achieve in Spain than even in Italy, whatever the complications of continued issue of censures by Roman tribunals for prelates in both the Italian and Iberian peninsulas.[35] In the Spanish kingdoms episcopal jurisdiction was circumscribed by royal defence of the jurisdiction of secular tribunals in appeals, from the end of the Council of Trent onwards, as well as by the competitive action of local secular justice. Nevertheless Ribera did not hesitate to use spiritual censures against lay authorities, even if his action lacked the drama of Borromean confrontation with civil government in the Ambrosian see.[36] The universal conflicts in the post-Tridentine church over the terms of the revised bull *In Coena Domini,* from the sixteenth to the eighteenth century, however, did include rare examples of brave Spanish prelates, including Quiroga himself, and Portuguese bishops, even after the Spanish succession in that kingdom, attempting to make the terms public. Such Iberian examples admittedly did not usually extend to preaching of the bull as publicly as at Santiago, where indeed sermons of specific Milanese inspiration were also published.[37]

The limitations imposed on the powers of Spanish bishops even after Trent arose not least from the generous exemptions from practical episcopal jurisdiction, for seculars and regulars as well as laity, provided by the sale of the *cruzada* bull on the one hand and the privileged status of the Inquisition and its numerous familiars on the other. In Portugal the extensive peculiars of the military orders, with their appropriated parishes, were also an obstacle to effective episcopal control, even in so rich and well-administered a see as Evora. Indeed this problem was arguably even more acute, at least in proportion to the size of dioceses, in Portugal than in Spain, where however the large enclaves under both military orders and monastic communities proved an equally frequent disturbance to pastoral care by bishops in Castile and above all in Aragon.[38] A few Spanish bishops attempted, with predictably small success, to maintain a right, as ordinaries, to investigate any possible heresy among the faithful of their diocese. The opposition of the Spanish Inquisition to any such claims was naturally adamant, while Spanish bishops after Trent received relatively little support from Rome in any clashes specifically with Inquisitorial authority. Archbishop Pedro de Castro, acting in the tradition of his precedessors in the see of Granada to confront boldly either Inquisitorial or local representation of royal judicial authority if the need arose, failed to secure Roman support for his plan to have the Inquisition remove the *sanbenitos* hanging in the cathedral. But his concern to encourage while controlling in person and in detail the work of new orders, that of the hospitaller brothers of John of God above all, was in the Borromean tradition, even if again not receiving always the fullest Roman support.[39] His outspoken letter to the king on the expulsion of the Moriscos, in the early seventeenth century, was also in the Ambrosian tradition of forthright comment on moral or public questions, even if he diverged from Ribera's final view on this specific issue of the Moriscos.[40] The cult that he established on the Sacro Monte of Granada and continued to foster financially even after his own translation to Seville was reminiscent of the Borromean care for the north Italian pilgrimage, mountains, and sanctuaries, despite papal caution over the "relics" that de Castro believed to have demonstrated the antiquity of the Marian doctrine, specifically promoted over a long period in Spain. While still at Granada he took great pains to try to establish Borromean standards for female conventual life, in the most difficult aspect of testing girls to determine their vocation or their mere subjection to family pressures. So too in his campaign to subject regular confessors to real episcopal examination and regulation, not least with regard to female penitents, against characteristic mendicant opposition and evasion, he again cited specific Borromean provincial legislation, as well as precedents from Valencia and the decrees of Carafa and Colonna at Naples and Salerno respectively.[41] After this translation to Seville, he took up, in extreme old age, the long-standing battle of archbishops of that see to discipline their cathedral and diocesan clergy, a struggle not made easier by relative episcopal neglect earlier in the sixteenth century and by Roman as well as royal intervention in the riches of the bishopric and its benefices. His occasionally forthright remarks on curial practice were indeed worthy of Borromeo, while consequent lack of adequate priests for the pastoral work of the diocese led him to compare Seville with the Indies themselves. His campaigns, continued at Seville, to reform female convents, reduce hospital provision to efficiently concentrated institutions, and circumscribe the notorious behavior of the city's confraternities and their public processions, all reflected Borromean ideals, even if meeting with the normal Spanish obstacles to reform on these three issues, as well as with curial complications. A further parallel, in all these aspects, was provided by his attempt to reduce the abusive expansion in the numbers of private oratories, which he had more successfully restrained at Granada, with a truly Borromean severity.[42]

Other Spanish bishops, after the Council of Trent, were more concerned perhaps to regulate hermits and hermitages in line with the Borromean regulation of lay devotion, especially where female hermits or mixed pilgrimages were concerned. Some were equally unafraid to draw attention, where necessary, to action in curial tribunals or by nuncios in Spain that disrupted episcopal attempts to impose Tridentine standards of clerical and lay discipline. While synodal decrees, intending to impose proper clerical dress and celibacy and to exclude suspect females from clerics' company were more marked by their necessary reiteration than by the famed severity from the start of Borromeo's regulations, the detail laid down with regard to clerical comportment or the furnishing of churches could sometimes recall the fineness of the Milanese legislation.[43] The Toledan conciliar provisions of 1582 included concern that the liturgical text should be clearly audible in church music, despite the fact that Spanish ecclesiastical practice, even at musical centers as important as Toledo itself and Evora, was more marked by the employment of lay singers and instrumentalists—to reinforce the clerical vicars and organists in cathedral use—in a tradition less restrictive than that adopted by Borromeo at least in Milan itself.[44] Borromeo's wider concern for the survival of Catholicism, under persecution elsewhere in Europe, was typified by his appointment of an exiled Scots bishop as his substitute at the basilica of S. Maria Maggiore in Rome. This Borromean concern found a reflection in Ribera's outright opposition to the Spanish peace with England and truce with the Dutch, in the early seventeenth century, for their subordination to reason of state of the absolute defence of Catholicism; it was also reflected in the employment by some Spanish bishops after Trent, among those prelates distracted by courtly duties or disabled by age and health, of Irish as well as native assistant bishops.[45] The creation of an Irish seminary at Santiago, as the result of archiepiscopal action there after Trent, was equally a parallel to Borromeo's concern for the education of priests for areas where diocesan seminaries could obviously not exist.[46] The Borromean sympathy with a more exclusive policy towards Jewish communities in the later sixteenth century, not least in Spanish-ruled Lombardy itself, also found an unexpected parallel in the enthusiasm of Archbishop Bragança of Evora, otherwise noted for the positive energy of his pastoral care, for the campaign against alleged Judaizers among the New Christians of Portugal that became marked after the Spanish succession there, conducted by the Inquisition of that kingdom.[47]

In both Castile and Aragon some bishops encouraged attempts, against mendicant opposition often, to enclose the poor or at least vagabonds within regulated institutions, in line with Borromean reserve towards unlimited casual charity. But many Spanish bishops, in the absence of adequate secular priests in sufficient numbers for real pastoral care, continued to employ mendicants, as well as the special abilities of the Minims and Capuchins, to supply parochial needs and to conduct, effectively, internal missions. Other bishops, in Andalusia and elsewhere in the peninsula, made greater use of Jesuits, although, in the face of changing royal policy as well as Roman and provincial complications, Ribera's hopes of using regular clergy to supply the specific demands of the Morisco parishes of his diocese and province were never fully realized. Indeed he latterly used Dominicans rather than Jesuits in his diocesan missionary work, even if his links with the society had at first been more conspicuously close than were those of Borromeo, perhaps, at least after he had left Rome for Milan.[48] In both Valencia and Castile it proved relatively easier to emulate Borromean regulation of exorcism and of emergency baptisms to be performed by midwives than to reproduce exactly the Milanese catechetical provisions. For Spanish reserve towards any vernacular translation of the Roman catechism, typified by the negative reaction of the 1582 Toledo council, necessitated more local provision, at diocesan level, or the use of texts such as those of Luis de Granada, for parochial instruction; this was distinguished from the episcopal licensing of formal preaching, where Inquisitorial authority could also be involved.[49] While Spanish synodal decrees did provide vernacular exposition of the essentials of the faith, and even of the Mass, the provision in Portugal was arguably more extensive, although Ribera tried to adapt his predecessor's catechetical text to the peculiar needs of the Morisco population of Valencia, despite his pessimistic view of the Morisco benefit from such exposition. His encouragement to the Capuchins to move more widely in Spain, after their Catalan confinement under Philip II, was balanced, in a Borromean way, by encouragement of contemplative, strictly enclosed orders, as well as re-formed activist orders; similarly, in Portugal, the prominence of the Jesuits, from before the Spanish succession, with royal as well as episcopal encour-agement, was balanced after Trent by episcopal encouragement of the Car-thusians and other older orders, as well as the Capuchins. Borromeo's concern to ensure intelligible vernacular preaching to the ordinary laity, distinct from synodal sermons to the clergy, was followed by Spanish bishops after Trent, in legislation designed to make even regulars preach in vernacular terms that the faithful could comprehend. Only in the Catalan areas of the Crown of Aragon did this raise special difficulties, not least in the reluctance of the Jesuits to use a language that might foster Castilian suspicion, royal, mendicant, and Inquisitorial, of the society's associations from the start with the peripheral dominions of the peninsula: the Basque country and Navarre, the Catalan heartland and Andalusia, as well as Valencia and Portugal.[50]

By contrast, Borromeo's campaign to enforce the new Tridentine stan-dards of matrimonial and sexual morality on the laity encountered other problems in its Spanish application. While bishops could attempt to impose, by diocesan legislation and the use of their own visitors and judicial tri-bunals, the Tridentine ban on "clandestine" marriages and the consequent penalties for matrimonial irregularity or cohabitation without benefit of the sacrament of the church, the Spanish Inquisition regarded, increasingly at the end of the sixteenth century in its various local tribunals, such affairs as its own business. While Italian post-Tridentine pastors might follow Bor-romeo's example in trying to outlaw prenuptial cohabitation and other matrimonial irregularities, the local tribunals of the Spanish Inquisition, still in the early seventeenth century, were conducting a campaign to eradicate from the mentality of the old Christian population, even the most humble and ignorant, the belief that "simple fornication" was not a sin, or at least not a mortal one. While Italian pastors concentrated on practice, Spanish In-quisitors concentrated on mental attitudes and expressions of belief, even more than on practice.[51] The distinct organization of the Spanish Inquisi-tion—with the unresolved doubts, even in Spanish specialists' minds, as to the precise nature of its extensive and varied powers, and the de facto subjection of the Inquisitors General themselves to royal appointment but also to dismissal—meant that even such prelates as Quiroga, who combined inquisitorial with episcopal, indeed metropolitan and primatial authority, were at times strangely lacking in effective power. By this paradox, even a figure like Quiroga, let alone one such as Ribera, lacked the extraordinary authority employed by Borromeo, in a variety of circumstances, as papal nephew, legate, apostolic visitor, archbishop, and metropolitan. The only figures in the post-Tridentine Iberian world whose accumulation of powers arguably approached those of Borromeo were the Portuguese examples, independently and distinctly, of Cardinal Henry, primate, archbishop, legate, inquisitor, and finally king; and of Archduke Albert, surprisingly conscientious in his roles as Spanish viceroy of Portugal, cardinal legate and inquisitor there, before his brief translation to the administration and titular occupancy of the primatial see of Toledo, in succession to Quiroga.[52] Despite the sympathy of many of the nuncios in the post-Conciliar decades, elsewhere in Spain bishops had to plead with Rome to support the reforms that they undertook, by Tridentine specification, against recalcitrant regulars or chapters, precisely as delegates of the Holy See. The nuncios themselves often, at this date still, were reforming diocesans of Italian sees, disciples or associates of Borromeo, as outstandingly in the case of Ormaneto, the reformer of Milan, Rome, and Padua.[53]

Ormaneto's long career, indeed, stretching back to Pole's Catholic reform council in the Marian restoration of England, even before his employment by Borromeo to prepare the way for archiepiscopal reform in Milan, was a specific symbol of Spain's place in the history of Catholic reform. For all the tragic failure of Pole's short-lived plans in Marian England and the fatal termination of the Toledan reforms begun by his former Spanish collaborator in London and Oxford, after Carranza's translation to the Spanish primatial see, the origins of this tradition were not lost. Even in discussion of the proposed legislation of Quiroga's 1582 provincial council, Pole's plans for the recording and where necessary recovery of church revenues and property were noted for imitation. Borromeo in Milan perhaps achieved more in fact in this crucial area of support for pastoral activity at a respectable level of clerical performance, compared with the repeated laments of Spanish bishops over the continued loss of economic means to laity and regular communities. But Spanish prelates at least showed the same insistence as Borromeo on the accurate keeping of diocesan archives, and, above all, of parochial records of economic resources as well as of spiritual obligations and of the status animarum of the faithful. Some bishops, in Spain and Portugal, after the Council of Trent, were indeed able to draw on impressively detailed accounts of the numbers of their diocesan parishoners, analyzed by age, with respect to the performance of Easter duties.[54] Yet at the heart of the sacramental life of the faithful in the post-Tridentine Church, a distinction of Italian and Spanish episcopal attitudes was perhaps evident. As more careful recent research has stressed with regard to both Italian and French traditions, Borromeo's rigor in casuistic questions was never intended to exclude the laity from relatively frequent communion, with due care and safeguards, of course. Proper confessional boxes in churches were introduced in Spain, especially for the confession of female penitents.[55] However, an occasional Spanish episcopal plea for the revival of exemplary public penance was perhaps as little productive as its Borromean counterpart of penitential prescriptions. But while contemporaries found explicable the concern of Ribera, Aliaga, Quiroga, and other Spanish prelates to exclude Moriscos and gypsies, of dubious faith, from communion, as opposed to the other sacraments administered in the course of the laity's lives, the more general suspicion among Spanish prelates of relatively frequent lay communion did not, arguably, end with the death of Archbishop Silíceo. The Jesuit encouragement of this, with interesting support from certain other nonmendicant orders, especially Benedictines, remained largely at odds with the view of lay piety found among the Spanish clerical hierarchy: an attitude that may have made even the austerity of Borromean spiritual standards seem positively generous. Yet pastoral solicitude, shared with Borromeo, was demonstrated in Spanish sees, where bishops attempted to enforce the limitations on unrestricted mendicant begging for the economic support of the laity and the impossible proximity or profusion of mendicant houses.

Not only in the outstanding examples, such as Valencia or Toledo, but elsewhere in the Iberian kingdoms after the Council of Trent, impressive episcopal regulation of diocesan life, in strict detail, could be found: this was true not only in Portugal, under the successors of de Martyribus at Braga or at Evora as a result of the heroic determination of Archbishop Bragança, but in the Spanish realms themselves, as at Cuenca, or in the exemplary enclosure of female convents under episcopal control at Jaén.[56] One of the most impressive examples, in Spain itself, indeed was provided by the relatively impoverished see of Cadiz, precisely during the recovery from the English raid that had destroyed even the original cathedral. Despite royal financial relief in this case, most Spanish cathedrals and their cult were often underfinanced as a result of royal financial demands, ordinary and extraordinary, growing greater in the seventeenth century, even if usually with papal compliance; quite apart from the effects of royal patronage on episcopal and capitular appointments,[57] the increasing annexation of prebendal revenues to Inquisition use, in Spain and Portugal, adversely affected liturgical and pastoral provision at Iberian cathedrals. Yet episcopal reference in Spain after the Council of Trent to the needs and actions of the Catholic monarchy was sincere as well as fulsome: not only in their distinctive dress were the Spanish bishops apart from the Borromean world.[58]

Notes

1. Broadsheet, "Ad perpetuam rei memoriam" (Rome, 1796).
2. Archivio Segreto Vaticano; S. Congregatio Concilii, Relatio, Visita Ad Limina: 848A, Valentin.(I). Cf. Inquisition report: Archivo Histórico Nacional, Madrid:

Inquisición libro 1280, 646r ff. Note also the dismissal, at the start of Philip IV's reign, of the archbishop's brother, Fray Luis Aliaga, from his position as Inquisitor General, as well as royal confessor and member of the Consejo de Estado: Archivo General de Simancas: Gracia y Justicia, legajo 621, 11r ff., August 1621 onward. Note also Molinos originally sent to Rome in connection with the cause of Simon: L. Kolakowski, *Chrétiens Sans Eglise* (Paris, 1969), p. 498.

3. R. Robres Lluch, *San Juan de Ribera* (Barcelona, 1960), p. 459.

4. R. Robres Lluch, "El Patriarca Ribera, La Universidad de Valencia y los Jesuitas (1563–1673)," *Hispania* 17 (1957): 510–609, pp. 512 f.

5. Robres Lluch, *San Juan de Ribera*, pp. 122ff. Cf. Ribera acting also as visitor of the university by royal appointment, under Philip II: Archivo del Reino de Valencia: Clero, legajo 89.

6. Robres Lluch, *San Juan de Ribera*, p. 226. Cf. Biblioteca Nacional, Madrid: MS 13019 for Quiroga.

7. Robres Lluch, *San Juan de Ribera*, pp. 471ff. Cf. Archivio Segreto Vaticano, Segret. di Stato, Spagna: 320, 22v, 94v, 116r, 117v; cf. Biblioteca Nacional, MS 6148, 105rff.

8. S. Congr. Conc., Relatio, Visita Ad Limina, 848A.

9. Robres Lluch, *San Juan de Ribera*, p. 61. Cf. Biblioteca Nacional, MS 13019, 6r; cf. MS 5788 (diocesan synodal decrees, Plasencia, 1624); MS 13033, 434r (Toledo provincial council, 1582–83); Archivo Histórico Nacional, Inquisición, legajo 4511 (Cuenca synodal decrees, 1602).

10. Archivo de la Corona de Aragon, Barcelona. Consejo de Aragon, legajo 651 (no. 83).

11. E. Olmos y Canalda, *Los prelados valentinos* (Madrid, 1949), p. 185. Cf. Robres Lluch, *San Juan de Ribera*, pp. 246ff. P. Boronat y Barrachina, *El B. Juan de Ribera y el R. Colegio de Corpus Christi* (Valencia, 1904), p. 54 and n. 18.

12. Biblioteca Nacional, MS 13124; cf. MS 13033. Cf. Archivo General de Simancas: Patronato Real, legajo 22, (no. 22–24), for Philip II's responsibility for the initial failure to create seminaries in Spain after the Council of Trent.

13. Robres Lluch, *San Juan de Ribera*, p. 411; cf. Archivo del Reino de Valencia: Cancillería Real, Cortes por Estamentos, Libros 524, 525.

14. *Indice de la Colección de Don Luis de Salazar y Castro*, ed. B. Cuartero y Huerta et al., (Madrid, 1951), 7.750. Cf. for Ribera's relations with the Jesuits and Capuchins: M. Batllori, "La santedat agençada de Joan de Ribera (1532–1611–1960), in *Catalunya a l'època moderna* (Barcelona, 1971), pp. 271–79, p. 278.

15. Robres Lluch, *San Juan de Ribera*, pp. 347ff. Cf. Archivo del Reino de Valencia, Libro 524.

16. Archivo de la Corona de Aragon, Consejo de Aragon, legajo 651 (no. 83); cf. Robres Lluch, *San Juan de Ribera*, pp. 396ff.

17. Archivo de la Corona de Aragon, legajos 594, 607, 651.

18. Archivo de la Corona de Aragon, legajo 686.

19. Biblioteca Nacional, MS 13019.

20. Archivio Segreto Vaticano, Segret. di Stato, Spagna, 322, 19r ff.; cf. 95r. Cf. Biblioteca Nacional, MS 13019, cf. MS13044; cf. Archivo de la Corona de Aragon, legajo 651.

21. S. Congr. Conc., Relatio, Visita Ad Limina, 370 A: Granaten (1).

22. Archivo Histórico Nacional, Clero, Legajo 443; Biblioteca Nacional, MS 6148. Cf. S. Congr. Conc., Relatio, Visita Ad Limina, 167A: Calaguritan. (1).

23. Vis. Ad Limina, 156, Burgen.; cf. M. Fernández Conde, *España y los Seminarios Tridentinos* (Madrid, 1948), pp. 79f. Q. Aldea, *Iglesia y Estado en la España*

del siglo XVII (Comillas, 1961), p. 122; cf. *Historia de la Iglesia en España*, ed. R. García-Villoslada vol. 4, *La Iglesia en España de los siglos XVII y XVIII*, ed. A. Mestre Sanchis (Madrid, 1979), pp. 76f.

24. Biblioteca Nacional (B. N. M.), MS 13019, 87r. ff.; cf. MS 13044, 128r ff.; L. Martz, *Poverty and Welfare in Habsburg Spain. The Example of Toledo* (Cambridge, 1983), pp. 71, 74, 82, 105, 139, 141, 147.

25. Vis. Ad Limina, 311, Elboren.; F. de Almeida, *História da Igreja em Portugal*, new ed. (Porto-Lisboa, 1968), 2:496, 499, 623.

26. J. I. Tellechea Idígoras, *El Obispo ideal en el siglo de la Reforma* (Rome, 1963), pp. 195 ff., 213ff. E. Cattaneo, "La singolare fortuna degli "Acta Ecclesiae Mediolanensis'" *Atti della Accademia di San Carlo* 5 (1982) 33–63, esp. p. 36; cf. F. Molinari, "Domenico Bollani (1513–1579) Vescovo di Brescia e i concili provinciali di S. Carlo," ibid., 65–114: ("Bollani") but cf. id., *Domenico Bollani (1514–1579) vescovo di Brescia e Carlo Borromeo (1538–1584)* (Brescia, 1983).

27. Vis. Ad Limina, 141, Bracharen.

28. B. N. M., MS 13019, 6v. ff., 100r ff.; MS 5788 (Plasencia), 47r ff., 197r; Archivo Histórico Nacional (A. H. N.) Inquisición, legajo 4511 (Cuenca), 113r ff.

29. B. N. M., MS 13044, 128r ff.; MS 5788; A.H.N., Inquisición, legajo 4511; cf. B. N. M., MS 6148, 24r ff.; Archivo General de Simancas (A.G.S.), Patronato Real, legajo; 22(22–1); cf. also B.N.M., MS 13019, 8r 9r ff., 13r ff.; MS 6148 103r ff.; Molinari, "Bollani," p. 77; Cattaneo, "La singolare fortuna," p. 36; Martz, *Poverty and Welfare*, p. 168.

30. A. G. S., Patronato Real, legajo 22 (22–32); cf. B. N. M., MS 13019, 6v ff., 8r; 6r; 2r ff.; 35r ff., 132r ff.; MS 13044, 34r ff., 128r ff. MS 6148, 32r ff.; MS 13033, 145r ff.

31. Vis. Ad Limina, 785 A, Tarraconen (1).

32. B. N. M., MS 13019; 13044, 128r ff., 156r ff.; MS 5788; A. H. N., Inquisición, Leg. 4511; cf. Cattaneo, "La singolare fortuna," p. 38; Archivio Segreto Vaticano, Segret. di Stato, Spagna (A. S. V. Spagna), 34, 283r ff.; A. G. S., Patronato Real, legajo 22 (22–1); cf. Martz, *Poverty and Welfare*, p. 105, cf. pp. 19f., 77, 164 ff.; Vis. Ad Limina, 394, Hispalen.

33. B. N. M., MS 6148 (Cordoba, Seville); Molinari, "Bollani," p. 94; cf. B. N. M., MS 13019; MS 5788; A. H. N., Inquisición, legajo 4511. Martz, *Poverty and Welfare*, pp. 17, 71, 83, 167; cf. 145, 182f.

34. Vis. Ad Limina, 704A, Salamantina (1); cf. 364, Gienen.; 193A, Carthaginen. (1); 354, Gadinen.

35. B. N. M., MS 5788; cf. L. Prosdocimi, "Il diritto nella formazione e nell'azione riformatrice di San Carlo," *Atti della Accademia de San Carlo*, 5 (1982): 15–25, esp. pp. 21, 24; Molinari, "Bollani," p. 85. A. H. N., Inq., legajo 4511.

36. A. G. S., Patronato Real, legajo 22 (22–1); *Colección de Salazar*, 7.908, 7.909. 7.910.

37. B. N. M., MS 6148, 32r ff.; Vis. Ad Limina, 370A, Granaten. (1); 315, Elven.; Almeida, *História da Igreja*, pp. 333f.; A. S. V. Spagna, 35, 298r ff.

38. Vis. Ad Limina, 311, Elboren.; cf. 370A, Granaten. (1); 193A Carth.

39. Vis. Ad Limina, 370A, Granaten. (1); cf. 263 A, Corduben. (1); cf. A. S. V. Spagna, 322, 95r ff.; A. G. S., Gracia y Justicia, legajo 621; J. López Martín, "Don Pedro Guerrero. Epistolario y Documentación," *Anthologica Annua* 21 (1974): 249–452; A. Marín Ocete, "El Concilio provincial de Granada en 1565," *Archivo Teológico Granadino* 25 (1962): 23–178; cf. id., *El Arzobispo Don Pedro Guerrero y la política conciliar española en el siglo XVI*, vol. 1 (Madrid, 1970). Martz, *Poverty and Welfare*, pp. 38ff., 152; cf. p. 78.

40. A. Domínguez Ortiz, B. Vincent, *Historia de los Moriscos. Vida y tragedia de una minoría* (Madrid, 1978), p. 188; cf. p. 140.

41. Vis. Ad Limina, 370A, Granaten. (1): A. S. V. Spagna, 322, 19r ff.

42. Vis. Ad Limina, 394, Hispalen.; A. S. V. Spagna, 320, 42r ff.; 322, 35r ff.; cf. J.L. González Novalin, "Ventura y desgracia de don Fernando de Valdés, arzobispo de Sevilla," *Anthologica Annua* 11 (1963): 91–126. Martz, *Poverty and Welfare*, pp. 79f.

43. B. N. M., MS 5788; A. H. N., Inquisición, legajo 4511; Molinari, "Bollani," pp. 88f.; cf. B. N. M., MS 6148, 103r ff.

44. B. N. M., MS 13033, 429r ff.; cf. MS 13019, 13r ff.; Vis. Ad Limina, 311, Elboren.; 805 A, Toletan. (1). Note also the use of instrumental as well as organ accompaniment in late sixteenth-century Seville, in the works of Guerrero, after the style of Victoria; continued there by Lobo, but found also elsewhere in the peninsula, including Evora apparently.

45. C. Marcora, "Un registro del cardinal nepote Carlo Borromeo conservato all' Ambrosiana," *Atti della Accademia di San Carlo* 5(1982): 205–18, esp. p. 218; cf. A. Palestra, "Spedizioni apostoliche affidate da Pio IV al Card. Carlo Borromeo," ibid., 159–203, esp. p. 184, no. 120 (*pace* nn. 30f.); Domínguez Ortiz, *Historia de los Moriscos*, p. 177; Vis. Ad Limina, 156, Burgen.; 249A, Conchen. (1).

46. Vis. Ad Limina, 246A, Compostellan. (1).

47. Vis. Ad Limina, 311, Elboren.; B. Pullan, *The Jews of Europe and the Inquisition of Venice, 1550–1670* (Oxford, 1983), p. 244; *The Jews in the Duchy of Milan*, ed. S. Simonsohn (Jerusalem, 1982), 1 : xxix, xxxii, 2 : 1441, no. 3308.

48. Martz, *Poverty and Welfare*, pp. 19ff., 70; cf. p. 213. Vis. Ad Limina, 2, Abulen.; 193A, Carthaginen. (1); 246 A, Compostellan. (1): 805A, Toletan. (1); 354, Gadinen.; 311, Elboren.; Batllori, "La santedat," p. 278. 1. Piqueras Albiñana, "Cartas de Felipe II en el Archivo del Real Colegio del Corpus Christi (Patriarca) de Valencia," *Primer Congreso de Historia del País Valenciano* (Valencia, 1973), 1 : 399–410; no. 24, cf. no. 30; cf. also no. 23. R. García Cárcel, "Trayectoria histórica de la Inquisición valenciana," in *La Inquisición Española. Nueva visión, nuevos horizontes*, ed. J. Pérez Villanueva (Madrid, 1980), pp. 411ff., esp. pp. 430f.; cf. Robres Lluch, *San Juan de Ribera*, p. 27; cf. Vis. Ad Limina, 848A, Valentin. (1).

49. B. N. M., MS 13019, 6v ff., 8r; MS 5788; MS 6148, 103r ff. MS 13033, 434r; A.H.N., Inquisición, legajo 4511; cf. Piqueras Albiñana, "Cartas de Felipe II," no. 18, cf. no. 33. Q. Pérez, *Fray Hernando de Santiago Predicador del Siglo de Oro (1575–1639)* (Madrid, 1949), pp. 182f.; cf. also pp. 45ff., 51f., 162. Molinari, "Bollani," p. 85. P. Rodríguez, R. Lanzetti, *El Catecismo Romano: Fuentes e Historia del texto y de la redacción* (Pamplona, 1982), pp. 281f.; cf. Vis. Ad Limina, 141, Bracharen.; G. J. Bellinger, *Bibliographie des Catechismus Romanus* (Baden-Baden, 1983), p. 238 for Portuguese translation (1590); no. 708.

50. Almeida, *História de Igreja*, pp. 445, 448; Archivo de la Corona de Aragon, Consejo de Aragon, (A. C. A.), legajo 594 (9/2). Robres Lluch, *San Juan de Ribera*, pp. 406ff., 433ff., 437ff., 439ff.; cf. pp. 442, 453f. Vis. Ad Limina, 311, Elboren.; 141, Bracharen.; cf. 111A, Barcinonen. (1), 785A, Tarraconen. (1); cf. 291 (Tortosa). Pedro de Ribadeneyra, *Vida del P. Francisco de Borja (Historias de la Contrarreforma)*, ed. E.Rey (Madrid, 1945), pp. 655ff.: p. 692; J. I. Tellechea Idígoras, *Tiempos Recios. Inquisición y Heterodoxias* (Salamanca, 1977), pp. 34ff. Cf. also Vis. Ad Limina, 364, Gienen.

51. J. M. Garcia Fuentes, *La Inquisición en Granada en el Siglo XVI* (Granada, 1981), pp. 119ff.; M. Jiménez Monteserín, *Introducción a la Inquisición Española* (Madrid, 1980), pp. 311 ff.; cf. p. 308. R. García Cárcel, *Herejía y sociedad en el siglo*

XVI. La Inquisición en Valencia 1530–1609 (Barcelona, 1980), pp. 270ff.; B. Bennassar, *L'Inquisition espagnole XV–XIX siècle* (Paris, 1979): J. Contreras, *El Santo Officio de la Inquisición en Galicia 1560–1700* (Madrid, 1982), pp. 627ff.

52. A. G. S., Gracia y Justicia, legajo 621; cf. A.H.N., Inquisición, libros 1280, 1251 (f. 408*v*). Almeida, *História da Igreja*, pp. 51 ff., 406; F. Caeiro, *O Arquiduque Alberto de Austria. Vice-Rei e Inquisidor-Mor de Portugal, Cardeal legado do Papa, Governador e depois Soberano dos Países Baixos* (Lisbon, 1961), pp. 85ff. A. G. S., Patronato Eclesiastico, legajo 147; A. S. V. Spagna, 322, 71*r* ff., 98*r*.

53. Prosdocimi, "Il diritto," p. 21; cf. Vis. Ad limina, 399A, Illerden. (1); 364, Gienen.

54. B. N. M., MS 13019, 8*v* f.; J. I. Tellechea Idígoras, *Bartolomé Carranza, Arzobispo. Un prelado evangélico en la Silla de Toledo (1557–8)* (San Sebastián 1958), pp. 36ff. Cf. B. N. M., MS 5788; A. H. N., Inquisición, legajo 4511; Vis. Ad Limina, 311, Elboren.; Molinari, "Bollani," pp. 69f., 77, 81.

55. M. Bernos, "Saint Charles Borromée et ses 'Instructions aux confesseurs': une lecture rigoriste par le clergé français (XVIe–XIXe siècle)," in *Pratique de la confession. Des pères du désert à Vatican II. Quinze études d'histoire* (Groupe de la Bussière), (Paris, 1983), pp. 185–200; Vis. Ad Limina, 370A, Granaten. (1); B. N. M., MS 5788; A. H. N., Inquisición, legajo 4511; cf. B. N. M., MS 13019, 9*r* ff.; Molinari, "Bollani," p. 69.

56. Vis. Ad Limina, 848 A, Valentin. (1); A. H. N., Inquisición, legajo 4511; cf. B. N. M. MS 6148, 103*r* ff.; MS 13019, 102*v*. A. Linage Conde, *El Monacato en España e Hispanoamérica* (Salamanca, 1977), p. 192. Vis. Ad Limina, 249A, Conchen.; 364, Gienen.

57. Vis. Ad Limina, 354, Gadinen.; A. G. S. Comisaria de Cruzada, legajo 516. Cf. C. Marcora, *I funebri per il Card. Carlo Borromeo nel IV centenario della morte 1584/1984* (Milan, 1984).

58. Vis. Ad Limina, 246A, Compostellan. (1); A. S. V. Spagna, 34, 220*r* ff., 588*r* ff.; cf. 35, 26*r*. Cf. C. Marcora, "Il cardinal Federico Borromeo e l'archeologia cristiana," pp. 115–54, *Studi e Testi* 235 (Mélanges Eugène Tisserant, 5: Archives Vaticanes, *Histoire Ecclésiastique* [Deuxième partie] (Vatican City, 1964).

The Influence of Carlo Borromeo on the Church of France

MARC VENARD

"DURING THE ENTIRE SEVENTEENTH CENTURY ST. CHARLES BORROMEO CAST on the church of France the great light of his pastoral genius."[1] At first sight this sentence of Paul Broutin would almost discourage further investigation. For to study the influence of Borromeo on France would be nothing other than to study the entire post-Tridentine reform in our country. Moreover, the diocesan or episcopal monographs regarding this theme continue to increase. Yet it is the same Broutin who in a preceding work invites us to investigate further: he writes, "The influence exercised by St. Charles in Italy and abroad has still not been exactly studied and exposed."[2]

Indeed perhaps this influence might best be assessed by our assembling the main themes under three perspectives: (1) How have Carlo Borromeo and his work been known in France? (2) On what points in particular can we recognize in France a Borromean pastoral influence, and are there not some distinctions or some significant nuances? (3) Can the causes of this influence be discerned? How was it that the personality and work of Saint Charles radiated beyond the Alps?

Between Borromeo and France the contact was first established, quite simply, by a few individuals. Some representatives of what was already called in this epoch "the school of the cardinal of St. Praxede" exercised under diverse titles a role in the church of France, and it was often a role of considerable importance. It is necessary to cite first the archbishop of Aix-en-Provence, Alexandre Canigiani. This Tuscan obtained his see as a sort of inheritance thanks to his being related to the queen mother, Catherine de' Medici. Destined to a career in the church, he had been placed, whether on account of sanctity or time serving, in the wake of Borromeo. French historians have never clearly determined what precisely was the status of Canigiani at Milan; they only repeat that he was one of the closest disciples of the celebrated cardinal.[3] That the example was, at any rate, fruitful the behavior of Canigiani at Aix surely attests: in a house ruled like a monastery he conducted a retinue in this austere life; with care he made the rounds of his entire diocese; he established a seminary.[4] But even before proceeding to his ecclesiastical residence, the archbishop of Aix sat in the Assembly of the Clergy, convened at Melun in 1579, where he at once knew how to impose his influence—less in the negotiations with the royal power for which his lack of experience in French affairs scarcely qualified him than in the internal debates of the assembly on the subject of Tridentine reform. The Constitutions of Melun about which we will have to speak again, incontestably bear his mark, that is to say the mark of Milan. Likewise five years later the archbishop of Aix, convening his provincial council, knew how to transmit there entire pages of the Milanese *Acta*.

If one is reduced to conjectures as to the precise relations between Canigiani and Borromeo, we are much better informed when turning to Giovanni Battista Castelli, who was nuncio in France from 1581 to 1583.[5] Castelli, who had served as canonist at the Council of Trent, had been since 1565 a close collaborator of Borromeo in the administration of the diocese of Milan. Promoter at the first provincial council, vicar-general since 1568, Castelli was often, in the absence of his patron, required to initiate measures, as is attested by a massive correspondence. Named bishop of Rimini in 1574, Castelli simply continued to practice as head of the diocese what he had learned at Milan: to pray, to visit dioceses, to hold synods. Moreover he was called by the pope to exercise in other dioceses the charge of apostolic visitor. "True reformer, Castelli bases himself at the outset in the tradition of the Council of Trent, but he has undergone the influence of the Milanese ecclesiastical milieux, formed by Charles Borromeo, nourished by piety, doctrine, rigorous renunciation. . . ."[6] Such is the pastor whom Pope Gregory XIII sent as nuncio to France in 1581. Thus it was natural that Castelli conceived his function to be as much a mission among the French bishops for prodding them to reform their church as it was a diplomatic representation at the court of France. During his sojourn, he increased his contacts with the bishops whom he considered the most influential or the most zealous especially in order to incite them to hold some provincial councils. He dreamed of extending to France the procedure that proved so efficacious in Italy, namely the apostolic visitations. He was preparing to realize one of his own in the single area that was not closed to him by "the Gallican liberties," to wit the three Lorraine bishoprics, when death interrupted his mission in 1583.

The idea of an apostolic visitation of the Borromean type on the frontiers of the realm was not to founder on that account. It was considered anew under Castelli's successor, Ragazzoni. But as the nuncio had not the time to undertake it himself, in 1585 Rome thought of sending another bishop, also of the school of Borromeo, Alexander Sauli, bishop of Aléria in Corsica.[7] It was a short-lived project that would have been able to effect a fruitful encounter between the church of France and one of the most interesting personalities of the Catholic Reformation in Italy, for Sauli's sense of the realities kept pace with his holiness.[8]

Although they failed to meet Alexander Sauli, the French still had in the person of the nuncio Girolamo Ragazzoni a thoroughly Borromean prelate.[9] This Venetian, who sat at the Council of Trent as coadjutor of Famagosta, made thereafter several apostolic visitations, especially in the diocese of Milan. A bishop of Bergamo in 1577 he was suffragan bishop to Cardinal Borromeo and sat in this role at the fifth and sixth councils in Milan. His intimacy with his archbishop is evident from his correspondence and by the fact that, departing from his nunciature in France, he stopped at Milan to obtain the counsel of Borromeo. Like Castelli, he also considered that the essential purpose of his mission as nuncio was to obtain a positive reception in France of Tridentine decrees and to win the clergy to the reform. He maintained continuous relations with Cardinal du Bourbon, archbishop of Rheims, who, as prince of the blood cut the figure, if unworthily, of head of the church of France; with François de Joyeuse, archbishop of Narbonne, shortly cardinal; with Guillaume Rose, bishop of Senlis; with the bishop of Paris, Pierre de Gondi. But the Assembly of the Clergy of 1585 also allowed him to work with the archbishop of Aix, Canigiani, as well as with the archbishop of Bourges, Renaud de Beaune, whose role in the following ten years was to be of capital importance.[10]

Nevertheless the influence of a nuncio in France cannot be compared with that exercised at the same time by his colleague at the post of Cologne or later at Brussels. There, a Bonomi, bishop of Vercelli, still another suffragan of Borromeo, presided over the provincial council of Cambrai in 1586—an event inconceivable in the kingdom of France,

All things considered, the church of France at the end of the sixteenth century knew several Italians trained or at least influenced by Borromeo. But was there an opposite current? Can it be said that some French prelates have met the archbishop of Milan and have been thereby marked? History has preserved but one case: it is that of the young François de La Rochefoucauld, who in 1579, at the age of twenty-one, passed through Milan and is likely to have been received by Cardinal Borromeo. By this encounter the young man is surely to have been marked for life, a life as a zealous bishop of Clermont, then of Senlis.[11] This personal connection appears to me well forged between the saintly archbishop of Milan and the prelate who in 1615 won the agreement of the Assembly of the Clergy of France to receive the decrees of the Council of Trent.

But after all, is it so necessary to pursue research in the human connections when the role of printing is still more important? If the work and personality of Borromeo were known in France, it is first and especially through the books that crossed the Alps.

From the first council of Milan (1566) the attention of the Catholic world was drawn to the work undertaken by the young archbishop. The acts circulated immediately upon its closure. Printed officially at Milan, they were reproduced at Brescia and at Venice. We know that the old nuncio Santa Croce, returning in 1566 into his diocese of Arles, brought a copy of the *Acta*.[12] And I have myself found in the Library of Avignon a copy of the Milanese edition. To judge by the library's holdings, copies from each of the succeeding provincial councils were likewise received there until 1582, when, while the archbishop was still alive, the first work appeared that brought together the full complement of the texts published under his episcopacy.

The *Acta Ecclesiae Mediolanensis*—whose immense reception everyone knows—was born. A superb edition was produced in 1599 by the patronage of Cardinal Federico Borromeo, cousin and successor of Saint Charles.[13] The work became well known throughout the Catholic world, which drank from it avidly, and the church of France wanted to have its own edition. This edition appeared at Paris in 1643 through the care of Monsieur Olier, curé of Saint-Sulpice. Later came the definitive edition, the great edition of Lyon (1683) in two folio volumes in which—significant testimony of the universality recognized in the work—the Italian texts of Saint Charles were translated into Latin. The *Acta* of Milan were henceforth available in all the episcopal and seminary libraries.

Yet one may ask if the life of Saint Charles, as propagated by printing, has not had a still greater impact than his work on the French public. It is known that the first book cast on the market had as its author Agostino Valier, bishop of Verona, faithful friend of Borromeo and brilliant writer.[14] Within a very short time, the book circulated everywhere. The archbishop of Aix, Canigiani, sent a copy of it to the canon of Cavaillon, César de Bus, who was then in search of his vocation; we know the reaction of the latter: "I have just received the history of that one whose mortal life I believe to have been changed into a better one, assuring you that in reading it, I have been so transported and suffused by so great a desire to do something in imitation of him that I will not grant sleep to my eyes nor repose to my efforts until I have achieved some beginning to this resolution of mine."[15]

For how many French ecclesiastics and bishops was the reading of the life of Carlo Borromeo, as for the canon de Bus, a shaft of light that revealed to them the sense of their vocation? At any rate they found more developments in the life of Borromeo by Bascapè (1592) or in that very official one which Giussano brought out on the occasion of the canonization (1610).[16] Let us note also that the edition of 1643 of the *Acta* included a *De vita et rebus gestis Caroli . . . archiep. Mediolani* that was undoubtedly for very many Frenchmen the source of their knowledge of Saint Charles.

Through men or through writings, one thing is certain: the reputation of Borromeo soon arrived in France, reputation as bishop, reformer, and saint.

Henry III echoed it before a delegation of French bishops as early as 1579: no need, he said, for the Council of Trent to reform the clergy "for we have in France from Borromeo and from Paleotto [sic] those who are worth as much as those of Italy."[17] And the death of Borromeo in 1584 did not pass unnoticed in France as the nuncio attested at the time.[18]

More remarkable, a veritable cult was soon established with respect to the saintly archbishop of Milan. This is evidenced by the following anecdote: returning from Rome in 1592 the archbishop of Vienne, Pierre de Villars, traversed Italy as a pilgrim; en route he paid reverence at the holy house of Loreto, to Saint Antoninus in Florence, Saint Catherine in Siena, Saint Antony at Padua. And, notes his biographer, "at Milan he visited also the sepulchre of Carlo Borromeo."[19] This cult was naturally confirmed after 1610 by the canonization. One is surprised by the popular eagerness for a saint who offers little hold to the collective fancy.[20] In 1615, for example, the consuls of Carpentras in the name of the community of citizens and inhabitants, asked their bishop that the public holiday of Saint Charles be celebrated in the city; three years later this bishop consecrated an altar to Saint Charles with some of the saint's vestments as relics.[21] An altar and relics also appeared at Martigues, in Provence: as early as 1619 the bishop authorized the establishment of a confraternity in honor of the saint.[22] In Arles some years later an extra stopping place was cleared: Saint Charles here also had his altar, his relics, his confraternity. Moreover he accomplished some miracles. In his visitation the archbishop had to intervene to forbid that some ex-voto be stuck up "without such miracles having been examined and approved by us beforehand."[23]

All these are local instances. In reality it does not seem that Saint Charles was the object of great popular devotion in France as a whole. The sole episode of his life that painting has popularized is his charity with respect to the plague-ridden.[24] But on the terrain of protection against the plague this place was already taken by Saint Sebastian and his rival Saint Roch. In fact where Saint Charles triumphed is in the clerical context. Regarding the devotion that the entire clergy of France rendered him, it will suffice for us to gather some scattered signs. Here is a history of the diocese of Vienne in Dauphiné, written in 1623 by a pious canon. Suddenly, after having recounted the pontificate of Pierre de Villars (1576–1587), he interrupts his discourse to note: "In this time flourished in the Church San Carlo Borromeo, Cardinal Archbishop of Milan, canonized and placed among the saints because of his virtues and miracles by Pope Clement VIII [sic]. His deeds during his life and miracles worked after his death are sufficiently luminous to have recourse to them and in reading of them to admire and to praise this great God in His Saints."[25] For the bishops of France Saint Charles inscribed himself in the line of the great models in succession to Basil, Gregory Nazianzen, Ambrose, and Augustine; but his is a model very much more immediate and imitable. All declared themselves instructed by him: François de La Rochefoucauld, François de Sourdis, Alain de Solminihac, who came to be called "the San Carlo Borromeo of France," and Henry Arnauld, bishop of Angers, who incessantly prayed for the spirit with which Saint Charles was animated in order to merit being himself "a worthy imitator of this saint."[26] In the possession of how many bishops of this time would one not find as with Cohon, bishop of Nîmes, a portrait of the archbishop of Milan?[27]

Moreover, young clerks in the seminary were brought up in the cult of Saint Charles whose patronage would be extended in France in the seventeenth and eighteenth centuries by a number of ecclesiastical institutions, including some feminine congregations. No other saint of the Catholic Reformation profited in France from such publicity.

Thus from the end of the sixteenth century the personality and work of Carlo Borromeo were known and admired in France. In the seventeenth century he was recognized as the model of the clergy and more specifically of the bishops. Recognized, admired, venerated, but in what measure imitated? We must now consider how the Borromean pastorate marked with its imprint the church of France in the epoch of the Catholic Reformation.

For that we need to return to the Constitutions of Melun in 1579.[28] The Assembly of the Clergy, desirous of remedying "the maladies" from which the Gallican church suffered, lays down a series of rules that, it says, will not be useless "either for prodding the provincial and diocesan councils or for correcting abuses." This is all the more necessary as one continues to await in France a promulgation of the Council of Trent's decrees. It is thus, the assembly specifies, in a spirit of charity and solicitous for the unity of the faith that it is fitting to observe henceforth the Tridentine canons. In short the initiative of the Assembly of the Clergy at Melun in 1579 is fully identical to that of 1615, so much celebrated by historians.

There follows a catalog of articles destined to guide the work of the provincial councils and synods. The references to the Council of Trent are constant, and numerous are the allusions to works that issued from it: the catechism, and the Roman missal, for example. But a quick scanning of these constitutions reveals that the order of the topics follows very closely that of the first council of Milan. Looking more closely, we recognize entire passages, literally recopied. Two examples will suffice. Concerning the first communion of children:

> Young people, before being admitted to receive such a great sacrament, will be trained for some time in the purity of the faith, in the practice and in the fruit of such a great sacrament. (Melun) When the young people will

want to receive for the first time the Eucharist, the priest will only admit them after having examined them diligently as to the nature and meaning of this sacrament. (Milan 1)

Concerning usury:

Curandum ne quid ex mutuo, vel depositis etiam apud Iudaeum factis, aliquid praeter sortem a quovis homine percipi ex convento, vel principaliter sperari possit; tametsi pecuniae sint pupillorum aut viduarum. (Melun)
   "Ex mutuo, vel depositis, etiam apud Iudaeum factis, nihil praeter sortem a quovis homine percipi ex convento, vel principaliter sperari possit; tametsi pecuniae ipsae sint pupillorum, aut viduarum. . . . (Milan 1)

Now as was foreseen the Constitutions of Melun served in their turn as the model for the councils that were held in most of the ecclesiastical provinces of France between 1581 and 1594. Regarding usury, for example, the councils of Bordeaux 1582 and of Embrun 1583[29] rehearsing as if to the letter the enumeration of cases presented by the text of Melun itself, as we know, imitated Milan. But after all it is hardly surprising that some bishops, most of whom had not sat at Trent, faced with the necessity of transmitting into their dioceses the decrees of the council, hastened to models that they had at hand.

That the Milanese model informed the spirit of all is evidenced in this reflection of the nuncio Castelli when he sent to Rome for examination and confirmation the acts of the council of Rouen that was held in 1581. This council was important: it was awaited for more than ten years because the archbishop was the Cardinal de Bourbon and his example was counted on for drawing along the others. "I have seen some pages of it," writes the nuncio; "it has neither the majesty nor the weight of the councils of Milan."[30]

In truth the proliferation does not cease. The last French councils of the sixteenth century are also the most Borromean: Aix in 1585, Toulouse in 1590, Avignon in 1594.[31] This time it borders on plagiarism: the article of the council of Aix on Christian doctrine, for example, is a collection of different passages from the councils of Milan joined end to end. The personal role of the archbishop Canigiani and the presence of some Italian prelates in the province of Avignon assuredly explain many things. But in the case of Toulouse we witness a veritable acclimatization favored by the wave of Ultramontane Catholicism that swept the church of France in the troubled years of the League. This example proves that henceforth in the reforming French clergy the identification between France and Milan was complete.

It is known that all the provincial councils were initially ineffectual. The political and social troubles and the divisions of the church of France prevented any execution of the reforming decrees. But one must avoid excessively minimizing their importance. All the recent historiography tends to show how the Catholic renewal of France in the seventeenth century was rooted in the restless and fecund period of the last third of the preceding century.

It is time, however, to tackle finally the epoch of realization. For that I propose to examine some characteristic traits wherein the French Catholic pastorate of the seventeenth century retained lessons from the archbishop of Milan.

At the foundation of Borromeo's action in Milan one notes the reorganization of the structures of the diocese. The institution of local vicars, itself borrowed from the experience of Giberti at Verona, is generally recognized as the key to the system. Especially in a large diocese, they constitute the indispensable intermediaries between the bishop and the parish clergy. Without repeatedly recapitulating the Milanese situation, all the French bishops were compelled to resolve the same problem in a similar fashion.[32] Two sorts of intermediaries offered themselves for their use: the archdeacons and the deans.

Since the Middle Ages the large dioceses of northern France had been divided into a certain number of archdeaconries. Originally assistants of the bishops, the archdeacons, aided by the absenteeism of the bishops, gradually adjusted themselves to an autonomous jurisdiction wherein they were no longer accountable to anyone. To impose on them anew their authority was for many of the reforming bishops a preeminent task that most often proved hopeless: at best they were only able to neutralize these irremovable dignitaries.[33]

In reality, it was from the rural deans that the bishops were able to obtain support.[34] Because of its dimensions (around forty to sixty parishes) the deanery responded very much better than the archdeaconry to the demands of effective government. More important still was the fact that the choice of the deans depended entirely on the bishop who was not even required to confer this title on the parish priest of the chief town but simply on that one who appeared to him, by his zeal and presence, to be the most worthy. Thus in order to control their dioceses, it was especially fitting that the reforming bishops effected to their own advantage a redefining of the deaneries, that they chose the deans with care, and that they committed to them all the necessary powers in order that they might assemble, visit, and correct the priests of their district, before punctually rendering their accounts through some reports which culminate at the episcopal council and annual synod. Too much neglected by ecclesiastical historiography, the rural dean was an essential agent of diocesan pastoral renewal.

Nevertheless governing a diocese, according to Borromeo, was not simply a matter of gearing down effectively the episcopal authority. It was even more a matter of offering to the clergy and to the faithful the personal and immediate presence of the bishop by the exercise of the visitation. In fact, this idea was already widespread in France even before the example of Saint Charles came to illustrate it and stimulate energies.[35] The actual contribution of the archbishop of Milan in the field of pastoral visitations was essentially a methodical practice regarding which the Constitutions of Melun since 1579 had recaptured the scheme: visitation to the premises of worship; inquiry concerning the clergy; inquiry concerning the faithful—all in a spirit that should inspire as much the preaching which the bishop ought to bring to these visitations as his behavior and that of his retinue.

If Canigiani was still something of an exception when he visited his diocese in 1582, in the seventeenth century in France the battle was won. All the reforming bishops were great visitors. When they themselves did not preach, they arranged to be accompanied or even preceded by preachers who imparted to their passage the character of a mission. Matching the example of Borromeo crossing the Alps, France also has her heroes of perilous routes, of whom François de Sales at the beginning of the century and Cardinal Le Camus at the end are the most celebrated. As to the method of visitation, the Abbé Baccrabère has perfectly shown us how François de Joyeuse at Toulouse in the last years of the sixteenth century and François de Sourdis at Bordeaux from the beginning of the seventeenth century followed up to the least detail the Borromean formulas.[36] These are extreme as well as early cases of imitation of the Milanese model. In the other dioceses it is for the most part not until the second half of the seventeenth century that we see appearing, one after the other, ever more detailed questionnaires for visitation. One further step was taken: these forms were printed so that the parish priest or visitor only had to fill in the blank spaces provided for responses. From the direct contact between the good pastor and his flock, the pastoral visitation, in passing through the stage of Borromean perfectionism, was transformed into modern bureaucratic paper work.

It would have been possible to deal similarly with another typical institution of the Borromean pastorate, also borrowed from Giberti: *status animarum*. It is known that the archbishop of Milan had enjoined his parish priests to keep lists, daily updated, of all their parishioners, having for each the following information: age, times confessed, times communicated, time confirmed, moral integrity. Thus the parish priest would be able to respond to the questions of the visitor when he was asked about the degree to which the faithful fulfilled their duties; and should the occasion arise he would also have to denounce to the superior authority the public sinners and the obstinately lapsed.

In what measure did the Milanese clergy faithfully maintain its registers of souls? This is not our problem. But for France the question has been recently raised by Georges Couton and Louis Michard.[37] It is certain that following upon the Roman ritual of Paul V and imitating the example of Borromeo, numerous French bishops prescribed in their synodal statutes that a *status animarum* be kept, and they inserted some models for it in their diocesan rituals. It is on this basis that Couton and Michard affirm that these books were frequently kept by the parish priests along with their registers of baptisms, marriages, and burials. But for my part I doubt very much that they did so. My first argument is that the archives very rarely impart such evidence for the France of the Old Regime. My second argument, the strongest in my opinion, is that the bishops or other visitors, in going through the parishes, never asked the parish priests to present this book to them, even though they did not fail to verify the registers of baptisms, marriages, and burials and of course the accounts for *fabriques.* Although the ultimate goal of the Borromean pastorate, in its concern for controlling all the souls confided to the responsibility of the bishop in order to lead them to salvation, the registry of souls did not succeed in passing into the French Catholic reform.

Model to the clergy, did Borromeo provide the church of France with a method of training priests? Frequently attributed to him is the merit of having been among the first to put into execution the celebrated Tridentine decree, *Cum adulescentium aetas,* and of having specified its content with some detailed regulations. It is true that a great many French bishops brought the diocesan seminary under their patronage. But in reality what continuity was there between the Milanese seminaries of Borromeo and those which flourished in seventeenth-century France?

The Constitutions of Melun on this point, as on so many others, drew from the *Acta* of Milan to project the model that the bishops of France were supposed to erect. The provincial councils, notably those of Rouen and Bordeaux, fitted their steps into its footprints. And there was effectively a certain number of seminaries created in France at the end of the sixteenth and at the beginning of the seventeenth century. But most strayed at the outset from the Milanese model in not securing studies locally, settling, rather, for sending their pupils to a neighboring college. In short all these seminaries, as Saint Vincent de Paul ascertained in 1644, were a fiasco.[38]

The diocesan seminaries succeeded in France from 1640 onwards only upon an entirely new basis that Saint Charles had not foreseen. At first they functioned as seminaries of ordinands, receiving for a short period of training the young people who were going to be promoted to the priesthood. Then progressively, gradually, as their material resources increased—thanks to the prosperity of ecclesiastical revenue in the seventeenth century—and the means of filling positions improved—thanks to the development of companies of specialized priests, Oratorians, Lazarists, Eudists, Sulpicians—their studies extended, constituting, toward the end of the seventeenth century, comprehensive programs of intellectual and spiritual training for young adults previously educated by the humanist college. In short it was scarcely before the second third of the eighteenth century that the entirety of the French clergy was subjected to the uniformizing mold of the seminary in the French manner.[39]

Yet without waiting for their clergy to be renewed by the seminary, many French bishops introduced into their diocese an institution that in fact came directly from Milan: namely, the "ecclesiastical conferences" which Borromeo called "local congregations." They gathered together the parish priests of a deanery (or frequently from a smaller area) for some monthly training sessions. Shaped at once for the purposes of exercises of piety and for the practical pastorate, the ecclesiastical conferences powerfully contributed to modeling the *"bon prêtre"* of the seventeenth and eighteenth centuries.[40]

For the simple faithful, one of the great innovations of Catholic reform was the catechism. Preceded in this respect by the Protestant reformers, the Roman Church desired in its turn that each Christian possess "the knowledge necessary for salvation" according to an oft-repeated expression. From the middle of the sixteenth century, in particular among the Jesuits, the Catholic catechism took shape, and after 1566 the catechism of the Council of Trent conferred its own inevitable reference upon it. But assuring in a practical manner the catechetical education of children was a matter of protracted suspense that for France required a full century.[41]

Confronted with the enormous problem of instructing the masses in his diocese, Carlo Borromeo resolved the matter by covering Milan and its diocese with a tight network of Confraternities of Christian Doctrine in which priests and the laity united their efforts. The example of Milan is at the origin of the catechetical vocation of the Canon César de Bus, who introduced at the outset in his diocese of Cavaillon, then at Avignon, some confraternities of Christian doctrine. It has been demonstrated how these were rapidly changed into congregations of priests.[42] The Constitutions of Melun in fact do not breathe a word about the confraternities of Christian doctrine that are nevertheless found again literally traced from the Milanese model in the provincial councils of Aix, Toulouse, and Avignon. Yet except for a brief beginning in this last diocese the Milanese confraternities of Christian doctrine did not succeed in becoming rooted in France.

In the kingdom, the catechizing of children was, depending on the locality, either the task of schoolmasters—they became the object of a vigilant control of faith and morals—or else more frequently the task of the parish priests. At times their tasks were linked, when the master conducted the children to the parish priest in order that he might initiate them in the Christian faith. Thus what was, under Borromeo, the general mobilization of Christians for instructing youth became in France the affair of a specialized personnel and, increasingly, of a clerical personnel. Not until the second half of the seventeenth century and the movement in support of the schools of charity did the elite become conscious of the lacunae in the system that allowed the entire stratum of the poorest urban people to escape instruction.

I would now terminate this general survey of the impact of the Borromean pastorate on France with a relatively negative picture, if it did not remain for us to speak about confession. Of all the work of Saint Charles none had in France the diffusion equal to his Instructions for confessors. In a recent work Marcel Bernos describes for us their astonishing reception.[43] Long unknown in France, to the extent that they do not figure in the edition of 1643 of the *Acta* of Milan, these Instructions, published by Borromeo in Italian in 1583, were revealed to the public by the *Fréquente Communion* of Antoine Arnauld. The archbishop of Toulouse, Charles de Montchal, had a first French translation of them published only in 1648. The book came at a ripe moment, at the high tide of the quarrel between Jansenists and Molinists. The Assembly of the Clergy, desirous of "placing a barrier in order to stop the current of new opinions which are leading to the destruction of Christian morality," then decided, in 1657, to have printed the *Instructions pour les confesseurs* at the expense of the clergy and to distribute them to all parish priests. "The success was striking. The editions will multiply and for each several printings. . . . They are not only proposed by each bishop but at times imposed as an imperative rule. Thus at Narbonne they are bound with the *Ordonnances synodales*, at Angers with the *Mandements* of Henry Arnauld and at Aix with those of Mgr. Grimaldi; at Alet they figure among the books that the parish priests must possess and whose presence is verified at the time of pastoral visitation. Knowledge of the *Instructions* becomes obligatory in certain seminaries."[44]

In practice from the middle of the seventeenth century until the victory of Liguori in the mid-nineteenth century all France was confessed according to the principles presented by Saint Charles. And for this to be accomplished, it was necessary for this practice to pass through another institution imported from Milan: the confessional. John Bossy a dozen years ago invited historians to follow from country to country the propagation of this remarkable piece of furniture.[45] Here I will only be able to establish for France some guideposts.

The first mention of the confessional from this side of the Alps is read in the synodal statutes of Carpentras in 1584;[46] but these were promulgated in the pontifical state under an Italian bishop. The Constitutions of Melun do not breathe a word of it, but it is not surprising that the confessional was discussed in the most Borromean provincial councils: Aix in 1585, Toulouse in 1590. The next logical step would be to follow the series of diocesan statutes in order to note there the appearance of the confessional. I have done this only for Normandy: the confessional was prescribed for the first time at Rouen in 1618 and at Evreux in 1644. Another track of research consists in turning up the first mentions of confessionals in the pastoral visitations, and this is in principle possible thanks to the national index currently being compiled.[47] This source proves that before the middle of the seventeenth century the visitors asked about the confessional in two categories of dioceses: first, the dioceses nearest Italy where the confessional seems to have penetrated as it were by contagion—the dioceses of Provence especially, caught in the crossfire between Milan and Avignon; secondly, some dioceses that had at their head one of the champions of Catholic reform—Bordeaux, Clermont, Chartres, Rodez, Toul. After 1660 the mention of the confessionals is encountered everywhere in France; henceforth they became part of the ordinary furnishings of every parish church that the visitors examined as much as altars and baptismal fonts. "Object of terror or of horror" increasingly carved by the local carpenter or sometimes artistically worked, the confessional was to the far end of the French countryside the most tangible and the most durable legacy of the Borromean pastorate. One cannot imagine the holy parish priest of Ars without his confessional!

* * *

Although you love the ancient discipline and doctrine of the Church, in particular of the Gallican Church, most illustrious archbishop, nevertheless I do not fear that these Acts of the Church in Milan which I offer you in a new edition seem to you little pleasing or useful. They are recent indeed but they have the worth of the purest antiquity, breathing its spirit, equalling its holiness. I do not say this on my own authority . . . but I have garnered this judgment from the general Assembly of the clergy of France which, having nothing more at heart than to restore piety and to defend the ancient discipline, has considered that there was nothing more urgent than to make all the dioceses of France to adopt the decisions of San Carlo Borromeo, especially those which concern the sacraments of penance and the Eucharist. For nothing more appropriate for the administration of the sacraments and the preaching of the word of God, nothing more fitting for the beauty and the neatness of churches, nothing more suited to the establishing of seminaries and to the ruling of an episcopal house was able to be proposed to the entirety of the Church of France than these statutes by which St. Charles has happily reestablished the discipline of his province.[48]

One will pardon me this long quotation extracted from the dedication of the 1683 edition of the *Acta* of Milan. For it splendidly presents the question that I would like now to tackle: How did it come about that the seventeenth-century church of France made of the sixteenth-century Italian archbishop its favored model? What accounts for the great success of Carlo Borromeo on this side of the Alps?

The first answer is to be sought, I believe, in the episcopal character of the personality and work of Borromeo. The essential aim of the Council of Trent on the disciplinary level had been the restoration of episcopal power. And it is precisely thus that it was understood in France, where, in the years which follow the council, the bishops pressed the royal power to receive the council, while the chapters and, in the shadows, certain religious orders dragged their feet and encouraged the resistance of royal officials. Catholic reform in France, more even than in other countries, was desired by some bishops and was realized by them. This was possible because from the reign of Henry IV they enjoyed the increasingly resolute support of sovereigns who, like James I of England, perfectly understood that the bishops whom they nominated were the most effective agents of monarchic absolutism.

The Borromean centralization, the rationalized and bureaucratized pastorate that Saint Charles tested at Milan—that is to say in the most developed economic and cultural space in the Europe of his time—surely captivated our French bishops and rising behind them the king. Whether they resided in large cities like Toulouse or Bordeaux or in "holes" like Vence or Senez, the prelates enjoyed enacting the role of the archbishop of Milan leading into heaven a flock—hierarchically organized, officered, and submissive.

More especially on one point in particular, the episcopal authority of Borromeo was exemplary; indeed it is a point that greatly affected the French bishops of the seventeenth century: namely, their relations with the regular clergy. The epic struggle of Saint Charles with the Umiliati encouraged many a bishop in conflict with exempt members of religious orders. For example, Henry Arnauld, bishop of Angers, symbolically chose the date of 4 November, Saint Charles's feast day, to publish in his diocese a pastoral letter against the regulars who sowed disorder by exaggerated compilations, "some injurious libels and some scandalous sermons."[49] All emulated Borromeo in his constant concern to maintain under his authority members of all religious orders, Jesuits as well as the mendicant orders, in their preaching and confessing. One of the reasons that pushed the Assembly of the Clergy to adopt the Instructions for confessors as an official manual was its limitation of the privileges of confessors from the regular clergy. In short, for the Gallican clergy Borromeo was living proof of the superiority of the secular over the regular clergy. Was he not canonized twelve years before Ignatius of Loyola, Theresa of Avila, and Philip Neri?

A third reason for the attachment of the Gallican Church to Saint Charles was his rigorism. Let us return once more to the Instruction for confessors. In the conjuncture of 1657 the text of Saint Charles served to provide arbitration for an important point: it allowed that the sinner driven only by attrition—that is to say fear of hell—could benefit from sacramental absolution. Thereby Borromeo closed the door on the Jansenists. But aside from this passage how many others, from the beginning of the sixteenth century, recalled the holy rigor of the primitive church, such as it was imagined in France. If the evocation of public penitence was for Borromeo only a utopian archaism, our French directed all their attention to what he advocated as conditions for absolution and to all the reasons that he maintained for delaying absolution. This further fed the quarrel between seculars and regulars, the former constantly reproaching the latter for absolving sinners with a facility that "enervates ecclesiastical discipline."[50]

But Borromean rigorism did not confine itself within the tribunal of penance. It dealt severely with all sorts of popular practices. Let it suffice for example to cite this passage of the third council of Milan concerning the celebration of festivals: "The bishop will forbid with care and he will do everything in order that not only balls and dances but also banquets, games and other profane entertainments do not publicly occur on these days whatever be the pretext which has established them."[51] For the French reader such a condemnation recalls the one that Guillaume Briçonnet produced in 1520 in his diocese of Meaux,[52] and which then ran through the entire French reform movement, Protestant and Catholic. Moreover Gallican piety identified without difficulty with the repeated condemnations that the archbishop of Milan cast against "superstitions," giving to this term an ever larger sense.[53] Even Borromeo's combat against Alpine witchcraft found a favorable echo in France, at least until the middle of the seventeenth century.

Popular religion includes also the confraternities. If one compares Milan to Paris or to Rouen in the peak years of 1570 to 1580, the bishops were equally severe with respect to these institutions that largely escaped their authority and competed with the parish.[54] Therefore on both sides the response was the same: to forbid to the old confraternities certain rites that symbolized their autonomy, to submit them narrowly to the parish priests, and especially to give to them as competitors some new confraternities, some confraternities of the Holy Sacrament particularly whose spirit and practices fit harmoniously into the pastoral subject of the hierarchical church.

On all these points the clergy of France—from the bishops of the sixteenth century assembled in provincial council down to the simple parish priests of the seventeenth century trained in the austere discipline of the French school, such as Jean-Baptiste Thiers[55] and the parish priest of Sennely[56]— were to be found in close agreement with the archbishop of Milan: they shared the same cultural distance with respect to the peoples entrusted to them; the same latent pessimism on the subject of human nature; the same acute sense of a pastoral responsibility that they ought not to share with any other; the same conviction that only a well-ordered flock can reenter the divine sheepfold.

Ideally, the church of France of the seventeenth century was entirely Borromean. In practice we have seen that the imitation had some limits and that the Milanese example is fairly far from accounting for the total French Catholic reform. But the great paradox is that from the Milanese model the Gallican church made a rampart against Ultramontanism.

Brought up in the school of Saint Charles, the French, clerics and laity cast a critical eye upon the Catholicism that surrounded them, including that of Rome. That began at Mediterranean Provence, where Madame de Sévigné was scandalized by the procession of the Holy Sacrament which uncoils itself at Aix; but it is true that this instance is rooted in a pre-Tridentine Middle Ages.[57] But at Rome itself, the capital of the Catholic Reformation, French travelers experienced varying degrees of astonishment before the pomp of pontifical ceremonies and the contempt for daily devotions. Take for example M. de Coulanges, the cousin of Mme. de Sévigné, who visited the Eternal City in 1658 and in 1690.[58] On Maundy Thursday he saw a procession of penitents passing: he ascertained there no authentic piety. At Christmas he made the circuit of the crèches, for the ceremony was still unknown in France: "There were some representations of the mystery made of waxen figures in all sizes; they were more suitable for attracting children than sensible persons; but at Rome all is oriented to spectacle, the crowd is included in these kinds of representations which last until after Epiphany." In 1690 M. de Coulanges dismissed with one word "the singular devotion of the Italians."

More significant still, when it is known how the Southern Netherlands were strained by the Catholic Reformation, is the brutal shock effected on the religious level by the change of sovereignty in the epoch of Louis XIV. Premier French prelates Bishop Gilbert de Choiseul at Tournai in 1670 and Fénelon, archbishop of Cambrai in 1695 had the same feeling of falling into a diocese where everything needed to be done with respect to ecclesiastical discipline.[59] This feeling was shared by the parish priests of French origin whom they introduced into the parishes, Alexandre Dubois at Rumegies,[60] François Desqueux at Lille.[61] In the words of the latter most of the priests of the great Flemish city were "idle, lazy, ignorant men"; as for the people, they were simple and credulous, "more inclined than any other to superstitions." Moreover we also have the reciprocal view of the Lille weaver Pierre-Ignace Chavatti concerning his new bishop and the clergy that surrounded him.[62] A century later the first French bishops of Corsica made some analogous judgments on the Catholicism of an island where the Tridentine reform nonetheless passes for having been a great success.[63]

Where do we go from here? Are we to say that this Catholicism à la française is nothing more than Jansenism? Is it being Jansenist for a bishop to want to reduce the influence of the regular clergy and especially the Franciscans of every obedience—Capuchins, Recollects, Minims? Is it being a

Jansenist to regard distrustfully the devotions that they propagate—scapularies, amulets, indulgence prayers, miraculous images, confraternities—and to impose episcopal control upon their preachers and their confessors? Is it being Jansenist to want to train the priests in seminaries? All that is what the French episcopate garnered from the heritage of Borromeo: this composite was developed in a cultural and social context where rigorism had some deep roots; and it imbibed in the successes of the French school a superiority complex of which it is not certain even today that the church of France has quite rid itself.

Notes

1. Paul Broutin, *La réforme pastorale en France au XVIIe siècle* (Paris and Tournai, 1956), 1:38.

2. P. Broutin, *L'évêque dans la tradition pastorale du XVIe siècle* (n.p., 1953), p. 103.

3. "S. Charles Borromée commancoit d'entreprendre l'illustre dessein qu'il avoit de reformer le Clergé. Canigeani fust l'un des premiers Prestres qui poussés du meme zele se soûmirent tres-volontiers à ses ordres, il fust enrôlé dans sa Compagnie, et dans cette école qu'un sçavant Prélat appelle la boutique de la sainteté et de la pieté; il en fust tiré pour venir reprendre dans nostre Eglise les saintes et salutaires maximes du Christianisme." J. S. Pitton, *Annales de la sainte Eglise d'Aix* (Lyon, 1668), p. 236. Recently, Jean de Viguerie has cast doubt upon the personal relations between Canigiani and Borromeo.

4. See Claire Dolan, *Entre tours et clochers. Les gens d'Eglise à Aix au XVIe siècle* (Sherbrook and Aix-en-Provence, 1981).

5. *Correspondance du nonce en France Giovanni Battista Castelli (1581–1583),* ed. Robert Toupin, (Paris and Rome, 1967).

6. Ibid., p. 15.

7. *Girolamo Ragazzoni, évêque de Bergame, nonce en France. Correspondance de sa nonciature, 1583–1586,* ed. Pierre Blet (Rome and Paris, 1962), p. 371. Sauli is actually cited, but as the text speaks of a bishop of Mariana, the learned editor has wrongly identified the personage as Nicolo Mascardi, bishop of Mariana from 1584 to 1599.

8. See the observations of Alexandre Sauli, bishop of Aléria, on certain decrees of the Mgr. Bishop of Mariana, apostolic visitor (1589), in *Documents relatifs à l'épiscopat du B. Alexandre Sauli, évêque d'Aléria,* published by Maurice Venturini (Bastia, 1886).

9. Cf. supra, n. 7.

10. F. J. Baumgartner, "Renaud de Beaune, Politique Prelate," *Sixteenth Century Journal* 9, no. 2 (1978): 99–114.

11. P. Broutin, *La réforme pastorale,* p. 40.

12. Enrico Cattaneo, "Il primo concilio provinciale milanese," in *Il Concilio di Trento e la riforma tridentina* (Rome, 1965), 1:215–76. It is to be noted that the archbishop of Avignon, Feliciano Capitone, possessed in his library, in 1575, a copy of the acts of the first provincial council of Milan.

13. In 1581, the rector of the Comtat Venaissin, Domenico Grimaldi, was named bishop of Savona. Under this title he was summoned to the sixth council of Milan; he

was not able to appear there in person, but he received a copy of the acts. Some years later, he deployed his reforming energy on the archbishopric of Avignon.

14. *Vita Caroli Borromei card. S. Praxedis* (Verona, 1586). The work had a dozen editions between 1586 and 1604.

15. *La vie du R. Pere Cesar de Bus . . .*, by P. J. Marcel (Lyon, 1619), p. 132.

16. It was translated into French in 1615 by M. de Soulfour.

17. *Correspondance de nonce en France Anselmo Dandino (1578–1581),* ed. Ivan Cloulas (Rome and Paris, 1970), p. 453.

18. "La morte del Sig. Cardinale di Santa Prassede dispiace ancora qui somma- mente, et massime al Re, per quanto intendo." Blet, *Girolamo Ragazzoni,* p. 139.

19. *Histoire de l'antiquité et saincteté de la cité de Vienne en la Gaule Celtique . . . , by Jean Le Lievre* (Vienne, 1623), p. 504.

20. François de Sourdis, young nominated archbishop of Bordeaux, came to Rome in 1599 and received from the pope as a relic the rochet that Charles Borromeo wore the day that he was the victim of an attempt upon his life; he was thus invited to take him as model (Broutin, *La réforme pastorale* 1:101).

21. Bibl. de Carpentras, MS 1364, fols. 586 and 1056.

22. Arch. municipales d'Arles, GG 14.

23. Bibl. d'Arles, MS 151, p. 208; and Arch. départ. des Bouches-du-Rhône, 3 G 296.

24. Sylvain Gagnière, in *L'imagerie religieuse avignonnaise* (Avignon, 1943), indi- cates (no. 225) a picture of the seventeenth century representing "the cardinal-saint on his knees at the foot of an altar, feet bare, rope around his neck, asking God for the cessation of the plague which afflicts Milan. On the altar, the holy ampula framed by two lit candles. Above, in a cloud, the angel replaces the sword in its scabbard. In perspective, through a bay, view of a quarter of Milan with corpses stacked and bedridden diseased under some tents."

25. Le Lievre, *Histoire de Vienne,* p. 498.

26. See Broutin, *La réforme pastorale,* passim; and Isabelle Bonnot, *Hérétique ou saint? Henry Arnauld, évêque janséniste d'Angers au XVIIᵉ siècle* (Paris, 1984), p. 150.

27. Robert Sauzet, *Contre-réforme et réforme catholique en Bas-Languedoc, Le diocèse de Nîmes au XVIIᵉ siècle* (Paris and Louvain, 1979), p. 234.

28. Edited by L. Odespun, *Concilia novissima Galliae* (Paris, 1646), pp. 85–119.

29. The decrees of the provincial council of Bordeaux are to be found in Odespun, *Concilia,* pp. 279–320. On the other hand this author has not been able to examine the acts of the council of Embrun of which most historians are unaware. They were, however, printed at Lyon in 1600.

30. Toupin, *Correspondance du nonce Castelli,* p. 150.

31. The councils of Aix and of Toulouse are in Odespun, *Concilia,* pp. 445–508 and 509–60. For Avignon, refer to the original edition (Rome, 1597).

32. The term *vicaires forains* in the Milanese sense is restored by Joyeuse at Toulouse, and by Solminihac at Cahors. Usually this term designated in France the official that a bishop appointed in the parts of his diocese that depended upon another civil jurisdiction than the episcopal city.

33. A good example in Thérèse-Jean Schmitt. *L'organisation ecclésiastique et la pratique religieuse dans l'archidiaconé d'Autun de 1650 à 1750* (Autun, 1957).

34. Rural deans or archpriests: the functions are the same and the words are often employed interchangeably.

35. Cf. M. Venard, "Les visites pastorales dans l'Eglise de France au XVIᵉ siècle:

évolution d'une institution," in *Les Eglises et leurs institutions au XVIᵉ siècle* (Montpellier, 1978), pp. 115–40.

36. Georges Baccrabère, "Visite canonique de l'évêque," in *Dictionnaire de Droit canonique* 7 (1965); and *Les paroisses rurales du diocèse de Toulouse aux XVIᵉ et XVIIᵉ siècles. Exercice du droit de visite* (Strasbourg, 1968).

37. Louis Michard and Georges Couton, "Les livres d'états des âmes. Une source à collecter et à exploiter," in *Revue d'Histoire de l'Eglise de France* 67 (1981): 261–75.

38. Cf. Venard, "Les séminaires en France avant saint Vincent de Paul," in *Vincent de Paul*, Actes du colloque international d'études vincentiennes, Paris, 1981 (Rome 1983).

39. There is no synoptic study of the seminaries in France since A. Degert (Paris, 1912). But for a very recent regional synthesis see Charles Berthelot du Chesnay, *Les prêtres séculiers en Haute Bretagne au XVIIIᵉ* (Rennes, 1984).

40. *Acta Ecclesiae Mediolanensis* (Lyon, 1683), 1 : 535–45. Solminihac, at Cahors, was without doubt the first French bishop to introduce these ecclesiastical conferences. Might not the idea have been suggested to him by Saint Vincent de Paul?

41. Jean-Claude Dhotel, *Les origines du catéchisme moderne* (Paris, 1967). Venard, "Le catéchisme au temps des réformes," in *Transmettre la foi. La catéchèse dans l'Eglise. Les Quatre fleuves*, pp. 11, 41–55.

42. Jean de Viguerie, *Une oeuvre d'education dans l'ancienne France. Les Pères de la Doctrine chrétienne en France et en Italie* (Paris, 1976); and Venard, *L'Eglise d'Avignon au XVIᵉ siècle* (Lille, 1980), pp. 1217–31.

43. Marcel Bernos, "Saint Charles Borromée et ses 'Instructions aux confesseurs'. Une lecture rigoriste par le clergé français (XVIᵉ–XIXᵉ siècle)," in *Pratiques de la confession*, ed. le Groupe de La Bussière (Paris, 1983), pp. 185–200.

44. Ibid., pp. 196–197.

45. John Bossy, "The Social History of Confession in the Age of the Reformation," *Transactions of the Royal Historical Society* 25 (1975): 29–31.

46. Wolfgang Reinhard, *Die Reform in der Diözese Carpentras* (Münster, 1966), p. 128. The indication given by J. Bossy ("Social History of Confession," n. 63) of a mention of confessional by the provincial council of Narbonne in 1551 derives from a misconstruing: "confessional" in this text signifies a document delivered by the pope who authorized his benefice holder to be absolved by any priest, including some reserved cases.

47. *Répertoire des visites pastorales de la France. Première série: Ancien Régime*, under the direction of Dominique Julia and Marc Venard. 1, Agde-Bourges. 2, Cahors-Lyon. 3, Mâcon-Riez. 4, La Rochelle-Ypres et Bâle.

48. *Acta Ecclesiae Mediolanensis* (Lyon, 1683). Dedication of Anisson to Maurice Le Tellier, archbishop of Reims.

49. Isabelle Bonnot, *Hérétique ou saint?*, p. 258.

50. "Le dit curé a représenté qu'il se commet beaucoup d'abbus dans les confessions par Mrs. les Religieux qui reçoivent les penitens qu'on rejette à cause du manque de disposition, ou dont on diffère l'absolution. . . . La facilité que les dits penitents trouvent dans les confessionnaux des dits religieux énerve toute la discipline d'Eglise, selon son sentiment" J. Ferté, *La vie religieuse dans les campagnes parisiennes (1622-1695)* (Paris, 1962), p. 383.

51. *Acta Ecclesiae Mediolanensis* 1 : 70. See also 1 : 172 for the condemnation of the rites of the first of May that Delumeau has translated in *La mort des pays de Cocagne* (Paris, 1976), p. 118.

52. Bishop's letter published by M. Veissière, from G. Bretonneau, *Histoire généalogique de la Maison des Briçonnets* (Paris, 1620), pp. 191–94.

53. Venard, "Dans l'affrontement des Réformes du XVI'e siècle. Regards et jugements portés sur la religion populaire," in *La Religion populaire* (Paris, 1977), pp. 115–25.

54. See for example the ordinance of the bishop of Paris concerning the confraternities in 1578 and the commentary on it by René Benoist, parish priest of St-Eustache: *De l'institution et de l'abus survenu ès confraries populaires: avec la réformation nécessaire en icelles* (Paris, 1578).

55. Cf. François Lebrun, "Le 'Traité des Superstitions' de Jean-Baptiste Thiers, contribution à l'ethnographie de la France du XVIIe siècle," in *Annales de Bretagne et des Pays de l'Ouest* 83 (1976): 443–65.

56. See G. Bouchard, *Le village immobile: Sennely-en-Sologne au XVIIIe siècle* (Paris, 1972). The work is chiefly based on the diary of its parish priest.

57. Noël Coulet, "Les jeux de la Fête-Dieu d'Aix, une fête médiévale?" in *Provence Historique*, no. 126, pp. 313–39.

58. *Memoires de M. de Coulanges*, published by M. de Mommerque (Paris, 1830).

59. Pierre Pierrard, ed., *Cambrai et Lille*, Histoire des diocèses de France 8 (Paris, 1978), p. 143 ff.; and Louis Trenard, "La vie religieuse à Lille au temps de la conquête française," in *Revue du Nord* 53 (1971): 33–61.

60. *Journal d'un curé de campagne au XVIIe siècle*, published by Henri Platelle (Paris, 1965).

61. Alain Lottin, "Réforme catholique et Contre-réforme en Flandre: un rapport secret de François Desqueux sur le clergé lillois sous Louis XIV," in *Revue d'Histoire de l'Eglise de France* 56 (1970): 297–325.

62. Lottin, *Vie et mentalité d'un Lillois sous Louis XIV* (Lille, 1968), pp. 203ff.

63. François J. Casta, *Le diocèse d'Ajaccio*, Histoire des diocèses de France 1) (Paris, 1974).

Borromean Reform in the Empire?
La Strada Rigorosa of Giovanni
Francesco Bonomi

JOHN M. HEADLEY

IN GERMAN-SPEAKING LANDS THE IMPLEMENTATION OF THE COUNCIL OF Trent encountered a context very different from that of Italy in general and of the archdiocese of Milan in particular. As Hubert Jedin has observed, the reform decrees contained much that in Germany was not applicable and little which could be instituted because of the growing confessional gulf. Failing a general acceptance of the Council of Trent by the Augsburg diet of 1566, Rome was thrown back upon a piecemeal establishment of the reform decrees to be achieved on an individual territorial basis. Although Gregory XIII, who manifested great concern toward Germany, sought to use his nuncios north of the Alps as instruments for the realization of the council, it was not until 1662 that such a strategically important archdiocese as that of Cologne saw the publication of the decrees.[1] Meanwhile supplementary approaches to Catholic reform would be developed in the work of the Jesuits and in the political support rendered by the rival houses of Habsburg and Wittelsbach.

Indeed the Tridentine decrees had never been cut to fit the German conditions. Beyond the fact of confessional parity left by the Peace of Augsburg in the imperial cities, those conditions were largely shaped by the distinctive phenomenon of the prince-bishop and by the unfortunate and all too prevalent tensions that existed between bishop and cathedral chapter. That the prince-bishop united in his person two quite different offices did not in itself prevent reform. Only much later in the seventeenth century do we find cases of prince-bishops such as Christoph Bernhard von Galen who at Münster consciously emulated Borromeo in promoting Tridentine reform.[2] But most were worldly minded, dynastically motivated creatures, more comfortable in the saddle than in the cathedral. There are in fact no instances of great reforming personalities who might serve as strong proponents of episcopal authority in a diocesan context fraught with heretical and confessional pitfalls and an intractable clergy. As evidenced by the early universal and long effective resistance by the canons of cathedral chapters and collegiate churches, the Tridentine reforms presented a dreadful challenge to established privilege and vested interests. The noble canons at Trier were fairly typical for the age in that they were unconsecrated, normally absent, yet prompt to wring individual favors or capitulations from the newly elected bishop.[3] Such conditions, generalized, served to strangle random episcopal inclinations to reform.

The unpromising terrain offered by the empire to ecclesiastical reform—whether Borromean or Tridentine or Roman, as promoted from Italy—helps to explain the poor reception given to the archbishop of Milan's works. It is hardly surprising that the translation of his writings into the vernacular is limited to a single German sermon published at Dillingen in 1575[4] and another at Munich in 1608.[5] More significant a test, however, rests with the original Latin, for the weight of Borromean reform was directed at the clergy. Here after a flurry of activity in Antwerp and Cologne in 1586–87, with the publication of two important editions of the *Pastorum instructiones* (discussed below), almost an entire century passed before German lands saw another publication of Borromeo's works, this time the *canones poenitentiales,* again from Cologne, in 1678.[6] Then, beginning at Vienna in 1737, a great surge of Borromean publications from Augsburg flooded the midcentury, no less than seven in the period from 1758 to 1767.[7] As for the *Acta* it remains unpublished on German soil.[8] Returning to the late sixteenth century, one may find in the pattern of publication pursued by David Sartorius of Ingolstadt mute testimony to the apparent absence of Borromeo's influence. During the last quarter of the century Sartorius, while including classical and patristic publications, emphasized current devotional, controversial, polemical works such as eight successive editions of Bellarmine's *Disputationes* and a German translation of the first part of Baronius's *Annales.*[9] He of course published Bascapè's life of Borromeo and even editions of Cardinal Paleotti's *De consultationibus sacri consistorii* and his *De imaginibus sacris*[10] but nothing from the pen of the great Milanese archbishop.

Turning away from this rather bleak scene and having duly lowered our expectations, we may ask whether Borromeo himself ever entertained any plans for reform in the empire and even more whether he acted upon them. To both questions a resounding affirmative can be given. By an extraordinary extension of the self through one of his closest associates, a vertiable alter ego, and by a conscious refashioning of the office of papal nuncio, Carlo Borromeo effectively prepared the instruments that might, if anything could, carry Tridentine reform into the hostile, intractable territories of the empire.

The man called upon to effect this almost insuperable task had been closely associated with Borromeo since their school days at the University of Pavia. Writing in the autumn of 1579 to Duke William of Bavaria, Giovanni

Francesco Bonomi introduced himself as one who had been a most intimate member of Borromeo's *familia* for the past twenty years. (*NBS* 2 : 451) With him at Rome in the early sixties, a member of the Noctes Vaticanae, while serving as an auditor, then as abbot of Nonantula, and after 1572 bishop of Vercelli, Bonomi received repeated advancement from his friend only because his driving capacities to promote reform within the Milanese context recommended him to his chief. Summoned to the task of mounting a visitation of the Catholic cantons, Bonomi relinquished his expanding nunciature in Swiss territories for the most prestigious one at the imperial court in 1581–84, during which period he intervened with masterful decisiveness in the Cologne crisis. Shortly thereafter he assumed this new post that, with his tenure beginning in October 1584, would make the Cologne nunciature permanent. During these crucial months it was Bonomi's prompt, forceful, and relentless activity that saved Catholicism in the northwestern part of the empire from silently slipping, as it were, into the Rhine. Preceded wherever he moved by his reputation for rigor, even more unsparing of himself than of others, Bonomi appeared to the cool, calculating Granvelle, bishop of Arras, as more zealous than prudent;[11] to the Protestant prince John Casimir as that furious horn among other instruments of Satan (*NBD* 1 :305). Dying in February 1587, Bonomi, like his great friend, had burnt himself out at a relatively young age in service to the church. It attests to the German commitment of Bonomi's last years that besides being the executor of Borromeo's devotional writings at the archbishop's death, he had also received a religious image from his friend which became henceforth his most treasured possession; this he gave at his own death to Duke William, the Wittelsbach prince whose support was rapidly becoming the fulcrum for Rome's leverage within the empire.[12]

If Bonomi presented himself as the man to whom both Borromeo and Rome looked for assuming ever greater responsibilities within the empire, the instrument he wielded and the office through which he operated was the nunciature. At this point we need to adjust our lenses, for if by Borromean reform we include a sense of archiepiscopal initiative—the efficacy of provincial councils, diocesan synods, and regular visitations in promoting an interpretation of Trent as an episcopally based and inspired reform—nothing could appear to be more diametrically opposed than the office of papal nuncio. For although pastoral functions were not entirely absent from the exercise of the office, the nuncio in the new age of territorial states and diplomacy was intended to engage the princes of Europe to Rome. As the primary agents of papal influence and control, the nuncios represented the outstanding expression of Roman centralism. Thus the reports of the nuncios to Rome, including the famous *Nuntiaturberichte*, would seem to be the last and easily the worst possible place to descry anything corresponding to what might be understood as Borromean reform. Furthermore it is in the sense of the preeminently political and diplomatic character of their office and work that Giuseppe Alberigo, seconded by Paolo Prodi, could refer to the resulting source material as providing "a reflection that is only marginal to the life of the church."[13] Our problem, however, proves to be more apparent than real. In the first place, Borromean and Tridentine reform cannot be divorced from that promoted by Rome, particularly during the pontificate of Gregory XIII who advocated the meeting of provincial councils and diocesan synods and the salutary practice of repeated visitation (*NBS* 1:119, 325–27, 340–41; *NBS* 3:231–32; 283; *NBD* 3:11, 25–26). Secondly, as a historical source the *Nuntiaturberichte aus der Schweiz* is distinctive in being preeminently pastoral and visitorial rather than political in character. Thirdly, such material gives evidence of a revamping of the nuncio's office in order to achieve clerical improvement and to regain the tepid Catholic and the wayward Protestant to the old church. In short, the evidence suggests a refashioned nunciature, designed according to visitorial priorities to address the specific needs of the Swiss cantons that in turn might serve as a stepping stone to greater Germany. As events would prove, the growing confessionalism within the empire proper and the German context of territorialism would transmute any exercise of such a nunciature and lead to a reassertion of political priorities.

*　*　*

Accompanied by G. F. Bonomi, the archbishop of Milan, already for a decade cardinal protector of the Swiss nation, undertook a visitorial swing through German Switzerland in mid-August of 1570, coming back through the Gotthard pass by early September. At the end of the month Borromeo submitted a long memorandum reporting on the conditions in the five Catholic cantons and their reform. He recommended first that a visitor or nuncio be sent to deal only with spiritual matters, expressly leaving aside secular affairs: he would address the disorders of the clergy by concentrating on the younger priests, urging them to give up their consorts, be more attentive to their office, and withdraw from secular professions, indecent clothes, and indiscriminate conversations abroad. Secondly, he recommended that a seminary be established which would be controlled by a Jesuit college situated at Constance whose stimulus might provide a "beginning in this holy work by opening the way for going further in order to bear fruit in those other peoples of Germany" (*NBS* 1:3–17). Two points need to be noted at the inception of what was to be the Swiss nunciature: (1) its essentially pastoral nature; and (2) its perception of the Catholic cantons with reference to greater Germany.

Because the three valleys of Riviera, Val Blegno, and Levantina, under the secular authority of the lords of the Graubunden, pertained to the archdiocese of Milan, problems of Swiss reform were right on Borromeo's

doorstep. But for most of the decade, powers in the Curia remained suspicious both of the need for and the effectiveness of any sort of visitation
here. Five months after his report Borromeo seems to have backed off from
his earlier suggestion as being inopportune. But by December 1577, with the
threatened annihilation of the three bishoprics of Chur, Basel, and Sion by
the Protestants (NBS 1:108), requests had come to Borromeo from many
leading Swiss laymen asking for intervention and support (NBS 1:108, 110,
115–16, 118). The new pope, Gregory XIII, more sensitive to German
problems, at the recommendation of Borromeo empowered Bonomi as
visitor and reformer for the bishoprics of Novara and Como (NBS 1:119).
The most difficult and delicate part of the assignment included the Val Telline
under the hostile lordship of the Graubunden. Necessity as well as wisdom
dictated extreme care. Bonomi explained in January 1578 that he did not
mean to exercise the power of punishment nor to condemn priests but
principally to console those poor Catholics, give some order to the
churches, and administer the sacraments (NBS 1:133–34). The Congregation of Bishops approved this low key approach (NBS 1::137), and
following up on this advice Borromeo advocated "a totally spiritual visitation more in keeping with the manner used in those early times [quei primi
tempi] namely of going about preaching, exhorting, admonishing, consoling
in the spirit of gentleness" (NBS 1:142).

As apostolic visitor Bonomi bore with him the direct authority of Rome,
yet much conspired during this visitation in the region of Tessin to confirm
the jurisdiction and control of the archbishop of Milan. In midsummer 1578
Bonomi told Borromeo that because the name of Rome is so hated he has
found it advisable to proceed as the delegate of the bishop of Como (NBS
1:144–45, cf. 158). On 10 August and as late as 23 September he confessed to
Borromeo that he still had not reported to the pope (NBS 1:154–56, 189).
Meanwhile his perception of the need and the value of a clever, pious,
prudent nuncio grew. Why, he asked Borromeo, should the pope care less
for Switzerland than for other parts of Germany (NBS 1:183, 189)? Indeed
the papacy had by 1580 invested in Germany the establishment of three
nunciatures—at the imperial court the oldest, at Graz the most recent, and a
roving amorphous one for southern Germany—not to mention the Collegium Germanicum and the Congregatio Germanica (NBD 1:721–30).[14]
By the beginning of the following year Borromeo, in communicating with
his agent in Rome, Cesare Speciano, reported that Bonomi had done so well
in Tessin that he proffered him as visitor for inner Switzerland. Then he
added that it might be useful to have a nuncio whose jurisdiction would
include the nearer reaches and areas of Germany as in the rest of Germany
(NBS 1:231–33). Shortly thereafter he imparted to Speciano his crystallizing
appreciation of the strategic importance of the Swiss cantons in relation to
Italy and northern Europe:

It is important to send a Visitor into those parts [the Catholic cantons] since our Lord [pope] with so much consolation of goods shows himself so prompt in helping these ultramontane nations, for he does not spare expenses as is seen in these great seminaries [Collegium Germanicum, 1552/1573; Hungarian College, 1578; English College, 1579] which he has erected in their service. I would believe that everything His Holiness may spend in helping these souls would produce much good and bear fruit, since, if they should leave the church—in that they serve as a sort of bastion for Italy—it would cause great damage. It is even a difficult matter for them to maintain their present condition without direct aid, given their ignornace of ecclesiastical censures and jurisdiction [*censure et potesta ecclesiastica*] not to mention their proximity and intercourse with heretics." (*NBS* 1 :251)

Conferring with Speciano in support of a permanent yet different sort of nunciature, Borromeo called for the maintenance of a nuncio in Switzerland but not according to the worldly model exemplified by those in France and Spain, for their political expenditures frequently became excessive and would cost the pope too much; rather one that would attend much more to spiritual matters (*NBS* 1 :271–72). Again to Speciano five weeks later in April 1579 Borromeo reaffirms the larger German, even European reference for such a nunciature. In encouraging the use of both names, visitor and nuncio, for such an enterprise, Borromeo emphasizes that the permanence of such a nunciature would have to depend upon its fruitfulness. If the results proved positive, the office might be applied in whatever other province or part of Christendom it appeared desireable (*NBS* 1 :316–17). And once having fashioned this nunciature, Borromeo would help to maintain it by constantly negotiating with Rome for its financial support (*NBS* 1 :344–45, 447–48, 538–39). Although Bonomi's reporting to Borromeo gradually shifted to the cardinal secretary, Borromeo felt it necessary to instruct his subordinate to send regular reports not only to the Congregation of Bishops but to the cardinal secretary (*NBS* 1 :540–41; cf. 486–88, 2 :399).

As nuncio and visitor to the Catholic Swiss cantons, Bonomi pursued a rigorous course of visitations that sought to root out concubinage among the clergy, restore the recognition of ecclesiastical jurisdiction, reaffirm the enclosure of nuns, and regularize the bestowal of benefices (*NBS* 2 :183–86). Bonomi's office of nunciature, dating from 27 May 1579, applied to all seven cantons, five of which pertained to the diocese of Constance; it would shortly be expanded to the dioceses of Basel and Constance itself (*NBD* 3 :xxiii). At times Bonomi could entertain loud praise for the laity as warm in their Catholic faith and exemplary in their moral life; in contrast he had uniform condemnation for a clergy lacking in moral leadership and sunk in perpetual concubinage (*NBS* 1 :463). Reform of the clergy became central. Reporting on the nunnery of Munsterlingen near Saint Gallen, he observed that heretics presented no problem; the problem lay with the priests, monks, and now the nuns (*NBS* 1:486–88). In his suspension, disciplining, and pursuit of concubinists, more than with any other clerical irregularity, he struck at a long-standing practice that defined the economy of many a parish priest attempting to live honorably with his domestic helper.[15] In this and in other respects Bonomi's zeal promoted a variety of oppositions highly instructive as to how his nunciature was perceived.

A confrontation developed in August at Wallis where the territorial council declared his visitation to be quite out of order and unnecessary. It violated privileges and ignored the fact that Wallis had "a thoroughly adequate prince in spiritual and temporal matters" (*NBS* 1:445–46). The prince-bishop soon followed: he interpreted the visitation as censure and as an innovation that could well cause the shipwreck rather than the increase of the faith *(potius causaret naufragium fidei quam non augmentum, propter novitatem rei).* New and unaccustomed burdens are not to be deftly imposed. To the bishop falls the task of maintaining clergy and laity in the right Catholic faith. To proceed with rigor might well invite civil war (*NBS* 1:455–58). Similarly from the abbot of Saint Gallen came word urging caution for, as he observed, "We are not in Italy nor even in the five Catholic cantons" (*NBS* 1:467; cf. also 1:710–12). While Bonomi replied sharply to the abbot's muffled stricture, he observed a month later that the nearer one gets to Italy the more prepared the clergy is to accept the Italic clerical discipline *(ad italicam clericalem disciplinam suscipiendam)* (*NBS* 1:491; cf. 472–73). The stock Germanic reaction both earlier to Borromeo's reforming activities and shortly to Bonomi's application of Trent was that it represented an innovation and an intrusion *(nuwerung und ingryff)* upon their old freedom[16] (*NBS* 1:117, 559).

Inspired preeminently by the issue of concubinage but obviously exacerbated by Bonomi's rigor, opposition culminated in September in a document expressing the complaints of the clergy of Uri, Schweiz, and Unterwalden. It was addressed to the legates of the three cantons as an appeal to the secular authority to protect the clergy from Bonomi's reformation (*NBS* 1:492–511, 607). The importance of the clergy's complaints derives from the fact that the document reveals a conflict over the interpretation and implementation of the Council of Trent, and in this conflict, wherein both sides claim to act in the interests of Tridentine reform, Bonomi is to be found on the papal side of the net over against the advocates of episcopal authority. A summary of the major points is in order:

Actions are being taken against the ancient custom of the Christian church, the statues and decrees of the fathers and finally of the Council of Trent. In claiming to promote this council among us, Bonomi is violating it, deforming, not reforming the church. According to sess. 24, chap. 3

bishops in their bishoprics by themselves or through their agents perform the visitation. "The bishops therefore as supreme pastors and *curatores* of souls ought diligently to see where defects exist among the sheep of Christ committed to them so as to emend, reform and institute all Christian discipline. It is even in the same council prescribed that no bishop whatsoever has authority to act episcopally in another bishopric" (496), which Bonomi now contravenes. He is not bishop of Constance nor his vicar. Local cases performed with moderation are and have been acceptable but not by a foreigner and most especially an Italian *(et maxime Italicum)* who is opposed to our German customs and sensibilities. Never is such a visitation read or heard of in Christian history. His agents are not experienced priests but unconsecrated associates. Much greater diligence is manifested in the administration of the sacrament at Constance than at Rome or in other Italian places. In Italy the greater part of the clergy neither speak nor understand Latin. The bishop of Vercelli himself preaches in Italian or Latin and has it translated into German by an interpreter. But we have our own native preachers of the Word of God. Bonomi has given indulgences in Italian which none understands and is counter to the doctrine of St. Paul (1 Cor. 14) and the Council of Trent (sess. 25). With these indulgence sellers the clock is turned back to the time of Martin Luther. Reformation of the clergy and of concubinage can be achieved by the bishop applying the Council of Trent sess 25, chap. 14. If the bishop of Constance (Cardinal Hohenems at Rome) should reside and display a good life, the community of clergy would follow suit. Just as in the New Testament a woman cannot have two husbands, likewise a church cannot have two bishops. Bonomi has his church at Vercelli, which he neglects. We are not his sheep. Reformation is not to be achieved with truculence, terror, and power nor through excommunication and suspension. Concubinage and children have become an economic necessity. Ideally, it should not exist but for most it is not given to castrate oneself for the kingdom of heaven. Removal of some of the burdens, such as entertainment of guests, would strike at the root of concubinage. The different climates of Italy and Germany compel different customs. Our garb needs to be not the long Italian tunic but that of middle length according to our forefathers. The (secular) lords are to be apprised as to the erosion of their own power in matters of appointments and in punishing priests. Now if the bishop of Vercelli will just withdraw to Italy, leaving us in peace and our ancient ways, all will be well.

But Bonomi's reform rolled on. After meeting the personal aspersions in writing, he chose to deal with the clerical assembly through his secretary. In Rome's official reprimand to Wallis, its bishop, and the abbot of Saint Gall, Gregory XIII said, in effect, cheer up and cooperate! If the pope himself wanted to visit them, would they reject it under the pretext that none had ever done it before (*NBS* 1:568–69)? Although appreciative of Bonomi's apparent success, particularly with respect to concubinage (*NBS* 1:533–34), Rome sensed the need to curb its nuncio's ardor, consequently requiring that he proceed more moderately, holding to *la strada men'rigorosa* (*NBS* 1:705–7; 2:343). The solid achievement in reviving and galvanizing Catholicism particularly in the five cantons and even beyond could be measured in the forceful imposition of higher standards upon the clergy, the reallocation of ecclesiastical properties such as poorly administered abbeys into seminaries and Jesuit colleges—Petershausen for Constance, several rich, badly administered ones in Baden, and two abbeys to be applied to the establishment of the Jesuit college in Freiburg (*NBS* 1:588, 2:315–17, 3:195)—and the sustained effort to have benefices conferred upon worthy individuals (*NBS* 3:231–32). Perhaps the crowning indication of Catholicism's new commitment to German lands was the establishment of the Helvetic College in June 1579—a product of the persistence of Borromeo. Pope Gregory's willingness to support it and situate it in Milan and to entrust its organization and direction to Borromeo, constituting it as part of the archbishop's *familia*, suggests a significant departure from Roman centralism (cf. *NBS* 1:128–32, 274–5, 277, 286, 289–90, 311–12, 314, 343–4; 2:16).

Among the several charges leveled by the three cantons against Bonomi, one proved particularly painful for the nuncio to answer: namely, that his flock was not here but back at Vercelli. Indeed the last eight years of Bonomi's life were to be spent in extremely demanding nunciatures that rarely allowed his return to Vercelli. The Swiss nunciature, lacking any domicile, kept him constantly on the road, moving from one hostelry to another (*NBS* 1:566–67, 580). Bonomi complained about the expenses and especially the fact that he was paying two hundred *scudi* per month at the expense of his Vercelli bishopric and yet was here on papal business and command (*NBS* 1:479–80). Although Borromeo would shortly manage to rectify this financial problem, the archbishop with a finer sense of ultimate priorities reproved his suffragan bishop by citing the case of his colleague Valier, bishop of Verona, who convoked two provincial councils in Dalmatia, not scrupling thereby to apply the revenues of his bishopric. (*NBS* 1:647–48). Yet Bonomi scrupled over more than just the finances of his nunciature. While impressed by the need for and effectiveness of nuncial action, he yearned that he might end his exile and return to his bishopric (*NBS* 3:254–55). More specifically he recognized that the conflict with his own canons was approaching a crisis and demanded attention (*NBS* 1:581). Soon thereafter at more distant posts—Vienna, Prague, Ratisbon—Bonomi pressed his request that he be allowed to return to his diocese: otherwise he would come to forget his pastoral duties; the faithful would suffer grave damage; and greater was the damage done by his absence from Vercelli than the fruits of his legation.[17] It all had a strangely Tridentine ring to it, but the need for his considerable talents called him always to larger tasks. Indeed only by disobeying papal commands would he be able to return briefly to his bishopric in 1585 (*NBD* 3:12–15).

An incident with the Protestants led to Bonomi's withdrawal from the Swiss nunciature, followed shortly by reassignment to the imperial court. In seeking a short cut to Freiburg, the nuncio had the imprudence to go through Bern (11 December 1580). The situation proved tense and awkward and culminated in Bonomi's at one point being met with snowballs and invectives in a city street. Bern's diplomatic embarrassment led on to increasing political tensions that fell just short of war (*NBS* 2:554–58, 586; 3:145–46; cf. also *NBS* 2:180–81). Rome was disturbed by the Bernese affair; it would have preferred that Bonomi had made the circuit and avoided the risk (*NBS* 3:61). Despite the cardinal secretary's reassurance that he would not be removed from the Swiss nunciature, Bonomi received word on 20 April 1581 that he would not go into Switzerland that year (*NBS* 3:96–98, 122–23). By the end of the summer he was ordered to assume the Vienna nunciature (*NBS* 3:197–98). While recognizing that the outrage of Bern and the decision of the assembly at Baden made his return impossible (*NBS* 3:182, 204–5, 239–40), Bonomi had begun to nourish a considerable attachment for these troubled cantons. When suddenly confronted with the prospect of being burdened with the visitation of Novara, he represented to Borromeo that the concubines of Helvetia as well as the witches and incantations of the Graubunden required his attention far more than the diocese of Novara (*NBS* 3:169). Hopefully, he inquired whether the imperial nunciature included in its competence Helvetia as well as the province of Germania (*NBS* 3:238). And although it did not, his concern for Swiss problems and affection for Swiss friends never disappeared from his correspondence (*NBS* 3:264–484, passim, esp. 340).

Toward the end of his Swiss nunciature, the bearer of Borromean reform had developed some instincts regarding the Protestants that would crystallize in the confessionally riddled, politically charged context of central Germany. Bonomi's native zeal gave him a keen eye for vacillations in matters of religion. In January 1580 he complains of Solothurn and its schoomaster as being *tutto Erasmiano* (*NBS* 2:34). Stemming from his Bernese experience he nurtured an even keener eye for heresy, hostilely expressed. In fact the city fathers had accused Bonomi of first using the term, while seeking to draw Protestants to Catholicism (*NBS* 2:554–62; cf. also 171–72). Although he hotly denied it (*NBS* 2:628, 631–32), the terms *heretici and heretici occulti* now occurred with increasing frequency upon his pen, and the categories of confessionalism began to take their toll. Locarno, he told the cardinal secretary, needed a Jesuit college (cf. *NBS* 2:628), for the city was creeping with secret heretics. Writing to Duke William of Bavaria in January 1581, while assuring him that Borromeo always included the Wittelsbachs in his prayers, Bonomi advised him not to suffer heretics to remain, for they bring perfidy, tumult, sedition, and a hostile mind (*NBS*, 2:50–53). Once established as imperial nuncio and while serving as second to Madruzzo, cardinal protector of Germany, at the Augsburg diet of 1582, Bonomi reported on meeting the Archduke Charles in Munich: indeed he is a fine fellow but would that he were somewhat more hard-nosed *(aliquanto durioris frontis)* that he might better confront the heretics. Then he urged the cardinal secretary that a brief be sent to the town council of Freiburg asking that the recent Catholic convert Ambrose Froben, "the first printer of Christendom," not be admitted as printer to the city, for he lacked *fede autentica (NBD* 2 :483, 492; cf. *NBS* 3 :63–65).

Of the two major issues consuming Bonomi's attention during the brief imperial nunciature—the Augsburg diet of 1582 and the notorious Cologne affair of 1583, the *Kölner Wirren*—the first afforded the papal nuncio ample opportunity to become acquainted with the complexion of religion in the central parts of the empire. Working closely with his superior, Cardinal Madruzzo, Bonomi revealed in his observations and recommendations the spiritual torpor that had fallen upon German Catholicism within a confused confessional matrix. With Madruzzo he found in the diverse parts of Germany the scattered remnants of Catholicism pressed under the Augsburg settlement of 1555 *(la pace de la religione),* made worse by the neglect and indifference of the leading Catholic princes. Indeed in this *provintia* there ruled a diversity of humors. Small wonder that Madruzzo took to reading Sleidanus's history in order to confirm his opinion about the *confessionisti (NBD* 2 :386–87, 571). Bonomi found it necessary to urge the dean of Aachen as leader of its Catholic party, if he cared for the liberty of his country and restored Catholicism, to send legates to Augsburg to act in support of the Catholic religion *(NBD* 2 :456–57). He joined Madruzzo in applying to Rome for a faculty enabling him to ordain clerics before the properly established age, for the country suffered from a dearth of priests; it would therefore be appropriate to concede the authority for a definite number such as twelve or fifteen *(NBD* 2 :527). At Rome the cardinal secretary seems to have grasped the nature of the confessional landscape: their letters had revealed the calamitous state of the clergy and cathedrals in Germany that he believed was due to timidity; they needed to support ardently the common cause *(NBD* 2 :547).

Between the two outstanding events of the Augsburg diet and the Cologne affair, Bonomi's handling of the imperial nunciature saw his usual ceaseless pursuit of visitation in the service of clerical discipline. Of the nineteen nuncios who held this office in the period 1573 to 1620 Bonomi has been deemed the most resolute champion of Tridentine reform and of Catholic restoration.[18] His time at Vienna and later at Prague was consumed by relentless trips within his jurisdiction that took him into Hungary for the founding of a Jesuit college[19]; Silesia to intervene in a long-standing dispute between the bishop of Breslau and his canons on the matter of electoral capitulations; and Bohemia where, by working in conjunction with the archbishop of Prague and other notables and by committing powerful elements at court beforehand, he devised a ten-point program for the reform of the entire kingdom—a plan that his successor could and did execute. In his report on the reform for Moravia and Silesia, Bonomi incorporated themes from his conversations with and instructions from Madruzzo of Augsburg and applied them to the church of Breslau: to recall the German bishops to their pastoral duty, exhorting them particularly to the visitation of their dioceses to establish seminaries and to effect the moral renewal of the clergy. The report dealt among other things with specifics peculiar to the confessional terrain: the burial of heretics, heretical godparents at baptisms, communion in both kinds, and mixed marriages.[20]

Bonomi's three nunciatures reveal a crescendo of requests for faculties empowering the nuncio to take effective action in certain instances, whether it be to absolve a troubled conscience or to confer a benefice or to discipline errant clerics. Rome was in the habit of doling out the requested faculty in an *ad hoc* fashion. With the imperial nunciature Bonomi significantly began to resort to requests of a universal character. In his report on the electoral capitulations exacted by the cathedral chapter at Breslau Bonomi suggested that a bull be issued which would be universal, making invalid the demands of canons during an episcopal vacancy, for such requirements not only limited the effective jurisdiction of the bishop but conflicted with the sacred canons.[21] More significantly in the continuing uphill struggle to assure the conferment of benefices upon good Catholics, the tensions between episcopal Tridentine reform and the salutary action sought by the pope's agent on the spot became evident. During the second half of the sixteenth century the nuncios at the imperial court enjoyed no right of provision to a recently vacant benefice. In order to prevent a conflict with the jurisdiction of the bishop, the Council of Trent had removed these formerly enjoyed faculties of presentation from nuncios with the result that, when a benefice became free, the nuncio had to propose his suggestion to Rome. The consequent delays exposed the situation to controversy, and in the interim the right of presentation could pass to the bishop who, by the Vienna Concordat of 1448, held the right on even-numbered months. Nuncios had repeatedly complained and sought faculties that would permit prompt, direct action. Bonomi now proposed to the Curia that this faculty generally inhere henceforth to the office of imperial nuncio in order to prevent the power of conferment from slipping into the apparently more casual, even negligent hands of the bishop in conjunction with his cathedral chapter.[22] Thus the confessional pressures of the German context joined to the continuing desire to effect Tridentine reforms produced at Bonomi's hands the irony that if Trent was to be realized, it would have to be violated.

Inevitably with the crisis occasioned by Gebhard Truchsess, archbishop of Cologne's desire to marry and to open up the entire archbishopric to

Protestant penetration, the political character of Bonomi's nunciature increased and continued into the Cologne nunciature, yet without prevailing. The magnitude of the crisis was not lost upon Henry of Navarre, who deemed the doings of Gebhard to be of greater significance for the ruin of the papacy than anything that had happened in Christendom for centuries. Yet except to note that the results served to affirm Roman centralism within the church, we cannot be concerned here with the politics that enfolded Rome, Munich, Madrid, Brussels, and Vienna in a collective act which saved Cologne and thus German Catholicism from this landslide.[23] Enough to say that it was Bonomi's capacity to take prompt, drastic, decisive action that made Rome's will effective at this critical juncture in a distant land. And when it came in October 1584 to establishing a regular nunciature at Cologne, Bonomi's own effective action, his deposition of Truchsess and purging of the cathedral chapter, recommended him to this important, if distasteful post (NBD 1:614–17). What Bonomi had earlier represented to the Emperor Rudolf as la chiave della Germania (NBD 1:336–37) and the cardinal secretary understood as being the biggest and most important legation that there had ever been in their times—"that place more important for the service of God and the increase of holy religion than any other at this time"—now became the bishop of Vercelli's burden (NBD 3:4, 11). Acting as a sort of ecclesiastical proconsul in a vast jurisdiction that included the dioceses of Cologne, Mainz, Trier, Speyer, Strassburg, Basel, Worms, Münster, Osnabrück, Paderborn, Liège, Luxemburg, Cleves-Jülich, and several other places in eastern Belgium,[24] Bonomi addressed the problem of Catholic restoration in these areas.

The papal nuncio had been instructed to begin by having the three electors hold provincial councils, leading off with Cologne where the new archbishop, Duke Ernst of Bavaria, would be the most docile and the others would follow (NBD 3:11). However, the seizure of Neuss by the Truchsess forces so upset all plans for reform on the lower Rhine that Bonomi had to turn into the Netherlands for any fruitful activity. Other matters seemed for Bonomi to militate against any quick assembly of provincial councils for Trier or Mainz: the former would have to include French bishops who had not accepted Trent and were not easily convenable at Trier; in the case of Mainz too many intractable bishops and unresolved problems prevented any assembly here. Flanders and Cologne itself appeared to be the best possibilities (NBD 3:25–26; cf. 97) In the prince bishopric of Liège he had the support of the general vicar, Laevinius Torrentius, and was able to set a diocesan synod for the autumn. He attended the gathering of the three spiritual electors at Coblenz later in August 1585; Mainz proved to be as disappointing as Trier was supportive. Westphalia and north Germany needed watching, where the four episcopal seats of Münster, Bremen, Paderborn, and Osnabrück were ripe for new installations. With Bremen, whose archbishop manifested the signs of going the way of Truchsess, Bonomi yearned to practice the same sort of *coup de main* on him that had been so effective at Cologne (*NBD* 1 : 583–85, 624). In October 1586 he held at Mons the provincial synod for Cambrai that, with its proclamation of the Tridentine reforms and its own legislation on questions of the pastorate, constituted one of the most striking achievements of Borromean reform, although in Francophone territory.[25]

With Cologne the negligence of the new archbishop and recalcitrance of the cathedral canons impeded practical reform. If the mood of the city and the general situation according to the assessment of the nuncio prevented a complete publication of the Tridentine decrees, at least those pertaining to matrimony, enclosure, and holy orders should be published (*NBD* 1 : 664). Admittedly laboring under the reputation of being *troppo rigoroso*, Bonomi persuaded the burgomasters to expel heretics from the city and not to permit their burials in the urban cemetery. Indeed hunting heretics was coming to supercede hunting concubinists but never to the neglect of clerical reform. Bonomi pressed the *Professio fidei* upon the Cologne canons with a vehemence that proved excessive (cf. *NBD* 3 : xxxvii). Particularly notable were his efforts here and elsewhere to magnify the dignity, richness, and solemnity of the liturgy and of religious ceremony. He regretted the absence of masses celebrated with deacons and subdeacons; consequently months passed in this prominent church without a mass being sung (*NBD* 3 : 62, 65–67). With undisguised satisfaction he tells of singing mass on Saint Peter's day 1583 before a great concourse who had never experienced it before or at least for the past forty years (*NBD* 1 : 636). Again to dignify the event by his presence and solemnize it for the edification of the people, Bonomi with his *famiglia* participated in this jubilee at Cologne in July 1585 by giving a short sermon in Latin, singing mass, and giving communion before a great concourse (*NBD* 3 : 104–5, 107–8). Although the jubilee itself, the bull *In Coena domini*, and the decrees of the council of Trent still remained unpublished, Bonomi derived some satisfaction from the good order of the great procession to which he had invited the burgomasters and from which he expected much spiritual fruit (*NBD* 3 : 116–18) To the new cardinal secretary, Rusticucci, Bonomi elaborated that the processions on Friday and Sunday produced such devotion never before witnessed among the people that the multitude of those confessing and communing occupied not only all the Jesuits but all the regular parish priests (*NBD* 3 : 123–25). In order to promote sung masses Bonomi apprised the cathedral canons of two scandals that demanded correction: (1) the same revenues were given to absent as to present canons; and (2) solemn mass was usually omitted because of the lack of canons able to sing the epistle (*NBD* 3 : 169–70). The papal nuncio clearly valued very highly this reaccustoming of the laity to the dignity and solemnity of religious ceremony wherein the emotional and aesthetic dimensions played their part (cf. *NBD* 3:141–42).

In order to preserve our focus upon the religious, pastoral, and educational, the properly Borromean features of reform, we cannot follow Bonomi into the camp of Parma before Antwerp there to negotiate the prince's intervention on the Rhine (*NBD* 3:90–94) nor to the lecture hall of Michael Baius at Louvain there to begin proceedings against the emerging specter of Jansenism (*NBD* 3:87–90, 100, 133–34, 179–80, 184–86), but rather to the printing house of Christophe Plantin there to lay the foundations for the later dissemination of Borromeo's works in the north (cf. *NBD* 3:167). Bonomi had hitherto not been unmindful of the printing press's value for the purposes of Catholic reform. In the autumn of 1580 he sent to various officials copies of the five Milanese Provincial Councils (*NBS* 2:401; 3:1; cf. also 2:220–21, 227, 250, 254; 3:19) Once at Cologne Bonomi embarked upon what appears to have been a well-designed program to make the voice of the Milanese school heard in the north. Having already published at Vercelli in 1579 the *Decreta generalia*, which included the reform decrees from his visitation of Como 1578–79 along with his own diocesan synodal decrees, he published the *Decreta* again in 1585 with the help of the learned Cologner Melchior Hittorp. The new edition, which had appropriated Borromeo's Latin address to the second session of the Fifth Provincial Council, was impelled by the desire to restore the collapsed clerical discipline.[26] By early February 1586 Borromeo's *Pastorum Instructiones* on preaching, the hearing of confession, and the administration of the Eucharist was well advanced in the presses of Plantin. The volume included additional material such as Borromeo's six sermons excerpted from the *Acta*, a table of the archbishops of Milan, and Bascapè's letter to Luis de Granada on the death of the cardinal. How did these materials come to Plantin's attention? A lengthy introduction by the vicar-general of Antwerp, Sylvester Pardo, provides explanation. Antwerp had fallen to Parma in July of the previous year. Bonomi arrived there at the beginning of November and stayed until the middle of the month. Beyond other activities he managed to distribute among pious and learned persons copies of materials from a book that he had brought from Italy. The work was considered so valuable for the needs of the strife-torn church of the Netherlands that he was prevailed upon to have it published in Antwerp.[27] From what we know of Bonomi, it would seem that he could well have set up the situation so that he might be prevailed upon. Apparently, however, he demurred on the idea of publishing the *Acta* unadorned and unsupported by materials that he expected soon from Italy. He chose the wiser course of publishing the more immediately useful *Instructiones* and its accompanying materials for the announced "purpose of both raising the minds of the clergy and retaining in the old religion the Christian people from these parts where nevertheless many and diverse heresies rage." Everything suggests that Bonomi was working toward the publication of the *Acta* by Plantin, but the death of the nuncio intervened. Instead Maternus Cholinus of Cologne brought out in 1587 a second edition of the *Instructiones* with supporting material that included Agostino Valier's life of Borromeo accompanied by further excerpts from the *Acta*. In the northern French, Netherlandish, and German editions of his works during the next two centuries, the presence of Borromeo's steadfast friend would persist.[28]

＊　＊　＊

In concluding let us attempt to bring into focus the salient questions that have promoted this inquiry into Borromeo's presence in Germany: Is there such a thing as Borromean reform apart from Trent and Rome? In all its subtle nuances, to what extent can Borromeo's reform be measured in properly religious, i.e., social, liturgical, psychological categories, and to what extent in institutional terms, i.e., the ecclesiastical structure and structures that best realize his quality of piety, devotion, holiness? What does it mean to have a Borromean bishop turned papal nuncio seeking to effect reform in an alien, intractable context? Certainly this investigation has not been able to discover in the bishop of Vercelli any division or tension between the episcopal and the papal, except that of physical limitation, namely, that he could not at once serve as a pastoral nuncio and attend to his pastoral responsibilities within his own diocese. Rather in Bonomi we discover the complete coalescence of Tridentine, Roman, and Borromean reform. Only at one point in a most intimate letter of November 1579 to Borromeo, who had been in Rome since mid-September, does he attempt to sort out the three levels of reform—episcopal, archiepiscopal, and universal:

> I am constrained to give you my opinion, although, subjecting it to your better judgment and obedience: I am of the opinion that you would do well not to stay long in Rome first because there is greater need for you in Milan than for any other person, a fact you do not consider, and secondly because, as you acknowledge to have confessed on other occasions, you do not accomplish much where you are not in command. . . . Moreover, pardon me if I presume, but I have very much at heart the affairs of Milan as my own at Vercelli, indeed even more so as from the former the latter derive their substance [*virtu*] and strength. I very much fear that after your departure things will proceed coldly. (*NBS* 1 : 643)

Nevertheless, whatever the insights and implications of this statement, they cannot represent the ultimate meaning of Bonomi's major work, for he stood at this time only at the beginning of his nunciature, and the whole German experience lay ahead. In successive nunciatures Bonomi would increasingly feel the need to have recourse to the supreme authority of

Rome, in order to realize reform in a difficult environment (*NBS* 1:199, 469–70, 472–73; 3:132–33; *NBD* 3:181). Painfully aware that few bishops in Germany were consecrated (*NBD* 1:663), he lit upon the inspiring notion of inducing the archbishop of Mainz to be consecrated by the hand of an apostolic nuncio—"since it would serve as a singular example in Germany" *(si come sarebbe di singolare essempio in Germania)* (*NBD* 1:585). The rough terrain compelled not only repeated reference to Rome but also to tougher, more direct means. In preparing the archbishopric of Trier for both visitation and council, Bonomi allowed that if the suffragan bishops prove refractory, the situation could be mastered by the authority of Rome and the piety of Lorraine and of Guise to whom the pope could appeal should the bishops cause trouble (*NBD* 3:41). The ecclesiological implications of Borromeo's reform would have to be forsaken in the German context. If Borromean piety was to be instilled and nurtured in a restored clergy and a reawakened laity, it would have to be through papal support. Here part of Bonomi's legacy would be the resulting friction between legate and bishop.[29]

When Bonomi departed the scene and the bishop of Basel lamented that the church in Basel and that in Germany as a whole had lost their greatest protector (*NBS* 3:478), two defensive confessional leagues were coming into being—the Catholic Landsberg and the Protestant Lüneburg (*NBD* 3:20–23, 33, 194–97, 205). In the German context and at the hand of Bonomi and the succeeding generation, Borromean rigor would be largely transmuted, not into a severe piety of seemingly Jansenist complexion as in France, but into a militant confessionalism. The Rudolphine world manifest in a late Renaissance humanist accord was dissolving before the hard realities of religious differences now being accentuated in Germany.[30]

Notes

The parenthetical references appearing in the text pertain to the following works:

NBS Nuntiaturberichte aus der Schweiz seit dem Konzil von Trient. 1. Abteilung: *Einleitung. Studien zur Geschichte der katholischen Schweiz im Zeitalter Carlo Borromeos*. Edited by H. Reinhardt and Fr. Steffens. Solothurn, 1910.

NBS 1 Vol. 1: *Aktenstücke zu Vorgeschichte der Nuntiatur 1570–1579. Die Nuntiaturberichte Bonomis und seine Correspondenz mit Carlo Borromeo aus dem Jahre 1579*. Edited by Fr. Steffens and H. Reinhardt. Solothurn, 1906.

NBS 2 Vol. 2: *Die Nuntiaturberichte Bonomis und seine Correspondenz mit Persönlichkeiten der Schweiz aus dem Jahre 1580*. Edited by Fr. Steffens and H. Reinhardt. Solothurn, 1917.

NBS 3 Vol. 3: *Die Nuntiaturberichte Bonomis und seine Correspondenz mit Persönlichkeiten der Schweiz aus dem Jahre 1581. Bonomis Tätigkeit für die Schweiz während seiner Nuntiatur in Wien und in Köln vom Sept. 1581 bis zum Februar 1587*. Edited by Fr. Steffens and H. Reinhardt. Freiburg (Schweiz), 1929.

NBD Nuntiaturberichte aus Deutschland nebst ergänzenden Aktenstücken. 3. Abteilung. Edited by the Preussische Historische Institut in Rom. Gotha, 1892–1909.

NBD 1 Vol. 1: *Kampf um Köln 1576–1584.* Edited by J. Hansen. Gotha, 1892.
NBD 2 Vol. 2: *Der Reichstag zu Regensburg 1576. Der Pazifikationstag zu Köln 1578. Der Reichstag zu Augsburg 1582.* Edited by J. Hansen. Gotha, 1894.
1. Abteilung der Görresgesellschaft. Edited by the Görresgesellschaft in coopera-tion with the Historische Institut in Rom, Paderborn, 1895.
NBD 3 Vol. 1: *Bonomi in Köln. Santonio in der Schweiz. Die Strasburger Wirren.* Edited by St. Ehses and A. Meister. Paderborn, 1895.
The author wishes to thank Professor Robert Bireley, S.J., of Loyola University, Chicago, for his careful reading and criticism of the manuscript.

1. Hubert Jedin, "Nuntiaturberichte und Durchführung des Konzil von Trient," *Quellen und Forschungen aus italienischen Archiven und Bibliotheken (QFAB)* 53 (1973): 180–213, esp. 197–202; August Franzen, "Die Durchführung des Konzils von Trient in der Diözese Köln," in *Das Weltkonzil von Trient,* ed. Georg Schreiber (Freiburg, 1951), 2:267–94, esp. p. 279.

2. Manfred Becker—Huberti, *Die Tridentinische Reform in Bistum Münster unter Fürstbischof Christian Bernhard von Galen 1650 bis 1687* (Münster, 1978), pp. 30, 79–80, 336. A luminous exception to the prevailing situation in the sixteenth century, although not consciously Borromean in character, is Julius Echter von Mespelbrunn, bishop of Würzburg. See Hans Eugen Specker, "Nachtridentinische Visitationen im Bistum Würzburg als Quelle für die Katholische Reform," *Die Visitation im Dienst der Kirchlichen Reform,* ed. E. W. Zeeden and Hansgeorg Molitor (Münster, 1967), pp. 37–48.

3. Hansgeorg Molitor, *Kirchliche Reformversuche der Kurfürsten und Erzbischöfe von Trier im Zeitalter der Gegenreformation* (Wiesbaden, 1967), pp. 36–40.

4. *Index Aureliensis (IA), Catalogus librorum sedecimo saeculo impressorum* (Baden-Baden, 1965–   ) 1/4, 581, no. 122. 518.

5. Suspecting that the sermon appearing in the 1608 imprint as no. 896b of Curt Von Faber du Faur's *German Baroque Literature* (New Haven and London, 1969), 2:109 had been misattributed to Carlo's cousin Federico, I consulted the Beinecke Rare Book and Manuscript Library, whose curator of the Yale Collection of German Literature, Dr. Christa Sammons, kindly confirmed my doubts and referred me to the new, more definitive *Bibliographisches Handbuch des Barock Literatur* by Gerhard Dünnhaupt (Stuttgart, 1980–81), 1:168. Although I have not inspected the Dillingen imprint, it is unlikely that the second is simply a reprint of the first as the audiences of the two sermons differ, the first being addressed to the laity, the later one to the clergy.

6. *Catalogue général des livres imprimés de la Bibliothèque Nationale,* Charles Borromée, no. 42.

7. Publications of Borromeo's works in Germany during the eighteenth century, as listed in The British Library (BL) and *National Union Catalog* (NUC):

Instructiones . . . ad confessarios (Vienna, 1737) (BL)
Instructiones pastorum (Augsburg, 1758) (BL)
Homiliae CXXVI . . . (Augsburg, 1758) (NUC)
Homiliae . . . sermones . . . noctes vaticanae . . . vita (Augsburg, 1758) (NUC)
Instructiones pastorum (Augsburg, 1762) (NUC)
Saluberrimae Instructiones (Augsburg, 1758, 1767) (NUC)
Editio novissima cui accessit . . . Versio Latina (Augsburg, 1758) (BL)
Monitiones et instructiones in Usum cleri (Vienna, 1760)

I have been unsuccessful in associating this burst of publications with any stiffening of attitudes against the Jesuits. Of the prefaces that I have been able to examine, none gives a clue. However James V. Melton in "Absolutism and the Eighteenth Century Origins of Compulsory Schooling in Prussia and Austria" (forthcoming, Cambridge University Press), Chap. 3 hints at the Theresian effort to effectuate the Counter-Reformation by reviving its Borromean features. Although no printer can survive for long without a market, the fact that six of the eight came from the same printing house, the Veith brothers, Augsburg suggests that the motives for promoting these editions may not have been unrelated to personal religious convictions. For the last of these I am grateful to Dr. Regina Mahlke of the Staatsbibliothek Preussischer Kultur-besitz, Berlin. Compared with the printed evidence for German interest in Carlo Borromeo, the architectural evidence is somewhat more impressive, culminating in the eighteenth century with the Karlskirche in Vienna, built by Fischer von Erlach during the years from 1716 to 1737. Immediately following the canonization of Borromeo, the medical doctor and lay theologian Hippolytus Guarinonius built out of his own means the architecturally charming Carlo Borromeo church at Volders that would exert its influence upon the style of later Bavarian and Bohemian churches. Cf. Jurgen Bücking, *Frühabsolutismus und Kirchenreform in Tirol 1565–1665* (Wiesbaden, 1972), p. 178. Cf. also the most recent study, *Kunst um Karl Borromäus*, ed. Bernhard Anderes et al. (Lucerne, 1983), which Professor Voelker kindly brought to my attention. Also in this respect I am grateful for the aid of Dr. Margrit Krewson of the Library of Congress.

   8. Among the catalogs, data banks, and librarians consulted I have been unable to discover a suggestion that the *Acta* was ever published in Germany. Although OCLC gives an *Opera omnia* of Carlo Borromeo (Augsburg, 1758) located at the Ryan Memorial Library, Saint Charles Seminary, Overbrook, Philadelphia, Pa., on inspection it proved to be the *Homiliae* 126 of 1758 miscataloged. I am here grateful for the cooperation of Sister M. John Aloyse, R.S.M. Indeed the argument *ex silentio* can be confirmed by an article that only later came to my attention: Enrico Cattaneo, "La singolare fortuna degli *Acta ecclesiae Mediolanensis*," *Atti della Accademia di San Carlo* 5 (1982): 33–63, esp. 53–58. While the editions of Milan, 1599, and Bergamo, 1738, seem from their prefaces to be responding to or directed toward an audience beyond the Italian peninsula, the only extra-Italian editions of the *AEM* are Paris, 1643, and Lyons, 1683.

   9. *IA*, 1/3, 189, no. 113.317 (Baronius); 1/3, 469–73, nos. 115.971, 115.979, 115.987, 115.992–3, 116.008, 116.017, 116.020 (Bellarmine). The heightened polemical and confessional character of the German context in the last years of Bonomi's life is reflected in the fact that Sartorius published in the years 1585–86 two editions of Bellarmine's *Iudicium de libro, quem Lutherani vocant, Concordiae* plus two more in German translation. *AI*, 1/3, 469.

   10. Paolo Prodi, *Il Cardinale Gabriele Paleotti 1522–1597* (Rome, 1967), 2:515, 551.

   11. *Correspondance du Cardinal de Granvelle 1565–1583*, ed. M. Charles Piot (Brussels, 1893), 10:377. Quoted in *Laevinus Torrentius: Correspondance*, ed. Marie Delcourt and Jean Hoyoux (Paris, 1950), 1:17.

   12. *NBD*, 3:lxi. The introduction to this volume by the editors, Ehses and Meister, includes the best available life of Bonomi (pp. xiv–lxiii).

   13. Quoted in H. Lutz, "Die Bedeutung der Nuntiaturberichte für die europäische Geschichtsforschung und Geschichtsschreibung," *QFAB* 53 (1973): 160–61. For the historiographical dimensions of the *NBD* see the same author's "Ver-

gangenheit und Zukunft einer klassischen Editionsreihe," *QFAB* 45 (1965): 274–324 and the articles in the same fascicle; for the immediate historical dimensions and the mechanics of the nuncial system at this time in the empire see the useful work by Felicitas Rottstock, *Studien zu den Nuntiaturberichten aus dem Reich in der zweiten Hälfte des sechzehnten Jahrhunderts* (Munich, 1980), which, probably because of the relative paucity of published material, has little to say about Bonomi's imperial and Cologne nunciatures, brief yet significant. It should be noted that with respect to Paolo Prodi on the importance of the nunciature, most recently in considering the political significance of this institution for the papacy, his opinion is expectably different. Cf. his *Il sovrano pontefice* (Bologna, 1982), pp. 308–10.

14. Although the Congregatio Germanica still remained a somewhat informal body subject to its chairman and the initiative of its members and not yet integrated into the curial administration, it nevertheless received decisive confirmation and support from Gregory XIII. Its purpose was to provide a continuous assessment concerning what measures might be taken to strengthen Catholicism in Germany. See the valuable study by Josef Krasenbrink, *Die Congregatio Germanica und die katholische Reform in Deutschland nach dem Tridentinum* (Münster, Westphalia, 1972), pp. 74–78, 95–96, 194.

15. Oskar Vasella, "Klerus und Volk in Kampf um die Tridentinische Reform in der Schweiz," *Historisches Jahrbuch* 84 (1964): 86–100, esp. 92–94. The traditional work on the origins and exercise of Bonomi's Swiss nunciature is Heinrich Reinhardt, *Studien zur Geschichte der Katholischen Schweiz im Zeitalter Carlo Borromeos* (Stans, 1911).

16. To what extent Bonomi's strenuous activities among the Catholic clergy of the Swiss cantons are responsible for the later image of Borromeo among Swiss Protestants would be difficult to determine. Nevertheless, the British Library possesses a copy of a scurrilous imaginary dialogue directed against Borromeo. Printed in 1656, anonymous, and without indication of place of publication, it is highly abusive and even scatological: *Synodus sanctorum Helveticorum Zusammenkünfte der fürnemsten Heiligen im Schweitzerland/nach dem man an ihre statt erwehlt und gesetz hat/den welschen Carolum Borromaeum*, etc. Written in rhymed couplets, the penultimate conveys the flavor and sense of its ringing doggerel:

Ein losen Hurensohn / ein kind des Antichrists /
Der in der Hellen sitzt / der in dem feüer ist.

(sig. Biii*v*)

17. Giuseppe Peraldo, "L'Applicazione della riforma tridentina nella diocesi di Vercelli durante l'episcopato di G. F. Bonomi (1573–1587)" (Ph.D. diss., Pavia, 1964–65), pp. 226–27; cf. also *NBS* 3:182. I am indebted to Dr. Luigi Avonto for making available to me both a xerox copy of this dissertation and an unpublished article also by Peraldo, referred to here (see infra, n. 27) as "Breve Nota." When he died rather suddenly from an unexpected dental infection, while teaching at the University of Naples, Peraldo gave every indication of being a very able historian and of completing an excellent biography of Bonomi. Peraldo correctly defined Bonomi's publishing program for Borromeo in the north and by discovering more of Bonomi's papers in the Graziana Archive, Città di Castello he had in effect solved the longstanding riddle of the lacuna for the year 1586 in the Ehses and Meister *NBD* 3. On this last point see Wolfgang Reinhard, "Katholische Reform und Gegenreformation in der Kölner Nuntiatur 1584–1621," *Römische Quartalschrift* 66 (1971): 18 n. 73.

18. Joachim Köhler, *Das Ringen um die Tridentinische Erneuerung im Bistum Breslau* (Cologne and Vienna, 1973), pp. 97, 99.

19. Giuseppe Colombo, "Notizie e documenti inediti sulla vita di M. Giovanni Francesco Bonomi vescovo di Vercelli," *Miscellanea di storia italiana* 18 (1878): 523–623, esp. 585.

20. Köhler, *Breslau*, pp. 46, 116–17, 160, 212, 330.

21. Ibid., p. 46.

22. Ibid., pp. 141–42.

23. Cf. Gunther von Lojewski, *Bayerns Weg nach Köln. Geschichte der bayerischen Bistumspolitik in der zweiten Hälfte des 16. Jahrhunderts* (Bonn, 1962), pp. 359–62, 397–99 et passim.

24. Colombo, "Notizie," p. 594.

25. Reinhard, "Katholische Reform und Gegenreformation," pp. 8–65, esp. 15–17.

26. The history of the publication and dissemination of the collections of Vercellese diocesan synodal decrees, the *Decreta generalia*, takes a place of equal importance with the dissemination of the Milanese provincial decrees. Today in the Cantonal Library of Freiburg can be found a copy of each of the published collections of the *Decreta* prior to 1579. See *Sinodi diocesani italiani, Catalogo bibliografico degli atti a stampa 1534–1878*, ed. P. Silvano da Nadro, Studi e Testi, 207, Vatican City, 1960), pp. 104 (1, 1573); 102 (2, 1574); 129 (3, 1575); 134 (4, 1576); 152 (5, 1578). Their presence here attests not only to Bonomi's deliberate diffusion of the Milanese school's reform but also to his warm friendship with the provost of the cathedral chapter, Sebastian Werro, to whom most probably he sent these decrees and who appears to have later translated a devotional treatise by Bonomi into German (*IA*, 1/4, 546, no. 122.160; *NBS* 3:1). The publication program for the *Decreta* in the north culminates with Hittorp's edition of 1585 by the Cologne printer Gottfried Kempen: *Reformationis ecclesiasticae decreta generalia, omnium ecclesiarum usibus accommodata, a Jo. Francisco Bonhomio . . . nuper in Comensis civitatis et diocesis visitatione aedita, nunc autem ad collapsam hoc tempori cleric disciplinam restituendam Melchioris Hittorpi, S. Cuniberti decani, cura ac diligenti revisa et recusa* (*NBD* 1:304; 3:xxiii).

27. Leon Voet, *The Plantin Press (1555–1589). A Bibliography of the Works Printed and Published by Christopher Plantin at Antwerp and Leiden* (Antwerp, 1980–83), 1:421–23; Peraldo, "Breve Nota," pp. 2–5. According to Sylvester Pardo's preface, "tum ad Cleri animos erigendos, tum ad populum Christianum his regionibus ubi tamen multae et diverses haereses grassantur, in antiqua religione retinendum."

28. The main outlines for this schedule of Borromean publication were charted by Professor Peraldo before his untimely death and kindly made available to me by Dr. Luigi Avonto through a copy of the unpublished article here designated as "Breve nota," pp. 5–11. However the crucial document, the dedicatory preface of the printer Cholinus to the doctor of theology and dean of Santa Maria "ad Gradua" at Cologne, Georg Brun, is readily available in the Achille Ratti (Pius XI) edition of the *Acta ecclesiae Mediolanensis* (Milan, 1890), 2:xxi: cui [Brun] novae auctiorisque editionis cura ab ipso Bonomio dicitur commissa et merito vertitur, quod sit "cum Episcopo Vercellensi unicus Borromaeianae pietatis ac zeli admirator et eiusdem magnum ac per augustum *Actorum* Mediolanensium opus, Domino Vercellense petente, indice copioso auxerit et praefatione elegantissima, adornaverit, quam Dominus Nuncius faceret plurimi et editori saepius commendaverit, fatereturque ipsum primum illi auctorem suasoremque fuisse, ut hae instructiones ex magno illo Borromaei opere

enchiridii forma separatim ederentur." On the apparent impetus given by Bonomi to the publication of Borromeo's works in the north and the continuity of his presence, see for example the preface of Franciscus Sylvius, doctor of theology and Regius professor in the academy of Douai, to his edition of the *Pastorum instructiones* (Douai, 1616), sigs. 4r–5r, pp. 135, 265, 453, and 462, and the Veith edition of the same work (Augsburg, 1762), pp. V–IX. Sylvius makes clear in the title itself the purpose of this edition: Nunc autem ad ecclesiarum Belgicarum usum accommodatae. He includes Bascapè's "Epistola de obitu Caroli Card. S. Praxedis" wherein Bonomi is mentioned: Tum vero scripta sua ad conciones pertinentia Vercellensi episcopo, quo neminem arbitror episcopum illi fuisse chariorem, neque etiam magis probatum (453). Also included (pp. 380–427) is the entire catalog of archbishops of Milan derived from Borromeo's fourth provincial council but taken over here from the Plantin 1586 edition.

29. A. Franzen, "Eine Krise der deutschen Kirche im 17. Jahrhundert?" *Römische Quartalschrift* 49 (1954): 56–111.

30. R. J. W. Evans, *Rudolf II and his World. A Study in Intellectual History 1576– 1612* (Oxford, 1973), passim.

Carlo Borromeo between Two Models of Bishop

GIUSEPPE ALBERIGO

THE LIFE OF CARLO BORROMEO SPANNED NEARLY HALF A CENTURY BETWEEN the late thirties and the mid-eighties of the sixteenth century. They were crucial decades for European history and for all the West: Charles V passed away and with him his imperial dream; the decline of the Moslem menace began; France, England, and Spain assumed a modern physiognomy; the discovery of the American continent ceased to be an "event," America becoming a "pole," even though subordinate to Europe. In the bosom of Christendom the second Protestant generation asserted itself and began the consolidation of the confessional division. Irenic hopes subsided and Roman Catholicism received at Trent the countenance that will characterize it down to the twentieth century.

In this intensely dynamic context the personal route of Carlo Borromeo seems a closed evolution marked by elements of continuity and of rupture, of tradition and innovation. At Borromeo's death, however, the West was entering upon a phase of settlement, tending toward inactivity and conservation, a phase particularly evident in the Christian churches. These general elements of the picture are essential for an adequate understanding of how the episcopal experience of Borromeo evolved and how very different were its successive phases.

If it is true that he was not born holy, it is likewise true that he was not born bishop, much less model bishop. Borromeo is the protagonist of a particularly complex journey that can be historicized in three successive phases, all markedly different. In the first place there was the Roman apprenticeship, that is, the six years spent at Rome (1560–66) as cardinal-nephew of Pius IV, during which time the young Borromeo received and made multifarious, appropriate spiritual requests and, at the end, chose to dedicate himself to being a bishop. There followed the Milanese period (1566–84) during which Borromeo tested and refined the received episcopal model and in the end incarnated a living example characterized by a profound unity between interior perfecting and pastoral commitment. With his death began the third phase, that in which Borromeo himself became the model imitated in a changed historical atmosphere.

The Model of the Young Borromeo (1560–1566)

In the first place it seems clear to me that the six Roman years were characterized by a notable evolution. The Carlo Borromeo of 1560 is almost irreconcilable with that of 1566. It is problematic to attempt to derive such an evolution from a single event by applying the classic category of radical and unexpected conversion.[1] From a historical point of view the sources document rather various successive moments of evolution or consolidation of the evolution; he seems to have been drawn by an uniformly accelerated movement.

A second given concerns the decisive import of the Roman evolution that would mark the entire subsequent life of Borromeo ever so rich with events and with further developments of his personality. The progress to maturity achieved in the intense Roman years would be irreversible. The years 1560–1566 do not constitute an episode and a parenthesis in the life of Borromeo but on the contrary a crucial period, even though not the only one.[2]

In the third place it is easy to observe that the substantial evolution that matured at Rome occurred under the influence of a number of factors. The most decisive seem to be his uncle, the pope, some exponents of two great and different religious orders—the Dominicans (G. Vielmi, F. Foreiro) and the Jesuits (G. B. Ribera)—some Portuguese ecclesiastics (B. de Martyribus) and some Italians (F. Foscherari, G. Morone). Other factors were events as the election and then the death of his uncle, the unexpected demise of his brother, and the experience of the Council of Trent.

Correspondingly one ought to consider that Borromeo's evolution involved different levels of his personality, from the cultural to the spiritual, from the ascetic to the ecclesial and to the pastoral. For some of these dimensions it is possible to indicate causal factors and moments of development; for others the reliable elements are still lacking. Significant at all levels, however, is the resounding reality of his familiarity with the Bible. The Caroline homilies attest to an abundant, sometimes even torrential, use both of the Old and of the New Testament reflecting a profound understanding of the texts. And yet it is not known when or from whom Borromeo received his Biblical initiation, which certainly was not accomplished at Pavia during his legal studies.

If more ought to be known about the Roman evolution, one can on the other hand be assured that Borromeo's essentially voluntarist temperament was not modified in these years; rather it seems that the responsibilities with which he found himself confronted confirmed and accentuated that characteristic.

We are confronted with a complex evolution, subjectively as objectively, that was freely and personally elaborated, producing a result greater than the sum of its causal parts, all the more so as in some cases contradictory factors have been involved. Borromeo performed—both instinctively and consciously—selections, blendings, rejections that are almost impossible to reconstruct, although one can begin to work inductively from their effects.

At Rome Borromeo was well situated to perceive the juggernaut of the abusive system that now constituted the prevalent disposition of the ecclesiastical world, contaminating all aspects of the life of the church. Decadence was inexorable, finding partisans and supporters everywhere. The struggle to break it and to extirpate it from the life of the church was as urgent as it was difficult and had no guarantee of success. The privileged observation post that the cardinal-nephew enjoyed afforded him no illusions in the matter. It required more than eliminating a few broken links in a sound system but intervening with clear determination to eliminate an extensive and ramifying degeneracy, determined to resist with all its powers. It was indeed the great force of decadence that underlined the precariousness and reversibility of a timid or not sufficiently intransigent reform. I am convinced that Borromeo's well-known severity arose in large measure from his consciousness that decadence always lay in ambush. Only a rigorous struggle against every trace of abuse, protracted in time and extended in space, would be able to achieve an effective and definitive overcoming of the unlawful practices and sustain this victory with habitual discipline.

In its complexity this situation brought the young Milanese ecclesiastic to the heart of one of the most intricate and decisive problems of his time, driving him to depart from a passive acceptance of the status quo and to realize that the future of the church could only be assured by the overcoming of the late medieval decadence and the attainment of a renewed countenance. The past did not provide a plan.[3]

A remarkable contribution was made by Bartolomeo de Martyribus and by the tradition of which he was the emblematic exponent. The encounter between Bartolomeo de Martyribus and Carlo Borromeo had an intense spiritual dimension centered on the importance of the council and the urgency of reform. The Portuguese succeeded in encouraging the Milanese in his ecclesiastical commitment by inflaming or at least by nourishing in him devotion to the church and to episcopal service. Thus it proved a crucial encounter for developing Borromeo's ideal of the bishop. He had certainly already become acquainted with men of great spiritual commitment, but perhaps he had not yet had the opportunity of meeting someone who presented to him in such a compact and therefore convincing way the living reality of a bishop fully dedicated, evangelically to the pastoral ministry.

The origins and the sources of the episcopal vision of De Martyribus ought also to be investigated. Indeed we already know about his Dominican training and his intimate relationship with Luis de Granada. But the issue involves a significant vein that has fed the great episcopal generations which illuminated the Iberian churches at Trent and made of Spain one of the epicenters of early Catholic resistance and then of renewal. The Savonarolan and Erasmian contributions have already been focused in this tradition that in 1563 went so far as unexpectedly to touch Carlo Borromeo at a significant moment of his evolution. That in April 1565 Borromeo should write to the archbishop of Braga, "Continually I bear you fixed in my mind and my heart and I do not propose to myself another model than your virtue for imitation" and again, "all is found in the Archbishop of Braga, all is excellent and worthy of highest praise," seems to transcend the limits of ecclesiastical courtesy, particularly so because acknowledgements of this sort did not customarily flow from the pen of Borromeo.

In the context of an extremely structured society that tended to grant an absolute role to authority, the hypothesis, that the church might be renewed around an episcopal order made of men disposed to enact their own supreme supernatural destiny in the commitment to being evangelically pastors, constituted a plan of great historical moment, destined to characterize Roman Catholicism for the following centuries.

The watershed, the point of no return for the Roman evolution, however, was the Council of Trent, its realization, its conclusion, its acceptance. Without this pinion the entire episcopal physiognomy of Carlo Borromeo crumbles, dissolves, ceases to exist. During all his life he acted *for* the council, *against* the precouncil and the anticouncil.

In this Borromeo objectively departed from the tradition of the "ideal bishop" to which subjectively and genetically he was also linked and by which he was formed, at least in part. The abstractions and the humanistic complacencies of the preceding literary treatises on the ideal bishop were surpassed by the Lombard temperament, but above all by the reference to the council, which attacks and replaces all preceding motivations.[4]

In this historical context, institutional, spiritual, and cultural, Borromeo preferred and exalted certain aspects of episcopal service. First the relationship between personal asceticism and episcopal ministry was greatly stressed, priority always being given to the demands of the ministry over those of an abstract pursuit of holiness. Borromeo increased his asceticism when he felt himself to be unequal to the service to be rendered. He chose not to be bishop *and* saint but saint *because* he was a bishop. Secondly there was the historical, but also ecclesiological perception of the pressing necessity of the local churches (diocese, province) and of their pluralistic dialectic as a phase following the unitary conciliar moment. Borromeo had to be thoroughly convinced—even for himself—of what he wrote in 1566 to Bonomi, that "being in his own particular church he will come to serve also the universal church with the example of his actions." His choice to go to

Milan was not obedience to necessity but a clear and fully conscious option, independently matured since the passing of Pius IV. Thirdly the centrality of the binomial constituted by residence/preaching was the typical "objective" virtue from which nothing and no one ever would dissuade the bishop. In this recognition we see Borromeo's capacity to identify the essential and to pursue it, subordinating to it all the rest.

From Model to Living Example (1566–1584)

The decision to go to Milan to be the archbishop was the sole authentic "conversion" in the life of Borromeo.[5] With that decision Borromeo definitively oriented his own life on ecclesiological, ascetic, and pastoral planes. As when in 1560 he had left Arona for Rome following a fortunate and fortuitous circumstance, so now he left Rome for Milan with an acute historical awareness and an inflexible determination. What guided him was "the spirit and light for the purpose of working, given to bishops and to the entire church in celebration of the Council of Trent for the reformation of the church" (spiritus et lumen ad laborandum, pro ecclesiae reformatione . . . datus episcopis et toti ecclesiae in Tridentini concilii celebratione). He was convinced of being Christi vicarius, like every bishop, that is caput et finis ecclesiasticae Hierarchiae . . . princeps ecclesiae[6]—formulations of transparent patristic inspiration. In his church he intended to be neither a noble nor a papal nephew, only pater, non dominus.[7]

At Milan Borromeo undertook a role not only new for him but long unfamiliar to the Catholic church. The eclipse of the pastoral commitment was so extreme as to have been considered a sunset; the living examples were thus rare and isolated, perceived as extravagant curiosities; the models outlined a few decades earlier appeared abstract and somewhat literary. In this conjuncture Borromeo initiated an entirely new pastoral experience, assuming as discriminate reference the conciliar decrees.[8] He showed how to put to account all the principal instruments from the Tridentine arsenal, from preaching[9]—exercised personally and in the vernacular—to residency[10]—observed with punctilio and not without sacrifice; from synodal activity—in the diocesan and provincial ambit—to his care for the training of the clergy[11] and for the discipline of the people.[12]

These pastoral instruments, classical as well as unusual, were animated and unified by Borromeo's unfailing devotion. His asceticism, his quest for holiness—unceasing and progressive—became articulated with the pastoral commitment; they did not degenerate into mere efficiency, yet they were stimulated by his efficiency in the process of achieving mastery. The common denominator of Borromeo's episcopal activity was the council, understood essentially as barrier and point of no return with respect to the decadence of the church and consequently as foundation for a new Christian discipline. The Tridentinum for Borromeo meant liberation of the church from abuses, an end to ecclesiastical transgressions; he did not ignore the doctrinal dimension of the council, but for him it was not central.[13]

The coherence of this vision drove Borromeo to accept, above all in the first phase of his episcopacy (1566–77), a struggle, bitter and not without blows, for the affirmation of the episcopal authority, the restoration of ecclesiastical immunities, the realization of reform. In these years Borromeo's voluntarist temperament found its own incentives in the opposition of the civil and the political authorities, that of the religious orders, and that from part of the clergy; on the other hand, it was also urged on by a growing popular consensus.[14] Quite a number of contemporaries, even among the most authoritative interlocutors of Borromeo, attempted to dissuade him or at least to moderate him in his "indiscreet zealous actions which do not link fancies with practice" with the risk of obtaining "less fruit in his administration since it becomes odious."[15] It seemed that his severity and the insistence on dictating legal rules might not be the most convincing pastoral method. For a long time it has been held that severity might have to be classified among the "virtues" of San Carlo; recently we have been asked whether this might not have been an error.[16] I believe that even this aspect may be historicized by relating it to the judgment that Borromeo gave on the gravity of the ecclesiastical decadence and on the corresponding fragility of a reform that has not profoundly rooted itself in the permanent structures of the church and of society. And on the other hand the multisecular efficacy of the Borromean pastorate seems to confirm the method that Carlo preferred and defended.

Nevertheless one may add that when the plague of 1576–77 upset Milan and bore the archbishop to new and unforeseen levels of commitment, he emerged from it with a complex revision of his own valuation of the historical moment, a revision rich with consequences also for his role as bishop. I formulate the hypothesis, namely, that in the second phase of his episcopacy (1577–84) Carlo had achieved a new level of maturity and of liberty. The long and dramatic trauma of the pestilence pushed him, as he would write in the *Memoriale,* to see in this the hand of God for effecting a caesura with respect to the past.[17] Actually in the years following there was a series of enterprises that gives the impression of a further shift forward of the "frontiers" of Borromeo's pastoral commitment. I allude to the sharpening of personal asceticism,[18] to the intensification of the preaching,[19] and above all to the decisions that would redefine relations with the political authority, such as Bascapè's mission to Madrid in 1580[20]—to realize more profoundly the physiognomy of the Ambrosian church in its shelter of the Ambrosian rite and foundation of the Oblates (1578)[21]—and Borromeo's efforts at Rome toward the institution of a cardinalatial congregation appointed to facilitate the bishops in the enforcement of the council.[22]

It seems that Borromeo abandoned the perspective of restoration of Christendom—that is of a society guided to salvation conjointly by the ecclesiastical and by the political authority—and came to see the function of the church as characterized rather by a concentration on Jesus Christ and his passion, which "is the base where ought to be established all those who want to treat of things Christian and spiritual with the people."[23] It seems that Borromeo set out on the final stretch of his journey with a more dynamic and complex vision of the life of the church and of the episcopal commitment. The Milanese experience fertilized and enriched the inspiration and the plan with which he had left Rome. The contact with social reality focused and refined the initial diagnosis and strategy.

Borromeo's Idea of the Bishop in the Church of the Counter-Reformation

Increasingly with the passing of years Milan had noticeably become a school for bishops to which all catholicity looked.[24] On the morrow of Borromeo's death one of his closest collaborators, the Minorite Francesco Panigarola, pronouncing the funeral oration, stated in a traditional but unambiguous language the specific content and universal significance of his life: "It was a marvelous dispensation of God that he should have lived in that [episcopal] state . . . so that he would have to be more fit for that great undertaking to which God called him for the reformation of the universal world (insofar as he was able to accomplish this task by his example)." The vocation of Borromeo manifested itself in his being bishop and in his being for the reform of the entire church. This emerged so evidently from the consideration of his life that on the same occasion Panigarola coined an extremely incisive expression for synthesizing the fundamental unity of the Borromean experience. The good friar as a matter of fact professed himself incapable of "describing that idea of the Bishop which he has expressed in his very self."[25]

The memory of Carlo Borromeo and of the idea of the bishop that he had realized not only imparted itself to the spontaneous resonance of his work but also found specific vehicles in the diffusion of the *Acta ecclesiae mediolanensis*[26] and in the various accounts of his life and death, culminating in the biographies of Bascapè (1592) and of Giussani (1610)[27] and finally in canonization.[28]

Of all this material there has been a good, even if not completely satisfactory, awareness. There exists also a moderate amount of information on the influence of the Caroline idea of the bishop in Spain,[29] in France,[30] in Germany,[31] and in Latin America.[32]

It seems to me important next to investigate critically the significance of a now customary "topos", according to which Carlo Borromeo is the symbol of the Counter-Reformation.[33] What was the idea of the bishop proposed by Carlo to the post-Tridentine church? Likewise what did Counter-Reformation Catholicism find in Borromeo that would cause it to elevate him as its own flag? Does the stereotype of the zealous and severe bishop, characterized by an unusual personal asceticism, by an intransigent moralization of social life, and by a struggle without quarter to heresy, do justice to the "idea" illuminated at Milan between 1566 and 1584?

Obviously the response can only be shaded and nuanced, taking into account the multivalent richness of the Caroline experience and at the same time the profound alterations of spiritual climate that came to pass in modern Christianity, indeed that began in the last decades of the sixteenth century and were modulated with many variations in diverse cultural areas.

At the moment of his death Carlo appeared very different from the youth called to Rome by the nepotism of a Medici pope and even more distant from the zealous prelate who set forth to Milan in 1566. The archbishop who died in 1584 had rediscovered what it means to be a bishop and has restored to the episcopacy social dignity and spiritual credibility. With others—from Bartolomeo de Martyribus to Gabriele Paleotti—he had attested to the capacity of Catholicism to produce great leaders, committed to a transparent evangelical allegiance and capable of exercising a spiritual direction capable of involving great masses of people.[34]

In particular Borromeo had seen with exceptional intensity the interdependence between the personal virtue of a Christian called to holiness and the ecclesial commitment of a bishop responsible for a Christian community. In him prayer, renunciation of self, and penitential asceticism were not particular individual exercises but energies placed at the service of the pastoral ministry. The participation with one's own people in preaching as in the visitation, the responsible exercise of the full weight of episcopal authority and at the same time the demand for a collegial coresponsibility, the respect for power both ecclesiastical and political but without estrangement, the unyielding struggle with decadence are all major aspects of an "idea" essentially unitary, of a response constructed day by day in order to confront the needs of a church that seemed destined to be overturned by history.

Again Borromeo composed this model having chosen to serve a church, to share its destiny, its history, its vocation in the communion of Catholicism. The Ambrosian church was not the inert stage on which an exceptional protagonist enacted a great drama. The holiness of Borromeo is tempered with his being bishop at Milan; the one without the other is only a phantasm, a mystification.[35]

Borromeo's idea of the bishop had attained to an exaltation of the pastorate as the means of overcoming of the fragmentation of the bishop-saint, bishop-statesman, bishop-diplomat, bishop-theologian, bishop-lord: a pastorate

that was synthesis and concrete unification of virtue and ministry, of evangelical sequel and of response to the times.[36]

One can recognize the debts that Borromeo owed to preconciliar petitions
for an ideal bishop and his umbilical dependence upon the Tridentinum, but
one still must grant that the type he incarnated had a considerable degree of
originality.

The reputation and the fortune of Carlo Borromeo were absolutely exceptional in time and in space. It is necessary to appraise him in the light of a
basic, critical warning. This involves being thoroughly aware that with the
conclusion of the Council of Trent and the crystallization of the confessional
division of European Christianity, there waned that stage of planning and
creativity which the minds between the fifteenth and sixteenth century had
traveled and of which Carlo was also a product, the mature and richest fruit.
In the final twenty years of the sixteenth century began a new period of
European culture and in particular of Western Christianity. It would be a
phase of normalization and of order, wherein both the spiritual and the
theological climate would be distinguished by certainty rather than by
inquiry.

The implementation of the Tridentinum would become the initiative and
finally the monopoly of the Roman papacy, while bishops and local churches
were relegated to a subordinate role, called to an obedience without coresponsibility. Robert Bellarmine and the school inspired by him would give
ecclesiological dignity to this empirical choice. The guarantees offered by the
ecclesial uniformity in opposition to the Protestant "variety" colored the
theological benefit of uniformity over pluralism. Uniformity and unity
seemed coextensive; pluralism became synonomous with irresponsible free
will.

The prudence that at Trent had advised treatment of only the doctrinal
points controversial to Catholics and Protestants was dismantled by the need
to oppose to the Reformation and to modern culture a theological system,
organic and complete, distinguished by certainty. All the spaces left open by
the council were closed, and almost always in its very name.[37]

The coherence of this great historical period—the Counter-Reformation—
also failed to realize the ideal of the bishop expressed by San Carlo Borromeo. With the same ease whereby the conciliar spirit and the conciliar
decisions were twisted to Counter-Reformation strategy, the memory of the
great archbishop of Milan suffered a similar treatment through selecting,
exalting, amputating, blurring. Thus the virtues were separated from the
pastoral commitment; the effort to promote the original characteristics of
one's own church without affecting the communion and obedience with
Rome became passive and inert subjection; the dedication to a struggle
without quarter for a new discipline in the church was reproposed in terms
of casuistic ethics.[38]

If it is recognized that the crumbling of the compact Caroline model favored its diffusion by assisting so many bishops in drawing liberally from it, we cannot fail to see that San Carlo was one of the poles of the encounter from which the Catholic Counter-Reformation went forth.

In this climate unfolded in just measure the reception of the Council of Trent and of the Caroline model. From them would be born contradictions and distortions along with impulses of extraordinary fecundity that modern Catholicism would carry down within itself through the centuries.

Notes

1. Bascapè dedicated to this connection between the death of Federico and the conversion of Borromeo chapter 5 of book 1: "He is consecrated to a holier conduct of life. Death of his brother. Reform of his life." Similarly Giussani has the title, "How he is made priest after the death of his brother." In the *Istoria del concilio di Trento,* Pallavicino confirms this point of view, maintaining that Borromeo performed the exercises of Saint Ignatius following upon his brother's death (l.19 c.4 n.9). The letters written by Carlo at this time do not reflect a particular spiritual impact occasioned by the death. Cf. P. Paschini, "Il primo soggiorno di S.Carlo Borromeo a Roma," in *Cinquecento romano e riforma cattolica* (Rome, 1958), p. 137. Cf. also A. Rimoldi, "La spiritualità di S.Carlo Borromeo," *Accademia di S.Carlo* 3 (1980): 101–9. More prudent is H. Jedin, *Carlo Borromeo* (Rome, 1971), p. 11. On Federico Borromeo see *Dizionario biografico degli Italiani (DBI)* 13 (1971): 31–33.

2. For the rest of this first part I refer to my lecture, "Carlo Borromeo e il suo modello di vescovo," forthcoming in the *Atti del Convegno di Milano* (May 1984).

3. It has been fashionable to present Carlo Borromeo as a restorer, while his attention was dedicated exclusively to the present.

4. Cf. H. Jedin and G. Alberigo, *L'ideale del vescovo secondo la riforma cattolica* (Brescia, 1985).

5. I use here "conversion" in its strong sense, that is as an event not only internal but also external, as an event that not only changed the spiritual and moral dimension of the life of Borromeo, but that has globally upset life itself. On the other hand one may think of Cardinal Paleotti's decision to transfer himself to Rome from Bologna in the last years of his life.

6. "Sylva pastoralis," 45 and 62, ed. C. Marcora, in *Memorie storiche della Diocesi di Milano* 12 (1965): 13–98. It involves a sort of introduction of Borromeo to the *Silvae clericales,* collections of citations made and caused to be made by Borromeo himself. Unfortunately the edition does not give information on the composition and the date of the same "Sylva pastoralis": Marcora records (p. 15) that according to Possevino, Borromeo had turned to the rearrangement of this material in 1584.

7. *Acta ecclesiae mediolanensis (AEM)* 2:159–60, 207–8, 252, 560, 857, 874, 881; cf. on this matter the rules of spiritual life for a bishop, where it is affirmed that he ought "to consider how the names of the episcopal office, which are bishop, pastor and father, show him what ought to be the bishop" (ed. Marcora, *Memorie storiche della diocesi di Milano* 8 [1961]: 382). As is noted, this preoccupation with being, as bishop, "father and pastor" not "lord" would be recovered many centuries later by Roncalli; cf. G. Alberigo, "Formazione, contenuto e fortuna dell'allocuzione

'Gaudet mater ecclesia'," in *Fede Tradizione Profezia. Studi su Giovanni XXIII e sul Vaticano II*, Testi e ricerche di scienze religiose, 21 (Brescia, 1984), p. 213.

8. In writing to Ormaneto on 5 July 1564, he indicates as criterion and guide for the imminent diocesan synod that each decree be opened by citing the Tridentinum (ed. Marcora, *Memorie* [1961], p. 489). Very explicit in this matter is a letter of Carlo Borromeo to Bartolomeo de Martyribus (Rome, 3 April 1565) in which he comforts him and encourages him to apply thoroughly the Tridentine decisions notwithstanding the opposition. Borromeo assures the archbishop of Braga that he can count on the support of the pope; cf. R. de Almeida Rolo, *L'évêque de la Réforme Tridentine* (Lisbon, 1965), pp. 403–4.

9. Again from Rome, where he had begun to train himself in preaching, he wrote to Ormaneto, 6 January 1565 (ed. Marcora, *Memorie* [1961], pp. 551–552) "not to want to serve in his sermons the glory of the world, but only God, by achieving the edification and winning of souls and not the display of doctrine where through seeking out dangerous disputes unity and the bond of charity are sundered and opportunity is given to the people to murmur; better and more laudable than competition and contention, it would be worthier of the good servants of the Lord to seek to toil principally for his praise and honor and for the welfare of the people, leaving aside all contention with words just as the Apostle says: Ad nihil utilis est nisi ad subversionem audientium, [2 Tim. 2:14] himself having in memory that precept of the same Apostle: Stultas et sine disciplina questiones devita, sciens quia generant lites, servum autem Domini non oportet litigare. . . ." [cf. 2 Tim. 2:23–4] In a letter of 12 February 1567 to A. Lino he explained why he preferred to preach from the altar and not from the pulpit (*Discorsi inediti*, ed. C. Marcora [Milan, 1965], p. 72). In 1578 he dissuaded the bishop of Lérida from serving in the confessional, for that would remove him from preaching (R. Lluch, "La congregación del Concilio y San Carlo Borromeo en la problemática y curso de la contrareforma," *Anthologica Annua* 14 [1966]: 117–18).

10. Residency would greatly determine a part of Borromeo's life, as can be attested by the fact that his abandonment of Rome for Milan was not entirely caused by the conclusion of the pontificate of Pius IV, but had motives and aims much more profound.

11. Concern for reform and the training of the clergy may have induced Borromeo, after having had contacts of a personal nature with various Jesuits, to desire the presence of the Society of Jesus at Milan. Nevertheless it would be precisely the anxiety for such training that would cause tensions between the archbishop and the fathers, about which there is still lacking a sufficiently critical study.

12. The commitment of Borromeo to reform of the Christian people was facilitated by the abundant and growing agreement obtained by him along with the fact of his own presence in the diocese; gradually the experience of his zeal and of his own severity became a guarantee of the determination of the archbishop to participate in the effort of reform.

13. It is striking that there has been no systematic study of the central presence of the council in the work of Borromeo. It would involve not only making an inventory—quite valuable—of citations of the conciliar decrees in the Borromean decisions, but also and above all analyzing the role that the Tridentinum has had in the pastoral commitment of the archbishop of Milan.

14. The conflicts provoked by the determination with which Carlo conducted his work of reform have become proverbial to the extent of constituting a commonplace that has to a certain degree polluted the image of Borromeo in historiography. Thus

the belief is often ventured that the clashes were the principal content of the commitment of Carlo, while they were in fact its vexing and tiring repercussions.

15. Bollani wrote thus on 12 May 1576 to his agent at Rome (Biblioteca Queriniana di Brescia, M.f. 2 4 m 7 c.109) and at greater length: "Tomorrow the second session with the name of the Holy Spirit will be done here and I hope also tomorrow at eight that the third session will be done; thus will be finished this council from which I do not know what fruit will be derived, given such a mound of decrees all being full of as much rigor as the cardinal wants to bestow on them. And he cannot be resisted in everything, although I with all modesty am moderating his work in part; he intends nothing other than to make another book, without ever seeing to its observance and in causing despair among all inferiors, failing thus to do the essential things: these indiscreet acts of zeal do not please me, which do not link fancies with practice. This lord is full of holy willpower, but in proceeding with so much rigor he causes no doubt less fruit in his administration, since it becomes odious."

16. F. Molinari, *Domenico Bollani (1514–1579) vescovo di Brescia e Carlo Borromeo (1538–1584). Linee di ricerca sulla pastorale post-tridentina in una chiesa locale* (Brescia, n.d.). The whole problem relating to Borromeo's severity has indeed been rigorously investigated with a detailed analysis of the numerous texts in which he himself pushes and defends his own manner in encounters with Gregory XIII, L. de Granada, the patriarch Ribera, and especially in the encounter with Bartolomeo de Martyribus, subject of critical analogies. Nor can it even be ignored that a contemporary wrote in 1566 to Borromeo himself: "It is certain to be wept that we live in times that holy things pertaining to the service of God appear to be fables and humors. . . ." E. Cattaneo, "Il primo concilio provinciale milanese," in *Il Concilio di Trento e la riforma tridentina*, vol. 1 (Rome, 1962), p. 249 n. 1. A. G. Roncalli has apprehended something in this respect, as A. Melloni documented at the Washington Borromeo Symposium of 1984.

17. *AEM* 3:710–824; G. Testori has been responsible for modern editions of it.

18. Interesting and significant is the *Scrutinium episcoporum* presented by Borromeo to the provincial council of 1579 for a most minute and pitiless examination of episcopal consciences; cf. Molinari, *Bollani e Borromeo*, pp. 83–88. Of analogous content, if with a didactic modulation, is a text edited by Marcora (*Memorie storiche della Diocesi di Milano* 8 (1961): 373–86), perhaps requested by Borromeo for Paleotti; cf. Prodi, *Il card. G. Paleotti* 2:11 n. 12.

19. See the letter of 2 April 1578 to Paleotti on this argument (ed. Prodi, *Il card. G. Paleotti* 2:91–92) occasioned by the opportunity to preach in Latin, as Paleotti did; although Borromeo did not, the letter is rich with many general hints.

20. P. Prodi, "Carlo Borromeo e le trattative tra Gregorio XIII e Filippo II sulla giurisdizione ecclesiastica," *Rivista di Storia della Chiesa in Italia* 11 (1957): 195–240.

21. Borromeo's point of view on the liturgical uniformity pursued by Rome is summarized with great clarity and efficacy in his letter of 28 July 1578 to Cesare Speciano, who represented him at Rome (ed. P. Mazzuchelli, *Osservazioni intorno al saggio storico-critico sopra il rito ambrosiano* [Milan, 1828], pp. 392–93). Cf. also C. Alzati, "C. Borromeo e la tradizione liturgica della chiesa milanese," *Accademia di S.Carlo* 3 (1980): 83–99 and *Statuti degli Oblati di S.Ambrogio*, ed. P. F. Fumagalli (Milan, 1984).

22. Cf. P. Prodi, "Charles Borromée, archévêque de Milan et la Papauté," *Revue d'histoire ecclésiastique* 62 (1967): 379–411.

23. Thus in a letter of Borromeo to Cardinal Valier dated 14 December 1582, in *S.Carlo Borromeo e il card. Agostino Valier*, ed. L. Tacchella (Verona, 1972), p. 86.

24. See also H. D. Wojtyska, "S.Carlo Borromeo e la Polonia negli anni 1578–1584," *Rivista di Storia della Chiesa in Italia* 38 (1984): 27–46.

25. F. Panigarola, *Oratione in morte e sopra il corpo dell'illustriss. Carlo Borromeo* (Brescia, 1585), A 4 and B 1. Now reprinted in C. Marcora, *I funebri per il card. Carlo Borromeo* (Milan, 1984), pp. 49–61; cf. M. Petrocchi, "L'idea del vescovo nel Panigarola," *Rivista di Storia della Chiesa in Italia* 8 (1954): 93–95.

26. Cf. E. Cattaneo, "La singolare fortuna degli 'Acta Ecclesiae Mediolanensis,'" *La Scuola Cattolica* 111 (1983): 191–217.

27. For the biography of Bascapè see the recent edition of the original Latin with Italian translation facing, ed. E. Cattaneo et al. (Milan, 1984). Cf. M. F. Mellano and F. Molinari, "La 'Vita di S.Carlo' del Bascapè: vicende della pubblicazione," *Ricerche di storia sociale e religiosa* 21–22 (1982): 125–89. The life prepared by G. P. Giussani was expressive of the milieu of the Oblates of Saint Ambrose, clerks regular founded by Borromeo. The first edition went out at Milan exactly in 1610 with the title *Istoria della vita, virtù, morte e miracoli di S.Carlo Borromeo*. Cf. G. Galbiati, "Per una ristampa della 'Vita di S.Carlo Borromeo' del Giussani," *Echi di S.Carlo Borromeo* 12 (1938): 559–60.

28. Always useful are the *Memorie e documenti sulla canonizzazione di S.Carlo* collected by C. Locatelli. On this also see C. Marcora, "Il processo diocesano informativo sulla vita di S.Carlo per la sua canonizzazione," *Memorie storiche della diocesi di Milano* 9 (1962): 706–30. More recently, the essay of A. Turchini, *La fabbrica di un santo. Il processo di canonizzazione di Carlo Borromeo e la controriforma* (Casale Monferrato, 1984) has chosen a sociological course whose value has been perceived by almost nobody.

29. Cf. R. Lluch, "S.Carlo Borromeo y sus relaciones con el episcopado iberico posttridentino," *Anthologica Annua* 8 (1960): 83–141; and also A. Huerga, "Fr. Luis de Granada y san Carlo Borromeo. Una amistad al servicio de la restauración católica," *Hispania Sacra* 11 (1958): 299–347.

30. Cf. P. Broutin, *La réforme pastorale en France au XVIIᵉ siècle. Recherches sur la tradition pastorale après le Concile de Trente* (Paris, 1956).

31. Cf. the lecture presented by E. Iserloh at the conference held at Modena through the support of the Fondazione S.Carlo (September 1984), which is now in process of publishing the proceedings.

32. Cf. E. Dussel, *Historia general de la Iglesia en America Latina*. 1/1 Introduccion general (Salamanca, 1983), pp. 372–80.

33. Cf. the synthetic evaluation of Pastor in *Storia del papi* 9 (Rome, 1929), pp. 80–81.

34. A relevant dimension for the second half of the sixteenth century is the growing inferiority complex that afflicts many Catholic milieus in facing the disconcerting capacity of the Protestant leaders to obtain an enthusiastic popular consensus and to put into circulation ideas, passwords, and rules of suitable behavior to promote not only adherence but participation and personal commitment. From this point of view Carlo Borromeo eminently showed that such capacity was not extinct in Roman Catholicism.

35. Only a complete knowledge of the Borromean body of correspondence and of other sources still unpublished will make it possible perhaps to focus on the degree of consciousness that Borromeo developed as to the significance of his commitment not at the "center" but in a "local church." Perhaps at the moment of his going to Milan from Rome the subjective aspect of this choice prevailed. Yet as early as 20 November 1566 the same Borromeo was writing to Bonomi that "stando a la sua chiesa particulare verrà a servire anche a l'universale coll'esempio de le sue attioni" (C. Mar-

cora, "I primi anni dell' episcopato di S. Carlo [1566–1567]," *Memorie storiche della diocesi di Milano* 10 [1963]: 533). It is also difficult to realize what may have been the consciousness of Borromeo at the end of his experience.

36. This characteristic of the "pastoralità" is in my way of thinking crucial in the contribution of Borromeo to modern Catholicism. He was, even in this matter, the most significant exponent of the new generation of Tridentine bishops. According to them the *salus animarum* was a precise and vital aim of the church and of the pastors in particular. That is what committed them to invest all their energies to make possible the profession of the faith, the exercise of the cult in spirit and in truth, and the effective practice of charity on the part of the faithful. Parallel to this attitude at Rome the *cura animarum* was given a rather ecclesiological-disciplinary interpretation, with the primary concern that bishops, clergy, and parishioners were faithful and obedient to the papacy, understood especially as a unified measure of Christian authenticity. Cf. G. Alberigo, "Profession de foi et doxologie dans le catholicisme des XVᵉ et XVIᵉ siècles," *Irénikon* 47 (1974): 5–26.

37. The relationship between the council and the documents edited and published at Rome in the following years, from the profession of faith and the catechism to the liturgical books, ending with the reform of the Curia by Sixtus V, would be attentively puzzled over.

38. I refer to my "Carlo Borromeo come modello di vescovo nella chiesa post-tridentina," *Rivista Storica Italiana* 79 (1967): 1031–52 and to "Du Concile de Trente au tridentinisme," *Irénikon* 54 (1981): 192–210.

Liturgy and Iconography at the Canonization of Carlo Borromeo, 1 November 1610

NIELS RASMUSSEN

THREE CHURCHES IN ROME CONTAIN IN THEIR TITLE THE NAME OF CARLO. They are all well known by Romans as well as by visitors, and they all belong to the first part of the seventeenth century. The first was begun in 1611 by the Barnabites and is known as San Carlo ai Catinari. The fresco by Guido Reni of San Carlo, which previously decorated its facade, has now been taken down and is kept in a back room of the sacristy but is still worth seeing. The next church to be constructed is the imposing Santi Ambrogio e Carlo, on the Via del Corso; the Company of the Lombards began it in 1612. The third church is the one that the Romans affectionately know under its dimunitive form, not San Carlo alle quattre fontane close to the Quirinal, but San Carlino, which had Borromini as its architect.

That three churches in Rome were built within not much more than fifty years and dedicated to the same saint calls for an explanation. That explanation is to be found in an event that took place in 1610 and which is to be the topic of this essay. That it *was* considered an event of major proportions is shown by the fact that the annual medal of the papacy for the year 1610–11 (the seventh year of the pontificate of Paul V) on its reverse designates exactly the same event as the most significant of the year. On the medal, which is by Moro, we see Paul V seated on the throne, on the side of which we see his coats of arms. The inscription glosses the commemorated event: "He [Paul V] places Cardinal Borromeo among the Saints. 1610" *(Inter sanctos refert Cardinalem Borromeum)*. That this session of our symposium can be de-

This paper, which was presented at the Washington Symposium, is an abbreviated version of the author's fuller treatment of the topic, to appear, under the same title, in the *Analecta Romana Instituti Danici* 15 (1986), with twenty-four illustrations and a publication of the expense-list of the canonization. *Scholarly references should be made to the full version.* The *Analecta* article will be available as an offprint at the Danish Academy in Rome: Accademia di Danimarca, Via Omero 18 (Valle Giulia), I–00197 ROMA.

voted to "the image of Borromeo in History" is due to this fact, that he was canonized, twenty-six years after his death.

But what does that signify? The church of the Catholic Reformation identified him as a model to follow and claims with regard to his sanctity immediately were voiced. These claims were formalized first by the publication of his lives, later by the canonical process in Rome (begun in 1604) and the demand of the Seventh Provincial Council of Milan in 1609 to Pope Paul V. It was to succeed in 1610. Professor Giuseppe Alberigo of Bologna has shown how the fact that really constituted the grandeur of Carlo Borromeo, namely that he was a model of a residing local bishop, in the course of the processes was somewhat lost and replaced by commonplace exaltation of traditional asceticism. This same attitude is apparent in the interdiction of iconographical representations of him in the vestments of a local archbishop: Rome decreed that he was always to be shown as a cardinal.

What does canonization entail? A complicated judicial process in many stages developed throughout the ages, and the final goal of that process was a judicial sentence, an announcement by the pope, that such and such in fact was a saint and should be venerated as such. It is from that solemn and definitive sentence that the celebration of the canonization develops, and it develops in a context which is dependent on judicial ritual as well as on ordinary Roman Catholic liturgical elements. That ritual has attracted many authors who have described it and few scholars who have explained it. One of these was the late Professor Theodor Klauser of the University of Bonn who in an article in 1938 studied the earlier periods of the development and disentangled some of its problems. He rightly distinguishes between the act of canonization proper and the celebration of the mass that follows that act. Concerning the former part this consists, for our period, of a triple postulation *(petitio canonizationis)* by the (cardinal) procurator, asking the pope to proceed. Twice the postulation is refused by a high prelate, the secretary of letters to princes, and more prayers are voiced. The third time no more delays are requested and the pope pronounces the solemn formula stating that it is "to the Honour of the Holy and Undivided Trinity for the exaltation of the catholic faith and the growth of the Christian Religion" that the Pope define such and such to be a saint, to be put into the calendar of the church and to be celebrated by the Church universal on such a day every year. This definition is pronounced by the seated pope with, normally, everyone else standing, which underscores the relation between this act and any other definitive act of judgment. Continuing in this line the cardinal procurator then asks the pope to order that appropriate proof for this sentence be given *(petitio documentorum);* the pontiff agrees by the word *Decernimus,* and the secretary of the pope orders the present apostolic protonotaries and notaries to make up the papal bulls. That part is concluded by the hymn of thanksgiving, the *Te Deum,* and by a prayer in which the intercession of the new saint is invoked for the first time. This first part of the canonization is something absolutely special in Roman Catholic worship and needed description. The second part is the celebration of the mass according to the ritual for the most solemn occasions, presided over by the pope himself. This second part has, however, one feature that is particular to canonizations: a very elaborate offertory during which not only bread and wine for the eucharistic sacrifice are given to the pope, but also other gifts of various sorts, as will be seen in the case which occupies us here.

Canonizations were truly exceptional events and have remained such until the 1970s when a distinct inflationary tendency appeared, blossoming in the 1980s. If they were not for other reasons infrequent, their price was prohibitive, and in the fifteenth to seventeenth centuries it was rare that a pope would preside over more than two at the most during a pontificate. This is exactly the reason why they become landmarks for the reign of a pope, and, happily for us who want to study them, they often are chosen by artists (or rather by their patrons, we can suppose) to be objects for iconographical or sculptural realizations. Paul V (1605–21) performed two canonizations: the first of the patron saints of the city of Rome—Francesca Romana, born in 1384, was canonized on 29 May 1608—and two years later, on 1 November 1610, the Borghese pope canonized Carlo Borromeo. The two events are recorded in frescoes in the end walls of the gallery of Paul V in the Vatican Library, and they are dated 1610–11 (fig. 1). The artist was Giovanni Battista Ricci of Novara (1537–1627). We may assume that he was present at least at the latter of the two events.

It is time now to look at that 1610 event, the canonization of Carlo Borromeo. We will not delve into the preceding process (the acts of which all have been edited) and whose last moments were in the three consistories in August and September of 1610. Instead we will try to analyze the written and pictorial material that describes the event itself. Some of the written documentation is printed: this is particularly the case for the work by the Milanese canon Aurelio Grattarola who in 1614 published his *Successi maravigliosi della veneratione di S. Carlo*. Grattarola was a member of the delegation of Milanese clergy sent to Rome, first in 1609 to request the canonization and then again in 1610 to the ceremony itself. The Spanish theologian Francisco Peña also wrote a description of the event in 1610. Other material is not printed and is less easily accessible. A liturgist first will look for the diaries of the papal masters of ceremonies, the records of celebrations from every occasion the pope celebrated or presided over. Two masters who have left written material participated on that day in 1610, Paolo Alaleone (1582–1632) and Giovanni Paolo Mucanzio. Alaleone, who ordinarily is not afraid of details, managed to complete his description in six pages and Mucanzio took less than two! But the latter refers to a description in a special book: *describitur in libro particulari*. No

Figure 1. Canonization of Carlo Borromeo, 1610, at the main altar, New Saint Peter's. *(Gallery of Paul V, Vatican Library, fresco by G. B. Ricci. Reproduced by permission: Monumenti, Musei e Gallerie Pontificie.)*

such work is recorded in the catalogs of the Vatican Library. As a great number of acts of canonizations came to Paris among the Napoleonic spoils and for some odd reason were never returned, I turned to the Bibliothèque Nationale, but our Saint Charles was conspicuously absent from the Roman collection. However, by a lucky chance, a little collection of canonization material showed up elsewhere at La Nationale, namely in that *fonds* which comes from Saint-Germain-des-Prés. Among these books was a stately volume consisting of 861 pages: this is the *liber particularis*, as the title page states, "compiled by Giovanni Paolo Mucanzio, Doctor utriusque juris, Master of Sacred Ceremonies and Secretary in the Sacred Congregation of Rites" (MS Lat. 12631). In that volume's last ten or eleven pages is found a list of expenses incurred by the event: gratuities to everybody, expenses for the decoration of the church, new vestments and dresses to the prelates. Such expense lists are relatively common at canonizations and a certain number of them have been printed. This one is not yet published (although it will soon be) and it has, together with the rest of Mucanzio's work and the book by Grattarola, been the most valuable of the written documentations.

As for the iconographical documentation, this will be discussed throughout the essay and thus needs no detailed presentation at this moment. It is enough to say that only four documents really can claim to qualify as source material, and, as we will see, this also is a qualified statement: two engravings by Matteo Greuter (1566–1638), one by Giovanni Maggi (1566–1618) (figs. 2 and 3) and the above-mentioned fresco by Ricci. All these are from 1610 or 1611 and thus contemporary with the event. When these sources do not concur, problems of interpretation arise, as will be seen.

With the relevant sources at hand we can now proceed to combine them and also, when needed, to contrast them. We will see that the result is an image of an overwhelmingly splendid church festival, a singular occasion in which elements of traditional worship mingle with the intricacies of the papal court ceremonial, all seasoned in the most characteristic baroque sense for splendor and festivity. We will first examine the space in which the canonization took place and then the liturgical action itself.

On October 27, a Wednesday, Paul V returned from the Quirinal to his winter quarters at the Vatican and that same week a delegation from Milan, presided by Federico Borromeo, the cousin, as well as cardinals and other prelates, arrived from the Provinces. The guests came to a church that had already been prepared for the solemnity. But they also came to a big construction site that gave great difficulties to the organizers, that is to say the masters of ceremonies.

On the morning of the feast of All Saints, Monday, 1 November, chosen to allow Carlo's own feast day to be celebrated on the fourth, the clergy of Rome awaited outside the Vatican palace but neither they nor the prelates could make the habitual grand entrance across the piazza, for fear of the "ruin of the Fabric" *(propter ruinam fabricae)*. Saint Peter's, indeed, had not yet been finished! The decision to add to the new basilica a central building, the *prolungamento* of Carlo Maderna, resulted in the laying of the new facade's foundation on 5 November 1607. Since then the work had proceeded with the haste characteristic of Paul V.

How the *fabrica* might have looked on that day is represented here. The degree of completion of the facade and of the passage between the two segments of the new church is open to discussion, but in between there certainly was a gap. There also were some steep steps up from the level of the old basilica to the new. And on the old *murus diversorius* of Paul III whose inside now had become a provisional outside, there was ample space for decoration. And it was indeed decorated. A mighty triumphal arch had been

Figure 2. Canonization of Carlo Borromeo. Interior of Saint Peter's; engraving by M. Greuter. *(Reproduced by permission: Gabinetto Comunale delle Stampe del Commune di Roma, Museo di Roma.)*

Figure 3. Canonization of Carlo Borromeo. Interior of Saint Peter's; engraving by G. Maggi. *(Reproduced by permission: Biblioteca Angelica, Rome.)*

built around Paul III's door leading up to the new church. Triumphal arches are highly significant for "occasional architecture" of the Renaissance and the baroque, and their symbolic signification should not be underestimated: although this topic is not yet fully researched, we might suppose that some kind of identification took place in the mind of the participants as they passed through the arch.

In this case, the decoration consisted in representations of all the saint archbishops of Milan. Apart from the anachronism, it was of course an impressive display, beginning with the apostle Barnabas and encompassing Saint Ambrose and Saint Carlo and thirty-five other archbishops.

The procession then went up the steps to the New Saint Peter's: seven outside the entrance and five inside, as has been shown by the excavations of our time. It was met by *suavissima musica,* as Grattarola says, at the moment when the chapter received it. For the rest of the musical repertory we are unhappily at a loss. One of our engravings, that of Maggi (fig. 3), gives us a glimpse of five cantors grouped in a balcony at the right central pillar. The account books and diaries tell us nothing about the repertory, but we do know that all the twenty-four cantors were functional. After the decoration outside, another view awaited them that must have staggered accustomed and unaccustomed visitors alike.

The permanent part of Saint Peter's first: the four pillars were hung with Raphael's tapestries, first executed, as is known, under Leo X for use in the Sistine Chapel. John Shearman, in his monograph on the tapestries, mentions their use on the processional route for the Corpus Christi procession. Grattarola's account adds to our knowledge of their use. But it is the nonpermanent, hence ephemeral, decoration of Saint Peter's that must have been astounding. Canonizations, like coronations, always took place on a specially built platform or estrade, ordinarily called the theater. The construction of the theater was entrusted to Girolami Rainaldi (1570–1655). A mighty twelve-sided enclosure surrounded the altar. Its main entrance was at the height of the first of the two central pillars, but its other end extended beyond the other two central pillars and approached the beginning of the apse. (See the engraving of Matteo Greuter [fig. 2] and that of Giovanni Maggi [fig. 3]). Although they concur, there are also some significant discrepancies. They both concur with the general description given by Grattarola: the theater consists of thirty-five arches, with pilasters and a running corniche on which an imposing number of candles are burning on greater and smaller chandeliers. Greuter, using a wider angle, also shows these on the corniche of the basilica and on the tambour of the cupola, and Grattarola tells us that on the former there were 412 candles and on the latter eighty, each weighing four pounds. The two engravings also show the series of paintings in gold chiaroscuro and in circular form hanging from the center of the thirty-five arches. Those on the entrance were double-faced, so there were thirty-nine in all. They were executed by the very prolific painter and designer Antonio Tempesta (1555–1630). They showed the life and the miracles of Saint Carlo and are lost today.

The main altar had been put in place and consecrated by Clement VIII on 26 June 1594. But the problem concerning the baldachin still had to await its definitive solution. The intermediary baldachin of Paul V consisted, as Irving Lavin says, of a tasseled canopy supported on staves held by four standing angels. It represented, in effect, a portable canopy such as was borne above the bishops; it was purchased in 1608 and was roughly nine meters high, a little less than one third of the twenty-nine meters of Bernini's definitive work.

But there are also discrepancies between Greuter and Maggi. One of these concerns perspective: Maggi seems to have used (if you will excuse me the expression) a zoom lens! A closer analysis, and with the help of the designs for the later canonizations in 1622 of Ignatius of Loyola, Isidore of Toledo, Theresa of Avila, Francisco Xavier, and Philippo Neri, shows that the Greuter engraving must be given greater credibility than the one by Maggi, but the arguments lie beyond the scope of this essay.

If we return to our scheme for the ritual used, we remember the bipolarity of a ceremonial divided in two parts: the juridical definition of sainthood on the one side and the celebration of the Eucharist on the other. It is this first aspect that is depicted on the two prints. Conveniently for the executing artist, there is seemingly no action going on. We have here clearly a representation of one of the three postulations.

The two prints, however, are not our only iconographical source for the liturgical action inside Saint Peter's. We will then now turn to the third source, the fresco executed by Ricci in the first of the two galleries of Paul V in the Vatican Library (fig. 1). It is frequently seen, but as it is on the last part of the trajectory in a visit to the Vatican Museum (although the galleries belong to the Library) it may not capture the viewer's full attention. These two galleries are decorated with representations of the many achievements of the Borghese pope, and the two major frescoes in the first of the two galleries depict two liturgical ceremonies, two canonizations: the canonization of Francesca Romana from 1608 and that of San Carlo. The two frescoes together are extremely interesting for the liturgist for they show that the artist—or, more probably, his patron—was very well aware of the bipolarity of the canonization ceremony. Very appropriately then, in the 1608 event is depicted, as seen from the southern transept of Saint Peter's, a scene from the first part of the ceremony, the proclamation segment; while, on the opposite wall, this time seen from the northern transept, is depicted a scene from Saint Carlo's canonization two years later. The boy whom we see in the 1608 scene in the corner to the right has grown up to be a young man with a little beard in the 1610 scene, for there is no doubt it is the same person. We also see a notable difference in the decoration of the two scenes: for Francesca Romana there is just a hanging of red and gold draperies from the walls, while in the case of San Carlo, the elaborate structure of Rainaldi's is clearly in evidence, with the Tempesta medallions hanging down from each arch. Let us then try to observe some of the components of this fresco and comment upon them. We can first try to remove the persons, looking only at the architectonic space. It is clearly shorter than the one seen on the engravings but this is normal: Ricci needed the two centers of the action, the altar and the papal throne, and he needs to paint persons, not architectonic space. Hence an inevitable reduction. The *quadratura* on which the cardinals are seated is not very square (unless Ricci has resolved the enigma of the circle!), but here again these lines fit well into the shape of the fresco painted on an endwall with a curbed roof. This space is "furnished" with objects and with persons. The liturgical objects are naturally centered on the altar but are also found elsewhere. Two of the *stendardi* are hanging from the roof. They show Carlo, as mandated by the rites, as a cardinal. Some of the candlesticks on the corniche are also showing. Concerning the ornamentation of the altar our expense lists refer to the pallium of *tela d'argento* and to four altar cloths, the first of *tela addamascata,* the second of *tela di Renzo,* the third of *Renzo finissima domandata pretiosa,* and the fourth of *Cambrino sotilissima.* Like all the other vestments and clothing these had been brought from Milan, certainly a way of letting the Milanese also enjoy the economic bonanza of the event. On the altar are placed liturgical objects and papal decorations. The altar cross is, according to Mucanzio, "that *preciosissima et speciosissima* Cross recalling and in memory of Cardinal Alexander Farnese about which one can never say enough.[11] Other liturgical objects are placed on the two credence tables, and a cleric is holding a cruet beside the nearest of these tables. Then the actors: Paul is sitting on his throne, not with the cope as in the Francesca picture but with the mass vestments into which he changed between the two segments of the ceremony. He is wearing the chasuble made for the occasion, which the lists describe as *"di drappo bianco con fondo riccamato tutto d'oro, ed d'argento con vaglissimo disegno, nel quale con belissima dispositione si vedvano tutte l'ensigne pontificie."* He is also wearing the pallium and a miter. Assisting him on each side are the two of the oldest of the cardinal deacons, the oldest of whom, Odoardo Farnese, is on this occasion occupied elsewhere (namely in the procession,) and somebody else is filling in for him. In our curbed *quadratura* are sitting the remaining cardinals. We can count fourteen of these. According to all of our written sources there were thirty-six cardinals present, but here again the exigencies of limited space easily excuse Ricci for his reductions. We salute in passing these cardinals, all bearded like Paul V; San Carlo disapproved of this custom as Professor Melloni will soon tell us, and he will recall the pertinent article on "San Carlo e l'uso della barba degli ecclesiastici" (1909) by the

young church historian, Angelo Roncalli. Are these actually the cardinals'
portraits? To this natural question we must unhappily answer that we do not
yet know. Paul V certainly is portrayed. But even in looking for more
prominent cardinals it does not seem possible to ascertain that Ricci had the
intention to be that exact. Among the ones we would like to be able to
identify are first Federico Borromeo, the cousin, but also Maffeo Barberini,
the future Urban VIII, and Roberto Bellarmine, the future saint. We will
return later to the cardinals in the procession. Among the other officials,
three clerics in the foreground are depicted in their new dresses, also courtesy of the Milanese. There is some reason to think that they are masters of
ceremonies and that the first is their head. In that case we would here have a
portrait of Paolo Alaleone. This is only a hypothesis, but in any case his
function in this place is not so much to carry a cruet in his left hand as to
point to something going on before him and to which we shall soon return.
The papal sacristan, although he is somewhat in shadow, can clearly be seen,
mitered. This is the famous and learned Angelo Rocca, the Augustinian
among whose works we also find a treatise on the rites of canonization
(1601), without doubt consulted for the event. Research in Rome is forever
indebted to Angelo Rocca, founder of the Biblioteca Angelica. The other
persons in this group call for less commentary, although we salute in passing
the ever present spectators, gesticulating so as to point compositionally to
the center of the fresco, the poor fellow with a cheap ticket in the right
corner, and the back of the Swiss guard.

Something is happening. In the midst of the *quadratura* a procession
advances from the altar toward Paul V. Happily, it includes fifteen persons,
all bearing gifts to present to the pope. Four cardinals can be identified
because they are fully vested: the deputy procurator Cardinal Taverna and
Cardinal Pinelli, oldest cardinal bishop of the Congregation of Rites: they
are both in copes; Cardinal del Monte, the oldest cardinal priest of the
congregation; and Odoardo Farnese, the oldest cardinal deacon. Accompanying them are either their manservants (clerical) or priests delegated from
the province of Milan. They present to the pope candles, loaves of bread,
gilded or silvered, and barrels of wine, gilded or silvered. Finally, Giovanni
Pietro Barco, canon of Saint Nazarius of Milan, presents a gilded cage
containing two turtledoves; Giovanni Pietro Barco, canon of Saint Ambrose
in Milan, presents a silvered cage with two pigeons; and Archpriest
Girolamo Settali of Monza presents (although we cannot see it) a multi-
colored cage containing various small birds, *ucelletti*. When these had been
received, Paolo Alaleone opened this last cage and the birds were set free.
According to Grattarola, in the general conflagration of wings throughout
the church, one *ucelletto* came to reside, during the rest of the mass, upon
the right arm of the cross.

This is then the end. The ceremony had begun at half past seven, one hour late, the proclamation of the new saint took place about twenty minutes to ten *(hora decisette meno quarto)*, and it was all over at a quarter to twelve. The *avviso* states that after vespers in the papal chapel (All Saints and All Souls), in the afternoon, Cardinal Borghese gave a great dinner *(pranzo)* for twenty-two cardinals. The musicians were relegated to the 'cafeteria' of the palace "dopo andammo tutti collegialmente a pranzo nel solito tinello dove fummo regalati honoratissimi." The next day the work resumed on the basilica and the banners left for their destinations. The following month, the *fabbrica* of Saint Peter's bought back the timber used for the *theatrum*, a theater that had cost 11,753 gold scudi to construct. It was salvaged for 1,050 scudi!

* * *

It is time to try to evaluate this stupendous ceremony. It is not easy. The simple solution would consist in speaking about either *"un triomphalisme pour toujours depassé"* or with the naïveté of a Ludwig von Pastor, speaking about the canonization of Francis of Paolo in 1519: "in the midst of these great and sublime ceremonies which has been used since the earliest ages in like circumstances!" Klauser has shown that liturgical action in relation to canonizations did not arise until after the first millennium of the Christian era. And the American liturgist, Robert Taft, has strikingly expressed what is the case in our rite: inordinate growth. He says, "It has been my constant observation that liturgies do not grow evenly, like growing organisms. Rather, their individual structures possess a life of their own. More like cancer than like native cells, they can appear like aggressors, showing riotous growth at a time where all else lies dormant!" Indeed, if we apply this notion to our ceremony of canonization we see that the loss of proportion is great: the merely juridical procedure became liturgical and expanded with the triple postulation, *instanter—instantius—instantissime,* and with specific prayer intercalated. And the offertory rite became so inflated that it overshadowed the rest of the eucharistic celebration about which neither Grattarola nor Mucanzio has a word to say.

But this negative judgment of lack of proportions and of inordinate growth must be weighed against another. The rite is fully of its time. A splendor without parallel characterized it. Mucanzio says he has never seen anything like it; it far surpassed the four preceding canonizations: *longissimo intervallo superavit.* And even without knowledge of Latin I think we all can grasp his meaning when he says that everything was being prepared *"ut merito summe huic actioni, pro Summo Presule, a Summo omnium viventium viro Summo Pontifice, in Summa et omnium Ecclesiarum Basilica, Principis nempe Apostolorum; omnes summo applausu respondere judicaverint."* The canonization of Francesca Romana two years before had cost about 19,000 gold scudi and was printed in 1893 by L. Pelissier who stresses that the scribe making it wrote in good faith: "Esso appare redatto con completa buona fede, con grande cura d'estattezza a senza alcuna idea d'ironia. Lo scrittore termina con una pia invocazione che ne prova tutta la sincerità." Two years later the expense list for the canonization of Carlo Borromeo does not stop at 19,000 gold scudi. That list goes beyond 31,143 gold scudi. With these expenditures the future of canonizations became even more difficult. The historian can agree with Pierre Delooz who, in his *"Sociologie et canonisations,"* writes that they were only possible where there was a very strong desire to contribute to them, which would always assure a popular support behind them.

But the extravagance is tempered by something else that relativizes it and even seems to be a necessary antidote to it. In speaking about the ephemeral baroque and the sumptuosities displayed for festivals, be they profane or ecclesiastical, Maurizio Fagolo dell'Arco notes the necessity of the touching detail: "in fin la meraviglia." And the German liturgist of the school of *Geistesgeschichte*, Anton L. Mayer speaks, in studying liturgy and baroque about how "things eternal loose their eternity, becoming present, transient, sensitive experiences." It is time to conclude.

If our judgment of a liturgy in the baroque period has thus received some serious qualification from the point of view of a liturgist studying it, that same kind of qualification is present when we compare the iconographical representation of the same ceremony. About three hundred feet from the fresco of Ricci, but one floor higher, in the stanze of Raphael, more precisely in the Stanza dell'Incendio, is the fresco of the coronation of Charlemagne. The most recent research attributes its architectural design to Raphael himself and the painting to Penni and the disciples. What a difference! The coronation is full of life, dramatic. The canonization is static: even though it depicts a procession, it has been frozen as by photography. The coronation is subtle: it purports to show the scene in Rome on Christmas day in the year 800; in fact it shows Francois Premier of France as pretender, supported by the papacy to obtain the imperial crown. All symbolism is absent from Ricci's fresco of the canonization. Decidedly, the art of the Counter-Reformation still had far to go before it could regain what had been lost as a result of the Sacco, the Reformation, and a certain reaction in the last part of the sixteenth century against Christian humanism.

History, Pastorate, and Theology: The Impact of Carlo Borromeo upon A. G. Roncalli/Pope John XXIII

ALBERTO MELLONI

I

EVEN AT THE END OF THE NINETEENTH CENTURY, CARLO BORROMEO RE-mained quite influential in the training of Catholic priests—and in a special way, among Italians, of the Lombard priests.[1] The image of Borromeo they had is, from a historical point of view, a myth. It derived from the choices that were made at the moment of canonization, over two and a half centuries before: the cardinal rather than the bishop, the ascetic rather than the reformer, the man of individual holiness rather than the leader of a local church. But it was at the very end of the century and in the beginning of the next that the demand for a more rigorous, critical knowledge arose within Catholic culture. This fact changed relations between church and history and led to a theological and spiritual process that could be considered completed in the papacy of John XXIII and the second Vatican Council.[2]

A. G. Roncalli belonged to this generation; he lived and transcended its experiences. Similarly he believed in the results of a direct approach to history in general and specifically to Borromeo and the Council of Trent. During his life he dealt often and variously with Borromeo: therefore we can today analyze the impact of Borromeo upon the culture of a common Christian man with an astounding career. This essay proposes to find a relation between this impact and the concrete pastorate of Roncalli, as a result of which an imperfect integrality has been conceived between Pope John and the heritage of the Counter-Reformation. Consequently I will approach Roncalli's era chronologically.

When Roncalli was young—at about this time we have the first documen-tary bases—he didn't approach Borromeo *in se*, but the San Carlo myth. Roncalli had a devotional background that must be considered from a biographical point of view as the oldest fact and the genesis of his develop-ment. It is just a variant of Catholic and Italian Tridentinism. The Bergamo seminary, although its characteristics were not well known at this time, emphasized the glamour of this devotion: this became a fertile memory for the future priest.[3]

The *Journal of the Soul* unfolds on a diachronic plane[4] the elements of a feeling that since Radini's death (1914) was central among Roncalli's devotions: in 1898 he complains of having omitted his confession, whereas Borromeo, on the contrary, took this sacrament twice a day.[5] Borromeo is often listed among his protectors.[6] Furthermore, during the period that Roncalli spent in the Roman seminary Borromeo is sometimes strictly associated with Ignatius,[7] but he is also a model for discipline and church government:

> On reflection I intend to apply myself everyday indeed and insofar as it is fitting to the great exercise of detailed examination. It is the solemn promise that I make to the always loving heart of Jesus as fruit of his holy withdrawal. I commit it into the hands of San Carlo, distinguished instructor of ecclesiastical education. And because the reverend superiors have wanted me to be attentive not only in my education but, as prefect, in my watching over others, I place this new year of scholarship under the auspices of the great archbishop, true model of instructors and generous heart of priest and apostle.[8]

Altogether, it seems that when Don Roncalli came back to Bergamo, he carried inside him quite a traditional and traditionally constituted devotion toward the archbishop of Milan. Nevertheless we all know that between 1902 and 1904 Roncalli met some of the most brilliant churchmen of the Italian scene: but he did not associate with people like Benigni and Buonaiuti; he did not write anything in the *Annali di storia ecclesiastica* published by Benigni in this period; he did not study problems concerning or involving Borromeo.[9] In spite of this, the more he silently refined his intellectual background which—a refinement that we could imagine as analogous to his process, as I have elsewhere[10] shown of assimilating his sources—the more he discovers history, as the emotion of the famous text about criticism and truth, in the *Journal of the Soul*, demonstrates.[11] So he arrived, between 1905 and 1910, at a double meeting with Borromeo: a historic and a pastoral meeting. I have used "double" lightly: Roncalli, as the secretary of Bergamo's Bishop Radini Tedeschi, was involved with an episcopal style that after Traniello is usually called "neoborromean." I need hardly mention the numerous synods and visitations all over Lombardy during these years, or the revival of the Provincial Council, or the challenge of the Lombard bishops to sever ties with the Romish praxis of extremist antimodernism.[12] Correspondingly Roncalli, teaching in the seminary,[13] with his special sensitivity for the local church that he never lost, approached Borromeo with a "certissima scienza"—as Achille Ratti wrote.

A double meeting. Yet both these aspects arose and developed together;

and the circumstances of Roncalli's finding of papers about Borromeo's visitation of Bergamo (Roncalli discovered these documents on 23 February 1906 when he was in Milan with Radini for the meeting of the preparatory commission of the Provincial Council) seem to me at the same time rather noteworthy.[14]

To understand what was for Roncalli the intrinsic worth, the depth and the weight of this approach to Borromeo, we must wait until 1909–10, when he started to publish his first articles. Nevertheless before this date we must briefly consider a very important lecture he gave in 1907 about Cardinal Baronius,[15] because it provides a clear example of the increasingly higher degree of critical consciousness in Roncalli at this date. In this text Roncalli defines the role of historicism within church history, a historicism that he applied when he criticized the stereotype of Borromeo's image as an ideological bias:

> In recent times, through a movement that has appeared to me to be a legitimate reaction to certain systems of hagiography whereby the saints have been grabbed by the hair and borne outside of all sensible society, even outside of themselves, and converted into demigods, we have gone a little too far in the opposite extreme, preoccupied more in studying the human element in the saints, omitting somewhat the work of grace. Still, I confess it, I have obeyed this prejudice of the moderns in studying Baronius; I have with him rather wanted to play the part of devil's advocate but in the end I have felt myself kneeling before that Christian virtue, exercised on the heroic level, before the sanctity of this cardinal.[16]

A crucial moment came in 1909: Roncalli made plans to publish the *Atti* that he had found three years earlier. Radini gathered in Bergamo—like Cardinal Ferrari in Milan—a commission to work with "prove storiche" for the coming celebrations. In each issue *La Vita Diocesana,* the diocese's review, provided news about the third centennial of Borromeo's canonization. On 4 November Roncalli published a first short article about devotion for Borromeo and about his own project.[17] As in his reading of Baronio he affirms that we must draw nearer to Borromeo, to approach "our soul to Carlo's soul, our life to Carlo's life, our time to his times. He [Carlo] wishes to be studied more, to be better known in his spirit, in his thought, in his institutions."[18] Roncalli thinks that thus we could have a deeper and more direct knowledge of the great cardinal:

> Perhaps we are accustomed to admire the great archbishop a little too much at a distance. The burden of the deeds of this true colossus of pastoral sanctity, the vastness of his dimensions, a certain indescribable rigidity in his appearance based on the impression that we ourselves have drawn from his austere life, from his energy and inflexibility. . . . But it is fitting to approach the great saint instead with confidence, to study him

minutely in every gesture of his person, in every step that he takes, in every word from his lips or from his pen, in every fold of his garments. . . .[19]

The young priest draws an analogy between the present and the broad Catholic reform movement in Italy of the sixteenth century, contemporaneous with Borromeo.

During 1910 there appeared at least three articles signed by Roncalli that cannot be ignored. In April the article on Borromeo and Bergamo's church appeared in the review that the commission gathered by Cardinal Ferrari published for the centennial year.[20] It is a quick look at contacts between Borromeo and Bergamo. At the very heart, obviously, there is a focus on the visitation. It is one of the most precise and erudite texts in the review.[21] Above all, it is important because here for the first time Roncalli suggests a crucial point of his perception of Borromeo: he thinks that Borromeo's ruthlessness is only a myth, based upon wavering feelings; therefore it must be rejected.

> All that does not alter the fact that the conditions of religious life and especially those of the clergy were not at that time so disgraceful. But it is precisely in the general revival following a little later that the long desired features which derive from that event now become recognizable. Since the truer results of the apostolic visitation of San Carlo to Bergamo can much more readily be perceived when there ceased or were removed the chief difficulties to the execution of the decrees that appeared from the beginning excessive and too hard, the clergy and laity come naturally to find themselves better disposed, calm with reflection having come to replace the earlier resentments. San Carlo, who saw much from a distance, wants what he wants and not only at Bergamo but also at Milan and everywhere. . . . A few years later the religious life was already formed by the spirit of those Milanese decrees which, adhering to the Tridentine disposition and to the synods, ought to become the point of departure of all that reform which the church of Bergamo succeeds afterwards in maintaining and on which is supported its present prosperity.[22]

We find another of Roncalli's articles in the special issue of *La Scuola Cattolica*, the review of the faculty of theology of Milan, during the summer of 1910: *San Carlo Borromeo e l'uso della barba negli ecclesiastici*.[23] Roncalli briefly discusses this banal subject; however, it is surprising that about so obscure a topic he tries once again to show Borromeo's lack of severity. He writes:

> Such a provision ought really not to have encountered much resistance, yet only two years later in the Fifth Synod (1578), there were ten to twenty priests attending who still wore beards. It might well be expected that San Carlo would use excessive rigor in demanding the execution of

the decree; however, to Bonomi, who by this time had become bishop of Vercelli, he wrote: "I approve very much that you go without beards; it displeases me that your Vercellese clergy do not follow your example. Nevertheless I cannot praise your announcement to treat harshly the disobedient and to solicit from the pope a decree in support."

He then adds how Borromeo awaited more advice, patiently overlooking for the time being the disobedience of some.[24]

He quotes also a memorandum that Baronius wrote for Borromeo in which the former made suggestions respecting freedom.[25] Here, in spite of the banal topic, Roncalli's stance is far from that of some articles in the issue,[26] which attempt to depict Carlo as a model for a cruel antimodernistic struggle. It might here be mentioned that in the next special issue of the review, about the freedom of the church in the sixteenth centennial of Constantine's Edict, Roncalli did not or could not write anything[27]. At the end of this essay he applies Carlo to his own times, as a model:

> Borromeo, writing to Speciano in Rome, said among other things: "Would that I might eradicate secret sins with such happy result as I have removed the beards of the clergy; for we should strive zealously for great advances on the pathway of the Lord. . . ." These words, repeated by us and applied to our times, seem to us the best conclusion to this brief note.[28]

Here it is possible to perceive a certain gap between the asceticism of Borromeo and the asceticism of Roncalli: in Borromeo's experience mortification was a moral task, at first a way to distinguish himself within the papal court, later an instrument to show his contempt for the world and to enforce the Tridentine reform; whereas Roncalli's asceticism is a theological one, a symbol of a spiritual attitude toward Providence.

On 30 November a few days after the special issue of the Bergamo's diocesan journal in honor of Borromeo,[29] close to the centennial's end, Roncalli gave a lecture—"discorso o saggio storico, "he says—about Borromeo and the origins of Bergamo's seminary. It was published in *La Vita diocesana* a few weeks later.[30]

This lecture is something like an official speech; nevertheless we find in it some very interesting general ideas. Baronius is introduced as the protector and the model of the young historian.[31] The times of the sixteenth century are referred to as "new times," with a dynamic meaning; and everybody knows how important this idea will be in Pope John's thinking.

> Indeed the beginning of modern times is characterized by that great blast of fresh air and renewal of classical intellectual life which is called humanism and which, while bringing many bad things, also brings a revival in

the general culture as to the need for a more vital priestly ministry equal to new demands.[32]

Roncalli says that he respects history in itself, "la storia schietta," as he called it.[33] He does not heed the great problems of the seminary, but at the same time he does not accept a judgment of severity on Borromeo's decisions: the behavior of Borromeo was

> One of those acts which were entirely appropriate for him and for his administration, one of those acts harsh in appearance and not to be judged by the standard of ordinary human prudence but that reveal themselves as most wise in their moral efficacy.[34]

For the next years one must recall only the book he published in 1912 about a fraternity of Bergamo, the Misericordia Maggiore.[35] Two years later, suddenly and unexpectedly, Radini died.[36] This fact and the outbreak of World War I mark a watershed between the young Roncalli and the mature one. After his "bishop and lord" died, Roncalli stopped the effort to publish the visitation with the proofing of the first volume.[37] There are many reasons for this: The war in itself, economic strictures resulting from the war, and his cold relations with the new bishop.[38]

Such was the dawn of Roncalli's knowledge of Borromeo. Only a dawn. Nonetheless if in Roncalli himself there are some points that could have influenced his pastorate and his theology, I think that it is appropriate to call attention to them now. Of course I will need to verify this tentative conclusion in the following texts and especially in the concrete fabric of his pastorate. But there are some problems I can see that come not only from Borromeo but surely also from Roncalli himself. The first concerns the relation with history; Roncalli stresses in many ways the congruency between Borromeo and his times. On this historical basis he refutes the image of a pitiless Borromeo. Borromeo becomes a model, a *forma*, of a fatherly and merciful behavior; in the field of modern research, this is quite an ideological but original attempt to understand, in the very meaning of the latin *intuslegere*, the great archbishop.

Last but not least, there is his focus on Borromeo as a bishop: as a way to present and receive Carlo's legacy this is not surprising. But for the contact with Radini and Ferrari, this historical profile could never have become a living project. It is odd to see *that* and *how* Roncalli, in 1916,[39] actually superimposed Borromeo on Radini's image; from a linguistic point of view there is a profound relation between the vocabulary that depicts Carlo as the *forma episcoporum*, and that which depicts Radini's episcopacy.[40] Radini and other bishops were inspired by Borromeo's model in their pastorate—but Roncalli goes further. In style, expression, and description he echoes texts and facts influenced by his Borromean readings.

II

To see the effect of Borromean studies within Roncalli's pastorate and theology we must wait until 1953, when he became patriarch of Venice, and then 1958 when he was elected pope. During the previous two decades and more he prepared a definitive edition of the *Visita*. Before we deal with it, we shall look at another work: it was prepared before the *Atti;* nevertheless, it was published after the first volume of them. It is the compact and precise essay on "Gli inizi del Seminario di Bergamo e San Carlo Borromeo," published first in *Humilitas* and reprinted in a small volume, with an introduction entitled *"Il Concilio di Trento e la fondazione dei primi seminari."*[41]

The lecture given in 1910 here is "completamente rifuso e steso in forma più documentaria." Roncalli recalls the early development of Bergamo's seminary: in his opinion its success was due to Borromeo—and there is something interesting in this eulogy, especially regarding the history of the seminary during the seventeenth, eighteenth and nineteenth centuries. Borromeo is depicted as "the" leader of the enforcement of the Tridentine reform:

> . . . The arrangements left by Cardinal Borromeo on the occasion of the apostolic visitation: those of an official nature are contained in the *ordinationes* sent to Bergamo at the conclusion of the visitation. They do not represent anything extraordinary. They are rather a summons to the more faithful execution of chapter 18 of the twenty-fourth session of the Council of Trent.[42]

He energetically criticizes once again as a myth the image of a hypersevere Borromeo:

> "These are normal vicissitudes of human existence. Old wine skins cannot be filled with new wine. And the history of all reforms is fraught with this difficulty and with these acrimonies. Let's say that this was the more or less general fate of the decrees of San Carlo: at first there was the struggle to comprehend their importance and their worth; then a difficult acceptance in an early stage, followed by a less displeased stage and finally a cordial, even enthusiastic stage. Time matures a new mentality; and the saints work for the centuries."[43]

Roncalli stresses that this myth is the result of a deep unconsciousness that Borromeo's contemporaries had regarding the situation. Then he points out how the more the contemporaries failed to grasp the gravity of the situation, the more Borromeo's congruency with history and its dynamics becomes fascinating in the perspective of his own situation: here there is all the "modernity" of Borromeo:

Still further progress would be slow; slow but certain, in perfect conformity of development with the great works that alter with the ages the
various epochs of their history.[44]

Also the appendix about the Council of Trent and the seminaries is quite
interesting: it allows us to understand the real knowledge Roncalli had of
Carlo's *Sitz im Leben*. It is surprising to see how close he is to the most
important protagonist of Catholic evangelism and how far he is from some
ideological "topoi": for example, when he denies the Jesuits a main role in
the birth of the seminary and says that Cardinal Pole led its foundation;[45] or
when he summarizes the six main points of the "sessio" 23 of the council as a
"novella pentecoste" and uses "nuovo" four times and "rinnovare" once;[46]
or when he shows the role of Cardinal Morone as a link between Borromeo
and the council and the role of the Italian bishops.[47] I think that this
dynamic and historicist attitude toward history is the right key to permit us
to analyze some "Tridentine" aspects of Roncalli's culture.

Yet let us turn to the five volumes of *Gli Atti della Visita Apostolica di San
Carlo Borromeo a Bergamo (1575)*. On 10 April 1936, in Istanbul—he had
arrived here sixteen months before from Sophia—Roncalli completed the
introduction to the first volume. He recalls the genesis of his work that will
come close to being two-thirds completed during the next three years. He
thanks many people whom I need not recall here. The three bases of the
work are historiography of the Cinquecento, of Borromeo and of Bergamo.

He stresses the "ringiovanimento" produced by the Council of Trent as
the main point of modern history and considers signs of this history—the
tradition of provincial councils, synods, and visitation.[48] Roncalli claims
that a few visitations—so interesting a reflection of "times in which the
religious life penetrated all manifestations of civil life"—are published.[49] The
Bergamo visitation will show

> the submission of the Tridentine legislation and of the spirit of the Catho-
> lic reform to the needs of a diocese that shows itself always wise, always
> provident, always mother.[50]

Roncalli knows that he is going to make an addition, "non mediocre
complemento," to Borromeo's biography; but instead of subjectively describing Borromeo the documents will show a living Carlo:

> History written by others is always somewhat the opinion and impres-
> sions of the one who writes it. Here instead in the acts of the visitation is
> San Carlo himself, alive, working, he himself at a distance of more than
> three centuries just as his own contemporaries encountered and venerated
> him. From these letters emerges the entirety of his person and there also
> revives around that person an entire world.[51]

From a methodological point of view, Roncalli as a historian knows that history can only perceive facts; but as a theologian he knows that Christian people are detectors of holiness, which objective history can never reach:

In the parade of documents his collaborators appear, listening to the voices, the voices of clergy and laity, men and women of all social classes that accept him, who recommend themselves, who receive admonitions and directions, who extol him as still alive; the Christian people always uniform in itself, in all times, always most alert to the passage of holiness.[52]

Once again Roncalli insists on a merciful image of Borromeo:

the superb art that he possessed of providing for everything with proper means, of expediting with order, with perfect organization, with calm, occasionally, not without contrasts but with great dignity and benignity even in the contrasts."[53]

To this date, the local aspect of the research is hardly perceptible: Bergamo is only an archivistic origin. The criteria for the work's implementation are briefly reconstructed: Roncalli was helped by his students to transcribe the manuscripts underlined by Roncalli himself in 1909;[54] after 1909 he is alone in the study.

This weakness in the framework of the research produces differences in the footnotes of volumes. In general the method was guided more by the exigencies of concrete situations than by a master plan.[55] On the basis of research done in 1910 Roncalli carried out the edition. Between 1910 and 1914, as I said, he had the proofs of the first volume, but they were interrupted.

Twenty years later, the situation warranted greater optimism: he thought that in ten years the volumes would be completed. Actually in 1937 the second volume, with the indices, was ready.[56] After this first part, P. Forno, Roncalli's assistant, worked hard to transcribe and prepare documents concerning Borromeo's visit to the town's surroundings.

After the death of this friend,[57] in the introduction to the third volume, Roncalli describes their research about Borromeo as informed by two ideas: "il servizio della verità e della Chiesa; l'amore fervido alla comune terra natale."[58] Once again the fertile couple "general-particular," "Borromeo-Bergamo," generates analyses. The process of spiritual refining that Roncalli had enacted to this date allowed him to recognize a link between "church" and "truth": "an idealità." But this goes beyond the limits of the visitation's edition, the next volume of which did not appear until 1946 brought peace: this was a dozen years after it was prepared, when the author had already been appointed nuncio in Paris.[59]

This delay was due to the general circumstances: but the delay of the last volume, which was not ready until 1958, was due to financial problems.[60] This fifth volume has an introduction in which memoirs and thanks are better organized.[61] Roncalli protests his fidelity to his method for so many years: the work is introduced as "an integral edition of general and fundamental bearing . . . for historical and scientific consultation." In a few words the analysis becomes a project about editions of visitations in Italy:

> This observation concerns an interest, nurtured by sympathy for the research and studies of native records, religious and civil, that appears always more vital from various proofs, and where the fervor toward wider horizons does not disdain, rather takes delight in occupying itself with the richest experiences of the past for application of the *magisterium vitae* which history continues to exercise for the common profit of human society. . . . To the graces of this last circumstance I owe the vital satisfaction, if I may be forgiven, of seeing this first attempt in Italy of an integral publication of general and fundamental bearing, placing itself by order of introduction through other individual and collective forces, especially in the sector of the post-Tridentine apostolic visitations, of the type most noted for Lombardy and carried out under the splendid name of San Carlo Borromeo.[62]

There were a few reviews of these volumes. During the 1930s only *Civiltà Cattolica*, *Archivio Storico Lombardo*, and *La Scuola Cattolica* published reviews, but sometimes it seems that the main topic is Msgr. Galbiati.[63] Only after 1958 did a critic focus on Roncalli.[64] Finally Giuseppe De Luca reviewed the visitation's edition,[65] because

> While these volumes speak of San Carlo and in appearance they are not proposed otherwise, in fact they bear testimony to the spiritual and pastoral formation of John XXIII.[66]

Pope John examined the article and annotated:

> 1.   The first part: good. 2. All that is written from that part up to the end of note 2 and at the beginning of 3 merits to be published in part because it is beautiful and interesting, but it is cumbersome for whoever wants to become acquainted with the volumes of the visitation of San Carlo and does not enjoy lingering amidst the personal notes of the *curriculum vitae* of the author, of the complex of sixteenth century bishops, of Cardinal Federico, of Bellarmine, and with still other charming distractions. . . .[67]

Pope John clearly introduces his Borromean interest as a particular phenomenon: it was not an intellectually unconscious choice, but a positive standpoint overlooked by historians both of Borromeo and of Roncalli. We could explain the lack of reviews about a pope's book by the lack of interest in Borromeo during the fifties: certainly at this time (and maybe also at our own time) the perception of a tie between historical knowledge and pastorate, which Roncalli assimilated in the first years of the century, was lacking.

III

Up to now we have talked about the meaning of Borromeo within the cultural and spiritual world of Roncalli. The emerging perception of Borromeo as a source also influenced Roncalli's pastorate. But how? To answer this question we must focus on the last ten years of Roncalli's life, because this period, i.e., the years 1953–63, are a turning point: within them as a shepherd he struggled directly with the church.

Above all, after the Venetian years, in which there developed many interests parallel to the Borromean one,[68] it is possible to put forward some hypotheses; it is possible to turn the results of the analyses into a hermeneutic meaning. From 1958 on, the texts are more revealing: in them his culture becomes a direct influence on his pastorate. About these years B. Ulianich has suggested some guidelines for a better periodization:[69] he has rightly seen within the speech "Gaudet Mater Ecclesia," at the opening of the council, the peak of the Roncallian pontificate;[70] but in his opinion the pontificate was a constant, slow, imperceptible development of Tridentine theology and ecclesiology. Ulianich's position is valid but not to the extent he carried it. My discussion of the impact of Borromeo and his historical image upon Roncalli allows us eventually to sketch a better profile of this process in the last years of his life.

I wish to underline three points: First, Pope John refers many times to historical studies. They are called "le bon compagnon de notre vie."[71] He points out their place within ecclesiastical disciplines; although during the audience for the Second Congress of Church History, he stresses history "in ordine," in order, to theology, and he quotes Carlo as an example.[72] He recalls his own experiences in the archives, from his youth up to the approval of the Accademia di San Carlo, founded for the never accomplished edition of Borromeo's epistles.[73]

In my opinion, it is important to remember the attention that Pope John showed in following the scholarly debate; I can only recall another private "review" he wrote about the well-known article that Roger Mols published first in the *Nouvelle Revue Théologique*, and secondly in *Ambrosius* (which obliged Cardinal Montini to apologize to the pope for it):[74]

> All is well said by this Father Mols in honor of the activity and pastoral wisdom of San Carlo Borromeo; but of his apostolic visitations, which were a true masterpiece of perseverance and of doctrine, there is not even a word, not even a citation. And needless to say the apostolic visitation of

Bergamo is published in five great volumes with great care and patience by Pope John XXIII himself.[75]

Secondly, Borromeo's link with the projects of 25 January 1959 is sometimes evident: especially during the first Roman synod.[76] Yet if this is true, we could try to answer one of the main questions about the relations between Pope John and the council: if Borromeo is an episcopal model, could we suppose that he influences the idea of episcopal dignity? And in this case would he become a model for relations between the pope, seen as bishop of Rome, and bishops gathered in council?[77] Clearly, I have no completely satisfactory answer at present for these questions; nonetheless it is impossible to overlook them. There is a documentary basis that forces us to answer them: "In his vigil over the Second Vatican Council one is forcefully reminded of San Carlo, so distinguished in his anxious solicitude for the conclusion of the Council of Trent."[78] Borromeo's activities are in Roncalli's mind "incomparable tests of paternal solicitude, of juridic doctrine, of perfect correspondence to the necessity of his time."[79]

Thirdly, it is also possible to realize the perception of Borromeo within the homilies of every 4 November, anniversary of the coronation of the pope: Borromeo here is a model not for bishops *in genere,* but "il grande maestro di tutti i vescovi dell' epoca moderna e contemporanea."[80] Borromeo is an example and an encouragement deeply concerning Vatican II:

> And allow us, venerable brothers, the joy of inviting your and our spirit to the contemplation of the luminous example and the most fervid encouragement that San Carlo Borromeo offers to the Catholic *episcopate* of all rites and of all nations of the world in support of the celebration of the Second Vatican Council.[81]

The "encouragement" comes from Borromeo's loyalty toward the Council of Trent, the enforcement of which he promoted; in this way the whole age of the Council of Trent becomes Borromeo's age.[82] But the encouragement comes also from his being a model of congruency between time and church:

> San Carlo brings to us all a precious encouragement. It is quite natural that changes of time and circumstances suggest various conducts and attitudes of external transmission and of reclothing of the same doctrine; but the vital substance is always purity of evangelical truth.[83]

IV

Now we are at the very heart of the problem and at the conclusions of the analysis.

Borromeo is a part of the theological, cultural, and spiritual "network" of Roncalli, and it is impossible to detach certain elements from its background. Sometimes it is hardly possible to differentiate the lines of this type of grid. For instance, as a historian, Roncalli had no inferiority complex regarding history and critical research. Besides other factors, is the positive approach of Roncalli to history as a science and to history as a reality due to his historical work *per se,* or could we suppose an effect of his main topic (i.e., Carlo) upon the method? In trying to understand Roncalli's attitude to history, which is more important—his experience as historian, no matter what the object of research might be? Or the concrete topic, Carlo Borromeo, who partly shaped this attitude? In my opinion it is clear that but for Borromeo we could not understand some important characteristics of the network itself. Consequently, the following conclusions are provisional, as is our overview of the network until a more comprehensive structure can be defined.

I am convinced that if in Roncalli's mind Borromeo was a reformer, he was also a criterion for understanding the Catholic reform. One scholar has recently attempted to find in Roncalli's famous choice of the word "aggiornamento" a way to steer clear of the "compromised" word "riforma."[84] This interpretation runs counter to Roncalli's thinking and theology: I do not believe that there is in the texts a clash between "reform" and "updating," as abstract concepts. On the contrary, the deep consciousness of the historical situation overcomes this surprising distinction. When Roncalli studies Borromeo, he tries to use an apt method for his topic: in other words, if Borromeo was a model to enforce the council *without* forgetting the historical situation, its impact upon Roncalli, from this particular point of view, would force Roncalli himself to study Borromeo *within* this situation. In such a case the Council of Trent, as a historical phenomenon, is no longer a frontier beyond which everything is a danger, everyone is an enemy. In such a case Borromeo is no longer a ruthless ascetic: and Roncalli, with great cogency, tries to explain why this myth, about the council and about Borromeo, arose within documents and Catholic sensitivity.

The way to read and to understand the Council of Trent is the more "Borromean" aspect of Pope John's theology: he looks at it as a moment of *renewal* of an ancient tradition, about discipline, seminaries, bishops, demanding enforcement within concrete situations.

Therefore the standpoint of Ulianich almost needs refining: the Roncallian way to approach the Council of Trent is not at all a legacy that withers away in the course of time. His Tridentinism is the product of a historical approach that can lead to the most various ends. The effect of the impact of Carlo Borromeo upon Angelo Giuseppe Roncalli illuminates more than we could expect the profile of both. "New wine is put into fresh wineskins, and so both are preserved."[85]

Notes

List of abbreviations:

G   A. G. Roncalli, *Il Giornale dell'anima* (Rome, 1964–84)
AVA 1–5   A. G. Roncalli, Gli atti della visita apostolica di S. Carlo Borromeo a
             Bergamo (1575) (Florence, 1936–58)
DMC 1–5   *Discorsi Messaggi Colloqui del Santo Padre Giovanni XXIII* (Vatican
             City, 1963–66)
CM   Biblioteca Civica A. Maj, Bergamo
AR   Archivio Roncalli, Loreto

   1. The "transfiguration" in the image of Borromeo, which took place within the
hardening of the council's aspirations for reform, remains an open problem: it was
vigorously proposed by G. Alberigo, "Carlo Borromeo come modello di vescovo
nella chiesa post-tridentina," *Rivista di Storia della Chiesa in Italia* 79 (1967): 1031–
52, sometimes harshly debated, but, as often happened in Borromean research, never
solved. The most recent work that I know, A. Turchini, *La fabbrica di un santo*
(Casale Monferrato, 1984), gives to a lot of well-collected issues insufficient critical
comprehension.
   2. The aspects of this process are self-evident: the development of historical
disciplines between the eighteenth and the twentieth century, its impact on both
clerical and academic culture, the institutional feedback of these phenomena; there is,
as far as I know, no exhaustive study about the problem; one can find an oblique
approach to it in research about the history of exegesis, e.g., W. G. Kümmel, *Das
Neue Testament. Geschichte der Erforschung seiner Probleme* (Freiburg and Munich,
1970); or in philosophy, e.g., P. Rossi, *Lo storicismo tedesco contemporaneo* (Turin,
1956); or about eminent historians, e.g., R. Manselli, "Ludwig von Pastor storico dei
Papi. Tradizione storiografica cattolica e metodologia storico positiva", *Studium* 75
(1979): 9–24 or some contributions in the volume *Monseigneur Duchesne et son
Temps* (Rome, 1975); or about that very large topic in relation to the concept of
Christendom effectively executed by D. Menozzi, "La chiesa e la storia", *Cristianesimo nella storia* 4 (1983): 69–106.
   3. Pope John talked about Borromeo as a saint familiar to him since his infancy.
As a matter of fact we know that in the Bergamo seminary Borromeo was one of the
most important "models". There are some references in the small book of spiritual
rules for future priests (the so-called "Regoline": within the manuscripts of the
Journal of the Soul there are three different redactions, and two of them were
published in the Italian edition of *G* in 1964): see R. Amadei, "Il 'Manuale del
maestro dei novizi,'" in *Cultura e spiritualità a Bergamo nel tempo di Papa Giovanni*
(Bergamo, 1982).
   Roncalli, when he was patriarch, gave a reference to his first historical readings
during the seminary period. See *Scritti e Discorsi* (Rome, 1958–59), 1:284: "Nei
ricordi della mia adolescenza c'è la lettura, quasi appasionata, di una bella pub-
licazione 'Nel primo centenario della nascita del card. A. Maj, Atti della Accademia
tenutasi in suo onore il marzo 1882 in Bergamo.' Fu quello il primo tuffo dell'anima
mia, curiosa e vaga in quel gran mondo di pergamene, palinsesti, antichissime
scritture."
   4. It runs from 1895 up to 1963.
   5. Giovanni Pietro Giussano, *De vita et rebus gestis Sancti Caroli Borromei*
(Milan: J. Marellus, 1751), 618d; 1015 says that Carlo, beyond the sacramental

confession that he took once a day, developed the habit of examining his own conscience once or twice a day.

6. "Protettori miei dolcissimi, san Francesco di Sales, Filippo Neri, Ignazio di Loyola, san Luigi, Stanislao e Giovanni Berchmans, sant'Alessandro martire, san Carlo Borromeo, intercedete per me" (G, 194).

"Sarà mio studio gradito esercitarmi, per quanto le nuove occupazioni me lo permettano, in quelle divozioni, per quanto minute sempre soavi ai miei dolcissimi santi protettori: ai tre giovanetti: Luigi, Stanislao e Giovanni Berchmans; a san Filippo Neri, san Francesco di Sales, sant'Alfonso de Liguori, san Tommaso d'Aquino, sant'Ignazio di Lojola, [sic] san Carlo Borromeo, ecc. ecc." (Ibid., 242).

7. "Mi raccomando alla protezione specialissima di santo Ignazio, di san Carlo Borromeo, mio singolare protettore in quest'ultimo anno dei miei studi teologici e della mia preparazione al sacerdozio, del soavissimo san Francesco di Sales" (Ibid., 224).

8. Ibid., 223.

9. I dealt with this period of Roncalli's life in my "Le fonti di A. G. Roncalli: il Giornale dell'anima," *Cristianesimo nella storia* 4 (1983): 103–72; for a general survey of the Roman milieu see V. Paglia, "Note sulla formazione del clero romano fra Otto e Novecento," *Ricerche per la storia religiosa di Roma* 4 (1980). The role of Roncalli's spiritual father was studied in G. Battelli, "Francesco Pitocchi (1852–1922)," *Spicilegium Historicum Congregationi Sanctissimi Redentoris* 41 (1983): 233–330 and idem, "La formazione spirituale del giovane A. G. Roncalli. Il rapporto col redentorista Francesco Pitocchi," in *Fede Tradizione Profezia. Studi su Giovanni XXIII e sul Vaticano II* (Brescia, 1984), 1–72.

10. A. Melloni, "Le fonti di A. G. Roncalli," 143–51, and also my recent "Formazione e sviluppo della cultura di Roncalli," in *Giovanni XXIII 1881–1963)* (Bari, 1987), 1–31. An English translation will be published in 1988 by Crossroads Publishing Co.

11. G, 231–32.

12. Within the research that the Istituto per le Scienze Religiose in Bologna is carrying out on Roncalli there will be a study about Radini: it is mentioned in G. Battelli, "L'episcopato italiano da Leone XIII a Pio X," *Cristianesimo nella storia* 6 (1985): 110–70. A first profile appeared in "G. M. Radini Tedeschi e A. Roncalli (1905–1914)," in *Giovanni Roncalli*, 33–62.

13. The following table shows the teaching role of Roncalli in the Radini years.

Year	Ecclesiastical History	Patrology	Fundamental Theology	Apologetics
1906–7	Roncalli			
1907–8	Roncalli			
1908–9	Pedrinelli	Roncalli		Roncalli
1909	Pedrinelli	Roncalli		‡Roncalli
1910–11	Roncalli*		Roncalli	Roncalli
1911–12	Roncalli			Roncalli
1912–13	Roncalli			Roncalli
1913–14	Roncalli	Roncalli†		Roncalli

*From first to third courses
†First course
‡Third and fourth course

14. "Mi recavo a Milano per accompagnarvi il mio vescovo e signore mons. Radini Tedeschi in occasione delle adunanze della Commissione preparatoria del Concilio Provinciale VIII. Queste si tenevano in arcivescovado intorno all'E.mo Metropolita

cardinale A. C. Ferrari. Solo pochi prelati vi avevano parte. Nulla di più interessante per me nelle ore di attesa, che di visitare il ricchissimo Archivio Arcivescovile che tanti tesori inesplorati rinserra per la storia della arcidiocesi milanese e non di quella solamente. Mi colpì subito la raccolta dei 39 volumi legati in pergamena recanti sul dorso: *Archivio spirituale—Bergamo*. Li esplorai: tornai a rivederli in visite successive. Quale sorpresa piacevole per il mio spirito: Incontrare riuniti insieme documenti così copiosi ed interessanti la Chiesa di Bergamo nell'epoca più caratteristica per il rinnovamento della sua vita religiosa, all'indomani del Tridentino, nel fervore più acceso della controriforma cattolica. Della Visita Apostolica di san Carlo alla mia città sapevo quel tanto che i biografi del Borromeo, il Bascapè ed il Giussano-Oltrocchi ne scrissero. Non molte cose in verità. A misura che il compito dell'insegnamento, la pratica degli archivi, l'amore agli studi storici mi rendevano famigliare a queste ricerche, più acuto si faceva in me il desiderio di vedere un materiale così prezioso e da tanti anni dimenticato messo a servizio della illustrazione storica mia patria" (*AVA*, 1 : xxix–xxx).

15. A Roncalli, "Il Cardinale Cesare Baronio nel III centenario della morte," *La Scuola Cattolica* 36 (1908): 3–29 (subsequently cited as "Baronio"). Msgr. Radini introduced his young secretary to Nogara, the journal's editor, that he might submit the lecture: G. De Luca reports the fact in an "avvertenza" following the second edition of Roncalli's lecture as a book (Rome, 1961). For a recent discussion see C. K. Pullapilly, *Caesar Baronius. A Counter-Reformation Historian* (London, 1975).

16. "In questi ultimi tempi per un movimento che mi parve di legittima reazione a certi sistemi di agiografia per cui i santi venivano presi pei capelli e portati fuori dalla società in cui vissero, fuori persino da se stessi, e convertiti in semidei, noi siamo, un po' troppo forse, passati all'eccesso opposto, preoccupati più di studiare l'elemento umano nei santi, trascurando un poco l'opera della grazia. Anch'io, lo confesso, ho obbedito a questo pregiudizio dei moderni, studiando il Baronio; ho voluto fare un poco con lui quella che si dice la parte dell'avvocato del diavolo: ma alla fine mi sono sentito piegare le ginocchia davanti alle virtù cristiane esercitate in grado eroico da questo Cardinale, davanti alla sua santità: (Roncalli, "Baronio," 13). It is easy to perceive the terrible gap between this approach to history and some contemporary stereotypes: thanks to the advice of one of my colleagues, Dr. S. Zampa, I can quote a passage full of this opposite conceptual framework from *Civiltà Cattolica* 50 (1903): 287–99: the author writes that "un santo è opera essenzialmente soprannaturale e divina, e quindi adoperarsi a rappresentarcelo, in una storia della sua vita, sotto l'aspetto naturale ed umano, è in qualche guisa studiarsi di svisarlo, facendolo diverso da quello che è. . . . Quelle vite, anzi quei leggendarii de' Santi, che convertirono a Dio uomini come il B. Colombano e S. Ignazio di Loyola, non erano certo scritti con tanta parsimonia di soprannaturale quanta, a senno di alcuni, se ne vorrebbe oggimai dagli agiografi."

17. A. Roncalli, "S. Carlo Borromeo ed il Clero nelle prossime feste centenaire," *La Vita Diocesana* 1 (1909): 317–20. In the same journal and year Roncalli published 6 other articles concerning Borromeo (49, 116, 137–39, 205–6, 391, 111).

18. "L'anima nostra a quella di S. Carlo Borromeo, la nostra vita alla sua, i nostri tempi ai suoi. S. Carlo vuol essere da noi più studiato, più conosciuto nel suo spirito, nel suo pensiero, nelle sue istituzioni" (Ibid., 318).

19. "Forse noi si è avvezzi ad ammirare un po' troppo a distanza il grande Arcivescovo. La decisione dei tratti di questo vero colosso della santità pastorale, la vastità delle linee, un non so che di rigido in apparenza fondato sulle impressioni che noi ci siamo fatti della sua vita austera e della sua energia ed inflessibilità. . . . Ma conviene avvicinare, invece, con confidenza il gran santo, studiarlo minutamente in

ogni atteggiamento della sua persona, in ogni passo che egli muove, in ogni parola del suo labbro o della sua penna, in ogni piega del suo abito." (Ibid., 318).

20. Members of the commission were A. Ratti, G. Nogara, G. Angeli, C. Gorla, C. Pellegrini, and C. Orsenigo.

21. A. Roncalli, "San Carlo Borromeo e la Chiesa di Bergamo," *San Carlo Borromeo nel III Centenario della Canonizzazione;* a letter by Ratti asking for this article and some other correspondence concerning Roncalli's study of Borromeo are in Biblioteca Ambrosiana W35 inf. 69–77. All the contributions had a very narrow topic, sometimes dominated by hagiographic purposes. About the role of A. Ratti, which is in my opinion also important to the understanding of some aspects of the future Pius XI, see a memorial of G. Galbiati, *Biobibliografia di Achille Ratti* (Milan, 1927), p. 108: "Nell'ottobre 1908, approssimandosi il III centenario della canonizzazione di San Carlo Borromeo, il Cardinale Ferrari, Arcivescovo di Milano, istituiva ed incaricava una commissione di valorosi ecclesiastici milanesi per curare la pubblicazione di un periodico diretto a preparare ed accompagnare la solenne circostanza che si avvicinava . . . . Fu redatto a cura di una commissione di cinque sacerdoti, uno dei quali fu Msgr. Ratti, ma questi fu più specialmente delegato alla direzione del periodico e quasi ad ogni numero contribuì con suoi scritti, firmati, P.A.R., par, S.A.R., qualcuno anonimo."

22. "Tutto ciò non toglie che anche a Bergamo la condizioni della vita religiosa e specialmente del Clero non fossero in quei tempi assai disgraziate. Ma è precisamente nel risveglio seguito un po' più tardi, che si devono riconoscere i frutti sospirati che derivarono da quel solenne avvenimento. Giachè i risultati più veri della Visita Apostolica di San Carlo a Bergamo si poterono scorgere assai meglio, quando cessate o rimosse le prime difficoltà alla esecuzione dei decreti che parvero dapprincipio eccessivi e troppo duri, il Clero ed il popolo si vennero naturalmente a trovare meglio disposti, poco per volta ad adattarvisi, essendo subentrata ai primi risentimenti la calma e la riflessione. San Carlo, che vedeva molto da lontano, volle ciò che volle, e non solo a Bergamo, ma anche a Milano e dappertutto. . . . Pochi anni dopo, la vita religiosa era già plasmata sullo spirito di quei decreti medesimi, i quali, accanto alle disposizioni tridentine ed ai sinodi, dovevano segnare il punto di partenza di tutta quella riforma che la Chiesa di Bergamo riuscì poi a mantenere e su cui si appoggia la sua floridezza presente" (Ibid.)

23. A. Roncalli, "San Carlo e l'uso della barba nei chierici," *La Scuola Cattolica* 38 (1910): 320–23. It was a special issue devoted to Borromeo with a preface by Cardinal Ferrari. The main aspects of Borromeo's profile were discussed here, from his activity as a reformer to his concept of pastorate, from his pedagogy to his asceticism, from his social thought to his institutions. The opening article was particularly noteworthy: one of the most famous Jesuits devoted to antimodernist hunting, Father G. Matiussi, wrote about Borromeo and dogma, introducing Carlo as the ideal antimodernist hero, may perhaps be assuming that not all Lombard bishops, especially Ferrari and Radini, showed the same zeal.

24. "Il provvedimento, a quanto pare, non dovette incontrare molte difficoltà, se due anni dopo, nel Sinodo V (1578) erano solo da dieci a venti i sacerdoti intervenuti che ancora portassero la barba. Nè S. Carlo per altro, poichè la cosa andava da sè, credette opportuno usar eccessivo rigore nell'esigere la esecuzione del decreto; anzi a Francesco Bonomi, che nel frattempo era divenuto vescovo di Vercelli, scriveva 'Approvo moltissimo che tu vadi senza barba; mi dispiace che il tuo clero vercellese non segua il tuo esempio: non posso però lodare il tuo avviso di trattare duramente i disobbedienti e di sollecitare un decreto del Papa in proposito.' E aggiunge poi come egli si atteneva a più miti consigli, dissimulando per allora pazientemente sulla

disobbedienza di alcuni" (A. Roncalli, "San Carlo e l'uso della barba nei chierici," 321).

25. The source is Calenzio's biography that Roncalli owned from 1907 on. I don't know when or where he lost it, but he surely did: actually in 1961 he asked De Luca for a new copy.

26. Especially the Matiussi article. The year after there was a new, again, indirect clash between Roncalli and the Jesuit: the latter gave a course at the Social School in Bergamo, full of threats and allusions to Bergamese modernism; this caused bitter controversies, and the bishop, Radini, asked for a confidential report from some clerics, among them Roncalli. The latter criticized with severity the style and the content of the lessons; the text was published by L. F. Capovilla, *X anniversario della morte di PP. Giovanni XXIII* (Rome, 1973), 57–61. I think that when Roncalli wrote "ammiravo da tempo la dottrina del P. Matiussi negli studi da lui pubblicati sui nostri periodici migliori" he referred also to the article about Borromeo.

27. One must remember that Roncalli drafted the letter of the Lombard bishop about the Constantine centennial!

28. "Il Borromeo, scrivendo allo Speciano in Roma diceva fra l'altro: 'Utinam latentia vitia tam felici exitu evellam, ut Cleri barbam expunxi: magnis enim profectibus in via Domini contenderemus. . . .' Queste parole ripetute da noi e applicate ai tempi nostri ci sembrano la miglior conclusione di questo breve appunto" (A. Roncalli, "San Carlo e l'uso della barba nei chierici," 323).

29. On 29 September 1910 the Bergamo Commission published a sixteen-page special issue, *Bergamo a S. Carlo Borromeo nel III Centenario della Canonizazzione (1610–1910)*. Roncalli reprinted there some of his contributions to the centennial, namely the introduction ("Il significato delle nostre feste," 1–2), three articles about the visitation's edition ("La Visita di S. Carlo Borromeo a Bergamo," 6–10; "Ricordi di S. Carlo," 12–13; "Un omaggio scientifico della Chiesa di Bergamo a S. Carlo Borromeo," 15–16), and probably another note ("L'opera principale di S. Carlo") on the Schools of Christian Doctrine, identifiable more because it is signed *r.* than because of the content. A long article about Borromeo and the Lombard churches remained unpublished.

30. A. Roncalli, "Le origini del Seminario di Bergamo e San Carlo Borromeo," *La Vita Diocesana* 2 (1910): 457–95.

31. Ibid., 460: "Ebbene non suoni troppo il confronto, nè alcuno mi voglia rimproverare, perchè a giustificarmi in qualche modo di aver accettato il compito non facile di parlare di S. Carlo Borromeo nella festa scolastica che il Seminario di Bergamo vuole in quest'anno dedicata, con nobile pensiero, a lui, io abbia osato rievocare qui sul bel principio questo ricordo del P. Cesare Baronio, quasi nell'intenzione di pormi oggi al posto dello storico insigne, o per lo meno all'ombra del suo esempio."

32. "Vero è che all'aprirsi dei nuovi tempi caratterizzato da quel soffio largo e rinnovatore di intellettualità classica che si disse l'Umanesimo e che insieme a molte cose cattive apportò pure un risveglio nella cultura generale di fronte al bisogno fattosi più vivo di un ministero sacerdotale pari ai nuovi compiti" (Ibid., 468).

33. A. Roncalli, "Baronio," 32: "Ma le ombre di un quadro—chi noi sa?— servono a dare maggior risalto ai personaggi principali. D'altra parte la storia è storia, e nella storia schietta e sincera della sua vita la Chiesa trova la sua più efficace apologia."

34. "Uno di quegli atti che erano tutti propri di lui e del suo governo, uno di quegli atti duri in apparenza, e che non vanno giudicati alla stregua della piccola

prudenza umana, ma che si rivelano sapientissimi nella loro efficacia morale" (A. Roncalli, "Le origini" 491).

35. A. Roncalli, *La Misericordia Maggiore di Bergamo ed altre istituzioni amministrate dalla Congregazione di Carità* (Bergamo, 1912), 133.

36. A. Roncalli, *Giacomo Maria Radini Tedeschi Vescovo di Bergamo* (Bergamo, 1916), 191–220.

37. The interruption of the visitation edition and the lack of books and articles do not mean that Roncalli stopped researching and lecturing on the topic: but for this aspect of Roncalli's life, for the moment, we know nothing except some titles from the rich chronology that S. Zampa is updating, published in L. F. Capovilla, *Giovanni XXIII. Quindici letture* (Rome, 1970). Actually Roncalli lectured in 1912 to the "Circolo S. Luigi," to the "Unione delle donne cattoliche"; we do not know anything but the topic of a lecture on 10 February 1918 in Milan about St. Catherine, on 15 February in Treviglio about Tasso's poem, "La Gerusalemme Liberata," on 12 November 1919 in Adrara about the sixth centennial of Cardinal Longo's death. The same is true for the lessons he gave in Rome in 1921 and 1923, and for the public lecture on 19 October 1924 at the "Arciconfraternita della carità al Verano." A better knowledge of these facts could be very useful in clarifying the appointment of P. Paschini to the chair of ecclesiastical history, as was often said, *instead of* Roncalli (but we do not know why he was in competition), and also in clarifying the appointment of Roncalli himself to the chair of patrology in Lateranense in November 1924, an appointment in evident contradiction to his immediately subsequent mission in Bulgaria. The historical commitment of Roncalli continued beyond the direct diplomatic engagement: the recent edition of some letters to don Giovanni Dentella (see John XXIII, *Il Pastore* (Padua, 1982) allows us to get the details of a work, very like the book about the Misericordia Maggiore, previously known only because of some allusions published in John XXIII, *Lettere ai Vescovi di Bergamo* (Bergamo, 1973), 39 and 52–53; it was a study on the expenses ("libro delle spese") of the canon Flaminio Cerasola (1562–1640) for a commemorative volume on the college founded with his heritage (1735). The Roman "Arciconfraternita dei Bergamaschi" (Roncalli too was a member until 1925) gave him permission to retain the manuscript in order to accomplish the study: the commemorative volume was published in 1935 as *Il Collegio Cerasoli. Commemorazioni Centenarie 1735–1935* (Rome, 1935); Roncalli's contribution is still unpublished in the *AR*.

38. Msgr. Luigi Maria Marelli (1915–1936).

39. See above n. 36.

40. I base this deduction on the Radini biography's concordance of the lemmas "esercizio," "sollecitudine," "cura," "vescovo," "ministero," "anima," and the themes "pastor-," "episc-," "sacerdo-."

41. A. G. Roncalli, "Gli inizi del Seminario di Bergamo e S. Carlo Borromeo," *Humilitas* 25 (1938): 988–1014. The manuscript is now in the archives of Bergamo's seminary; the typed text in *AR* "San Carlo," D5. For the pages I refer to the second edition, *Gli inizi del Seminario di Bergamo e S. Carlo Borromeo. Note storiche con una introduzione su Il Concilio di Trento e la fondazione dei primi Seminari* (Bergamo, 1939), dedicated to A. Bernareggi, former editor of *Humilitas* and then Bergamo's bishop.

42. ". . . le disposizioni lasciate dal card. Borromeo in occasione della Visita Apostolica. Queste nella loro parte ufficiale sono contenute nelle *Ordinationes* mandate a Bergamo a visita conchiusa. Non rappresentano nulla di straordinario. Sono piuttosto un richiamo alla esecuzione più fedele del capo XVIII della Sess. XXIIII del Tridentino" (Ibid., 60).

43. "Ordinarie vicende delle cose umane. Non si possono riempire le otri vecchie di vino nuovo; e la storia di tutte le riforme è fatta di queste difficoltà e di queste asprezze. Si può dire che questa fu la sorte quasi generale dei decreti di san Carlo. Dapprima si stentò a comprenderne l'importanza ed il valore: poi opposizione alla loro esecuzione: poi accettazione in un primo tempo faticosa, in seguito meno sgradita, e infine cordiale e persino entusiasta. Il tempo matura le nuove mentalità ed i santi lavorano per i secoli" Ibid., 68–69.

44. "Anche i progressi ulteriori saranno lenti: lenti ma sicuri, in perfetta conformità di sviluppo con le opere grandi che mutuano coi secoli le varie epoche della loro storia" Ibid., 82.

45. Ibid., 8n.

46. Ibid.

47. Ibid., 24–25.

48. *AVA* 1:xxxiv.

49. "In tempi in cui la vita religiosa penetrava tutte le manifestazioni della vita civile" (Ibid).

50. "Il piegarsi della legislazione tridentina e dello spirito della riforma cattolica ai bisogni di una diocesi che si mostrò sempre saggia, sempre provvidente, sempre madre" (Ibid., 1:xxxvi).

51. "La storia scritta da altri è sempre un poco pensiero ed impressione di chi scrive. Qui invece, negli atti della Visita è san Carlo stesso, vivo ed operante, lui a distanza di oltre tre secoli, quale lo accostarono e lo venerarono i suoi contemporanei. . . . Da quelle carte balza la sua figura tutta intera, ed insieme con essa è tutto un mondo che si ravviva intorno a lui" (Ibid.).

52. "Nella successione dei documenti si scorgono i suoi collaboratori, se ne ascoltano le voci, le voci del clero e del popolo, uomini, donne di tutte le classi sociali che l'accolgono, che si raccomandano, che ricevono ammonimenti ed indirizzi, che lo esaltano ancor vivo; sempre eguale a se stesso il popolo cristiano, sempre sensibilissimo al passaggio della santità" (Ibid.).

53. "L'arte squisita che egli possedeva di provvedere a tutto con mezzi adatti, di riuscire con ordine, con organizzazione perfetta, con calma, non senza contrasti talora, ma con grande dignità e bontà anche nei contrasti" (Ibid., 1:xxxvii).

54. Roncalli himself points out that popular demonstrations following the execution of a Spanish anticlerical, Francisco Ferrer, on 13 October 1909, interrupted research; see E. Ragionieri, "La storia politica e sociale", *Storia d'Italia,* ed. Einaudi (Turin, 1979), 1936.

55. The practical inspiration was P. Tacchi Venturi, *Storia della Compagnia di Gesù* (Rome, 1922). On 4 July 1934 Roncalli wrote to don Dentella (see *Il Pastore,* 240–44) and recommended to him as methodological basis L. Fonk, *Il metodo scientifico* (Rome, 1909), but here "method" meant the external dignity of the edition.

56. In *AVA* 5:vii, Roncalli says that the first volume was almost ready in 1910. This notwithstanding, the letters between Roncalli and the publisher showed that it was only after 1934 that the project was practically resumed.

57. P. Forno died on 19 November 1938 in Bergamo.

58. *AVA* 3:viii–ix.

59. He knew of his appointment during the night of 6 December 1944; he was in Paris on 30 December 1944. About this period see A. Latreille, *De Gaulle, la libération et l'Eglise Catholique* (Paris, 1978), and E. Fouilloux, "Uno straordinarie ambasciatore?" in *Giovanni XXIII,* 63–91.

60. The typographer's bill was not paid for a long time.

61. It is impossible to say if the different exposition depends on better hindsight or

on a certain confusion and nostalgia. The manuscript of the "Introduzione" is in *AR* "San Carlo," A5; a copy of the typed version is in *CM*, with a minute of Roncalli's letter to the publisher, namely S.E.S.A.'s president Dr. Brizio, on 6 August 1958. The preface by Cardinal G. B. Montini was requested with a letter on 17 November 1958 (see John XXIII, *Lettere 1958–1963* [Rome, 1978]).

62. "La constatazione riguarda un interessamento che da vari indizi appare sempre più vivo, fatto di simpatia per ricerche e studi di patrie memorie religiose e civili e dove il fervore religioso verso orizzonti più vasto non disdegna, anzi prende gusto, ad occuparsi delle ricchissmie esperienze del passato ad applicazione del *magisterium vitae* che la storia continua ad esercitare a comune profitto della umana convivenza. . . . Alle grazie di questa ultima circostanza debbo il vivo compiacimento, che mi si vorrà perdonare, di vedere questo primo tentativo in Italia di una pubblicazione integrale di portata generale efondamentale, disporsi in ordine di avviamento per altri sforzi individuali e collettivi, specialmente nel settore delle Visite Apostoliche post-tridentine sul tipo di queste più note di Lombardia che recano in fronte il nome splendente di S. Carlo Borromeo" (*AVA* 5 : viii–ix).

63. *Civiltà Cattolica* 88 (1937): 553–54; G. Barni, *Archivio Storico Lombardo* 3 (1938): 479–89; C. Castiglioni, *La Scuola Cattolica* 46 (1938): 100–103.

64. L. Chiodi, *Bergomum* 33 (1959): 103–7; it is strange that this journal, which reviewed the lecture on Baronio (2 [1908]: 48), the beginning of the study on Borromeo (5 [1911]: 77), and the book on "Misericordia Maggiore" (6 [1912]: 156), did not comment on or review the edition of the visitation until 1959!

In October 1960 L. Chiodi was involved by the pope himself in the project of publishing Barbarigo's pastoral visit of the diocese in 1658–64; it was never accomplished (see John XXIII, *Lettere 1958–1963*, 268–70).

The most important Italian journal of church history at the time published only in 1960 a short comment, signed by A. Stella (see *Rivista di Storia della Chiesa in Italia* 14 [1960]: 470–71).

65. *L'Osservatore Romano*, 1 January 1960, reprinted in *Giovanni XXIII in alcuni scritti di Don Giuseppe De Luca* (Brescia, 1963), 29–49. See the most recent consideration of this important priest and scholar in the forthcoming proceedings of the congress organized by G. De Rosa, *G. De Luca, H. Bremond e la storia della spiritualità* (Vicenza 1984).

66. "Mentre questi volumi parlano di san Carlo e in apparenza altro non si propongono, di fatto testimoniano sulla formazione spirituale e pastorale di Giovanni XXIII" (*Giovanni XXIII in alcuni scritti*, 31).

67. "1. la parte d'ingresso bene. 2. tutto ciò che è scritto da quella parte fino alla fine del n.2 e l'inizio del 3 merita d'essere stampato a parte perchè bello e interessante: ma è ingombrante per chi vuol conoscere i volumi della Visita di S. Carlo ecc. e non ama attardarsi fra le note personali del curriculum vitae dell'A.: del complesso dei vescovi del sec. XVI, del card. Federigo, del Bellarmino: con altre pur vaghe distrazioni. . . ." (*Giovanni XXIII in alcuni scritti*, 28 or John XXIII, *Lettere 1958–1963*, 491).

68. There are interests and problems that sometimes fascinated Roncalli and paralleled his central study of Borromeo; it seems to me that they are taken from Borromeo's experience. Among them are, of course, Lorenzo Giustiniani and Gregorio Barbarigo during the ten Venetian years. I perfectly agree with G. Cracco, "Nel solco di Roncalli e De Luca: prospettive di ricerca su Lorenzo Giustiniani," *Rivista Diocesana del Patriarcato di Venezia* 68 (1983): 3–7, who has stressed some fundamental points: he points out that there is a "singolare affinità" between Giustiniani and Radini, and he thinks that this is the very origin of Roncalli's attitude

toward the first patriarch; in other words the bishop's profile (a Borromean image) seems to be at the root of this interest. I think that the same is true for Barbarigo: about him Roncalli was already reflecting in June 1911 when he drafted the historical footnotes for a speech that Radini gave in Padua (see L. F. Capovilla, *Giovanni XXIII Quindici Letture*, 528). Among the reasons for such parallel interests, I wish to add a sensitivity for the saints of the local church, as I pointed out in my "Le fonti" See also S. Tramontin, "Venezianità del card. Roncalli," *Cultura e spiritualità*, 329–50.

69. B. Ulianich, "Un papa, un itinerario," *Bozze 79* 1–2 (1979): 31–76.

70. "Ma è nel discorso dell'11 ottobre che Giovanni XXIII riesce a chiarire a se stesso la dicotomia tra dottrina da un lato e disciplinare, pastorale, pratico dall'altro, superandola dall'interno. . . . Qui si ha la piena rivelazione del faticoso cammino dell'aggiornamento" (B. Ulianich, "Un papa"). G. Alberigo has commented on and I myself have published a critical synoptic edition of the manuscripts and the final text, "L'allocuzione *Gaudet Mater Ecclesia* (11 ottobre 1962)," *Fede Tradizione Profezia* (Brescia, 1984), 187–283.

71. *DMC* 3:341, speech to the Bibliotheca Historica Medii Aevi.

72. *DMC* 3:10 and 407.

73. Letter to Cardinal Montini, 27 March 1962, in L. F. Capovilla, *Giovanni e Paolo. Due Papi* (Brescia, 1982), 139–41; about the idea of a Borromeo Academy see the personal note of the pope on the same day in John XXIII, *Lettere 1958–1963*, 530.

74. R. Mols, "Saint Charles Borromée pionnier de la pastorale moderne," *Nouvelle Revue Théologique* 89 (1957): 600–622, 715–47. translated in Italian for *Ambrosius* suppl. 1961; the letters are in L. F. Capovilla, *Giovanni e Paolo*, 135.

75. "Tutto ben detto da questo padre Mols in onore della attività e sapienza pastorale di S. Carlo Borr.: ma delle sue Visite Apostoliche che furono un vero capolavoro di pazienza e di dottrina, neanche una parola, neanche una citazione. E. dire che la visita apostolica di Bergamo è pubblicata in cinque grossi volumi e chi l'ha pubblicata è il papa Giovanni XXIII in persona con grande cura e pazienza" (L. F. Capovilla, *Giovanni e Paolo*, 136, manuscript's copy edited above).

76. *DMC* 1:129–33 presents the manuscript of this speech, very close to the final text, although at the last moment some parts were changed in the authorized version (see E. E. Y. Hales, *Pope John and His Revolution* [London, 1965], 98). The link between this speech and the Borromean model is exactly in the instruments that the pope chooses for ruling the church, namely a synod for Rome's diocese, a council for the church, an updating of the code of canon law as byproduct of the council. The first Roman synod was never studied as to its sources, its models, its preparation and celebration, that is, as a four centuries' delayed obedience to the Council of Trent. Also in this specific case, the episodes and the texts assembled by P. Hebblethwaite, *John XXIII Pope of the Council* (London, 1984), offer only a superficial impression: neither he nor any other scholar profoundly analyzes the substantial relations between the Roman synod and the two synods that Roncalli celebrated in Bergamo and Venice. A. Cairoli, the postulator of Pope John's beatification, quoted during a congress in Bergamo some passages of the personal journals of the pope that could significantly clarify the context of the synodal speeches and some other papers published in the appendix of John XXIII, *Lettere 1958–1963*.

77. About the relationship between the Council of Trent's image and the Vatican Council's project, B. Ulianich ("Un papa," 57), wrote: "Giovanni XXIII ha dinanzi agli occhi il movimento di riforma interna alla Chiesa voluto dal Tridentino e realizzato dai vescovi riformatori. Egli pone l'accento in maniera assai intensa, sul

rinnovamento della 'disciplina ecclesiastica.' Categorico è il suo silenzio su una analogia con la parte definitoria del concilio stesso." There is a lot of description, but there is no serious study about Pope John's desire to be bishop of Rome.

78. "In questo pervigilium del Il Concilio Vaticano, come non pensare a San Carlo, cosi distinto nelle sollectitudini ansiose per la conclusione del Concilio di Trento" (*DMC* 4 : 27).

79. "Saggi incomparabili di paterna sollecitudine, di giuridica dottrina, di perfetta corrispondenza alle necessità del tempo suo" (Ibid.).

80. *DMC* 2 : 8. The five speeches are: *DMC* 1 : 10–14; *DME* 2 : 3–8, 368, 531–33; *DMC* 3 : 499–500; *DMC* 4 : 17–32, 621–26; *DMC* 5 : 5–14, 284–86. Just before the first homily he wrote to Montini: "Sto sul punto di scendere a S. Pietro per la grande cerimonia. Penso a S. Carlo, al suo successore, ed ai Milanesi tutti insieme clero e popolo. Ho voluto nell'ordine del grande rito un piccolo posto per l'omelia brevissima [completely unusual!] perchè mi premeva di ricordare S. Carlo il cui nome feci aggiungere nella invocazione litanica" (see John XXIII, *Lettere* 1958–1963, 47–48).

81. "E lasciateci, venerabili fratelli la gioia di invitare il vostro e il nostro spirito alla contemplazione del preclaro esempio e al più fervido incoraggiamento che S. Carlo Borromeo offre all'episcopato cattolico di tutti i riti e di tutte le nazioni del mondo a proposito della celebrazione del Concilio Vaticano II" (*DMC* 5 : 10).

82. "Alla gloria di S. Carlo fece splendido onore e fu motivo merito eccezionale l'essersi egli trovato a serizio della Chiesa nella occasione di un Concilio, di cui non potevasi oltre protrarre la celebrazione, e in condizioni di contribuire in forma provvidenziale al suo successo definitivo, a poi consacrare circa venti anni della sua vita santa e santificatrice—dal 1565 al 1584—alla felicissima realizzazione, come abbiamo detto, attraverso le visite pastorali ed apostoliche, celebrazioni di Concilii Provinciali e di Sinodi Diocesani, a tutta ristorazione della vita ecclesiastica, che segnò del suo nome benedetto un'epoca—l'epoca di S. Carlo—che grazie al Signore, ancora si prolunga a nostra fiducia nell'avvenire" (*DMC* 5 : 13).

83. "S. Carlo aggiunge per noi tutti un prezioso incoraggiamento. E' ben naturale che novità di tempi e di circostanze suggeriscano forme ed atteggiamenti vari di transmissione esteriore e di rivestimento della stessa dottrina: ma la sostanza viva è sempre purezza di verità evangelica" (Ibid.).

84. Ph. Levillain, "Le pontificat de Paul VI," *Paul VI et la modernité dans l'Église* (Rome, 1984), 17.

85. Matt. 9 : 17.

The Resources of the Ambrosiana for the Study of Borromeo

CARLO MARCORA

THE AMBROSIAN LIBRARY, WHICH TAKES ITS ORIGINS FROM THE MUNIFICENCE of Cardinal Federico Borromeo, cousin of San Carlo, became by means of the same founder the rich depository for all the documents that Cardinal Federico himself succeeded in gathering and, following his example, what the doctors of the Ambrosiana were able to recover. The announcement of these documents' existence and location is all the more necessary in as much as Aristide Sala in his vast publication of Caroline documents, largely drawn from the Archivio della Curia Arcivescovile Milanese, noted not without regret an excessive caution on the part of the Ambrosiana to participate in the publication of his Caroline documents. Now these hesitations no longer exist, and as long ago as 1936 a catalog was printed entitled: "Opere manoscritte di S. Carlo Borromeo possedute dalla Biblioteca Ambrosiana."[1] It is opportune, it seems to me, to proclaim the wealth of the Ambrosiana.

1. The Correspondence

(A) LETTERS TO SAN CARLO

The Ambrosian Library possesses 35,971 letters addressed to San Carlo Borromeo. This is not all the correspondence received by him; in fact the correspondence of his early youthful years has remained in the Archivio del Principe Borromeo, which is now located at Isola Bella.[2] Thus whoever examines the materials of the Ambrosiana will realize that the correspondence running from 1560 to 1565 is sparse; these are the years of residence at Rome as cardinal-nephew, and much of this correspondence has not come to the Ambrosiana but remained in the Vatican. The same may be said about letters sent to the cardinal-archbishop: some are present in the Curia Arcivescovile di Milano.

It also ought to be noted that the correspondence of San Carlo held by the Ambrosiana did not arrive all en bloc, but at different times, in waves, sometimes many years apart; this explains why there has not yet been an arrangement in strict chronological order. It is of use to know a little about the chronology of the arrival of these letters at the Ambrosiana.

In Borromeo's will Msgr. Ludovico Moneta was named heir of the documents of San Carlo and in case Moneta predeceased Borromeo the charge devolved upon Msgr. Giovanni Fontana and Grifidio Ruberti:[3] for all practical purposes the letters of the archbishop were secluded by Moneta. In 1588 Moneta, in writing to Federico Borromeo, shows himself to be a little reluctant to hand over the correspondence of San Carlo, fearing that thus might be violated the just caution that still ought to prevail, because too many correspondents were still alive.[4] Not only had he collected all that remained in the private workroom and archive of San Carlo, but San Carlo's writings were sought from heirs, estates, and even from private individuals: this last occurred in the cases of Msgr. Fontana and of Msgr. Giovanni Franscesco Bonomi, bishop of Vercelli.[5]

San Carlo himself had taken care that the letters and memoranda sent by him should not be dispersed; for that reason when Msgr. Nicolò Ormaneto ceased to be his chargé d'affaires at Rome because he was named bishop of Padua, Borromeo wrote to him, asking him to send back to him all his letters and papers, in order that they might not pass into the hands of others, on account of the weighty matters that they treat.[6]

Other letters would come to the Ambrosiana through the hands of Archdeacon Angelo Marchesi, a nephew of San Carlo's biographer, the Barnabite Carlo Bascapè, once correspondent of San Carlo and afterwards bishop of Novara.[7] Cardinal Federico himself had over time acquired a group of letters that he consigned to his assistant, Gerolamo Alfieri, canon of Santa Maria della Scala in Milan.[8]

From the letters cited by Angelo Marchesi it may be deduced that: (1) the writings of San Carlo remained for some time in the hands of Bascapè, who in all probability made many copies of them: these copies constitute the five volumes conserved at Rome by the Barnabites in their Curia Generalizia (Via Pietro Roselli, 5) under the title of *Lettere di Governo;* (2) the original letters of San Carlo, which were in the hands of Bascapè, were restored by Marchesi, but for the moment they became the property of the Father Oblates, who only later passed them over (as we will see) to the Ambrosian Library.

Toward the middle of the seventeenth century at the Ambrosiana, Stefano Canziani, oblate and doctor of the library from 1658 to 1667, the year of his death, was charged with compiling the alphabetical index of the correspondents and, further, a register, as the prefect of the Ambrosiana, Pier Paolo Bosca, attests: "Cantianus arranged an index for the letters of San Carlo along with the substance of each of the letters, which labor he enjoyed most, consulting these documents kept in the many volumes."[9]

The volumes of letters were then only thirty-four, as can be deduced from a statement of the curators under the date of 4 December 1634. Concerning the business "of doctor Canziani after . . . the index of surnames and the overhauling of the writings" were committed to him, it is said that "one judged it expedient and conforming to the will of the Most Excellent Founder that he apply himself to make an index or inventory of the notable things in the letters of San Carlo which, distributed in thirty-four large volumes, are held in the library. On account of the information on affairs and important negotiations which are contained in these letters this work cannot help but be of much utility to the public."[10]

The historian Giovanni Battista Fornaroli writes on the matter of Canziani: "One of his first charges was that of reducing to order the letters of San Carlo and forming the index. There were then very few; hence he squeezed them all into only two volumes, placing in one the writings from 1560 to 1577 and in the other those from 1577 to 1584." The latter year, 1584, is that of the death of San Carlo.[11] The assignment assumed by doctor Canziani was interrupted by death, and only in 1687 in the session of 4 January did the curators mandate that doctor Francesco Bicetti be engaged in compiling the index of the "nineteen volumes of letters of San Carlo which were unidentified in the Library.[12]

He had to deal with the thirty-four volumes on which Canziani had worked previously of which nineteen still remained to be systematized. This can be confirmed by the catalog of manuscripts of the Ambrosiana compiled at the beginning of the eighteenth century.[13] Finally in 1721 the Ambrosian Library obtained from the Oblates, who then had their mother house beside the present church of San Sepolchro adjacent to the Ambrosiana, a promise that they would give to the library a considerable number of letters received and expedited by San Carlo.[14] Toward 1757 Argelati wrote to the Ambrosiana that the number had already risen to seventy-five volumes;[15] thus the collection possessed almost definitively what the Ambrosiana presently possesses. The major part of the letters received from San Carlo and conserved at the Ambrosiana are in the volumes marked *F 36 inf.* up to volume *F 175 inf.* The collection resumes with volume *F 183 inf.* and continues up to volume *F 184 inf.*[16]

The volumes are bound in pasteboard and half maroon leather (34 × 23 cm.). Some of these volumes were split for greater convenience; thus the second bears the number of the preceding with the addition *bis.* Sometimes in the flyleaf there is the notation of this rearrangement, which was accomplished by the prefects Achille Ratti (Pius XI) and Luigi Gramatica; this latter even adds the date of the execution of this work. Of these volumes the doctors of the period made an index for correspondents and for subjects that has remained incomplete.[17]

A simple list with names of correspondents for every volume was compiled by Adolfo Rivolta, formerly official scribe of the Ambrosiana; this inventory or list was compiled between 1914 and 1919. This title was later bestowed upon it: "Index-Inventory of the Correspondence of San Carlo Borromeo by order of codex and folio for each codex with the number of the individual letters (designated at the left of the folio of each codex) contained in each codex and (machine printed thereon) the progressive numbers of all the letters constituting the same body of Correspondence. There are included, beyond the letters addressed to the Saint also some letters written by himself to others both autographs or copies." In the library this inventory bears the signature *Cons. F. VII, I.*

(B) LETTERS OF SAN CARLO

At the Ambrosiana there are also San Carlo's missive letters or letters in reply. As previously mentioned, the saint himself at the death of some of his correspondents sought to recover what he had written to them. Cardinal Federico Borromeo and later the doctors of the Ambrosiana requested of the possessors of these letters that they forward them to the Ambrosiana, but the result was meager.[18] Instead the Ambrosiana possesses many drafts; they occupy twenty-four volumes and are organized chronologically (signatures P. 1 *inf.*–P. 24 *inf.*). On these folios, written by secretaries, Borromeo made deletions and revisions in his own hand. From these drafts one sees his meticulous nature, the personal intervention for revision in every document from the most solemn to the missive addressed to a person of the lowest rank.

From these letters can be drawn much chronological information on the life of the saint: from the dates and place designations the shifts in his location can be closely followed. Unfortunately this collection of drafts must have suffered many vicissitudes, for at some points there appear to be folios lacking, as a result of which it is difficult to guess the addressees and sometimes also the dates. Of all this vast body of letters received and sent, the Ambrosiana has compiled a card index in alphabetical order by correspondent.

All scholars desire that this catalog be published as a most useful instrument for the study of the Borromean epoch, not only in Milan but also in the Roman church as a whole.

> The utility of this immense index is truly inestimable: an entire epoch, among the most important in the history of Christianity, is there conserved and reflected or at the least may be consulted simply through the names of persons: it is the epoch in fact of the Counter-Reformation: politics and religion; Catholic morality and public prayer of the church, discipline of the clergy, ecclesiastical institutions, Christian reeducation of

the laity, relations with the civil authority, jurisdictional conflicts . . .
matters pertaining to the Swiss cantons are all subjects touched or treated
at length in the forest of Caroline letters.

We use here phrases from the public announcement for the index of correspondents of San Carlo as presented by the Ambrosian collection.

The following announcement appeared in volume 11 of the *Fontes Ambrosiana*, edited and researched by the Ambrosian Library in 1936. Unfortunately the plan claimed as imminent was never realized, nor is the reason
known; perhaps it was the eternal reason of poverty that always grips the
Ambrosiana. The impelling motive still remains valid that "this repertory
signifies a not unimportant passport in the preparation of the materials that,
in its time, will give to us in definitive form the true history and the genuine
physiognomy of San Carlo, which today because of the vastness and man-
ifold nature of the subject and of that period, unfortunately we do not
know."

The validity of this assertion is still greater today given the fact that
through the index for the addresses from the epistolary drafts we are better
able to reconstruct the thought and action of Borromeo. In treating the
letters of San Carlo one needs also to take into account the letters written to
the assistants of San Carlo: for example, the volume "Lettere di diversi scritte
a Monsignor Nicolò Ormaneto Protonot. Apost. Agente di S.S. in Roma
1563–1567" (signature S.Q. + II, 17), a volume of 425 folios. The succeeding
volume of 407 folios (signature S.Q. + II, 18) includes the years 1568–70,
while another manuscript of 542 folios contains the letters addressed to
various members of San Carlo's *familia* (signature S.Q. + II, 16). There is
also a volume of letters of 379 folios addressed to San Carlo's vicar, Msgr.
Giovanni Battista Castelli (signature S.Q. + II, 19). There are two other
large volumes: the first of 448 folios (signature S.Q. + II, 23) and the other
of 479 folios (signature S.Q. + II, 24) are *"Lettere volanti [sic] di diversi
scritte a Mons. Bernardo Carniglia Protonotario Apostolico ed Agenti del Sig.
Card. Arcivescovo di Milano Carlo Borromeo in Roma."*[19] Two other volumes are entitled "Memoriali, suppliche, relazioni di diversi scritte al Sig.
Card. ed Arcio. di Milano Carlo Borromeo" (signature S.Q. + II, 25–26).
The first volume consists of 615 folios, the second of 624. Nor should we
neglect three other manuscripts (signature S.Q. + II, 31–33): *"Lettere diverse de varie persone dirette ad alcuni amici & parenti in Milano ed anche
esteri ritrovate nell' ammasso di quelle dirette a San Carlo Borromeo."* These
are most interesting writings, which complete the correspondence of the
saint, portraying for us those living in his ambience, but unfortunately they
are neglected by almost all the scholars of San Carlo, probably because they
are not well known.

2. The Sermons

One of the new functions that San Carlo introduced into the pastoral activity of the bishops was preaching, because, sad to say, there were only a very few bishops in his time who preached. We have not as many sermons as we have schemes for sermons; these are from his hand in the form of genealogical trees, whence comes the name *arbori* or *arbores* with which he designated them. These folios, which the saint himself considered so precious as to make of them testamentary objects bequeathed to the bishop of Vercelli (Bonomi), were gathered by Cardinal Federico Borromeo and put into eight albums. These schematized plans or *arbori* are themselves in Latin, although Borromeo preached in the Italian language.

A description, folio by folio, of each of these albums has been published.[20] Thus we can study the method by which he developed the sermon, the source from which it derived, since frequently the source is mentioned, where the sermon was given, and in what year and on what feast day. There are eight such albums designated *F.189 inf.* to *F.197 inf.*

There are furthermore some manuscripts that contain the sermons of San Carlo written down by a secretary as he heard them pronounced; unfortunately these sermons are themselves in Latin, while we know that Borromeo preached in Italian. For all these manuscripts of the second type, the first being that of the *arbores*, descriptions and indexes have been published and in the eighteenth century Giuseppe Sassi, prefect of the Ambrosiana, published a good number of them in a truly splendid edition.[22] Others, above all the early sermons, have also been published.[23]

3. Spiritual Treatises

Linked with the sermons are the manuscripts of the *Silva Pastorales*. Borromeo, in order to prepare himself for preaching, collected phrases and precepts from the Bible and from ecclesiastical authors. One of the first biographers of San Carlo wrote: "He had devoted the greatest study to these clerical materials, and the same year that he died he had achieved a sort of concordance of an infinite number of pericopes from Holy Scripture and from the Holy Fathers pertaining to whatever an ecclesiastical person might want, supplying him with excellent materials for dealing with ordained and ordinands, before baptizing, at confirmations, at consecrations of churches, altars or similar matters, and if time might have been left him to digest perfectly and order his work, he intended to call it *Sylva Pastoralis.*"[24]

Of these diverse manuscripts only one, the shortest, has been published, yet the description of the others has also been given.[25] Even these manuscripts, which concern the spiritual physiognomy of the bishop and of the clergy, are often neglected by scholars who prefer other sources, although Borromeo probably considered publishing this *Sylva*. The fact that it is not an autograph of the saint, although in some manuscripts are to be found his corrections, does not affect its worth; rather the copies in a clear hand make more likely the hypothesis of its intended publication.

Another treatise left almost complete by Borromeo concerns the method for preaching well. Here we have some *arbores*, a few drafted by his own hand and also by some of his collaborators. These were sent later on to Cardinal Agostino Valier, bishop of Verona, in order that he then might draft the text, which in fact was prepared, but San Carlo had by this time died. This manuscript has recently been published.[26]

And there is also a document concerning spiritual exercises according to the Ignatian method: "*Modus quomodo tradenda sunt puncta et diversa exercitia spiritualia.*"[27] There is no one complete treatment but a few notes, and they have been explained at length by Achille Ratti (Pius XI) who, besides manuscript *D. 325 inf.*, also touches upon a second manuscript, *D.240 inf.*, more fully.

Another small treatise is on the sacraments of orders, extreme unction, and matrimony; it has recently been published.[28]

4. Documents on His Life

While much information can be derived from the documents cited up to this point, direct witnesses for the life of Carlo Borromeo are not lacking. Very significant is the evidence rendered in the diocesan and apostolic proceedings when it involved conferring the honors of the altar.

It is not appropriate here to rehearse the history of San Carlo's canonization, already set forth by its greatest promoter, the oblate Marc' Aurelio Grattarola.[29] In actual fact there were two proceedings: the first initiated at Milan in 1601 by instigation of the Congregation of the Father Oblates; the other, the so-called apostolic proceeding begun in 1606. In large part they cover the same ground; nevertheless a comparison among the various witnesses is always worthwhile, because sometimes notable differences are to be perceived. Of these manuscripts there has already been published the description of the first proceeding, namely the diocesan, desired by the Father Oblates.[30] There is also a group of documents bearing upon the canonization that contains letters of Grattarola or by others addressed to him which do not appear in his book, already cited, *Successi meravigliosi della venerazione di S. Carlo*. Among these documents one finds a biography of San Carlo drawn up by the same Grattarola, which remains unpublished.[31] The witnesses called for the proceedings are numerous and authoritative. There are to be noted prelates, his collaborators, but not few are the number of laymen, doctors, magistrates, and nobles, who bear witness to the sanctity of Carlo Borromeo, recounting episodes and judging events.

For particular events in the life of Borromeo relevant documents include the diploma of graduate in both laws Borromeo gained at Pavia.[32] On the other hand there remains unpublished the diploma of Roman citizenship conferred by the Senate of Rome on 1 July 1561.[33] It is necessary to record also some diplomas regarding privileges conceded by Pius IV to his two nephews Federico and Carlo, especially to the latter; of these diplomas we still have no study.[34]

A dramatic event in Borromeo's life was the attempt upon it by means of an arquebus shot that struck him on the evening of 26 October 1569; on the motive we have some manuscripts.[35] Another salient event is the visit of San Carlo to the church of Santa Maria della Scala, which enjoyed royal patronage and thus presumably was considered exempt from the jurisdiction of the archbishop.[36] There are few specific documents conserved at the Ambrosiana on the event of the plague of 1576.[37]

Also for the pastoral visitations the Ambrosiana has almost nothing because these acts and reports are to be found in the Archivio della Curia Arcivescovile of Milan. Nevertheless we may indicate here some manuscripts in this category: for the visitation to the Valle Mesolcina,[38] for some convents,[39] and for the city of Cremona.[40]

There are not a few conclusions that can be drawn from this review.

1. In the first place an authoritative biography of Borromeo is not possible today if the vast archival materials here amassed are not consulted. If scholars limit themselves to a single group of documents, they risk presenting a San Carlo *ad imaginem et similitudinem nostram*, thus failing to describe the historical phenomenon in the light of all its possibilities. So many times the major pieces of information are acquired from letters addressed to his collaborators rather than those written directly to the petitioner. For the letters it is necessary to know the bibliography, because a not insignificant number have been published either wholly or in extensive extracts.

2. Research conducted in other libraries and archives is necessary, and we point out especially: the Archivio della Curia Archivescovile di Milano, where there are not only letters and acts of pastoral visitation but, above all, documents bearing on jurisdictional controversies; the Vatican Archives; and the Archivo de Simancas. In mentioning these we are not excluding other archives of a public nature as well as private family archives, particularly those of noble families.

3. For what concerns our special theme—sources in the Ambrosian Library—it can be argued that the catalog of letters that this holds should be published: this edition, given the financial means or courageous editors, will easily be realized.

4. More difficult, on the other hand, is research for materials in other archives and above all the complete edition of texts; here, however, there exist means and scholars not only Italian but from all countries where there flourishes the study and love of history, transcending geographical and political confines.

If our conference, to whose organizers I present most hearty thanks, will not only align themselves with these proposals but give assistance toward their realization, a milestone in the study of San Carlo will indeed be achieved.

Notes

1. Aristide Sala, *Documenti circa la vita e le gesta di S. Carlo Borromeo* (Milan, 1861), 3:126–29. The list of manuscripts concerning San Carlo is in Agostino Saba, *La biblioteca di S. Carlo* (Florence, 1936), 81–86.

2. For a list of San Carlo's correspondents from the letters conserved in the archive of the Borromeo family, see Adolfo Rivolta, "Epistolario giovanile di S.Carlo Borromeo," *Aevum* 12 (1938): 253–80; "Corrispondenti di San Carlo (1550–1559)," *Aevum* 13 (1939): 556–670. Cf. Carlo Marcora, "Lettere giovanili di S. Carlo (1551–1560)," *Memorie storiche della diocesi di Milano* (Milan, 1967), 14:393–563.

3. Giacomo Bascapè, *L'eredità di S.Carlo Borromeo all'Ospedale Maggiore di Milano* (Milan, 1936), 76: "Item lego, volo, iubeo et mando quod statim post obitum meum Rev. D. Ludovicus Moneta vel ipso tempore obitus mei defuncto, Rever. D. Joannes Fontana Archipresbiter Ecclesiae Mediolani, vel eo etiam tempore obitus mei defuncto, Rever. D. Grafidius de Rubertiis, ordinarius ecclesiae mediolanensis habeat et accipiat ac habere et accipere valeat propria auctoritate. . . ." For information on Ludovico Moneta, see Carlo Marcora, "Mons. Ludovico Moneta collaboratore di S. Carlo in una sua biografia coeva," *Memorie storiche della diocesi di Milano* (Milan, 1963), 9:445–94. Msgr. Giovanni Fontana was then bishop of Ferrara.

4. Biblioteca Ambrosiana MS *G 140 inf.*, letter 213 of 7 December 1588: "Oltra di ciò vado pensando che non senza causa il Sr. Cardinale di S.ta memoria ha lassato nel suo testamento che tutte le littere di missive quanto responsive venessero nelle mie mani il che si può interpretare essere fatto acciò che niuno le vedesse. Questo è quanto mi occorre. Però se il parere di V.S.Ill. ma e altrimenti la mi comanda che essequirò."

5. By letter of 26 February 1587 Giovan Antonio Caresana announced to Federico Borromeo the death of the bishop of Vercelli and added: "Ha legato a lei et a Mons. Ill.mo di Verona le scritture che gli lasciò il S.to Cardinale et ritornando io a Vercelli si metteranno tutte insieme per seguire noi quanto sarà in piacere et del sudetto Ill.mo et di V.S.R.ma" (*G 138 bis inf.*, fol. 1099). *G 138 inf.* fol. 793 (letter 201, of 20 May 1587 from Moneta to Cardinal Federico): "Se haverò le scritture et di qua (Milano) et di Vercelli ne haverò quella cura che conviene per l'obligo che ho con V.S.R.ma" (*G 138 bis inf.*, fol. 793). In his turn Msgr. Giovanni Fontana, archpriest of the cathedral of Milan writes on 10 June 1587 to Federico: "Mons. Rev.mo di Vercelli di bona memoria haveva dato ordine e reiterato molte volte con lettere sue che Mons. Rev.mo Arcivescovo mi consegnasse i libri e le scritture ch'erano di Mons. Ill.mo S. Prassede di beata memoria, ma non fu possibile ch'io potessi recuperar se non gli Arbori delle Prediche quali in esecuzione di quanto V.S. Ill.ma m'ha comman-

dato con la sua delli XXX del passato ho consignati a Mons. Moneta con altre scritture ch'io havevo ricuperate da Mons. Bellino, ho ritenuto la Selva [sic] Pastorale qual desidero grandmente di vedere et la supplico a lasciarmela alcuni mesi. . . ." (*G 138 bis inf.*, fol. 961).

    6. *F. 43 bis inf.*, fol. 305 (letter of 18 July 1570): "Non mi parendo bene che le lettere che io ho scritte a V.S. et le scritture con esse si sono mandate alla giornata, vadino in man d'altri per le materie gravi che trattano, non mi par che le lasci a Roma in man d'altri; ma più tosto aspettarò che si contenti di inviarle qua à me; et prima che parta la prego à dar fine à quelle poche cose mie, che restano da risolvere."

    7. Giuseppe Boffito *Scrittori Barnabiti* (Florence, 1933), 1 : 95–117 has provided us with a precious piece of information on Bascapè and his literary endeavors; Baldassare Oltrocchi, *Ragionamenti apologetici in risposta alla scrittura contro la traduzione latina della Vita di S. Carlo* (Milan, 1753), 62, imparts the letter now conserved at the Ambrosiana (*G 200 inf.*, 49): "Ill.mo e Rev.mo Sig.r e Pad.on mio Col.mo. Quando Monsignor Vescovo mio Zio doveva scrivere la Vita del Beato Carlo, ebbe da Monsignor Moneta le lettere del Beato, e altre scritture per tale effetto: e dopo averle vedute, e servitosene, quasi la metà di quelle, come meno importanti, e necessarie restituì, e di presente devono essere in San Sepolcro legate in tanti libri. L'altra parte ritenne presso di se per provare e verificare, quando fosse stato il bisogno, le cose da lui scritte nella suddetta Vita. Ora credendo egli non essere più di bisogno, incominciò egli stesso a ordinarle per rimandarle a V.S.Illustrissima, ma sopravvenuto dalla infermità, nè potendo ciò per se stesso eseguire, commise a me in conformità del desiderio suo, che dovessi finire di accomodarle, ed inviarle poscia a V.S.Illustrissima con avvisarla di due cose: l'una che tra queste lettere ce ne sono parecchie scritte di proprio pugno del Beato, ed una buona parte da lui stesso corrette: l'altra, che la scelta e disposizione non è fatta perfettamente ne sono legate molto bene, in modo che non abbiano bisogno di nuova diligenza, e nuova cura per essere in miglior maniera scelte e meglio legate. Vi si aggiunge poi che oltre alle lettere e scritture rinchiuse ne' Libri, ce ne sono molte in foglj sciolti, le quali si sono compartite per i suoi anni al meglio, che si è potuto, e tra queste vi sono alcune buone lettere, ma molte duplicate, che si trovano nei Libri legati: ed oltre di queste ci sono altre scritture diverse nell'involglio attaccato alla Cassa più picciola, le quali sono per lo più o di riforma, o di giurisdizione. Si mandano adunque a V.S. Illustrissima tutte le suddette lettere, e scritture in due Casse ferrate, l'una più grande dell'altra, ed in uno involglio di canepa attaccato alla Cassa più picciola; e questo è quanto Monsignor Vescovo può dare a V.S. Illustrissima delle scritture, e lettere del Beato, che sono queste, che io invio a V.S.Illustrissima di commissione sua. . . . Di Novara li XVI di Febraro MDCIX. Di V.S. Ill.ma e Rever.ma Unil.mo e Devot.mo Servitore M. Angelo Marchesi Archidiacono."

    8. Bibl. Ambrosiana, Archivio dei Conservatori, carton 21, fascicle 5.

    9. P. Paulus Bosca, *De origine et statu Bibliothecae Ambrosianae Hemidecas* (Milan, 1672), 161: "Cantianus descripto ad literas Divi Caroli indice atque singularum epistolarum sententia, qui labor plurimum iuvat interrogantes ea monumenta compluribus voluminibus contenta."

    10. The quotation is taken from the notes of Luigi Gramatica, prefect of the Ambrosiana (1914–24), *C 322 inf.*

    11. Ettore Fustella, "Biografie dei sacerdoti che si fecero oblati dal 1644 al 1666 scritte dal P. Gio Battista Fornaroli," *Memorie storiche della diocesi di Milano* (Milan, 1969), 16 : 192.

    12. From the cited notecards of Msgr. Gramatica, *C 322 inf.* For biographical

information on Francesco Bicetti de' Buttinoni, see Carlo Castiglioni, "Dottori dell'Ambrosiana," *Memorie storiche della diocesi di Milano* (Milan, 1955), 2:32–33.

13. Bibl. Ambrosiana, *I 134 sup.*, fol. 10.

14. In the Archive of the Curators (i.e., administrators) adjacent to the Ambrosiana there is a manuscript register: "1705 / Libro/ Nel quale si registrano / Di / Tempo in tempo Le / Congregazioni / De Sig.ri Conservatori / Del / Collegio Ambrogiano / E / tutti li Decreti / Che / In esse si fanno." Under the date 21 June 1721 is read: "Finalmente il S.r Dottore Bibiotecario richiese se doveasi le lettere scritte da S. Carlo che in hoggi si conservano in Biblioteca unitamente alle risposte da esso Santo ricevute e delle quali se ne è formato l'indice unire a quelle di S. Sepolcro con procurare quelle che si ritrovano pure in S. Sepolcro e compensare allo stesso con libri che abbisogna la Libreria di S. Sepolcro, fu stabilito doversi la cosa intendere tra il S.r Preposto Repossi et il S.r Dottore Bibliotecario e che tra essi s'agiusti e concerti quello stimerano bene sciegliendo anche un terzo quando bisogni per consulto." Fornaroli, biographer of the Oblates, speaking of the provost general of the Oblates, Repossi, wrote: "Aveva la libreria di S.to Sepolcro molte lettere manoscritte di S. Carlo, più ancora di lei ne aveva la Biblioteca Ambrosiana. Fu stimato conveniente d'unirle tutte insieme in una raccolta sola. Espose pertanto il Prevosto Generale Repossi nel Capitolo del 3 settembre 1721 Congregationem Bibliothecae Ambrosianae petere a Domo S. Sepulchri la cessione delle lettere di S. Carlo da lei possedute promettendo in compenso altri libri arbitrio prudentis viri. La risposta del Capitolo fu rem totam committendam esse prudentiae ipsiusmet Praepositi Generalis. Il cambio fu eseguito. La Biblioteca acquistò la raccolta compita delle lettere manoscritte di S. Carlo, degna veramente d'una biblioteca pubblica fondata dal gran Card. Federico Borromeo e la Libreria di S. Sepolchro acquistò libri più utili all'uso di chi doveva servirsene per i suoi studi" (2:413). The manuscript is held by the Oblates of via Settala.

15. Argelati, Bibliotheca Scriptorum, 2, cols. 274–75: "Quoniam praesenti saeculo earundem Epistolarum suppellex admodum crevit inductis ad eamdem Bibliothecam pluribus aliis quibus volumina, quae ultra XXXVI vix numerabantur, ad LXXX redacta sunt. . . ."

16. Frequently some codices of the Ambrosiana are erroneously cited with large capital letters of the alphabet and the number, omitting the designation *inf.* (inferior) or *sup.* (superior), the signature thus remaining incomplete.

17. The indexes prepared in the seventeenth and eighteenth centuries by doctors of the Ambrosiana correspond now to the following manuscripts: (a) *F.176 inf.* = 550 folios; (b) *F.177 inf.* = 512 folios; (c) *F.178 inf.* = 449 folios; (d) *F.179 inf.* = 41 folios; (e) *F.180 inf.* = 222 folios; (f) *F.181 inf.* = 251 folios; (g) *F.186 inf.* = 262 folios. [The editors have here omitted six pages of dense description concerning the specific features of these indexes that would largely be of interest only to the committed researcher who would find them available at the Ambrosiana.]

18. Important are the MSS *I 139–141 inf.*, three manuscripts (30 × 23 cm.) bound in leather with lines in gold. In the anterior and posterior plate is the coat of arms of the Borromeo family. There are letters from Pius IV and from San Carlo to the pontifical legates sent to the Council of Trent and from the legates or others to the saint. *I 139 inf.* includes 290 folios and has documents running from 1560 to 1561. *I 140 inf.* has 546 folios and concerns the year 1562. *I 141 inf.* has 304 folios and covers the years 1562 and 1563. In the flyleaf appears a note: "The letter of February 7, 1562 was inserted on May 2, 1911, given by the most illustrious Signor Marchese Gioachino d'Adda Salvaterra. A. Ratti." In many of these letters only the signature is autograph. *S.P. II.261* contains an autograph letter of San Carlo to Pius IV (19

August 1563), obtained as a gift from the provost of Canzo (province of Como), Camillo Fino (28 February 1962). *F.188 inf.* (now *S.P.II, 261*) contains autograph letters of San Carlo. It includes detached folios and is contained in a ceremonial cloth bound in red paper boards. It contains the following letters:

1. To Msgr. Ormaneto (10 November 1568)
2. To Msgr. Ormaneto (29 June 1569)
3. To Pius IV (29 October 1569) (in copy)
4. To Msgr. Carniglia (28 March 1576)
5. To Cardinal Farnese (28 August 1563)
6. To Count Giberto (father of San Carlo) (1551)
7. To Msgr. Speciano (6 July 1577)
8. To Msgr. Speciano (17 July 1577)
9. To Msgr. Speciano (6 November 1577)
10. To Msgr. Speciano (9 October 1577)

F.183 inf. is a manuscript in paperboard binding (34×22cm.) including 213 folios. From fol. 2 to fol. 62 there are contained letters sent by San Carlo, with autograph signature. From fol. 65 to fol. 213 are copies of letters from the young San Carlo. These letters have been published: see Carlo Marcora, "Le lettere giovanili di S.Carlo," *Memorie storiche della diocesi di Milano* (1967), 14:393–563. Also the manuscript *S.Q. + II,7*, bound in half leather and paper including 233 folios (33×22 cm.), contains copies of letters of San Carlo: *Lettere della gloriosa memoria del Cardinale S.to Carolo Borromeo* is read in fol. 1. The letters run from 13 June 1562 to February 1564. MS *0.264 sup.* has 26 folios (31×24cm.). It is virtually a facsimile album containing the photographs of eight letters addressed by San Carlo at diverse times to Cardinal Sforza and to Duke Giacomo Buoncompagni. The originals of these letters are in the Archivio Buoncompagni di Roma. They are letters from 1562 to 1583. *F.184 inf.* and *F.184 bis inf.* are two volumes bound in half leather comprising 619 folios, including letters of San Carlo in which only his signature is autograph. Most are addressed to Speciano and to Carniglia. *G.46 inf.* of 36 folios (27.5×21.5 cm.) contains as copy "*S. Caroli Borromaei Mediolani Archiepiscopi Epistolae ad varios Europae Principes, Episcopos ac Optimates conscriptae a Jo. Baptista Amalthaeo, qui illi erat a Secretis.*"

19. For Carniglia cf. Luisa Bertoni, "Carniglia Bernardino," *Dizionario Biografico degli Italiani* (Rome, 1977), 20:488–90.

20. *Discorsi inediti di S. Carlo Borromeo nel IV Centenario della sua entrata in Milano*, ed. Carlo Marcora (Milan, 1965), 12:25–50.

21. Ibid., 41–48.

22. *S. Caroli Borromaei S. R. E. Cardinalis Archiepiscopi Mediolani Homiliae nunc primum e Mss.Codicibus Bibliothecae Ambrosianae in lucem productae Joseph Antonii Saxii Praefatione et Annotationibus illustratae* (Milan, 1747).

23. See n. 19 supra.

24. Giov. Battista Possevino, *Discorsi della vita del beato Carlo Borromeo* (Rome, 1591), 46.

25. Carlo Marcora, "La sylva pastoralis di S. Carlo Borromeo," *Memorie storiche della diocesi di Milano* (Milan, 1965), 13–98.

26. Carolus Borromeus, *Ordo tractationis De Oratione* (Milan, 1968). Cf. Carlo Gorla, "I trattati spirituali di S. Carlo," in *S. Carlo Borromeo nel terzo centenario della Canonizzazione 1610–1910* (Milan, 1910), 488–91.

27. Achille Ratti, "San Carlo e gli Esercizi Spirituali di Sant'Ignazio," ibid., 482–88.

28. Carlo Borromeo, *Trattato sui Sacramenti dell'Ordine del Matrimonio dell'Unzione degli Infermi* (Milan, 1984).

29. Marco Aurelio Grattarola, *Successi meravigliosi della veneratione di S. Carlo, Cardinale di S. Prassede et Arcivescovo di Milano* (Milan, 1614). For biographical information on Grattarola, see Argelati, *Bibliotheca Scriptorum Mediolanensium*, bk. 1, pt. 2, cols. 703–7. Ettore Fustella, "Biografie dei sacerdoti che si fecero oblati al tempo di S. Carlo (1578–1584)," *Memorie storiche della diocesi di Milano* (Milan, 1965), 12:179–91. Carlo Pasetti and Uberti Giansevero, *Cenni biografici del ven. Servo di Dio Marco Aurelio Grattarola* (Lecco, 1911).

30. Carlo Marcora, "Il processo diocesano informative sulla vita di S. Carlo per la sua canonizzazione," *Memorie storiche della diocesi di Milano* (Milan, 1962), 9:76–717.

31. *X 295 inf.–X 298 inf. Grattarola Marco Aurelio, oblato. Scritture appartenenti alla vita e miracoli del Beato Carlo Borromeo raccolte per la Canonizzazione di San Carlo* (1610). The biography of which we speak is in *X 295 inf.*, fols. 145–332 and continues in the manuscripts *X 296 inf.*, fols. 352–391 and *X 298 inf.*, fols. 1–40.

32. Luigi Gramatica, *Diploma di laurea in diritto canonico e civile di S. Carlo Borromeo* (Milan, 1917).

33. Parchment 1217. There exists a photographic reproduction in *Echi di San Carlo* (Milan, 1937–38), 207.

34. *Y 131 sup.; N. 133 inf.*

35. *Z 399 sup.* (6) "*Relatione de tutto il successo occorso nell'archibugiata tirata all'Ill.mo et Rev.mo Card. Borromeo arcivescovo di Milano.*" Another copy is in *R. 125 sup.*, fols. 112–19; *P 271 sup.*, fols. 161–82. *Trotti 41*, fols. 97–108: "*La vera Relatione del successo occorso dell'Archibugiata tirata all'Ill.mo et Rev.mo Cardinale Borromeo Arcivescovo di Milano et della cospiratione d'alcuni Prevosti Humiliati contra sua Persona.*" This is, however, the transcription of the small printed work, "In Milano per Gio. Battista Pontio Stampatore alla Dovana del 1569 a di 27 ottobre." Cf. Luigi Anfosso, *Storia dell'archibugiata tirata al Cardinale Borromeo (S. Carlo) in Milano la sera del 26 ottobre 1569* (Milan, 1913). Carlo Castiglioni, "L'Ordine degli Umiliati in tre codici illustrati dell'Ambrosiana," *Memorie storiche della diocesi di Milano* (Milan, 1960), 7:26–35.

36. Ilario Corte "Notizie della Ducale, Regis, Imperiale Collegiata di S. Maria della Scala raccolte dalle scritture dell'Archivio del Senato di Milano." MS (29.5 × 21.5 cm.) of 82 folios (Signature: *A 189 sup.*). See also *B 180 (sussidio)*. MS *G.167 sussidio* expressly treats the "*Visita fatta alla chiesa di S. Maria della Scala in Milano.*" There is also a fascicle including copies of various documents concerning the foundation and privileges of that church.

37. MS *S.80 sup.*, fols. 163–64 published by S[acerdote] A[chille] R[atti] [Pius IX] "Lettera di un Padre Cappucino scritta da Milano nell'infierire della peste," *S. Carlo Borromeo nel terzo centenario*, 327. In MS *D.216 inf.*, fol. 136, is found "Relatione fatta a S.Ecc. da li Conservatori della Sanità di Milano sopra i successi della peste, settembre 29 1576."

38. *D.216 inf.*, fols. 70–75. There are attached other documents for the foundation of seminaries, fols. 76–83.

39. *D.348 inf.* (Monastero del Bocchetto, Monastero Maggiore, Lambrugo, Cremella).

40. *G.269 inf.*

Contributors

GIUSEPPE ALBERIGO, Secretary for the Istituto per le Scienze Religiose, has written widely on the Catholic Church in the Tridentine and in the modern period.

AGOSTINO BORROMEO, Università di Roma, has been engaged in extensive archival research in both Italy and Spain on Philip II and his bishops and has produced many important articles on the relations between the church and the Spanish monarchy in this period.

ERIC W. COCHRANE (1928–1985), to whose memory this volume is dedicated, taught history at the University of Chicago and was an outstanding authority on the late Italian Renaissance, upon which his several renowned studies focused.

PAUL F. GRENDLER, University of Toronto, has written several important studies on Italian Renaissance culture with particular attention to primary and secondary education.

JOHN M. HEADLEY, University of North Carolina, Chapel Hill, has published on Luther, Thomas More, the Habsburg Empire and more recently on European problems of the early seventeenth century.

CARLO MARCORA is doctor of the Ambrosian Library and one of the founders of the Accademia di S. Carlo.

ALBERTO MELLONI, Istituto per le Scienze Religiose, who studied under Professor Alberigo, has recently prepared a computer concordance of A. G. Roncalli-Pope John XXIII's writings and has published many articles on his career and thought.

JOHN W. O'MALLEY, S.J., Weston School of Theology, is best known for his important study of humanist rhetoric, *Praise and Blame in Renaissance Rome,* and is currently writing a history of Christian preaching.

ADRIANO PROSPERI, professor of modern history, Institute of Historical and Juridical Discipline, University of Bologna, has published widely on the subject of the Catholic and Counter-Reformation in Italy.

NIELS RASMUSSEN, O.P., University of Notre Dame, has devoted his scholarly research and publishing to all aspects of the liturgy and is contributing the chapter "Liturgy, Liturgical Arts" to John W. O'Malley's forthcoming *The Counter Reformation: A Guide to Research.*

JOHN B. TOMARO, with whom the idea of the conference originated, wrote his dissertation at the University of North Carolina, Chapel Hill, on "The Papacy and the Implementation of the Council of Trent," wherein he treated Archbishop Borromeo.

ROBERT TRISCO, a scholar of both American and European church history at the Catholic University of America, has recently written extensive articles on aspects of the Council of Trent.

MARC VENARD, Université de Haute Normandie, is one of the foremost authorities on the institutional life of the church in France during the early modern period and is currently working on a repertory of pastoral visitations during the Old Regime.

E. CECILIA VOELKER, College of Architecture, Clemson University, is completing a translation of Borromeo's *Instructiones fabricae,* book 2 and a revision of book 1 together with supporting commentary and analysis.

A. D. WRIGHT, University of Leeds, has published a comprehensive study of the Counter-Reformation, which has established his prominence in the subject and manifested his specific interest in and mastery of its Spanish aspects.

Index

Buonaiuti, Ernesto, 278
Bus, César de (canon of Cavaillon), 211, 218
Buser, Thomas, 41

Cairoli, A., 298 n.76
Calini, Muzio (archbishop of Zara), 52
Callot, Jacques, 35
Calvinism, 15, 58
Canigiani, Alexandre (archbishop of Aix-en-Provence), 208, 210, 214, 216
Canisius, Peter, 57
Cantimori, Delio, 33
Canziani, Stefano, 301–2
Capuchins, 200–201
Carafa, Carlo, 47
Carbone, Ludovico, 165–66
Cardinal secretary, 233, 238, 241. See also Borromeo, Carlo: as cardinal nephew
Caresana, Giovan Antonio, 308 n.5
Carniglia, Bernardo, 304, 311 n.18
Caro, Annibale, 69, 80 n.6
Carranza, Bartolomé de (archbishop of Toledo), 202
Casale, Giambattista, 43, 168
Cassinese congregation, 125
Castelli, Giovanni Battista (nuncio), 209, 210, 214, 304
Castellino da Castello, 158, 162–63, 165, 168, 169
Castro, Pedro de (archbishop of Granada), 21, 193, 198–99
Cateau-Cambrésis, Peace of, 13, 31
Catechism: Roman, 200; Tridentine, 213, 218
Catherine of Siena, Saint, 212
Catholicism, 11–12, 19, 25, 88, 93, 103–4, 118, 126, 199, 200, 223, 230, 237, 238, 257, 262 n.34, 263 n.36, 284
Catteneo, Enrico, 120
Celle, parlamento of, 43
Cerasola, Flaminio, 295 n.37
Cerralbo, marquess of, 98
Cervini, Marcello (later Pope Marcellus II), 32
Chabod, Federico, 32, 43
Chapter, cathedral, 228–29, 240, 241
Charlemagne, 276
Charles (archduke of Hapsburg), 238

Charles V (Holy Roman emperor), 86, 92
Chavatti, Pierre-Ignace, 223
Choiseul, Gilbert de (bishop of Tournai), 223
Cholinus, Maternus, 243
Ciapponi, Lucia A., 187 n.32
Cicada, Giovanni Battista (cardinal of San Clemente), 49
Ciceronianism, 145, 146
Clement VIII (pope), 31, 212, 272
Clergy, 18, 112–35, 163, 186 n.15, 199, 215–18, 229, 234–35, 241; regular, 123, 124, 130–35; regular, in Spain, 193, 196–97 (see also Religious orders); secular, 191, 221. See also Borromeo, Carlo: and clergy, regular and secular
Cognor, Antonio (bishop of Bruganto), 51–52
Cohon, Denis (bishop of Nimes), 213
Collegio Borromeo, 191
Collegium Germanicum, 232–33
Cologne nunciature, 230; crisis, 230, 238–41
Colonna, family of, 199
Concubinage, 233–35, 241
Confessional, 179, 193, 202–3, 219–20, 260 n.9
Confraternities, 99, 131, 133, 134, 163, 188, 212, 222, 227 n.54, 282; and Casacce, 37. See also Schools of Christian Doctrine
Congregatio Germanica, 232, 247 n.14
Congregation: of Bishops, 75, 76, 77, 232, 233; of the Council, 71, 75, 76, 77, 83 n.45; of Rites, 77; 186 n.14, 267
Consilium de emendanda Ecclesia, 113
Constantine's Edict, 281
Contarini, Gaetano, 37
Contarini, Gasparo (cardinal), 34, 113
Cornaro, Luigi (cardinal), 52
Corpus Christi: college of, 190–91 feast of, 191, 271
Coulanges, M. de (cousin of Mme de Sévigné), 223
Council of Italy, 107 n.51
Council of Trent. See Trent, Council of
Councils: of Cambrai, 210, 241; in Italy, 265, 278–79, 298 n.76; provincial and diocesan, in France, 210, 213–14, 217,

Orsenigo, Cesare, 162
Osio, Giambattista (bishop of Rieti), 51

Pacheco, Francisco (cardinal), 87
Paleotti, Gabriele (archbishop of Bologna), 39, 40, 71, 142, 143, 149, 165, 177, 195, 212, 229, 257, 261 n.19
Palestrina, Giovanni de, 40
Pallavicino, Pietro Sforza, 259 n.1
Palludius, Niels, 140
Palmio, Benedetto, 146, 148
Panigarola, Francesco, 43, 77, 148, 256
Papacy, 48, 77–80, 193, 232, 264; papal bulls, 165, 187 n.28, 198, 241; Roman centralism of, 12, 230, 236, 240, 261 n.21, 263 n.36. See also Curia, Roman; individual popes
Pardo, Sylvester (vicar-general of Antwerp), 242, 248 n.27
Parish, 131, 163–69, 215, 216, 217, 218, 220, 241
Parma, duke of, 242
Pachini, Pio, 47, 295 n.37
Pastor, Ludwig von, 103, 275
Paul III (pope), 268–69
Paul IV (pope) (Gian Pietro Carafa), 33, 34, 40, 93, 199
Paul V (pope), 103, 264–74
Pelagianism, 19, 144
Pelissier, L., 275–76
Peña, Francisco, 266
Peraldo, Giuseppe, 274 n.7, 248 nn. 27 and 28
Philip II (king of Spain), 14, 52–53, 73, 127; and Capuchins, 201; ecclesiastical policy of, in Milan, 85–104, 130; and seminaries in Spain, 204 n.12
Pilgrimages, 198–99
Pinelli (cardinal), 274
Pirri, Pietro, 40
Pius IV (pope), 14, 47–63, 68–69, 87, 92, 172, 251–54, 307, 310–11 n.18
Pius V (pope), 87, 103, 128, 165, 189
Pius VI (pope), 188
Placet, 92, 93, 107 n.46
Plantin, Christophe, 242, 249 n.28
Poggiano, Giulio, 18, 83 n.50, 122
Pole, Reginald (cardinal), 33, 120, 202, 284
Politi, Ambrogio Catarino, 35
Possevino, Gian, 186 n.13, 259 n.6
Priuli, Lorenzo (patriarch of Venice), 165

Prodi, Paolo, 12, 28–29, 40, 42, 231, 247 n.13
Professio fidei, 241
Prosperi, Adriano, 24, 27
Protestants, 49, 232, 237, 244
Pseudo-Dionysius, 115

Quiñones, Fernández de (count of Luna), 55
Quiñones, Juan de (bishop of Calahora), 57
Quintilian, 146
Quiroga (cardinal), 21, 191, 193–94, 195, 196, 198, 201, 202, 203

Radini Tedeschi, Giacomo Maria (bishop of Bergamo), 26, 278, 282, 293 n.23, 297–98 n.68
Ragazzoni, Gerolamo (bishop of Famagosta), 172, 209–10
Rainaldi, Girolami, 271, 273
Raphael (Raffaele Sanzio da Urbino), 271, 276
Ratti, Achille (later Pope Pius XI), 248 n.28, 278, 302, 306, 310 n.18
Rebiba, Scipione (cardinal of Pisa), 62
Reform: concept of, 18, 24, 30 n.3, 34, 72, 123, 234–35, 239, 243, 289. See also Borromeo, Carlo: and reform
Religious orders, 110–11 n.95, 125, 133–34, 192, 200
Reni, Guido, 264
Requesens, Don Luis de Zúñiga y (governor of Milan), 73, 95–96, 98, 99, 108 nn. 59 and 61, 132; on heretics as rebels, 111 n.99
Reserved Sacrament, 190, 195
Reuchlin, Johann, 140
Ribera, G. B., 15, 68, 251
Ribera, Juan de (archbishop of Valencia), 21, 188–90, 191, 192, 193, 194, 196, 197–99, 200, 201, 203, 261 n.16
Ricci, Giovanni Battista, 266, 268–74, 276
Rite: Ambrosian, 177–78, 195, 198; of Braga, 195; Roman, 193, 195
Rivolta, Adolfo, 303
Rocca, Angelo, 274
Roch, Saint, 212
Romana, Francesca, 266, 272, 273, 275
Roman missal, 213
Roncalli, Angelo. See John XXIII